Peter Norton's
DOS 5.0 Guide
Fourth Edition

Peter Norton

Brady Publishing

New York   London   Toronto   Sydney   Tokyo   Singapore

The first edition of this book was published under the title:
MS-DOS and PC-DOS: User's Guide

 Brady Publishing

Simon & Schuster, Inc.
15 Columbus Circle
New York, NY 10023

Manufactured in the United States of America

1 2 3 4 5 6 7 8 9 10

Library of Congress Cataloging-in-Publication Data

Norton, Peter, 1943
    [DOS guide]
    Peter Norton's DOS guide / Peter Norton.—4th ed.
      p. cm.
    Includes index.
    1. Operating systems (Computers) 2. MS-DOS. 3. PC-DOS.
  I. Title. II. Title: DOS guide
  QA76.76.063N68 1991
  005,4'46—dc20   91-4046
  ISBN 0-13-663048-0   CIP

ACKNOWLEDGMENTS

With my thanks, to
Harley Hahn
Scott Clark
and
Kevin Goldstein.

As always, my continuing thanks to
William Gladstone
and his staff at Waterside Productions

and to Burt Gabriel and the people at Brady Publishing.

TRADEMARKS

LIMITS OF LIABILITY AND DISCLAIMER OF WARRANTY

Screen shots in this book were prepared using Hijaak, a product of Inset Systems. Thanks to Carol Barth and Greg Reynolds at Modern Design for their expertise.

Thien - Thuy Tran
07/2000

CONTENTS

Chapter 14   Hard Disk Setup   177

Chapter 15   Working with Subdirectories   189

Chapter 16   Organizing Your Hard Disk   203

Chapter 17   Advanced Disk Commands   223

Chapter 18   The DOS Data Security System   241

Chapter 19   Pipeline Tricks   259

INTRODUCTION

This book is about getting started with DOS—the disk operating system for the family of IBM-compatible personal computers—but it doesn't stop with DOS. It is about much more, because there are two halves to this book, even though you won't find them broken out in separate sections. One half of the book—the part you would expect to find—teaches the things you need to know about getting started with DOS and getting the most out of it. The other part, equally valuable, teaches what you need to know in order to be a wily, smart, and effective user of a small personal computer.

On the one hand, this book tells you about DOS and how to make good use of the commands that are built into it. On the other, it also gives you information on such topics as how to choose intelligently among the hundreds of programs offered for sale. Both halves of this book are based on something that sets it apart from many others: practical advice. In these pages, you'll find out how to make your personal computer work for you. You'll learn what works and what doesn't, what to buy, what to use, and none of this advice is theoretical; it's based on 25 years of experience working on all kinds of computers, from personal computers to mainframes. The last 10 of those years have been dedicated to working with personal computers, often ten hours a day or more, six or seven days a week on projects ranging from programming to writing articles and columns for PC Week and PC M*agazine,* to all the myriad tasks that a personal computer can do that contribute to running a company. This book is a result of that experience, leavened with a healthy dose of common sense—something we all rely on, and something this book will help you develop when dealing with DOS and your personal computer.

Help When You Need It

Perhaps you are the enthusiastic first-time owner of a personal computer. Perhaps your work is forcing you to use a computer you aren't really sure you want to deal with. Perhaps you are considering getting a computer, and you want to learn a little of what computers are all about (and how to spend your money wisely). If you fit any of these three descriptions, then this book is for you.

This is a help book for beginning computers users—people who will be working with the family of IBM-compatible personal computers. How can you get the most help from it?

- If you are completely new to computers and don't understand them at all, read Chapter 1. It explains the fundamental ideas about how a computer and its operating system (DOS) work. Also, use the narrative glossary in Appendix B; it defines some of the most commonly-used technical terms related to computers, but it ties the definitions together in a narrative rather than dictionary-like form, so it's easier to read and understand.

- Check the chapter headings. They will guide you into the material you need.

Most of all, this book is here to help you through the small traumas of beginning to use your computer. Every new experience brings its pleasures and pains, but the pains tend to come first. And the problems of "computer phobia" are now legendary. Whether you are a reluctant beginner or a starting enthusiast, this book will help you make your use of DOS easier. Computers are for everyone.

This book won't, by the way, go into the overly technical details of using DOS. Your computer's manuals do that nicely. What it will do is help you understand what those manuals are about and, more importantly, it will help you get started. And it will do something more that your computer's manuals cannot, or dare not, do: It will give you advice about what's good and bad in software that you may be thinking about buying.

Variations in DOS

Like everything else mankind has created, DOS has a history, and this history is reflected in the version numbers, such as 3.10 and 5.00, which indicate what edition of DOS you have. You need to know at least a little about these version numbers to know where you stand with DOS.

The major changes to DOS are reflected in the whole numbers, like the five in version 5.00. The lesser numbers indicate minor, less important changes in the progress of DOS. Of course, there are improvements and additions made in each version of DOS; the only really important thing is that you have a version no earlier than 2.00. The one-series was really the infancy of DOS. If by any chance you have one of those, you should trade it in for a newer version, but it's unlikely that you do. Whatever version of DOS came with your computer, it's almost certainly the right one for you to use.

The most popular versions seem to be 3.10, 3.20, and 3.30. Quite likely, you have one of these or the newer 4.00 or 5.00. This book describes the features of the latest version of DOS, 5.00. If you have an earlier version, a few of the things I mention here may not apply to your computer and to your DOS. Not to worry, as long as you have a version later than the one-series, you should be fine. If it is at all possible, I'd personally recommend that you update your DOS to version 5.00.

There are several ways you can find out what version of DOS your computer is using. One way is to look at your DOS manual. It will have the version number on the cover or title page. There are also two ways your computer can tell you which version of DOS it has. When you start up your computer with DOS, you ordinarily see the version number at the beginning of your session. There is also a DOS command called VER that tells DOS itself to report its version number to you. I'll be discussing how to start your computer with DOS and how to use the VER command early in the book.

In Appendix A, we will take a closer look at the various DOS versions. We will discuss why there are a number of versions and what differences you can expect when you change from one version to another.

DOS and Your PC

Just before I end this introduction and plunge with you into DOS, let's pause to define two terms: *DOS* and *the family of IBM-compatible personal computers.*

DOS is the name used by IBM for the main operating system that runs on the IBM PC family. DOS was created for IBM by Microsoft, a leading company in software for personal computers. Microsoft also provides versions of DOS for many other computers; these other versions are usually called MS-DOS (short for Microsoft DOS).

To distinguish their version of DOS, IBM calls it IBM DOS (the old name was PC-DOS). Whether we call it DOS, IBM DOS, PC-DOS, or MS-DOS, we're essentially talking about the same thing. The differences between DOS for one computer and DOS for another are quite minor.

However, since this book is for use with IBM-compatible computers and the IBM version of DOS, we'll follow the IBM standard when there are differences between one version of DOS and another.

Now, what about the computers that use DOS? There are now three basic families of IBM computers that use DOS: the PS/2 series, the newer PS/1 series, and the original personal computers: the PC, PC XT, and PC AT. While all three of these families use the same DOS and run the same software, most of the PS/2 models have different internal hardware—collectively, these are known as Micro Channel computers. IBM itself no longer makes the original personal computers, but many other companies make a range of compatibles.

IBM's PS/2 and PS/1 families have themselves grown quite large. At the low end, there are economical machines that offer performance similar to the original PC AT. At the high end, there are very powerful machines, like the PS/2 models 90 and 95, which are designed for intensive computing or for supporting a computer network.

The original PC family's—and more recently the PS/2 family's—vast popularity has seen them grow far beyond what IBM itself offers. Other companies have broadened our choices by producing models that are highly compatible with the IBM products and offer combinations of features that aren't exactly matched by any IBM model. Notable among these extended members of the family are many models by Compaq, Tandy, Toshiba, Dell, and Epson. In truth, there are more good variations on the old workhorse PC AT than we could wiggle a floppy disk at. All of these machines can be considered legitimate members of the full PC family; they all use the same DOS that you'll learn about in this book. Thus, when I refer to a "PC" or to a "personal computer," I mean any machine that runs DOS—that is, any member of one of the IBM or IBM-compatible personal computer families.

1

BASIC COMPUTER
CONCEPTS

Introduction

To use your computer successfully you need to have an idea of what it is and how it functions. By this, I don't mean the computer technician's understanding of what's going on under the cover of your machine. I mean just a simple, practical, working idea of what's what: the sort of working knowledge that you need of a car in order to be a safe driver—not what a mechanic needs to know, but what a driver needs to know.

This chapter will lay out some basic computer concepts for you. We'll cover these concepts in four parts: First, we'll look at the computer metaphorically, as if it were a human office worker. Then, we'll consider what this "office worker" can do and what it can't. Next, we'll look at the importance of an operating system like DOS. Finally, we'll wrap up this chapter with a practical matter—the two quite different ways you can use your computer.

The Computer as Worker

The best way I know to explain how a computer works, to help make sense of its parts, and to show how they work together, is to pretend the computer is an office worker. Let's suppose you are at work. Your boss tells you that you will have a new personal assistant with only one responsibility: to help you with your work. But, the boss tells you privately, this assistant isn't very bright. Conscientious, yes; hard-working, yes; but bright, intelligent, imaginative? Absolutely not. A helper to assist with whatever you ask to be done, but one who has to be given instructions in laborious detail. A worker with lots of energy but absolutely no initiative, no common sense, no independence.

You don't need me to tell you the identity of your new assistant: obviously, it's your computer. Let's see, then, what your computer assistant has to offer, what it needs to get any work done, and what you'll have to do to get any useful work out of it.

Parts of the Computer

Your computer has, as they say, an electronic brain. This brain (and as you'll see, it's a "pea brain," for sure) goes by various names in computer terminology. Basically, it is the **central processing unit**, or just the **processor**, for short. This "brain" is the central, fundamental part of a computer, and sometimes people refer to just this one part as being the computer itself. That description is pretty accurate, but naturally it can be confusing to refer to one of many parts as the computer, so I'll mostly call it the **processor**.

If we choose to ignore intelligence and creativity, which even the most sophisticated artificial intelligence can't give to a machine, we can say that your computer's processor is analogous to a brain. It is a fair analogy, because the computer's processor, like a person's brain, is what has the ability to comprehend and carry out instructions.

So far, then, we have your computer assistant's brain: the processor. What comes next? If your assistant is going to get any work done, it needs a place to work. For an office worker that place would be a desk. What part of your computer is its work space, its desk? You might be surprised to find it is the part we call the computer's memory.

Memory

Now, we all know that a person has a memory, and most people have heard that a computer also has something known as its memory, so it is natural to think that the computer's memory is analogous to our own. Wrong. Our memory is where we remember things; it is our brain's more or less permanent record of information. In contrast, the memory of a computer is not a permanent record of anything. Instead, the computer's memory is the area it uses as a work space. The memory is where the computer places the information it is working on at the time. This is just like the desk of an office worker. When people perform work, information is spread out on as much of the desk as is needed. When the work is finished, the desk is cleared and made ready for another task. So it is with the computer's memory: the computer uses its memory on a temporary basis. When the current job is done, most of memory can be cleared for another task.

This analogy between the computer's memory and an office worker's desk goes even further. In principle, all of your desk is work space, but part of it is probably taken up by a telephone or a pencil cup. It is the same way with a computer's memory. On the whole, most of the memory is available as working space for the computer, but certain parts of the memory are dedicated to one specialized use or another.

Some things that you do at a desk require very little space. You don't need much space to scribble a letter. But if you are writing a report, you need more space—space for your writing pad, for your notes, for a dictionary. Nearly any desk has room for that sort of work. But if you are doing a very complicated task, let's say some complex accounting job that requires looking up information in all sorts of account books and journals—then you need much more space. Maybe more space than there is on an ordinary desk.

Things are the same way in a computer's memory. First, the more complicated the task, the more memory the computer needs as working space. Second, like desks, computer memory usually comes in standard sizes. With a computer, memory size is measured in characters (or **bytes**, in computer terminology). The units of measurements are **kilobytes** and **megabytes**. One kilobyte, often abbreviated as KB or K, is exactly 1024— 2 to the power of 10—bytes. One megabyte, or MB, is 1,048,576—2 to the power of 20—bytes. Although a byte can hold any kind of information, for convenience we can think of each K as being about a thousand characters; that is, about the amount of space taken up by 175 words of English, approximately the size of this paragraph. Similarly, we can think of each MB as about one million characters, slightly more than the size of this book. A typical amount of memory in a personal computer is between 640K and 2MB (2048K). Although some PCs have less memory than this, the trend today is towards greater flexibility and, therefore, larger amounts of memory.

But back to our analogy. There is another way that a computer's memory is like a worker's desk. For common, simple tasks, not much of the memory/desk is used. For more complex jobs, more and more memory is used until, finally, we encounter some job that is too large to fit into the available space. This is why it is good to have plenty of memory in your computer; since memory is relatively cheap, having plenty is inexpensive insurance against bumping up against a problem that is too large to fit. And again, as with an office worker, having more work space generally doesn't affect how fast the work gets done—speed relates to the worker's brainpower. The size of the work space mostly affects how large and complicated a job can be done.

So far in understanding the parts of our computer, we've covered the **processor** (brain) and the **memory** (desk/work space). What about the rest of the computer parts? Let's consider what **disk storage** represents to your computer.

Disk Storage

Disk storage is the computer's equivalent of the office worker's filing cabinet. Disk storage comes in several forms: flexible **floppy diskettes**, rigid disk cartridges, and both nonremovable and removable **hard disk**

systems. Depending on which one you're talking about, these may be called disks, diskettes, fixed disks, hard disks, Winchester disks, cartridges, or minidisks. Functionally, they all do the same job for our computers. They act as a place to store information when the computer is not actually working on it. The information can be either data or programs. When the computer is working on the information, it is in memory (on the desktop); when the computer is not using the information, it is in disk storage.

Disk storage not only acts like a filing cabinet for the computer, it even borrows some of the terminology of filing cabinets. Within disk storage, our information is organized into **files**. Each file contains whatever kind of data is appropriate to its purpose: written text, accounting numbers, sets of instructions (**programs**) for the computer, and so on. When the computer needs information from a file, it *opens* the file, reads it or writes to it, and then *closes* the file.

Here, the computer terminology closely matches what human workers do with files. There is only one major difference in the way a computer uses a file and the way a person does. If you or I work with a file from a filing cabinet, we generally place the whole file folder on our desk. The computer's way of using a file is different. The computer's processor can only work with information that is in memory. So, a computer with a limited amount of memory has to work with small sections of a large file at a time—similar to our taking only one page at a time from a folder.

Peripherals

I've already mentioned that computers "read" and "write" when they're working with files. They can read and write in another sense, too, and even talk on the telephone. They do this through what are called **input/ output (I/O) devices**, or **peripheral devices**.

A personal computer usually has a display screen to write information onto, and it often has a printer as well. A printer is the computer's equivalent of having a typewriter at hand. Both the display screen and the printer are I/O devices. The computer does most of its reading (other than from its disk filing cabinet) from its keyboard. It reads what we type on the keyboard. The disk storage on a computer is another I/O device.

The computer also can use the telephone line to talk to other computers or write to distant peripheral devices (for example, writing through a telephone line to a printer that is located somewhere else). To use a telephone line, a computer needs special parts to connect it to the phone lines. These special parts are called a **communications adapter** and a **modem**; they perform the translation necessary to change computer talk into telephone talk and back again. These parts, the adapter and the modem, may be built into your computer, or they may be attached separately. The communications adapter can also connect some brands of fax machine to your PC.

In addition to those I've mentioned, there are many other possible types of I/O or peripheral devices that can be connected to your computer. Many of them are designed for special purposes. There are **laser printers**, which can print anything from extremely detailed pictures to typesetting-quality text, and **plotters**, which are designed to draw pictures using colored pens. There are special input devices that the computer can read, such as a **mouse**, which allows you to carefully control the position of a pointer on the display screen, and makes tasks like editing documents and creating pictures much easier.

That is basically the full set of a computer's parts: the processor (brain), the memory (desk), the disk storage (filing cabinet), adapter and modem (telephone), printer (typewriter), and so on. That is the **hardware**—the physical computer as worker. What about the computer software we hear so much about?

Software

The analogy of our computer as a faithful, but not very bright, assistant helps to explain **software**—computer programs—as well. Normally, people have a general education, general mental skills, and knowledge that we call job skills. A computer has few job skills of its own, but this loyal, if dim-witted, assistant can do anything that we can explain in meticulous detail.

The computer doesn't know how to do anything by itself. It needs programs to tell it what to do—this is one assistant that literally "goes by the book." To accomplish any work, the computer must first turn to its disk file for the program instructions that will tell it exactly what to do.

When we use the computer, our first step in getting it to work is to tell it which program—which book of instructions—to follow. The program can be anything that people have taught computers to do, from accounting calculations to game playing. (Some of the programs we run on our computers are aids to make it easier for us to write more programs.)

Introducing DOS

One of the programs a computer can run is a master program, a program that makes it easier to run other programs. This master program is called an **operating system**, and it is the computer's equivalent of a human worker's general education or an office worker's general office skills. If you or I were working as clerks in an office, we would be expected to have training in specific jobs, such as bookkeeping. For jobs like these, a computer has programs that tell it how to do specific work.

But as clerks we would also be expected to know how to do common, ordinary things: sharpen a pencil, close an envelope, or even how to find things in a filing cabinet. These types of very basic skills are given to a computer by its operating system. The operating system takes care of the ordinary tasks that all programs need to carry out. Notice that I used the word "basic," not "unimportant." It is the operating system that handles the very important task of taking care of the filing cabinet, the computer's disk storage.

And so we come to the main subject of this book: an operating system, the Disk Operating System, called DOS.

The Computer at Work

Now we are ready to see how a personal computer works as a whole. To make things easier, we'll keep to our analogy of the dumb-but-faithful computer assistant.

When we arrive at the office and first need our computer, we turn it on. Our assistant reports to work. The first task we give it is to start up its operating system. Our assistant has forgotten almost everything overnight, so its first task in the morning is to take its general instruction manual (operating system) out of the filing cabinet (disk storage), and place it on its desk (memory).

Once the computer is running, our assistant is ready for work and we can tell it what to do next. We give it the name of a program. This might be a word-processing program, such as Microsoft Word, or it might be a spreadsheet program, such as Lotus 1-2-3. Given the name of the job to be done, our worker can take the specific instructions (program) out of the filing cabinet (disk) and get everything ready on its desk (memory). For a while, we have our computer help with that kind of work. When we're done, we tell it to put the program away. When we want to do something else, we give our computer the name of another program—and so it goes.

As the computer works for us, it uses its disk storage to fetch and save our information. It uses the display screen to speak to us; it uses the printer to give us a written record; it uses the keyboard to take our commands. It may use the telephone line to pass information to and from another computer or a fax machine. But whatever it does, it is still just a simple helper.

What a Computer Can and Can't Do

There are times when a computer can be very helpful and times when it is more of a nuisance than an aid. We have to teach it how to do things (which is laborious), and we have to learn the limitations of its ways (which can be equally time consuming). For some jobs, it helps; for others, it doesn't.

On the whole, a computer can be very useful, but it pays to remember that there are some things it can do and many, many things it can't. Even more important, there are many things you might try to do with a computer that are better done by hand.

First, let's consider what the computer can do. It's a real whiz at arithmetic—fast and unfailingly accurate. Arithmetic is what computers do best. In fact, when you are using a computer for something else, such as writing a letter with a word-processing program, most of what the computer is doing behind the scenes is arithmetic. So when we need arithmetic done, the computer is just dandy at it. The computer's most famous and best success with arithmetic has been with **spreadsheets**, such as Excel and Lotus 1-2-3.

Actually, a spreadsheet is a fine example of computing at its best: It is quick and handy, and it makes it possible for many people to do all sorts of financial planning and numeric calculations, which they wouldn't have even tried before there were programs like this. Doing the kind of work that a spreadsheet does, only doing it by hand, was so difficult that we might as well say it was impossible. In short, computers can make impossibly lengthy calculations as easy to do as scratching your nose.

Another thing computers are very good at is record keeping, but only certain kinds of record keeping. With their large disk storage, computers can save large amounts of data. And under the right circumstances, computers can be efficient about searching out just the information that we need. But it is also true that many kinds of simple record keeping are more work to keep on a computer than they are to keep by hand.

This is something worth knowing. Once you fall even a little in love with what a computer can do, it is easy to become infatuated and try to get it to do everything for you. Beware. You don't turn to your computer to add 2 + 3, but you do use it to add the square roots of a hundred numbers—that's more in its line of work. It's the same with keeping records. If you have any information that is reasonably easy to keep organized by hand, then it would probably be more work to use your computer to keep track of it. On the other hand, when your manual records get out of hand, it's time to call in the computer.

People are still learning how to master the talents of computers, and so we are expanding the range of things it is practical to have computers do for us. Some things that don't even fit into a computer's natural skills of arithmetic and record keeping have turned out to be very good things to have a computer do, anyway. The best example of this is **word processing**, which means computer work related to the written word: accepting written text, changing (editing) it, keeping track of it, checking its spelling and grammar, and formatting it so the printed pages are nice and tidy. This is one type of work that the computer learned (through programming) how to do fairly recently, and yet it has become one of the computer's greatest successes. So there are now, and will be in the future, many jobs a computer can do well, even though they don't involve much computation.

There are some jobs, though, that computers can't and may never be able to do, and these include anything that involves intelligence and judgment. Computers do very well by rote. Although artificial intelligence may make a computer seem intelligent, when a task calls for imagination, intuition, or creativity, it is, at least for now, a job for people—perhaps a job with which a computer can assist, but still a job for humans.

What it all boils down to is this: You can expect your computer to be able to handle any task that is mechanically straightforward, but you can't expect it to perform any job that involves judgment. Likewise, you can expect success with your computer in any work that falls in the right scale—neither too big for your computer to handle, nor too small for it to be worth putting on your computer. Don't blame the machine if you ask it to do something it was not meant to do.

The Importance of an Operating System

So far you've seen what a computer is and the sorts of things that it can do, and you've had a little bit of explanation of the role of the computer's operating system, DOS. But that is all; at this point, it might seem that the operating system is no big deal. Actually, the operating system is a very big deal, and for several reasons.

First, an operating system is very important because it sets both the environment in which you interact with the computer and the environment in which your programs work. That means the operating system establishes the working character of your computer, as much as or more than the particular kind of computer you have. Likewise, the operating system sets many of the practical limits of your computer's usefulness, just as the specific hardware does.

The operating system animates your computer. Without it, your computer is a useless hunk, like a car with no fuel. With it, your computer takes on both life and a particular character. Your friends who grew up in big cities have different characters and styles, on the whole, than your friends who grew up in the country. It's the same with operating systems. With one, your computer will have one style; with another, it will have another style. And because this style permeates much of your interaction with your computer, the character of your operating system affects the way you use the computer.

Here's another reason why your operating system is important. Computer programs will not work with just any operating system. They generally have to be matched to the operating system used by the computer on which they run, and this means the number of programs available for your computer is heavily influenced by the popularity of the operating system that it uses. Thanks partly to the enormous success of the IBM Personal Computer, which pioneered the DOS operating system, and partly to the strong reputation of Microsoft, DOS has become the dominant operating system for the current generation of personal computers.

Yet another reason why our operating system is important has to do with the future. An operating system can either be open to expected developments in computing, or it can cut itself off from the future. Again, fortunately for us, DOS has a well-planned and orchestrated future ahead of it, based upon a compatible family of operating systems.

There's a related advantage, too. When you change from one personal computer to a newer one, you do not want to have to discard all of the computer skills and experience you have acquired. Here again, DOS is a plus. Because it is the dominant operating system in its part of the computer world, the chances are great that your next computer will use either DOS or OS/2 (which has many of the same commands as DOS). This *upward compatibility* ensures not only the usefulness of your skills, but probably the usefulness of your programs as well.

2

GETTING STARTED
WITH DOS

Introduction

Life often seems topsy-turvy when you are getting started at some new endeavor—usually it seems as though you need to know everything at once. What do you learn first? What do you do first? We'll grapple with this problem, as you learn how to get started with DOS.

The very best way to start using DOS and your computer is to do it with someone else. If you can find a patient someone who knows the ropes, ask this person to lead you by the hand through the basic steps. With the help of an experienced friend or co-worker, you can skim the rest of this chapter. The second best way to start is to continue reading.

Setting Up DOS

There are some fairly important things you need to do before you get started with DOS. Well, not really before you get started, but still quite early in the game. But you can't, or shouldn't try to, do these early steps, which have to do with safeguarding your DOS system, until you are at least slightly comfortable with your computer.

If this is beginning to sound like the "chicken or the egg" riddle, it's not. So that you don't feel lost right at the start, this is what you are working toward: First, you're going to get a little working knowledge of diskettes and how to prepare them. Second, you're going to learn about hard disks and how to make the best use of them. Then, you'll discover how to install DOS on your own computer and what DOS does when you work with it.

Once you have an idea of what you should do, you are going to do it. You'll step through the basic operations for both diskettes and hard disks: formatting, copying, testing, and, of course, using them. Let's get to work.

What You Need to Know First

The very first things you need to know are these:

- How DOS settles in at its desk when it begins its working day
- How you tell DOS to do some work
- What special problems you face when starting out
- How the safeguards work against these problems
- What setting up diskettes and hard disks is all about

Let's begin with what DOS does when it starts its working day. When your computer "wakes up," it doesn't know very much, because it doesn't have an ordinary program loaded into it. Your computer does, however, have two special built-in programs it can rely on, and it does know how to do two things: how to perform a self-testing routine to see that things are in working order, and how to start up an operating system. This start-up program is usually called a **bootstrap loader**, since it pulls DOS up "by the bootstraps."

This bootstrap operation works in two stages. First, the tiny program built into your computer goes to work. This simple start-up program reads the very first part of a hard disk or a diskette which, if it has been prepared for start-up, is where DOS has left a program of its own—a program that knows how to get DOS itself all set up. The program in your computer doesn't actually know anything about DOS. It just knows how to read the beginning of a disk and run whatever it finds there as a program. The program doesn't know, or care, if it is starting DOS or some other operating system. It just reads the beginning of a disk, where DOS's own starting routine is.

The second part of this start-up routine, which is part of DOS, is just smart enough to get the rest of DOS going; it reads the rest of DOS from the disk and voilà—DOS is running. All this goes on behind the scenes, however; you don't see the details. You just watch the computer working away until DOS is started up.

When you first set up your computer, you specify the time and date. It is a good idea to put in the exact time and date because DOS will keep track of when your data is created, and such information can become very important later on. Once DOS is installed on your computer, the operating system automatically takes the time and date from the battery clock inside the system unit. That way, you won't have to enter them every time you turn on the computer.

If you turn on your computer for the first time and DOS is already installed, someone—perhaps a technician from the store where you bought the system, has already set up DOS for you. In this case, the time and date will already be set. If they are incorrect, you can change them by using the TIME and DATE commands, which we will cover in Chapter 8.

If you are using an old PC, you may be asked to specify the time and date each time the system starts. If this is the case with your computer, DOS will ask you for the date by displaying a message like the following:

```
Current Date is Tue 1-01-1980
Enter new date (mm-dd-yy):
```

You enter the date using a hyphen (-) or a slash (/) to separate each component. For example, for July 8, 1991, you can enter either 7-8-91 or 7/8/91. Notice that you do not have to enter the day of the week—DOS will figure that out on its own.

If you are asked for the time, the message will look something like this:

```
Current time is 0:00:01.23
Enter new time:
```

You enter the correct time using a colon (:) to separate the hours from the minutes. You can add an a or p at the end of the time to indicate AM or PM. For example, for 2:30 PM you would enter 2:30p.

If you have an older version of DOS, it may not accept an a or p. If this is the case, you will need to specify a PM time as if you were using a 24-hour clock. For example, for 2:30p you would type 14:30.

By the way, notice the date and time that we used in our example: January 1, 1980 at 12 midnight. This is the time that DOS will revert to if, for some reason, it cannot find the proper date and time. This could be the case if you are using an older PC that does not have a built-in clock.

What is the significance of January 1, 1980? We might consider it to be the start of the personal computer era. True, IBM did not actually introduce the first PC until August 12, 1981, but perhaps computers have a long gestation period.

After the preliminaries are taken care of, DOS is ready to go to work. Depending on how your system is set up, you may see a short message showing the version of DOS that you are using. A typical message looks like this:

```
IBM DOS Version 5.00
```

Date, time, and starting message. This, in simple terms, is how DOS begins its working day. Next, let's see how to tell DOS to do some work. The process is a simple, if very terse, dialogue between DOS and you. DOS tells you it is ready to accept a command, and then you tell DOS what to do.

Getting DOS to Work

DOS tells you it is ready for a command by displaying what is called the DOS **prompt**, which, literally, prompts you to type in a command.

The typical prompt is a capital letter C, followed by a backslash, followed by a greater-than sign:

```
C:\>
```

The C part of the prompt indicates which disk drive DOS is using to get and save information. You might see another letter of the alphabet, but the effect is the same. (We'll dig further into what this letter means in Chapter 3.) The \ part of the prompt indicates that we are currently working in the main directory—called the root directory. (We will cover what this means in Chapter 15).

When you see the DOS prompt, then you know you are talking to DOS and it wants you to tell it what to do; it wants an instruction. On the other hand, if you see something else on the display screen—a non-DOS prompt—you know it isn't DOS that's waiting for a command, it's some other program asking for instructions.

When you turn on your computer and you see the DOS prompt, you know that DOS is ready to start work. However, some systems are set up so that a specific program will begin automatically every time the computer is turned on. If your system has been organized in this manner, you will start working with a program rather than with DOS.

In particular, it may be that your system is set up so that when you turn on your computer you will begin working with the DOS Shell—a special program that is included as part of DOS. The purpose of this program is to make it easier for you to control your PC. We will discuss the DOS Shell and how it works in Chapter 31. For now, all we want to mention is that if your computer automatically starts the DOS Shell, your screen will look something like Figure 2-1 or Figure 2-2.

If this is the case, you can ask for a DOS prompt by pressing <Shift-F9>. (That is, you hold down the <Shift> key and press the <F9> key.) At any time, you can return to the DOS Shell by typing:

```
EXIT
```

So, one way or the other, you will see the DOS prompt. The prompt is DOS's part of the dialogue. To actually get DOS to do some work, you must give it a **command**. What are commands and what can they do? In the simplest terms, a command is the name of a program that you want the computer to carry out. That program/command might be the name of a program you've written, or it might be the name of a program you've bought, such as Lotus 1-2-3, the Norton Commander, or Word-Perfect. It might be the name of a program that is a part of DOS itself, such as TIME, which shows you the current time and lets you change it if you want. Finally, it might be a **batch file**, which I'll be explaining in

Chapter 11. (A batch file contains a list of commands that are automatically executed, one after another, just as if you had typed them in from the keyboard.)

Essentially then, you might say there are four types of commands: your own programs, store-bought programs, DOS's own programs, and DOS batch programs. If you're a little bit fuzzy on the distinctions at this point, don't worry about it. Dividing commands into four categories just gives us a way to think about them logically. Although there are significant differences between the categories, basically they are all just programs that we can tell DOS to carry out for us.

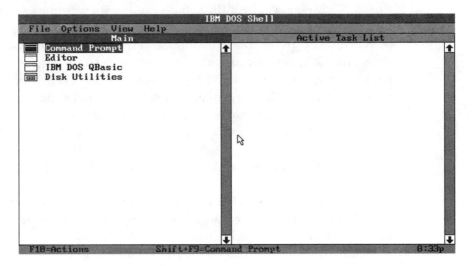

Figure 2-1. *The DOS Shell (5.0)*

Now, how do you get commands to work? It's simple: You type in the name of the command and press your computer's <Enter> key. DOS takes it from there, figuring out what type of command it is, finding the program, and making the program work. DOS does it all. All you have to do is type in the command name.

When you type commands to DOS, you will find that DOS is flexible. First, you can use either **lowercase** (small) or **uppercase** (capital) letters. Most of the time, you will use lowercase because it easier—you do not have to hold down the <Shift> key. However, in this book, we will use upper case when we show commands because, in a book, it is easier to read.

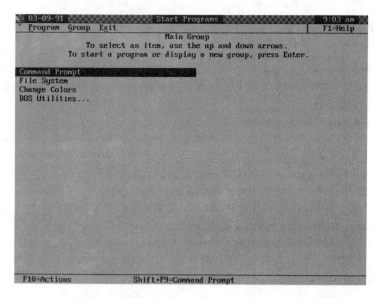

Figure 2-2. *The DOS Shell (4.0)*

In between the different parts of a DOS command you put a space by pressing the <Space> bar. If you want, you can use more than one space. You can also use a tab or more than one tab.

Here is an example. The following command will copy all the files from a diskette in drive A to a diskette in drive B. (We will meet this command in Chapter 9.)

```
COPY A:*.* B:
```

Here are three more commands that, as far as DOS is concerned, are equivalent:

```
copy a:*.* b:
COPY    A:*.*    B:
COPY    a:*.*    b:
```

One last point. You finish by pressing the <Enter> key. This tells DOS that the command is complete. For this reason, we often speak of **entering** a command. In this book, when we say enter a command, we mean type the command, then press <Enter>.

Giving Yourself a Sense of Security

So far you've seen how DOS gets started, and how it takes commands from you. Now, what are the special problems I mentioned at the beginning of this chapter? How serious are they, and how do you protect yourself?

The problems actually are few, and are mostly concerned with the possibility of losing data. It's pretty hard to break the computer itself, short of dropping it out the window, or pouring coffee inside it. If you were driving a car, rolling along at a good speed, and then suddenly shifted into reverse, you'd break your car pretty quickly. Driving into a tree would do a lot of damage, too. But you can't break a computer by "bad driving." You can damage it by physical abuse, but not by typing the wrong thing at the keyboard.

The major problem you face as a computer user is losing your only copy of some information. You can lose data in two ways. One is by physically damaging a diskette on which the data is stored, the equivalent of taking a phonograph record and breaking it. The other is by mistakenly telling the computer to throw data away, the equivalent of taking a cassette recording of some music and erasing it. In fact, the reason I developed my UnErase programs (that come with the Norton Utilities), was to help people retrieve data that they had accidentally erased.

There are ways you can reduce the chance that you'll do the computer equivalent of breaking a record or erasing a tape, but the most important safeguard against losing data is simply to keep extra copies around. That is the reason why you should regularly make a backup copy of your data onto diskettes. (We will discuss the details of doing this in Chapter 15.) Similarly, if someone were to give you a diskette containing important data that you need to change, the very first thing you should do is make a copy of the diskette. You can start working with the copy knowing that if you do anything wrong, the original is safe.

As you can see, before you can begin to get down to work with DOS you need to understand the basics of setting up diskettes. Once you do, you will be able to copy data onto blank diskettes whenever the need arises. But a blank diskette cannot be used just as it comes out of the box—a diskette must first be formatted.

Formatting

What is formatting? It is something like taking a piece of paper and ruling lines on it to give you guidelines to make your handwriting even. In

Keep Pace with
Today's Micro-
computer
Technology with:

Brady Books
and
Software

Brady Books and software
are always up-to-the-
minute and geared to
meet your needs:

- Using major applica-
  tions
- Beginning, intermedi-
  ate, and advanced
  programming
- Covering MS-DOS and
  Macintosh systems
- Business applications
  software
- Star Trek™ games
- Typing Tutor

Available at your local
book or computer store or
order by telephone:
(800) 624-0023

///BradyLine

You rely on Brady's bestselling computer books for up-to-
date information about high technology. Now turn to
BradyLine for the details behind the titles.

Find out what new trends in technology spark Brady's authors and
editors. Read about what they're working on, and predicting, for the
future. Get to know the authors through interviews and profiles, and
get to know each other through your questions and comments.

BradyLine keeps you ahead of the trends with the stories behind the
latest computer developments. Informative previews of forthcoming
books and excerpts from new titles keep you apprised of what's going
on in the fields that interest you most.

- Peter Norton on operating systems
- Winn Rosch on hardware
- Jerry Daniels, Mary Jane Mara, Robert Eckhardt, and
  Cynthia Harriman on Macintosh development, productivity, and
  connectivity

Get the Spark. Get *BradyLine*.

Published quarterly, beginning with the Summer 1990 issue. Free exclusively to
our customers. Just fill out and mail this card to begin your subscription.

Name _____

Address _____

City _____ State _____ Zip _____

Name of Book Purchased_____

Date of Purchase _____

Where was this book purchased? *(circle one)*

   Retail Store   Computer Store   Mail Order

*Mail this card for
your free subscrip-
tion to BradyLine*

F
R
E
E

70-66304

College Marketing Group
50 Cross Street
Winchester, MA 01890

ATT: **Cheryl Read**

the process, any information which might have already been on the paper will be erased.

A brand-new disk is like a blank piece of paper. Before your computer can use a disk, it needs the equivalent of guidelines written onto it to create a framework for your data. Formatting creates this framework. In addition, formatting sets up an empty directory. As we will see in Chapter 10, this directory will be used to hold the names of your files. Thus, before you can use any disk, it must be formatted. If you try to use an unformatted disk, you will get an error message.

Most modern computers use two types of disks: small, removable **diskettes** and larger, high-capacity **hard disks**. We will learn more about disks in the next two chapters. For now, what is important to understand is that you will store most of your data on a permanent, built-in hard disk. This way your files will be available to you instantly, whenever you turn on your computer. You will use diskettes when you want to make copies of data for safekeeping or for convenience. For instance, if you need to mail a copy of a file to a friend, you would copy the file from your hard disk to a diskette and simply mail the diskette. At the other end, your friend would read the file from the diskette. If he wanted to use the file repeatedly, he would copy it to his hard disk.

When you format a disk, you can specify that you want to include a copy of DOS on the disk. Why is this important? At the beginning of this chapter, we explained how, whenever you turn on your computer, the bootstrap loader gets your system up and running by reading DOS from a disk. If there is a diskette in the first diskette drive, the bootstrap loader will look for DOS on that diskette. Otherwise, it will look for DOS on your hard disk. Most of the time, your diskette drive will be empty when you turn on the computer and the system will start from your hard disk.

In order for any of this to work, the disk you start from must have been previously formatted and it must contain a copy of DOS. Thus, when you format a new disk, you include DOS if you think that you will be starting the computer from that disk. When you install DOS, the installation program automatically formats your hard disk and then copies DOS to it. (We will discuss this process in more detail in Chapter 6.)

As a rule, you do not include DOS on each disk that you format. After all, your hard disk is always there and will always be available to start the system. However, there are two cases in which you may want to install DOS onto a diskette. First, if your computer does not have a hard disk you will have to start from a diskette. This is the case with certain small laptop computers and with older PCs that do not have hard disks.

Second, you may find it handy to have a diskette from which you can start DOS in case something happens to your hard disk.

Aside from these two cases, it is doubtful that you will ever need DOS on a diskette. Thus, when you format a disk you rarely specify that DOS is to be copied. This will save space as the DOS files do take up room.

One last point. When you format a disk that has already been used, all the data on that disk will be erased. This allows you to reuse old diskettes. Similarly, if you were to give an old PC to a friend, you could completely clean off the hard disk by formatting it. On the other hand, it is all too easy to format a disk and then discover that you have accidentally wiped out valuable information. People often ask, it is possible to recover data that has been lost through formatting? (Usually, they ask the question after the accident.)

The answer is yes, in some cases it is possible to get back data from a formatted disk. We will discuss this important topic—recovering lost data—in Chapter 19. For now, let's end our short background tour of DOS and continue by learning about diskettes.

3

UNDERSTANDING DISKETTES

Introduction

It used to be that personal computers had only one type of disk—the floppy diskette. Now there are several types of disks, each with its own variations. In this chapter, we will take a short guided tour of the world of diskettes, pausing a moment at each important stop. You will then learn about the steps you need to follow to prepare a diskette for use.

Understanding Diskettes

A diskette is sometimes called a **floppy disk** for a good reason. If you were to cut it open you would find a thin, round, brown piece of plastic. The plastic is covered with a metal coating and is indeed flexible.

The original diskettes had a soft cover and the whole thing could be bent. New style diskettes come in a hard cover for greater protection. Although the insides are still flexible, the term floppy has now been mostly replaced by the word diskette.

Types of Diskettes

If we wanted, we could distinguish the two families of diskettes by their cover: hard or soft. However, it happens that all hard-cover diskettes are 3 $1/2$ inches wide and all soft-cover diskettes are 5 $1/4$ inches wide, so the way we tell them apart is by referring to their size in inches. (By the way, the 3 $1/2$ diskettes are the same size as the ones used in an Apple Macintosh computer. However, Macs store data differently and you cannot simply interchange the two types of diskettes.)

The 3 $1/2$ inch diskettes come in three variations and 5 $1/4$ inch diskettes come in two variations, so actually there are five different types of diskettes. The following table which goes from newest to oldest summarizes the details. The sizes, expressed in MB and KB, are approximate. Remember, KB stands for kilobytes, thousands of bytes, and MB stands for megabytes, millions of bytes.

As you can see from the table, the largest capacity diskettes—the 3 $1/2$ inch, 2.8 megabyte ones—are the newest. In fact, they are so new that they are not yet in widespread use. The most common diskette is actually the 3 $1/2$ inch, 1.4 megabyte one.

Throughout the history of PCs, diskette capacities have grown ever larger. That is why there are now five different types of diskettes. (Indeed, there are even two very old diskette types that we did not include in the list.) Eventually, we can expect that 2.8 MB diskettes will become the standard. However, when this occurs what will happen to all the old diskettes? Will we still be able to use them?

Fortunately, IBM and Microsoft have recognized this problem and have decreed that new diskette formats must be upwardly compatible with the old diskettes of the same size. Thus, if you you have a 3 $\frac{1}{2}$ inch diskette drive that uses 2.8 MB diskettes, the same drive can use 1.4 MB and 720 KB diskettes. Similarly, a 3 $\frac{1}{2}$ inch, 1.4 MB drive can use 720 KB diskettes; and a 5 $\frac{1}{4}$ inch, 1.2 MB drive can use 360 KB diskettes.

Table 3.1. *Diskette Variations*

	Size	*Type*	*Capacity*
(newest)	3 1/2 inch	hard-cover	2.8 MB
	3 1/2 inch	hard-cover	1.4 MB
	3 1/2 inch	hard-cover	720 KB = 0.7 MB
	5 1/4 inch	soft-cover	1.2 MB
(oldest)	5 1/4 inch	soft-cover	360 KB = 0.35 MB

This means that if you want to upgrade to a new diskette format—say, when you trade in your computer for a new model—you will still be able to use all of your old diskettes. The only exception is that if your computer uses the old 5 $\frac{1}{4}$ inch diskettes and you buy a modern machine that uses 3 $\frac{1}{2}$ inch diskettes. In this case, the old 5 $\frac{1}{4}$ inch diskettes will not fit into the new 3 $\frac{1}{2}$ inch drive. This is a good argument for using only 3 $\frac{1}{2}$ inch diskettes (which should remain the standard for some time to come). Above all, do not buy a new computer that uses only 5 $\frac{1}{4}$ inch diskettes—you will be starting off with old equipment and dooming your system to instant obsolescence.

Using Diskette Drives

All PCs come with at least one diskette drive. It is not necessary to have two drives, although an extra drive does come in handy.

In order to keep all your drives straight, DOS refers to each one by a letter, A, B, C, D, and so on. The letters A and B are always reserved for diskette drives. If you have only one diskette drive, it is known as both drive A and drive B.

For example, say that you have two diskette drives and you use the COPY command to tell DOS to copy all the files from drive A to drive B. You insert the appropriate diskettes into the correct drives and DOS will copy from one to the other.

However, what if you have only one diskette drive and you enter the same command? DOS will use the drive as both A and B by having you switch the diskettes back and forth. When DOS wants to use the drive as A, it will tell you to insert the first diskette. When it wants to use the drive as B, DOS will tell you to insert the second diskette.

In other words, if you have only one real diskette drive, DOS will maintain the pretense that there are two drives, as long as you cooperate by switching the diskettes in and out as necessary.

Preparing Diskettes for Use—Formatting

As I explained in Chapter 1, you must format any disk before you can use it. The procedure is simple: All you need to do is enter the DOS FORMAT command and specify which drive contains the disk to be formatted.

Let's start by learning how formatting works with diskettes. We will then move on to hard disks in the next chapter.

If you already have DOS working on your computer, you can take some blank diskettes and try it right now. If not, just read through this section to see how it all works.

Making a Diskette Bootable

The FORMAT command is easy, just the word format followed by the name of the drive that contains the disk that you want to prepare. For example:

```
FORMAT A:
```

Remember, as we mentioned in Chapter 2, we show all our examples in upper case, but you can type commands in either upper- or lower-case. For instance, if you were to enter the previous command, you could have easily typed:

```
format a:
```

There is also a variation of the format command that I want you to know about. Remember how I explained that if your computer does not have a hard disk, you will need to boot DOS from a diskette? This diskette, like all others, must be formatted before it can be used. Only in order to make the diskette "bootable," FORMAT has to copy DOS onto the diskette after the formatting is done. To tell FORMAT to do this, you need to specify /S (for *system*) at the end of the command:

```
FORMAT A: /S
```

If you normally boot from a hard disk you can leave out the /S when you format diskettes. After all, DOS will take up room on the diskette, and why waste the room if you are never going to use it? If you normally boot from diskettes you might want to format several of them using /S.

Here is an example. Say that you have bought five programs that you will be using regularly. If you have a hard disk, you will copy all the programs to it. When you turn on the computer, DOS will boot from the hard disk and you will them start the program you want.

If you do not have a hard disk, you will prepare five separate diskettes, each of which holds one program. You will boot the computer from a special DOS boot diskette. Once DOS is started, you will swap diskettes, putting in the one that holds the first program you want to use. You will then start the program from that diskette.

However, if you put DOS on the program diskettes when you first format them, you can start DOS from them directly. This means that you can boot the computer and then start your program without having to swap diskettes. You will find this to be a great convenience.

If you format a disk in the usual manner (without /S) and later decide to add DOS, you can do so by using the SYS and COPY commands. (We will explain how to do this in Chapter 10.) Unfortunately, this will only work with the newer versions of DOS. If you are using a version before 4.0, you can only add DOS to a disk when you format it.

For this reason, some people who work only from diskettes format all of of them with /S. However, this is wasteful: The DOS files that the FORMAT /S command places on a disk do take up space, reducing the amount of room you have for your own purposes.

Entering the FORMAT Command

So far, we have shown you two versions of the FORMAT command:

```
FORMAT A:
FORMAT A: /S
```

Notice that whenever you give the name of a disk you put a colon after it. In fact, we can consider that all disk names have two parts, a letter and a colon. Within a DOS command, you will always have to include the colon. Make sure that you do not put a space between the letter and the colon. For example, it would be wrong to enter:

```
FORMAT A   :
```

After you type the command, press the <Enter> key and the FORMAT program itself comes into play. When FORMAT is ready to start the actual formatting process, it will stop and ask you put your diskette into Drive A. The message will be similar to the following:

```
INSERT NEW DISKETTE FOR DRIVE A:
AND PRESS ENTER WHEN READY...
```

(If the message you see is not exactly the same, don't be concerned. That's one of the minor variations among different versions of DOS.)

There are two reasons why FORMAT pauses and asks you to insert the proper diskette. First, if you only have one diskette drive and no hard disk, you will need to start FORMAT from your DOS diskette and swap in the diskette to be formatted. By pausing, DOS allows you to make the swap. Second, FORMAT is giving you one last chance to change your mind and abort the process before the data on the diskette is destroyed.

If you do decide to stop the command at this point, hold down the <Ctrl> (Control) key and press <Break>. (This is sometimes referred to as pressing <Ctrl-Break>.) The <Break> key will be near the top right-hand corner of your keyboard. It will be the same as either the <Pause> key or the <Scroll-Lock> key, depending on which style of keyboard you have on your computer.

By the way, you can stop any DOS command by pressing <Ctrl-Break>. But be forewarned, the computer works so fast that sometimes it has finished all or part of the command by the time you can press the keys. To avoid trouble, check what you have typed *before* you hit the <Enter> key.

Volume Labels

After you insert the blank diskette and press <Enter>, the FORMAT program will work away, formatting the diskette. When it is finished, FORMAT will ask you to specify a **volume label** for the diskette.

As you might imagine, it is a good idea to put an identification label on the outside of every diskette. A volume label is an internal label that DOS keeps for you stored *inside* the disk. Whenever you ask DOS to show what files are on a disk, DOS will also display the volume label. This helps you keep track of which disk is which.

The volume label can be up to 11 characters. If you use lower case letters, DOS will convert them to upper case. If you are formatting spare diskettes to keep in reserve, a good volume label to use is EMPTY. When the time comes to change the volume label, you can do so using the LABEL command.

If you are using an old version of DOS (before version 4.0), the FORMAT command will not automatically ask you for a volume label. If this is the case with your system, you can force FORMAT to ask for the label by using /V at the end of the command. For example:

```
FORMAT A: /V
```

With DOS 4.0 or newer, you can specify the volume directly as part of the command by specifying a colon and the name after the /V. Here is an example:

```
FORMAT A: /V:EMPTY
```

(Be sure that you do not accidentally put a space between the colon and the name.) If you specify the volume label as part of the command, DOS will use the name automatically and will not ask you for a label when the formatting is complete.

The FORMAT Report

Once the formatting is complete and you have set the volume label, FORMAT will display a little report on its work. The exact nature of the report will depend on your computer and upon the type of diskette that you are formatting. Here is a typical message, displayed by an IBM PS/2 computer after formatting a 3 $\frac{1}{2}$ inch high-capacity diskette:

```
1457664 BYTES TOTAL DISK SPACE
1457664 BYTES AVAILABLE ON DISK

    512 BYTES IN EACH ALLOCATION UNIT
   2847 ALLOCATION UNITS AVAILABLE ON DISK

VOLUME SERIAL NUMBER IS 3D22-15F5
```

The most important parts of the message are the first two lines. The next two lines describe the technical details of how the storage is organized.

The last line shows the Volume Serial Number—a unique identification number that the newer versions of DOS assign automatically. This is different from the volume label that you yourself choose. The volume serial number will come in handy if you ever need to identify a particular diskette, but aside from that, you can ignore it.

Quick Formatting

From time to time you may want to reformat a disk. For instance, if you have finished using a diskette, formatting is a fast way to erase all the data on the diskette so that you can use it again.

To help you, DOS 5.0 introduced a new option for the format command. When you specify /Q (quick) with your command, DOS will perform a special quick format. Using /Q can save a lot of time as formatting generally takes awhile. However, this option will work only with DOS 5.0 or later and only with disks that have previously been formatted.

Here is an example of the FORMAT command using /Q:

```
FORMAT A: /V:EMPTY /Q
```

In this case, FORMAT will perform a special quick format on the diskette in Drive A. Once the formatting is complete, a volume label named EMPTY will be written to the diskette.

4

UNDERSTANDING HARD DISKS

Introduction

In the last chapter, I discussed diskettes. Let's turn our attention now to their big brothers: the hard disks. In this chapter, I will introduce you to hard disks and show you how to prepare them for DOS and for storing files. At the end of the chapter, we will meet some other types of disks, including one that doesn't really exist.

Understanding Hard Disks

Remember that I told you that if you opened a diskette you would find the actual recording surface to be a flexible piece of thin plastic. Hence the old name, floppy disk.

If you opened a hard disk you would find three important differences: First, as the name implies, the actual disk—the surface on which data is recorded—is hard. In fact, it is a rigid platter coated with magnetic recording material.

Second, where a diskette has only one thin, flexible disk (with two surfaces), a hard disk usually has more than one rigid platter, making for several recording surfaces.

And third, a hard disk is completely sealed against the outside air and dust. Usually, hard disks are installed in the computer and are not removable.

In the same way that a diskette is sometimes referred to as a floppy disk or a floppy, there are several other names used for a hard disk:

- fixed disk
- hard file
- Winchester disk

The last two terms are of IBM origin. *Hard file* is a term that will sometimes appear in IBM manuals and advertising literature. Presumably, someone thinks that hard file is a more intuitive expression than *hard disk*.

Winchester disk is a term of historical interest. When IBM was first developing what we now call the hard disk, the internal code name was Winchester. And when the disks first started to appear, they were known informally by that name.

Hard Disk Storage Capacity

The first hard disks held 5 or 10 MB (megabytes) of data. You will remember that, in Chapter 1, I explained that 1 MB is 1024 K bytes or 1,048,576 bytes. So 10 megabytes is over 10 million bytes. At the time hard disks debuted, this seemed like an enormous amount of storage. In fact, the diskettes that were used at the time held only 360 K bytes, so that a 10 MB hard disk could hold more than 28 diskettes worth of data.

However, by today's standards such sizes are puny. Modern hard disks range from 30 MB to hundreds of megabytes. And we are even starting to see disk systems whose size is measured in gigabytes. (1 gigabyte = 1024 megabytes = 1024 x 1024 kilobytes = 1024 x 1024 x 1024 bytes which is approximately one billion bytes!)

For your own use, I would recommend at least 30 MB, but the more the better. Although it may seem unlikely that you will sit at the keyboard and generate tens of millions of characters of data, you will not regret buying extra space. Modern programs often come with many files and it is not uncommon to use several megabytes installing some large new piece of software.

Using Hard Disks

In the last chapter, I explained how DOS uses letters to refer to disks, and how the letters A and B are reserved for diskettes. This means that your hard disk will be known as C. If you have a second hard disk, it will be known as D and so on.

Remember that if you only have one diskette drive, it is known as both A and B. This means that your first hard disk is always C even if you only have a single diskette drive.

Partitioning a Hard Disk

You already know that diskettes must be formatted—prepared—before they can be used by DOS. The same is true for hard disks and, in fact, you use the same program, FORMAT. However, before you can format a hard disk there is another step that must come first: You must partition the disk.

Partitioning allows you to divide a hard disk into one or more on logical disks, called **partitions**. For example, say that you have a 50 MB hard disk. You might choose to divide it into two partitions, the first having 30 MB and the second having 20 MB. In this case, the 30 MB partition would be known as drive C and the 20 MB partition would be known as drive D. As far as you are concerned, each partition acts like a separate disk even though you know that, physically, there is only one real drive.

The question is, why would you choose to divide a disk into more than one partition? There are three reasons:

First, you may want to put another operating system on your computer. For instance, some people will want to be able to use both DOS and a Unix operating system on the same computer. Each operating system is separate and has its own separate file system residing in its own partition.

With OS/2, on the other hand, you have two choices. You can either share the DOS file system or use a separate OS/2 file system. If you decide to share a single file system between DOS and OS/2 you will need only a single DOS partition. If you want to use a separate OS/2 file system you will need a separate partition. Some people choose this alternative because it allows them to use the OS/2 high-performance file system which is not compatible with DOS. (If you are interested in OS/2, we will be comparing it with DOS in Chapter 35.)

If you do want to install more than one operating system, read the instructions carefully. Some operating systems—for example the Unix systems—need to be installed *before* DOS. Others—such as the Pick operating system—need to be installed after DOS.

The second reason why you might want to partition a hard disk is for organization. One large hard disk can hold many thousands of files. You may find it convenient to divide the space into more than one logical disk. For example, you might create two partitions, one for programs (the C disk) and one for your data files (the D disk). Or, if your computer is being used for two distinct purposes—say, two completely separate businesses—you may choose to have each business use its own partition.

The third reason to partition a hard disk is not as important as it used to be. Up until IBM DOS 4.0, you could not make any partition larger than 32 MB. When hard disks were small this was not much of a limitation, but as disks grew in size people found it necessary to divide their disks into more than one partition just to be able to use all the space.

Fortunately, that limitation has been removed and you can organize your hard disk as you see fit. DOS 4.0 allows hard disk partitions up to 512 MB. DOS 5.0 allows partitions up to 2048 MB (2 gigabytes). In addition, DOS 5.0, unlike earlier version, directly supports the use of more than two hard disks.

Using the FDISK Command

To create and manage the partitions on a hard disk you use the FDISK (fixed disk) command. The form of this command is simple, just the name:

```
FDISK
```

The FDISK program is menu driven and easy to use, but make sure you read the directions in your manual before you start. FDISK will allow you to:

- display a summary of what partitions currently exist on your hard disk
- create new partitions
- delete old partitions
- change which partition will automatically boot when you turn on the computer

The last point may need some explanation.

When you turn on the computer, the bootstrap loader (see Chapter 2) will try to boot from a diskette in the first diskette drive. If there is no such diskette, the loader checks the partition information on your first hard disk and determines which partition is active. The operating system then boots from that partition.

For example, say that you have installed both DOS and UNIX on your system. If the DOS partition is active, DOS will boot when you turn on the computer. If the UNIX partition is active, UNIX will boot. You can use FDISK to switch back and forth.

But beware—you must be very careful when you use FDISK. When you delete a partition, all the data is gone forever. There is no way to get it back. In certain circumstances it is possible to get back data if you accidentally reformat a hard disk (see below). But it is always impossible to recover from deleting the wrong partition.

Partitioning is something that you should do once and forget. In fact, there is a good chance that the store where you bought your computer has already partitioned the hard disk for you. If you set up a computer for someone else, I recommend removing the FDISK program. (Unless of course, you are working with a sophisticated user who will be switching from one operating system to another.)

Examples of FDISK Summaries

Here are two examples of FDISK summary reports. The first report is from FDISK under DOS 5.0. It shows a disk that has a single large partition:

```
CURRENT FIXED DISK DRIVE: 1

PARTITION STATUS TYPE VOLUME LABEL MBYTES SYSTEM USAGE
 C: 1        A    PRI DOS   NORTON      31   FAT 16  100%

TOTAL DISK SPACE IS 115 MBYTES (1 MBYTE = 1048576 BYTES)
```

The second example is more complex. In this case, I installed OS/2 and AIX (a type of UNIX) on the same hard disk, and then used DOS to create an additional partition. This situation is probably more complex than anything you will encounter.

In the next case, the summary report is from FDISK, DOS version 3.3. Notice that the report from this older DOS is more confusing than the newer style report, above.

```
PARTITION STATUS   TYPE    START  END SIZE
     1         N    NON-DOS    0    0    1
     2   C:    A    PRI DOS    1   10   10
     3         N    EXT DOS   11   24   14
     4         N    NON-DOS   25  114   90

MAXIMUM CAPACITY OF THE FIXED DISK IS 115 CYLINDERS.
```

In this example, partitions number 1 and 4 were created by the AIX installation program (which I ran first). During the installation, I specified that a certain amount of space was to be set aside. Later, I used this space to create partitions 2 and 3.

Partition 2 is an OS/2 partition; partition 3 is a DOS partition. However, since OS/2 and DOS use the same type of file systems, FDISK describes them both as DOS partitions. Partition 2 is called the primary partition; partition 3 is called the extended partition. (These details are explained fully in your manual.)

Notice that the status of partition 2 is active and the status of the other partitions is non-active. This means that when I turn on the computer, it will boot from partition 2—that is, it will boot OS/2. If I want to start AIX, I would have to use FDISK to activate partition 1, and then reboot.

Formatting a Hard Disk

Once a hard disk is partitioned, you must format each partition. Usually, you will use only one large partition. However, if you have more than one DOS partition, each is considered a logically distinct disk and each must be formatted separately.

You use the FORMAT command exactly as I described in Chapter 3. Just remember that your first partition must be formatted with a /S so that a copy of DOS will be placed on it, making it bootable. The other partitions should be formatted without /S as there is no reason for them to contain DOS.

Here are some examples: Say that you have one hard disk partitioned as one large DOS partition (the usual case). The disk will be known as drive C, and you will use the following FORMAT command:

```
FORMAT C: /S
```

If you are using an older version of DOS, you might want to utilize the /V option to force FORMAT to ask you for a volume label (see Chapter 3).

```
FORMAT C: /S /V
```

Here is another example: You have a large hard disk that you have decided to divide into three partitions, all of which you will use with DOS. They will be known as drives C, D, and E, and you will use the following format commands:

```
FORMAT C: /S
FORMAT D:
FORMAT E:
```

One last example: You have two hard disks. You decide to keep the first one as one large partition but divide the second hard disk into two partitions. In this case, DOS considers the partition on the first hard disk to be drive C and the partitions on the second hard disk to be drives D and E. The format commands are the same as the last example.

Built-in Safeguards

Formatting a hard disk is much like formatting a diskette but with two built-in safeguards for your protection.

First, if you are reformatting a partition that has already been format-ted, the newer versions of DOS will make you type in the volume label before they proceed. This keeps you from accidentally erasing an enor-mous amount of data. That is, if you do want to reformat a partition, DOS sees to it that it is a deliberate act on your part and not a mistake.

Second, before the actual formatting starts, FORMAT will display a message similar to:

```
WARNING. ALL DATA ON NON-REMOVABLE DISK
DRIVE C: WILL BE BE LOST!
PROCEED WITH FORMAT (Y/N)?
```

Since you are formatting a hard disk partition (which contains a large amount of data) and not a relatively small diskette, FORMAT is giving you one last chance to confirm that this is really what you want to do.

The Format Report

Once the formatting process is complete, FORMAT will display a short report, just as when you format a diskette. Here is a sample report. It shows the results of formatting a hard disk that has been prepared as one large partition (drive C) using the following command:

```
FORMAT C: /S
```

The report is:

```
120315904 BYTES TOTAL DISK SPACE
   110592 BYTES USED BY SYSTEM
120205312 BYTES AVAILABLE ON DISK

     2048 BYTES IN EACH ALLOCATION UNIT
    58694 ALLOCATION UNITS AVAILABLE ON DISK
VOLUME SERIAL NUMBER IS 1C63-11FD
```

The first three lines show how big the partition is, how much space is taken up by DOS, and how much space is left to be used. In this case, you can divide these three numbers by (1024 x 1024) and convert them to megabytes. If you do, you will find that the partition contains 114.7 MB, of which DOS uses 0.1 MB, leaving 114.6 MB for general use.

The next two lines describe the technical details of how the storage is organized. The last line shows the volume serial number—a unique iden-tification number for this disk (see Chapter 3).

Defective Areas on the Disk

When you prepare a disk, FORMAT marks any defective areas as bad so that they will never be used to store data. This means that if a disk does have some bad areas, you can still use the rest of the space. If this happens, you will get a message as part of the FORMAT report showing how many bytes were bad.

If this happens with a diskette, it is a good idea to format over again. If the problem recurs, throw away the diskette. It is unusual to have a diskette that won't format 100% correctly. Your data is worth much more than the cost of one diskette.

With a hard disk, the story is different. Hard disks can hold many megabytes of data and it is not uncommon for some of those bytes to be bad. In the example above, I was able to format almost 115 MB with no defective areas. However, it is common for hard disks to have a small percentage of bad bytes.

Here is a general rule: You can feel comfortable accepting a hard disk that has up to 1% to 2% of its space marked as bad. However, if more than 2% of the bytes are bad, you may want to return your disk as being unacceptable.

Recovering Data from an Accidentally Formatted Hard Disk

As I mentioned above, if you accidentally repartition a hard disk, there is no way to restore any of the data. However, if you accidentally reformat a hard disk partition, there may be a way to recover. Here is why:

When you format a diskette, FORMAT completely erases all the data on the diskette. But when you format a hard disk partition, FORMAT marks the space as being available without actually destroying the information. One reason is that it would just take too long to physically expunge every byte of data on a large hard disk. So although it looks as if the data is gone, it is actually still there.

If you ever accidentally format a hard disk partition, you will need to take special steps to recover your data. Starting with version 5.0, DOS provides commands (MIRROR, UNFORMAT) that you can use in such an emergency. We will discuss these commands in detail in Chapter 19.

In order for the UNFORMAT command to work well, you should have previously used the MIRROR command. If you did not, you can still use UNFORMAT but it will probably not be able to recover your data completely.

If you would like a more sophisticated way to protect yourself, you can use the UNFORMAT program that comes with the Norton Utilities. (Many people prefer this program to the DOS commands.) Norton UNFORMAT is especially important if your version of DOS does not come with an unformat facility. The instructions for using this program are in the Norton Utilities manual.

Just one word of warning: If you do accidentally format a hard disk partition, the safest thing to do is to turn off your computer and don't let anyone near it until you have read the instructions for using your unformat program.

Other Types of Disks

So far, we have talked about two types of disks: diskettes and hard disks. But there are several variations that you might run into that we should discuss. Their sizes range from small to extremely large but at heart, like all disks, their chief purpose in life is to store and recall data.

Removable Hard Disks

As you know, hard disks, unlike diskettes, are built into the computer. Since the disk surfaces reside in a controlled environment within hermetically sealed containers, they can be designed to be faster and store more data.

Now, however, it is possible to get the best of both worlds. You can buy special hard disk drives that use removable cartridges. Typical sizes would be 20 or 40 MB (although this is bound to increase). This means that you can have the convenience of a portable storage medium (like a diskette) along with the speed and size of a hard disk.

In most cases, you will do just fine with one standard hard disk. However, in certain situations removable hard disks offer three important advantages.

First, if you use a lot of storage, but not all at the same time, a removable hard disk with cartridges is more convenient than an enormous hard disk. For example, if you have several large databases, you might keep each one on a separate cartridge. If you check the prices, you will see that once you buy the special disk drive, the cost of the cartridges, per megabyte, compares favorably to the cost of diskettes.

Second, removable cartridges provide portability. For instance, you can carry 40 MB on a business trip without having to struggle with an armful of diskettes.

Third, it is easier to maintain security. Sensitive data can be stored on a cartridge that can be removed and locked in a secure place. (Of course, this works both ways. It is a lot simpler to steal a catridge than a built-in hard disk.)

Optical Disks

Optical disks are based on technology that uses lasers to write and read data. The disks themselves look much like the compact disks that you would use with your home stereo system. The main advantage of optical disks is that they can hold an enormous amount of storage—hundreds of megabytes on the same size disk that might hold one record album! And the cost per megabyte is definitely competitive.

To use optical disks you must have a special drive, and, as you might imagine, special software. DOS is designed to work only with diskettes and hard disks.

Basically, there are three types of optical disk systems: The first, CD-ROM (compact disk—read-only memory) uses disks that can be read but not changed. It is not uncommon to find CD-ROMs that hold up to 600 MB of data.

CD-ROM disks are created from master disks that contain data that will be mass-distributed. For example, a book wholesaler may send out a new CD-ROM catalogue to retail stores every month. Microsoft Corporation sells CD ROMs that contain a wide variety of reference works and literature.

The second type of system uses optical disks that are blank when you buy them. You can write on them, but only once; they are not erasable. These types of disk systems are known by the exotic name of WORM (write once—read mostly).

WORM systems represent a halfway point between CD-ROM disks, which cannot be changed, and fully erasable disks. WORM systems are generally used for archival storage in situations where you need to write information once and keep it as a permanent, unalterable record. For example, law firms find it useful to save data on a medium that can be neither erased nor tampered with.

The third type of optical disk system uses fully eraseable disks that behave, from your point of view, much like hard disks. That is, you buy blank disks on which you can write, read, and erase as many times as you want. And each disk might hold 200 to 600 MB!

Fully eraseable optical disks have yet to replace hard disks which are still cheaper and faster. However, when the time comes, the optical disks will provide enormous improvements over the current technology.

Floptical Diskettes

As a disk rotates within a drive, there must be a way to keep track of the disk's position at all times. To allow this, there are special markings on the surface of the disk that are used as reference points. As the disk moves, the position of these markings are sensed.

It happens that one of the limitations to how much data can be stored on a disk is how closely and how well-defined these reference points can be written. With regular diskettes, the tracking marks are written magnetically. However, if the marks are written optically, using a laser, the system works better and much more data can be stored.

A floptical diskette looks like a regular 3 1/2 inch diskette. And indeed the data is written and read in the much the same way. However, the special tracking marks are written onto the diskette, using a laser, before you buy them. And where a regular 3 1/2 inch diskette holds 1.44 MB or 2.8 MB of data, a floptical diskette holds 10, 20, and even 40 MB.

The name *floptical* is a contraction of floppy and optical. Floptical diskettes are still new and, as yet, there are no well-accepted standards. However, like the erasable optical disks—some of which also merge optical and magnetic technology—their potential is great.

Virtual Disks

The last kind of disk, a virtual disk, is a contradiction: It isn't really a disk, and yet it's the fastest disk of all. It holds the smallest amount of information, and yet it can be more useful than a large optical disk. It works the same way as any other disk and yet it disappears when you turn off your computer. It is the most expensive type of disk and yet you can't buy one.

When you look in the mirror, what you see is called a virtual image. A virtual disk is called by the same name because it too seems to exist, but it really isn't there. Here is how it works:

You specify to DOS that it is to take a portion of your memory and simulate a disk. (The details are described in Chapter 29, The Configuration File.) This disk, a virtual disk, behaves just like a real one, and you can use it to store and read files in the normal manner. Because a virtual disk resides in memory, it is often called a RAM disk. (RAM stands for Random Access Memory.) A less common term is electronic disk.

The peculiar characteristics of a virtual disk come from the fact that it is simulated by DOS using memory. First, it is unlikely that you will be able to spare more than a few megabytes for a virtual disk (if that), although even the smallest hard disk has 20 or 30 MB.

Second, since a virtual disk resides in memory, it is empty when you start, and it disappears when you turn off the computer. To use a virtual disk, you must first copy to it or create files on it. And, if you change those files, you must save them to your hard disk before you power down.

Third, if you compare the cost of memory to that of a hard disk, you will see that, byte per byte, a virtual disk costs much more than a regular disk.

However, as I explained in Chapter 1, Basic Computer Concepts, DOS can directly use only 640 K bytes of your memory, and most computers come with more than that. For example, if your computer has 2 MB— 2048 K bytes—of memory, you have 1408 K bytes (2048–640) that can be used for other purposes. You could use this space to create a virtual disk of about 1.3 MB.

Here is an example of how you might use a virtual disk: Say that your word processor has a spelling checker that uses a built-in dictionary stored on disk. Every time you check a word, the program must read from the hard disk. To speed this up, you can copy the dictionary to the virtual disk and direct the word processor to look there. Now, whenever you check a word, the program reads the dictionary from the virtual disk which, because it is in memory, responds faster than a regular hard disk.

5

INSTALLING DOS

Introduction

So far, we have oriented ourselves to DOS and have learned about disk-ettes and hard disks. Now, we can move on to the last step that will prepare us for using DOS.

In this chapter, I will show you the proper way to copy DOS from your master diskettes—that you get when you buy DOS—onto your personal computer system. This process is called **installing** the operating system.

It may be that you do not need to bother with this at all—the person from whom you bought your computer may have prepared everything: partitioning, formatting, and installation. If you turn on the computer and DOS starts, this is the case.

Nevertheless, I suggest that you still read this chapter. We will discuss how DOS used to be installed and then move on to how DOS is installed today. Even though you may have little work to do yourself, the principles are important for you to understand.

However, before we install DOS, let's take a moment and see exactly what we are dealing with.

The Parts of DOS

In order to really understand DOS you need to understand its parts. Think of DOS as having two parts, each made up of a number of files.

1. The main part of DOS, consisting of three programs.
2. A large number of auxiliary programs and files.

The three main programs have different names depending on what type of DOS you are using. If you are using PC-DOS (IBM DOS) the main DOS programs are:

- IBMBIO.COM
- IBMDOS.COM
- COMMAND.COM

If you are using MS-DOS (for non-IBM computers), the same programs are called:

- IO.SYS
- MSDOS.SYS
- COMMAND.COM

IBMBIO.COM (or IO.SYS) provides the basic facilities for handling the input and output (I/O) devices. In fact, BIO stands for basic input/output: IBMDOS.COM (or MSDOS.SYS) is the main DOS program that generally runs everything. COMMAND.COM is the command processor. This is the program that reads your commands from the keyboard and decides what to do to carry out your requests. If you are used to the Unix operating system, here is a rough analogy: IBMDOS.COM is the kernel, IBMBIO.COM contains the basic device drivers, and COMMAND.COM is the shell.

Installing DOS

Installing DOS means copying both parts of DOS to the disk from which you plan on booting your system. Normally, this means copying the DOS files to your hard disk. If you need to be able to boot DOS from a diskette—say, if your computer does not have a hard disk—you need to copy both parts of DOS to that diskette.

When we format a disk using the /S option (see Chapters 3 and 4) the FORMAT command copies the three main programs after the disk is formatted.

However, there are a great many other, auxiliary files that DOS uses. If you have only the three main files, you can boot DOS and use a limited number of DOS commands; but in order to use the rest of the DOS commands, you need access to the rest of the DOS files. (I will explain why in detail in the next chapter.)

How DOS Used to be Installed a Long Time Ago

In the olden days (before 1983) IBM-compatible computers did not have hard disks and everyone had to boot from a diskette. The steps in installing DOS were as follows:

1. Make a copy of the DOS master diskette that you got when you bought DOS.

   (As you might imagine, it is a much better idea to work with a copy than with your only original.)

2. Use the copy of the DOS diskette to format a blank diskette.

    (You use the FORMAT command with /S in order to copy the three main DOS files. It is this blank diskette that becomes your new boot diskette.)

3. Copy the second part of DOS—the auxiliary files—to the new boot diskette.

There were variations to this scheme, but basically the idea was simple: format a diskette and copy files to it. In fact, under certain circumstances, there was even a way (using the DISKCOPY command, see Chapter 9) to do all of this in one step.

When hard disks became available, there was one more step to add: As I explained in Chapter 4, you must partition a hard disk before you can format it. So, with a hard disk, the steps were:

1. Make a copy of the DOS master diskette that you got when you bought DOS.

2. Use the DOS diskette to partition the hard disk.

3. Use the DOS diskette to format the hard disk.

4. Copy the second part of DOS—the auxiliary files—to the hard disk.

How DOS Used to be Installed Not So Long Ago

By the time DOS 3.0 came along, things had become more complex. Most people had hard disks which meant that partitioning and hard disk management was the norm.

Another consideration was that IBM had enhanced DOS to be convenient for people to use in many different countries. There were now various keyboards for different languages and DOS needed to know which one you were using. Furthermore, DOS needed to know what country you were in so that it could display the time and date in the appropriate format.

This meant that, unless you were using the default American keyboard and language, you needed to place certain commands in your two configuration files, CONFIG.SYS and AUTOEXEC.BAT. (I will explain these files fully in Chapter 12 and 28. For now, all you need to know is that you set up these two files to tell DOS how you want to configure the details of your particular system. For example, you put the command that specifies which language you are using into the CONFIG.SYS file; and the command which specifies which keyboard you are using into the AUTOEXEC.BAT file.)

To make things easy, IBM developed a new command, SELECT. You used this command to perform the bulk of the installation, including formatting the hard disk and copying many of the DOS files. The name comes from the fact that you use the program to select which configuration you will be using.

So, with an operating system from the DOS 3 family, the installation steps were:

1. Use the DOS diskette to partition the hard disk.
2. Use the DOS diskette to run the SELECT command.
3. Copy the remaining DOS files to the hard disk.

Note: Unlike the olden days, we did not start by making a copy of the DOS diskettes (by now, there were several). When you install software to a hard disk, you rarely use the master diskettes again and it is not really necessary to copy them. Just make sure that they are stored in a safe place.

How DOS Is Installed Now

As you might imagine, DOS is more complex than ever. Nowadays, there are many more details to consider during an installation. However, in the face of this complexity, IBM has made life easier. Starting with DOS 4.00, the SELECT program was enhanced to do all the work for you. For DOS 5.0, the name of the program was changed to SETUP. Once again, the installation program was completely rewritten—this time, to automate even more of the entire installation process.

The installation program is now menu-driven, which means that it presents you with a series of screens (menus) asking you to make choices as to what you want. (For example, if you want, you can tell the installation program to install to a diskette instead of a hard disk.)

During the installation process, the installation program will tell you when to switch diskettes. All you have to do is follow the instructions. However, it is important to understand that even though the program is doing all the work for you, it is still performing the standard procedures necessary to install DOS:

1. Partition the hard disk.
2. Format the hard disk.
3. Copy the DOS files to the hard disk.
4. Create personalized configuration files (CONFIG.SYS and AUTOEXEC.BAT).

Although DOS installation is now completely painless, I recommend that you take a few minutes to read the startup documentation before you begin. After all, our goal is not just to get the job done, but to understand what is happening.

So, having explained the entire DOS installation process for DOS 4 and DOS 5, let me summarize it as follows:

- Read the documentation.
- Insert the installation diskette, turn on the computer, and follow the instructions.

And now, let's move on to the next chapter where you will begin to learn about the magic words that will make the computer your personal servant—the DOS commands.

6

FUNDAMENTALS OF DOS COMMANDS

Introduction

Before you can move on to really start looking at the DOS commands, you have to learn the fundamentals of how they are laid out and used. In this chapter, we'll pause to master the basics of DOS commands. My real goal in this book is to help you become familiar with DOS: to speed you as quickly as possible toward thinking of DOS as an old friend, a needed tool that you use easily and with hardly a second thought. One thing that will help you most in getting comfortable with DOS is an understanding of how important disk drives are to DOS.

DOS is, after all, a disk operating system, and disks are at the core of the way DOS operates and organizes itself. If you want to understand DOS, you need to understand the way DOS thinks about disks.

Keeping Track of Drives

One of the first things you need to realize about how it works is that DOS focuses more on the disk drive than on the actual diskette or hard disk. Whether your computer has a hard disk, or one or two diskette drives, DOS needs a consistent and uniform way of keeping track of this disk gear. It does this, as you saw in Chapter 2, by giving a letter "name" to each of the drives.

The first drive is referred to as A, the second as B, and so forth. As I mentioned in the last chapter, DOS will turn a single diskette drive into a "let's-pretend" pair of drives, A and B. Many DOS command operations need two disk drives and when there is only one drive, it is easier and more consistent for DOS to fake a second drive, B drive, than to try to do everything with only the A drive. In other words, if you have two diskette drives, the first will be drive A and the second will be drive B.

As we mentioned earlier, your hard disk partitions are named drive C, drive D, drive E, and so on. Many people set up their system so that their hard disk is one large partition. If your system is like this, most of the work you do will center around this single partition which DOS will call drive C.

Later, in Chapter 16, we will discuss strategies for organizing your hard disk. At that time, we will explain how you might want to divide your hard disk into two partitions, one for your programs and one for your data. If you do this, your work with DOS will center around drives C and D.

Regardless of how you choose to partition your hard disk, your work with diskettes will use drives A and B.

Such background aside, let's assume you have a diskette you want to work with. If you put that diskette in your A diskette drive, then you tell DOS to look to the A drive to find what is on that diskette. You'd get the same result if you put the same diskette in the B drive and told DOS to look there. The point is simple: DOS doesn't know what you're doing with diskettes, which you might even be switching around behind its back. DOS *does* know what's what with the disk drives, so that is where its focus is.

This means that whenever you do anything with data or programs on a disk, you have to let DOS know which drive you want it to look to. You do this by typing the drive letter, followed by a colon, like this:

```
C:
```

This tells DOS to work with drive C. You'd do the same for one of the diskette drives; for drive A by typing:

```
A:
```

or for drive B by typing

```
B:
```

(By the way, DOS will happily take either upper- or lowercase letters and treat them the same.)

When any of your computer manuals refer to the **drive specification**, they are referring to the drive letter, followed by a colon. So remember, A:, C:, and so on are also known as drive specifications. As a matter of fact, since you will almost always need to type a colon after the name of a drive, I like to think of the drive as having two names. The letter, A, B, C and so on is the first name; the colon is the second name. As with people, the same last name, in this case, the colon, shows that all drives are members of the same "family." However, unlike a person's name, there is never a space between the drive's first name and the colon.

The Default Drive

Much of what you do with the computer involves disk data, so it could be a real nuisance to have to keep typing in the drive specification all the time. DOS simplifies the process by having what's called a **default drive**—a drive that DOS looks to, unless you say otherwise. DOS keeps track of the current default drive, and any time you or a program refer to a disk without giving a drive specification, DOS assumes you intend to use the default drive.

I've already mentioned that DOS prompts for commands with something like this:

```
C:\>
```

So you're probably able to guess that the C in this prompt refers to the current default drive. If the default drive were changed to A, DOS's prompt would be:

```
A:\>
```

This prompt is really quite clever, when you think about it. Since the default drive can be changed, it's very helpful to have DOS remind us of where the default is. But it would be a nuisance to have DOS repeatedly display a message such as:

```
THE DEFAULT DRIVE IS NOW C:.
```

Instead, the DOS command prompt is a compact, handy, and unobtrusive way for DOS to remind you of the current default drive. And actually, the prompt tells you more than just the default drive. It also tells you what directory you are in. Directories are explained in Chapter 13, so don't worry about them for now. In these examples, the backslash [\] is telling us that we are in the main (or *root*) directory. So, a prompt of:

```
C:/>
```

is really telling us:

```
THE DEFAULT DRIVE IS C: AND YOU ARE IN THE MAIN DIRECTORY.
```

If you are using a version of DOS before 4.0, or if you do not have a hard disk, the prompt will not show directories. You will just see the drive letter followed by a colon. In any case, as I will explain in Chapter 14, you can always change the prompt according to your preferences.

What if you want to change the default drive? It's simple: Just type in a drive specification all by itself. DOS interprets the drive specification as a command to change the default drive and away you go. Here is an example:

Your prompt is currently:

```
C:\>
```

which means that your current drive is C, your hard disk. You want to change to the first diskette drive, so, after making sure that there is a diskette in the drive, you enter:

```
A:
```

DOS changes drives and displays the new prompt:

```
A:\>
```

Your default drive is now drive A.

Whenever you are working with disks, you have free choice: Use the default drive or specify a different one. In fact, you can specify the drive even if it is already the default—there is no harm in that. The upshot is, if you want to be very specific about a drive, for whatever reason, you can type the letter of the drive you want to use, followed by a colon, and it will work just fine, default or not.

Internal versus External Commands

The next thing to cover about commands in general is where they come from. As I've mentioned, commands that we ask DOS to carry out are, in one way or another, programs. The question is: What kind of programs are they and where are they located? This brings us to the topic of internal versus external commands.

DOS faces a quandary you might never think of. In itself, DOS has a large number of services, or commands, available for us to use. Given a choice, we would like to have these command services on tap, instantly, at all times. But for us to have this, the programs that provide these services would have to be resident in memory. That means they would be taking up a lot of our computer's working memory space all of the time—when we were using them and when we were not. On the other hand, we want to have as little as possible of our computer's memory (its working desktop) taken up by these command programs that we might or might not need to call upon, because we have plenty of other uses for the memory.

The conflict is obvious, and to resolve it DOS provides us with a compromise. A handful of the smallest and most useful command programs are a resident part of DOS. These are called the **internal commands**. They are in memory all the time, once DOS has been read from the disk and started up. And because they are in memory, they are always available—DOS "knows" these commands and can call upon them as easily as you can muster up your name or telephone number. Two examples of internal commands are COPY (to copy files) and VER (to remind you which version of DOS you are using).

All of the other command programs in DOS are called **external**, and they are kept on the disk until they are needed. When you call for one of these commands, DOS must refer to the disk to "refresh" its memory, much as you might look up the recipe for your grandmother's holiday cookies. The 5.0 version of DOS has 77 commands that perform 88 different functions. Of these 77 commands, 29 are internal and 48 are external.

Here is how it all works. You will remember, from Chapter 5, that the main part of DOS consists of three programs. One of these programs is COMMAND.COM which is sometimes called the command interpreter. It is COMMAND.COM that displays the DOS prompt and then waits for you to enter a command. When you enter a command, it is COMMAND .COM that reads what you have typed and carries out your request.

The internal commands are the ones that are built into COMMAND .COM. The external commands are carried out by separate programs, one program for each command. For example, the FORMAT command is carried out by the FORMAT.COM program. When you install DOS, all of these programs are copied to your hard disk.

Whenever you enter a command, COMMAND.COM checks its list to see if the command is internal. If so, COMMAND.COM itself will carry out your request. If the command is not internal, COMMAND.COM will look for a program that has the same name. If such a program is found, it will be executed on your behalf. When the program is finished, control returns to COMMAND.COM. In either case, once the job is done, COMMAND.COM displays the DOS prompt and waits for you to enter another command.

Here are two examples. First, you enter the following command to copy all the files from the diskette in drive A to the hard disk C. (For now, don't worry about the details.)

```
COPY A:*.* C:
```

Once you press the <Enter> key, COMMAND.COM looks at what you have typed. In this case, the COPY command is recognized as being internal so COMMAND.COM carries out your request directly.

Now, consider this example. You enter a command to format the diskette in drive A.

```
FORMAT A:
```

Again, COMMAND.COM checks to see if this is an internal command. However, in this case, FORMAT is an external command. That means that COMMAND.COM cannot carry out your request directly. Instead, COMMAND.COM looks on the disk for a program whose name is FORMAT. Since FORMAT is an external command such a program exists. COMMAND.COM finds the FORMAT program (FORMAT.COM) and starts it executing.

For the most part, you don't have to worry about which commands are internal and which are external. All you have to do is make sure that DOS knows where to look for an external command. You do this by setting the *search path*, which we will cover in Chapter 13. (Actually, with modern versions of DOS the installation program does this for you automatically.)

Thus, DOS can always carry out internal commands, but it can execute external commands only if it can find the corresponding programs. Normally, the programs are stored on your hard disk. If your computer does not have a hard disk you have two choices: either you use only the internal commands, or you make sure that whenever you enter an external command the diskette in the drive contains the external command programs. In some cases, you might have to swap diskettes, especially if you have only one diskette drive. (As you can see, having a permanently available hard disk is a big advantage.)

If you ever enter the name of a command that DOS cannot find you will see the following message:

```
BAD COMMAND OR FILE NAME
```

When you see this message it might mean that you have entered the name of a legitimate command that, for some reason, DOS cannot find. However, the most common problem is that you have misspelled the name of the command. For example, if you enter:

```
FORAMAT A:
```

DOS will look for an external command named FORAMAT. So, the first thing you must do when you get the "Bad command" message is check what you typed as a command name—it may not be what you intended.

To finish this section, take a look at Table 6-1 which shows all the DOS commands, classified as internal or external. The batch commands are special internal commands that we will look at in Chapters 10 and 11.

Table 6.1   A List Of All The External And Internal DOS Commands

External	Internal	Internal Batch
APPEND	CHCP	CALL
ASSIGN	CHDIR (CD)	ECHO
ATTRIB	CLS	FOR
BACKUP	COPY	GOTO
BREAK	CTTY	IF
CHKDSK	DATE	PAUSE
COMMAND	DEL (ERASE)	REM
COMP	DIR	SHIFT
DEBUG	EXIT	
DISKCOMP	FOR	
DISKCOPY	LOADHIGH (LH)	
DOSKEY	MKDIR (MD)	
DOSSHELL	PATH	
EDIT	PROMPT	
EDLIN	RENAME (REN)	
EMM386	RMDIR (RD)	
EXE2BIN	SET	
EXPAND	TIME	
FASTOPEN	TYPE	
FC	VER	
FDISK	VERIFY	
FIND	VOL	
FORMAT		
GRAFTABL		
GRAPHICS		
HELP		
JOIN		
KEYB		
LABEL		
MEM		
MIRROR		
MODE		
MORE		
NLSFUNC		
PRINT		
QBASIC		
RECOVER		
REPLACE		
RESTORE		
SETVER		

(continued)

Table 6.1   *(continued)*

External	*Internal*
SHARE	
SORT	
SUBST	
SYS	
TREE	
UNDELETE	
UNFORMAT	
XCOPY	

Common Command Notation

There is a standard format for asking DOS to carry out commands, a format usually called the command **syntax**, which governs the way we are supposed to enter commands. This section will explain the normal way you request DOS commands. Unfortunately, there is a little too much variety in the way you can enter commands, and that can lead to some confusion about the best way to express commands. I'll try to clear all that up here.

First, all commands follow this basic format:

```
COMMAND-NAME PARAMETERS-IF-ANY
```

In Chapter 8 we will learn about the COPY comand; for now, though, here is an example of how you would use COPY to copy all the files from the diskette in drive A to the diskette in drive B:

```
COPY A:*.* B:
```

The command name was COPY and two parameters were needed, the first indicating what to copy from (A:*.*) and the second showing what to copy to (B:). That's the most basic part: A command begins with the name of the command, followed by whatever parameters are needed.

In addition, some kind of punctuation must be used to separate the command name and the parameters. In the examples so far, I've always used spaces, but DOS allows—in fact, sometimes requires—other punctuation marks, including commas, semicolons, and certain other symbols.

It is best, for various reasons, to use the space character, the comma, and the semicolon. You'll probably get the best results and have the fewest problems if you always use the blank <Space> character to separate commands and parameters, except for one special circumstance, which I'll discuss next.

Most commands need only one or two parameters, but sometimes you may need to give DOS several parameters, which must be listed in a specific order. If you omit any of these parameters you must tell DOS that you've deliberately left them out. I won't bother with the details right now, but here's an example of the type of command I'm talking about. It's called the MODE command, and you use the following format to tell DOS how to send or receive information through a connection to a modem or a serial printer:

```
MODE CONNECTION-NAME 1ST,2ND,3RD,4TH
```

Notice that the first through fourth parameters are separated by commas. DOS needs information about all four parameters, but for various reasons you may not need to enter all four. If, for example, you only needed to tell DOS about parameters 1, 3, and 4, your command would look like this:

```
MODE CONNECTION-NAME 1ST,,3RD,4TH
```

To tell DOS you're quite aware of parameter 2, you type the comma that holds its place in the list.

While most commands need only one or two parameters, some special command programs, such as compilers for programming languages, need a longer list of parameters, some of which may be left off. For this kind of command, there is a very useful convention: Each of the parameters is separated by a comma. If a parameter is being left off, then two commas appear in a row. When no more parameters follow (even if there might be more), a semicolon indicates the end of the list. Here is an example showing how this is done:

```
COMMAND 1ST,2ND,,4TH,,6TH;
```

Notice that the third and fifth parameters don't appear, but the commas serve to hold their places, so that it is clear that the fourth parameter is the fourth parameter.

When you need to specify command parameters in this special way, do so. Otherwise, for simplicity, I recommend that you always use spaces to separate a command name from its parameters, and to separate the parameters from each other.

Setting the Switch

There is one more thing you need to know about how commands and their parameters are written. Some commands divide their parameters into two categories: regular parameters and those that are called switches. This short list gives you a simple way to understand what switches are:

- **Commands** indicate what is to be done (for example, copy data).
- **Parameters** indicate what the command is to act on (for example, what data to copy).
- **Switches or options** indicate how the command is to be carried out (for example, should the copy be checked for correctness).

To make it easier to separate *parameters* (what to act on) from *switches* (how to carry out the action), DOS uses a special notation: The switch is preceded by a special character.

The standard switch identifier is a slash (/), and that's what all the programs that make up DOS itself use. Most other programs do, too. (Just to make life more complicated, though, let me warn you that some programs identify their switches with a hyphen, -, instead.) In this book, for consistency, I'll show the slash format, which is the normal DOS form.

Here is an example. In Chapter 3, we used the following command:

```
FORMAT C: /S /V
```

In this case, FORMAT is the command; C: is the parameter, and /S and /V are switches.

Like /S, switches are usually very short and simple—typically just a slash and a single letter. The whole idea of a switch is to tell DOS to do or not do some variation on the basic operation. For example, the /S switch in the FORMAT command told it to include a copy of the operating system on the formatted disk and the /V switch requested a volume label. Similarly, the COPY command has a /V switch which tells it to verify that the copy can be read properly. As you can see, the same switch—in this case, /V—can have a different meaning with different commands.

Sometimes switches are called options because they allow you to specify optional features for a particular command. In this book, we will use the two terms, switches, and options interchangeably.

Files and File Names

Most DOS commands perform some operation on either an entire disk or on files stored on a disk, so most parameters are either a disk specification (telling the command which disk to do its operation on) or they are the names of some files.

I'll go over all the details of file names when we cover disks in more detail in Chapter 13, Understanding Disks. But since you're going to be seeing them a lot as we go over the DOS commands in the chapters in between, here is a quick summary that will give you some background and give you a head start when you come to Chapter 13.

Data on a disk is organized into **files**. For identification, each one has a file name. On any one disk, each file name must be unique so that files don't get confused. The name of a file actually has two parts called the **filename** proper and the **extension**.

The filename must be at least one character, and it can be as long as eight characters, but no longer. A filename can be made up of letters of the alphabet, digits, and some punctuation marks and special symbols (details in Chapter 13). You can't use a space character as part of a filename, nor can you use any of the characters that are used to punctuate a command and its parameters. You can use upper- or lowercase letters in filenames, but DOS treats them as if they were all uppercase. Here are some sample filenames:

```
FILENAME
12
A
ABC123
```

The extension to the filename is a short appendage added on after the filename. The two are separated by a period, so a filename and extension look like this: FILENAME.EXT. The extension is three characters at most, and it's optional. A file must have a filename part, but it doesn't have to have an extension part. If there is no extension part, drop the period that is used to separate the two parts.

The intended purpose of an extension is to indicate the category the filename falls into. It is an informal—not a mandatory—way of indicating what type the file is. In Chapter 13 you'll see some of the more common categories.

Here are some more examples of file names, with and without extensions, to give you more of an idea of what they can look like:

```
FILENAME.EXT    (this is as big as they can get)
A               (this is the minimum size for a file name)
12345678        (numbers are OK)
NEW-DATA        (hyphens are OK)
NEW_DATA        (underscores are OK, too)
ADDRESS.LST     (file name can indicate a file's contents)
JULY.91         (another informative file name)
```

It is a little confusing to have a file's complete name called a file name, and part of that name be called a filename (with no space), but that is the terminology used with DOS, so we have to live with it. Whenever you run across either term, slow down and be careful to see what is being referred to.

Wildcard Characters

There is a way to refer to more than one file at a time—through a mechanism known as **wildcards**, or (more officially) **global filename characters**.

Wildcards give you a way of partly specifying a file name so that several files may match the specification. For example, in the section on switches, we saw a copy command with a file specification of *.*, which meant any filename and any filename extension. If you had typed it as *.COM, that would mean any filename, but only if it had the extension COM.

There are actually two wildcard symbols: the asterisk (*), which you've already seen, and the question mark (?), which you haven't encountered yet. Either or both can be used in many ways in file specifications, but we'll leave the details to Chapter 13. For now, just remember that you can use *.* as a way of saying any filename with any extension.

With this basic information under your belt, let's move on to look at some of the commands that DOS provides for us.

7

ELEMENTARY COMMANDS

Introduction

In this chapter, you'll begin learning the commands DOS gives you to work with and control your computer. I'll begin with the commands that are easiest to understand and the ones most commonly used, and work up to the more complicated ones in following chapters.

To make the commands (and DOS) easier to understand, I'll cover them by topic rather than in alphabetical order. I won't cover the precise details of how each command works. That's a subject that properly belongs to your DOS manual, particularly since some of these commands can vary a little from version to version. What I will do here is make sense of these commands for you, and give you tips and handy hints about how to get the most from them (and how to avoid problems with them, as well).

Asking DOS For Help

Perhaps the most important commands are the ones that assist you. Starting with DOS 5.0, there are several important ways to ask DOS for help. Unfortunately, the older versions of DOS do not have these commands.

To get the basic information, just enter:

```
HELP
```

DOS will display a long list, showing each command with a short description. The list will be·in alphabetical order by command name.

The HELP command is handy when you need to perform a particular task and you are not sure which command to use. As an example, here are the first few lines of the list:

```
APPEND    Allows applications to open data files in
          specified directories as if they were in the
          current directory.
ASSIGN    Redirects requests for disk operations on one
          drive to a different drive.
ATTRIB    Displays or changes file attributes.
BACKUP    Backs up one or more files from one disk to
          another.
BREAK     Turns extra CTRL+C checking on or off.
```

```
CALL       Calls one batch file from another.
CD         Displays the name of or changes the current
           directory.
```

As you might imagine, there are so many commands that the entire list is pretty long. For this reason, HELP displays the list one screenful at a time. At the bottom of the screen you will see:

```
---MORE---
```

This means that there is more to come. When you have finished reading what is on the screen, you can press any key to continue. In this way, you can page through a quick reference of all the DOS commands. Once you find the command you need, you can abort the listing by pressing <Ctrl-Break>.

A second way to ask DOS for assistance is to request a summary of a specific command. To do this, enter HELP followed by the name of the command. For example, to ask for help in using the TIME command, enter:

```
HELP TIME
```

You will see:

```
DISPLAYS OR CHANGES THE SYSTEM TIME.

TIME [time]

TIME with no parameters to display the current time
setting and a prompt for a new one. Press ENTER to
keep the same time.
```

In this way, you can ask for help concerning any DOS command. As another example, you can get help on the HELP command itself by entering:

```
HELP HELP
```

These summaries are especially useful when you are working with commands that have a lot of options. There may be times when you need to use a seldom-used option that is difficult to remember. Using the HELP command is a lot faster than looking things up in the DOS manual. If you want to see a summary that shows a lot of options, enter:

```
HELP FORMAT
```

As a convenience, DOS 5.0 provides a second way for you to ask for a command summary. Each command will recognize the option /? as being a request for help. This will work for any DOS command. For example, here are three pairs of equivalent commands:

```
HELP TIME
TIME /?

HELP HELP
HELP /?

HELP FORMAT
FORMAT /?
```

Three Simple Commands

Let's get started with the three simplest commands in DOS. They're called CLS, VER, and MEM, and they're handy and easy to use. All you do is type the command name and press the Enter key.

CLS

The CLS command stands for "clear the screen," and that's exactly what it does. It wipes the screen of everything on it and finishes up by displaying the DOS prompt in the top left-hand corner. You might wonder why you'd need a command to erase the screen. In practice, especially when you come to rely more and more on DOS, you'll find CLS can be useful in removing on-screen leftovers and distractions, and giving you the equivalent of a brand-new sheet of paper to work on. And, as you'll see in Chapter 10, Batch File Basics, you can use the CLS command as part of a batch-execution file, clearing the screen automatically so you can have DOS display something else.

If you're at your computer, here's a simple example you can try. Set yourself up so you are at the DOS prompt. You should see something like this:

```
C:\>
```

Now, enter the TIME command:

```
TIME
```

The output of this command will be similar to the following:

```
CURRENT TIME IS 2:54:00.89P
ENTER NEW TIME:
```

As we saw in Chapter 3, TIME is showing you the current time and asking you if you want to change it. In this case, just press the <Enter> key. The time will remain as it is and you will once again see a prompt:

```
C:\>
```

Now that you screen has some output on it, let's try out the "clear the screen" command. enter:

```
CLS
```

You will notice that everything is cleared and a new prompt is displayed in the top left-hand corner of the screen.

VER

Now, on to the VER command. As I mentioned, VER lets you find out what version of DOS you are using. This command is helpful when, for example, you're using someone else's machine and want to find out what version of DOS is on that person's computer. (You may need this information, because some commands and application programs will only work with certain versions of DOS.)

Like CLS, VER is easy to use. Just enter:

```
VER
```

You will see a message that looks something like this:

```
IBM DOS VERSION 5.00
```

There is very little, if anything, you can do to make VER self-destruct. The same is true of CLS, but here's a tip for you. If you've been working with lists of files or file names or you've been creating files with DOS (you'll see how later), check what's on the screen before you use CLS to wipe it out. You may find you've erased something you wish you hadn't. I've done it.

MEM

The last of the three simplest DOS commands is MEM. As its name implies, MEM will tell you about the memory in your computer. All you have to do is enter:

```
MEM
```

As we will see in Chapter 29, no matter how much memory your computer might have, DOS can use only 640 kilobytes as general purpose memory. Any extra memory, the so-called extended memory, can be used only in certain specific ways. We will cover all of this in Chapter 29.

When you enter the MEM command you will see a summary that looks something like this:

```
 656384   BYTES TOTAL CONVENTIONAL MEMORY
 655360   BYTES AVAILABLE TO IBM DOS
 623712   LARGEST EXECUTABLE PROGRAM SIZE

7602176   BYTES TOTAL CONTIGUOUS EXTENDED MEMORY
      0   BYTES AVAILABLE CONTIGUOUS EXTENDED MEMORY
5225472   BYTES AVAILABLE XMS MEMORY
          IBM DOS RESIDENT IN HIGH MEMORY AREA
```

In this example, our computer has 8 megabytes, about 8.4 million bytes. However, as we mentioned, DOS can only use 640 kilobytes directly as general purpose memory. In this case, out of these 640 kilobytes, we have 623712 bytes available to run programs. (This is about 610 kilobytes.) The rest of the space is taken by DOS itself and other associated programs. (We also see that we have a little over 7.6 million bytes of extended memory, but we will put off discussing such details until Chapter 29.)

The MEM command is available only with DOS 4.0 or newer. Before DOS 4.0, the command to check memory was CHKDSK. As you might guess from the name, the main use for this command is to check disks. In fact, we will meet CHKDSK more formally in Chapter 9 when we discuss the basic disk commands.

What is important here is that, after displaying a report having to do with your disk, CHKDSK will throw in a free two-line memory report. So, if you enter:

```
CHKDSK
```

you will see a disk report, followed by two lines that look something like this:

```
656360 TOTAL BYTES MEMORY
623712 BYTES FREE
```

The CHKDSK command is available in all versions of DOS so you can use it whenever you want. However, if your DOS has the MEM command it is usually a better choice for two reasons: First, MEM displays a more informative report; second, MEM is faster than CHKDSK because CHKDSK has to check out your disk before it can issue a report.

The Calendar Commands

As we saw in Chapter 2, DOS keeps track of the date and the time of day. That's a very handy feature for all sorts of reasons, but one of the best is that every time you create or change some information on a disk, the disk data is marked with the current date and time. This marking can be extremely valuable to you in answering questions such as: "Which of these files did I work on last week?" or "Which of these diskettes has the latest changes to my report?" (You'll find out how to get these answers in Chapter 9, when we cover the DIR command.)

Just as with paper files, I've found that it's occasionally a lifesaver to know that all of my files are accurately stamped with the date and time, and there's hardly a day when I don't find it at least useful to see time stamps on my files.

Date and Time

To make it possible to display, enter, or change the date and time, DOS has two special commands called, naturally, DATE and TIME. These commands work independently, so you can enter or change either one without affecting the other.

DATE and TIME both operate in the same way, and both can be used in either of two ways. The first, which we might call interactive, occurs when you just enter the command name, with no parameters. Using DATE as an example, you would type:

```
DATE
```

As you've seen several times already in this book, DOS responds by telling you its current understanding of the date and asking for a new date, like this:

```
CURRENT DATE IS FRI 12-21-1990
ENTER NEW DATE (MM-DD-YY):
```

At that point, you can either type a new date or just press <Enter> to leave the date unchanged. Similarly, you can change the time by entering the command:

```
TIME
```

DOS will show you the current time and invite you to change it.

```
CURRENT TIME IS 3:10:42.84P
ENTER NEW TIME:
```

You can either enter a new time, or press <Enter> to leave it as it is.

The other way to use the DATE and TIME commands is more direct. If you key in the command name, followed by the date or time, and press <Enter>, DOS will just change the date or time without displaying or requesting anything else. Here is an example of how we would use DATE and TIME this way:

```
DATE 12-21-1990
TIME 3:10P
```

Here are some tips and notes on the DATE and TIME commands:

- When you type the date you can choose to punctuate it with either hyphens (-) or slashes (/). You punctuate the time with colons (:).

- You can leave leading zeros off the figures. So, for example, January can be entered as 1, rather than 01.

- When typing the date, you can leave off the century—the 19 in 1987.

- When typing the time, you can leave off the seconds, or both minutes and seconds, if you want.

- You can use a or p at the end of a time to indicate AM or PM (for example, 10:30a, 3:10p). You can also leave off the a or p and use a 24-hour clock (for example, 10:30 and 15:10). **Note**: some older versions of DOS use only a 24-hour clock and do not give you the option of specifying AM or PM.

- There isn't any normal way to have DOS display the current date or time without having it ask you for a new value. There is a trick you can use; you'll learn about that in Chapter 19 when we discuss the FIND command.

- Under normal circumstances, if DOS is running when midnight passes, it automatically changes the date.

- DOS is smart enough to keep track of leap years.

The DATE and TIME commands are internal, so you can use them at any time, regardless of what you have on your disks.

Whenever you set the date or time, DOS automatically resets the date and time on your battery clock. This means that you will not need to reset it the next time you start the computer.

And there you have it—a few gentle, but useful commands to get you started with DOS. You know how to clear the screen to get a blank slate, you can find the version number of any copy of DOS, you can check up on your computer's memory, and you can check on or adjust DOS's knowledge of the date and time. Now let's move on to more interesting and valuable commands.

8

BASIC FILE COMMANDS

Introduction

I've made a point of emphasizing that most of the work DOS does is related to disks and the files on them. It's time to learn about the most fundamental and useful commands you can use with your disk files: the basic file operations. Just what are these things you'll want to do with files? Most of the time you'll want to make duplicate copies of them, get rid of those you don't want any more, display them, change their names, and compare them to see if two files are the same. Let's begin with copying.

Copying Files

The COPY command starts out as something very simple—a tool to make copies of disk files. But it adds enough variations on the theme of copying that it ends up serving three distinct purposes.

The most straightforward type of copying just duplicates files from one disk to another. Here's an example that tells DOS to copy a (hypothetical) file named THISFILE from the diskette in drive A to the diskette in drive B:

```
COPY A:THISFILE B:
```

Here is another example using wildcard file names (which we discussed in the last chapter):

```
COPY A:*.* B:
```

to copy all the files (*.*) from the DOS diskette in drive A to the formatted diskette in drive B.

You can use both characters and wild cards in a file name. For example, you could copy all the files that begin with the letters XYZ like this:

```
COPY A:XYZ*.* B:
```

You can see there are many variations on this idea, but basically any COPY command in the form:

```
COPY drive:filename drive:
```

results in the same thing: DOS duplicates the files onto a different disk, but under the same name as on the original disk. Since you haven't told

DOS anything but the drive specification for the target, COPY uses the same file names.

You can, if you want, specify the names of the target files so that DOS not only copies them, but gives them different names from the originals. For example:

```
COPY THISFILE THATFILE
```

would make a copy of a file named THISFILE, and the copy would be named THATFILE.

Notice a big difference between this command and the one preceding it; it doesn't specify any drives (such as A: or B:). In this case, DOS uses its default drive for both the source and the target. That means both copies, THISFILE and THATFILE, will be on the same disk. The names are different, so the two files can coexist on one disk with no problem.

The point to remember here (aside from how to copy) is this: If the copy is being made without any change of name, COPY requires that the source and target be on different disks or directory because DOS won't let you have two files with the same name in the same disk or at least in different directories (see Chapter 9). If the name is being changed on the copy, however, then the target file can be anywhere: either where the source is or, if you specify a different location, somewhere else.

For example, you could copy THISFILE from drive A to drive B and name it THATFILE at the same time by typing:

```
COPY A:THISFILE B:THATFILE
```

So far you've seen two of the three different uses of COPY: making duplicates on other disks, and making duplicates under a different name on either the same or a different disk. There is yet another use for COPY: combining the contents of several files into one. This combining operation is advanced and can be tricky, which means you shouldn't try it until you have become more experienced in using DOS. But you should know about this feature of COPY so when you need it, you can study it. Here is an example of how this use of COPY works.

Suppose you have two files, XX and YY, and you want to combine their contents into another file, ZZ. This copy command could do the trick:

```
COPY XX+YY ZZ
```

You should know that there are dangers and pitfalls in doing this kind of copying, and there are some special rules to follow. In particular, you need to make sure the files you're combining actually exist (if one doesn't, DOS won't stop to tell you there isn't any such file). You must also check whether the file you're copying to exists on the disk. If it does, the files you're combining will replace, not be added to, the information that's already there. For instance, in the last example, if the file ZZ already existed, it would be replaced. When you need this use of the COPY command, be careful.

Basically, no matter what kind of copying you are doing, the COPY command will proceed whether or not there is already a file with the target name. If there isn't a file with the target name, then a new file will be created. If there is one, it will be overwritten, which could destroy some valuable data. There is no warning that an existing file is about to be destroyed, so be careful with all copies: This is one of the ways you can clobber your valuable data.

On the other hand, except when you combine files, COPY does require that the source files be there and that's natural enough. How can you make a copy of something that isn't there? COPY will let you know if it can't find the source file you claim you want copied by showing you the message "File not found".

Deleting Files with DEL and ERASE

If you can duplicate files (create new copies) with COPY, you'd expect that you can intentionally remove files as well, and you can. For that operation there is the DEL/ERASE command. This is one command, but with two different names: DEL, or delete, and ERASE. Either command name will cause DOS to throw away a file.

You can remove files one at a time or en masse, using wildcard file names. In the latter case, obviously there's a danger if you mistakenly tell DOS to remove all the files on a disk or within a directory by using the wildcard filename *.*, meaning all files. To protect you from that one possibility, DEL/ERASE will pause to ask if you are sure that's what you want to do. For example, if you type:

```
DEL *.*
```

DOS will ask:

```
ARE YOU SURE (Y/N)?
```

That's your only chance to back out. If you type <Y> and press <Enter>—all gone.

All other file deletion commands proceed without warning, however, so a command like this will proceed automatically:

```
DEL *.BAK
```

So will this:

```
ERASE THISFILE
```

and this:

```
ERASE MYFILES.*
```

If You Delete the Wrong File

The data from erased files is, in fact, still on the disk. DOS doesn't literally go through the chore of wiping out every trace of a deleted file; instead, it just flags that file's space on the disk as "ready for occupancy" and writes over the old data as it goes through the process of storing new information.

Because the deleted information is still on disk then, it can sometimes be recovered by a clever unerase program. If this kind of program is available for your computer, buying it could be one of the best investments you can make, because the program acts as an insurance policy for your data. Starting with version 5.0, DOS includes just such an unerase program, the UNDELETE command. We will cover this command in Chapter 18.

When I got my first personal computer there wasn't any such unerase program available for it, so one of the first things I did was write one. That program saved the day for me many times, and I have a stack of letters from other people, thanking me for creating a tool that helped them rescue their data, too. If you would like a copy of the latest version of my Unerase program, it comes with the Norton Utilities.

Accidentally deleting a file is only one way to lose data. Another way is to mistakenly format a disk that contains information. Again, with DOS version 5.0 or later, there is a command to help you. The command is UNFORMAT and we will cover it in Chapter 18. If you would like a more sophisticated tool, or if you are using an older version of DOS, you can use the data recovery programs that come with the Norton Utilities.

Reformatting is a handy way to provide yourself with a blank diskette, especially when your supply is running low, but if you're going to do this, take some precautions. You might try putting an X on the label of any diskette you no longer need, or you might store old diskettes in a separate box or drawer.

One technique that we particularly like is to use the volume label to indicate that a diskette is available. As we explained in Chapter 3, the volume label is an internal name that you can assign to a disk. This name is displayed whenever you use the DIR or VOL commands (see Chapter 9). You can specify a volume label whenever you format a disk. Once a disk is formatted, you can change the volume label by using the LABEL command (Chapter 9).

We suggest that you use a volume label of EMPTY to indicate that a diskette can be used for new data. For example, if you decide that you do not need the files on a diskette, change its volume label to EMPTY. The next time you need a new diskette, it will be easy for you to remember that this diskette is available. Similarly, if you decide to format a few diskettes for spares (a good idea), start them off with a volume label of EMPTY.

Such a scheme can save you a lot of grief. For example, suppose that you need a new diskette right away and you can't remember if you have any spares. You can check your diskettes one at a time by using the DIR or VOL commands. If a diskette has a volume label of EMPTY you know that it is available; otherwise, you know that the diskette contains data that you still need. Without an organized method for keeping track of spare diskettes it is all too easy to delete files that you really mean to keep.

Of course, whenever you decide to use a spare diskette, your first move should be to use the LABEL command to change the "EMPTY" volume label to something else.

There are other ways to protect yourself here, too, but it's still a little early in the game to go into those details. You'll find more information on the dangers of erasing and formatting, and some tricks to safeguard yourself against these dangers later. At this point, just keep these two rules in mind:

- Make sure you know what files you're deleting and why, before you actually remove them, especially if you are using wildcards to delete more than one file with a single DEL command.

- Make sure any diskette you reformat truly contains expendable information. (The DIR command in Chapter 9 will help you out here.)

Making Sure That You Are Deleting the Correct Files

Deleting the wrong file can have disastrous results, so let's spend a few moments taking about two things that you can do to make sure that you are not making a mistake.

Generally speaking, the most serious deletion errors occur when you use a wildcard to delete a whole set of files; you may not realize that you really want to keep some of the files described by the wildcard.

Here is an example. You think that you want to delete all your files that have an extension of BAK, so you enter:

```
DEL *.BAK
```

It happens that you have two such files, NAMES.BAK and PHONE.BAK that you want to delete. However, you have forgotten that you also have another file, ADDRESS.BAK, that you want to keep.

Unfortunately, once you enter the DEL command, all these files are gone, and DEL does not even display a message telling you which files have been erased. You might not realize that ADDRESS.BAK is missing until weeks later when you look for it and find that it has mysteriously disappeared. The solution, of course, is to be extra careful whenever you enter a DEL command that uses a wildcard. But you can go one step further.

In Chapter 9, we will be meeting the DIR (directory) command which you can use to give you a list of whatever files you specify. For example, to display the names of all the files with an extension of BAK you can enter:

```
DIR *.BAK
```

The DIR command only displays information, it does not change the files in any way. Thus, before you delete files using a wildcard, you can use the same wildcard with DIR to see exactly what files will be matched. Then, you'll know exactly what files DEL would delete if you were to give it the same wildcard.

In our example, the previous DIR command would list all of the files with the BAK extension:

```
ADDRESS.BAK
NAMES.BAK
PHONE.BAK
```

Now, we are tipped off that the command:

```
DEL *.BAK
```

would delete all of these files. We can avoid a problem by carefully deleting only the files we really want to erase:

```
DEL NAMES.BAK
DEL PHONE.BAK
```

We'll talk a lot more about the DIR command in Chapter 9. For now, let's move on to the second way that you can be sure to delete files correctly.

At times, it would be nice if DOS would list the names of each file it is ready to delete and, one by one, ask your permission to go ahead. This is exactly what the /P (permission) option tells the DEL command to do. For example, if you are working with the same BAK files that we just mentioned and you enter

```
DEL *.BAK /P
```

DOS will display the name of the first file that matches the wildcard and then pause:

```
C:\ADDRESS.BAK, DELETE (Y/N)?
```

At this point, DOS is asking, do you want to delete this file? Press the <Y> key for yes, or the <N> key for no. (Do not press <Enter>.)

As it happens, ADDRESS.BAK is the file that you want to save so you press the <N> key. DOS will leave the file intact and move on to the next one. You will see:

```
C:\NAME.BAK,    DELETE (Y/N)?
```

In this case, you do want to delete the file so press the <Y> key. DOS deletes the file and continues:

```
C:\PHONE.BAK,    DELETE (Y/N)?
```

You press the <Y> key to delete the third file. Finally, the DEL command finishes. The screen shows:

```
C:\ADDRESS.BAK, DELETE (Y/N)?N
C:\NAME.BAK,    DELETE (Y/N)?Y
C:\PHONE.BAK,   DELETE (Y/N)?Y
```

You have successfully deleted two out of three files.

In Chapter 11, we will show you how to use the DEL /P command within an automated procedure called a batch file. But now, let's move on to another important file command, the one that lets us change the name of a file without changing its contents.

Renaming Files with REN

Related to both copying and erasing files is a DOS command to change the name of a file. REN, short for rename, will change a file's name as long as the name isn't currently in use by another file in the same directory. (Directories are explained in Chapter 14). Renaming is done like this:

```
REN old-name new-name
```

For example, if you had a file named DRAFT and you wanted to change the name to FINAL, the command would be:

```
REN DRAFT FINAL
```

Like other commands, you can use wildcards with REN to rename several files at once. For example, you could change every file with an extension of XXX to YYY, like this:

```
REN *.XXX *.YYY
```

or any variation on this idea.

Displaying Files with TYPE

So far you've seen how to copy, delete, and rename files. Suppose you're not quite sure what's in a file you're planning to copy/delete/rename. It would be nice to take a look and verify what's in it. Can you do so? Sometimes—with a command called TYPE. TYPE is a handy way to get a quick look at the contents of a file, because it writes a copy of a file onto the display screen of your computer. In fact, TYPE is really just a COPY command, with the target of the copy being your display screen instead of another file.

The file you want to see, however, must be something reasonable to look at. It has to contain display characters; it must be what is called a text file, or else what appears on your screen will be all or partly nonsensical. TYPE is done like this:

```
TYPE SOMEFILE.TXT
```

(You'll have to give DOS the full file name, including the extension if the file has one.)

One last thought on the TYPE command—if you tell DOS to display a file that is not a text file, you may be surprised to see and hear a string of indecipherable symbols and strange beeps. Don't worry, you haven't broken anything. Just let the command run its course, and remember not to use TYPE on that file again.

Using the <Pause> Key to Display Long Files

If you are displaying a file that is longer than the size of your screen, the lines may go by so fast that you cannot read them. In this case, you have two choices: First, use the <Pause> key to pause the display; second, send the output of the TYPE command to a special program that will display the output one screenful at a time. Here is how it all works.

The simplest way to read a long file is to make use of your PC's built-in <Pause> key. (If you have an old computer without a <Pause> key, you will use <Ctrl-Numlock>. That is, hold down the <Ctrl> key and press <Numlock>.) The <Pause> key will freeze the program that is displaying output. You can restart the program by pressing any key except <Pause> — for instance, by pressing <Enter>. Here is an example.

You want to display a very long file of text named LONGFILE.TXT. When you enter:

```
TYPE LONGFILE.TXT
```

the lines whiz by so fast that you can't read them. So, you type the same command:

```
TYPE LONGFILE.TXT
```

but just before you press the <Enter> key, you position your hand over the <Pause> key. You press <Enter> and, a moment later, you press <Pause>. The display is now stopped.

Once you have read what's on the screen, you can press any key (except <Pause>) to continue. A good key to press is <Enter>. When the display restarts, you can wait a moment and press <Pause> again.

This might sound complicated, but it really isn't. All you have to do is type the TYPE command and then, without pressing <Enter>, position your right hand so that your thumb is over the <Enter> key and another finger is over the <Pause> key. You can now go back and forth, pressing <Enter> and <Pause> to start and stop the display.

By the way, the <Pause> key does not just pause the display, it actually stops the program that is executing (in this case the TYPE program). This means if you can use <Pause> to temporarily stop any program, regardless of how much output it is generating.

Using the MORE Filter to Display Long Files

Although using the <Pause> key is simple, you may find it a bit much to keep pressing keys, back and forth, every time you want to display a long file. An alternative is to send the output of the TYPE command to a special program that will display the output one screenful at a time. This program is called MORE. (The MORE command is one of several DOS programs that are called filters. We will discuss this topic in detail in Chapter 19.)

To send the output of a command to the MORE filter you type the command, followed by the vertical bar character (|), followed by the MORE command. It looks like this:

```
TYPE LONGFILE.TXT | MORE
```

Your output will be displayed one screenful at a time. At the bottom of each screen you will see the message:

```
--- MORE ---
```

(This is where the name MORE comes from.)

Once you are finished with the current screen, you can display the next screenful by pressing any key. Many people find it convenient to use the <Space> bar. Thus, by using the MORE filter to display a long file, you can press the <Space> bar and page through the file, one screenful at a time. If you want to abort the command, simply press <Ctrl-Break>.

By the way, there is an alternative way to use MORE to display a file. Enter the MORE command, followed by a less-than character, followed by the file name. For example:

```
MORE < LONGFILE.TXT
```

This command tells DOS to read the input for MORE directly from the file you specify. We will cover all the details in Chapter 19.

Comparing Copies of Files

When you make copies of files with the COPY command, you may want to confirm that the copy is exact. To be honest, there is little reason to check a copy you have just made; the copying process is extremely reliable and it is very unlikely that there will be any errors in copying, unless the copying procedure itself tells you there were problems. The main reason for comparing copies of files is to find out if the copies contain any discrepancies—small changes, perhaps, that you might have forgotten about.

COMP, FC, and DISKCOMP

There are three comparison commands, COMP and FC, to compare files individually, and DISKCOMP, to compare entire diskettes (we'll cover it in the next chapter). The file comparison program checks the contents of files to make sure that they match.

Here is how file comparison is done with COMP. You provide the names of two files to be compared. If the two copies have the same name, but are on different disks, then you needn't specify the name of the second file. Just tell DOS where it is located by giving a drive specification. Here are two examples of how you would start a file comparison:

```
COMP ORIGINAL COPY
COMP A:FILENAME B:
```

For instance, imagine you've just duplicated a very important file named CONTRACT in order to preserve the original but make some changes to the copy. You've learned to have faith in DOS, but just to be on the safe side you want to know that the duplicate, named REVISION, is starting out as an exact copy of the original. That's when you would use the first of the two preceding examples:

```
COMP CONTRACT REVISION
```

Likewise, if you had copied CONTRACT from drive A to drive B, keeping the same file name, your command would be:

```
COMP A:CONTRACT B:
```

You can also use wildcard filenames to compare a group of files automatically. There are many ways this can be handy; one of the handiest is in comparing all of the files on one disk with all the files on another, to see if they're the same. Using COMP, you can compare all the data between the two disks like this:

```
COMP A:*.* B:
```

As mentioned, when you compare files you usually have one of two things in mind: Either you want to check that the files exactly match or you want to figure out what the differences are. Of the two, you're best off only checking to see whether the files are exact duplicates. You can also find out what the differences are, but the information may be useless to you. Here's why:

COMP does report any difference it finds between two files, but only in the most exasperatingly technical way. If it finds a difference, it reports both the location of the difference and the difference itself in hexadecimal notation, which is base-16 math. For most people, hex is just plain confusing. So in ordinary circumstances use COMP to tell you if the files it's comparing match exactly. If COMP does report differences, make your check the old-fashioned way: by comparing paper copies.

There's also one instance in which COMP will simply refuse to continue: If COMP finds that the files it's comparing are of different lengths, it will stop right there, without comparing any of the contents. If COMP finds 10 differences in the content, it won't try to hunt for a place where the files match up again, it will just stop. Next to smarter file comparison programs, our COMP seems rigid and dumb. Still, it's part of DOS and it is good for finding out if two files match exactly, even if it's not very helpful in showing us the substance of any differences.

Fortunately, starting with DOS 5.0, the COMP command has options that vastly increase its usefulness. As we mentioned, COMP normally displays the differences it finds in hexadecimal. If you would like to display the options in decimal—that is, using regular base 10 numbers—just specify the /D option. For example:

```
COMP FILE1 FILE 2 /D
```

The /D option is useful when you are comparing numeric data. If your file contains regular text you can use the /A option instead. This tells COMP to display differences as characters. For example:

```
COMP OLDTEXT NEWTEXT /A
```

(The "A" stands for the ASCII code, which we will meet in Chapter 13. As we will see, DOS uses the ASCII code to represent characters.)

The next two options help you work with specific lines in a file. /L tells COMP to display the line number each time it finds a difference, and /N tells COMP to look at only certain lines. When you use /N, you follow it by an equal sign and a number. COMP will start at the beginning of the file and look at that number of lines. When you use /N, COMP automatically assumes you want to see line numbers so you do not have to use /L.

For example, to compare the first 20 lines of the two specific files, you can use:

```
COMP OLDTEXT NEWTEXT /N=20
```

Finally, the /C options tells COMP to ignore any differences between small and capital letters—that is, differences between upper and lower case.

Of course, you can combine any of these options as you see fit. For example, the following command compares the first 15 lines of the files OLDTEXT and NEWTEXT, lists differences as characters, ignores differences due to case, and shows the line number where each difference occurs:

```
COMP OLDTEXT NEWTEXT /N=15 /A /C
```

The second command to compare files is FC (for file compare). Unfortunately, unless you have a new version of DOS (5.0 or later), the FC command is available only with MS DOS, not with IBM DOS. In fact, this is the only DOS command that you can use with one DOS and not the other.

In its basic form, you use FC about the same as COMP. For example, to compare the files ORIGINAL and COPY, you would use:

```
FC ORIGINAL COPY
```

However, unlike COMP, if you compare files with the same name on different disks or in different directories, you must specify both names. For example:

```
FC A: CONTRACT. DOC B: CONTRACT. DOC
```

Like COMP, the FC command has a whole set of options that you can use. Be careful though, most of the options have different names, even those that perform similar to COMP options.

Unlike COMP, which shows you differences in hexadecimal as a default, the FC command assumes that you have textual data. That is, by default, FC assumes that your files contain characters.

With such files, it is often useful to abbreviate the output when you make a comparison. The /A option does just that. Instead of displaying all lines that are different, /A displays only the first and last line for each set of differences. For example:

```
FC OLDFILE NEWFILE /A
```

The /L option tells FC to assume that the file contains characters and to try to match up corresponding lines. Each time a mismatch is found, FC will examine the file, line by line, and try to resynchronize the data. Unless you are making a binary comparison (see below), FC provides this service by default so you d not normally need to use /L. If you want to control how many consecutive lines FC must match in order to consider the files to be synchronized, you can use a / followed by that number. For example, if you use:

```
FC OLDFILE NEWFILE /5
```

it tells the FC that, when trying to match up the lines after a difference has been found, it should look for 5 lines in a row that match. By default, FC looks for only 2 lines in a row.

The next two options are similar to what we encountered with the COMP command. /C tells FC to ignore any differences due to upper or lower case, and /N displays line numbers. (Notice though, that the option is /N, not /L as with COMP.)

Normally, DOS expands any tab characters that it finds. The assumption is that there are tab stops at each eighth character position. That is, DOS acts as if there were tabs set at positions 1, 9, 17, and so on. When FC compares files, it normally replaces tab characters with the appropriate number of space characters before making its comparisons. (Of course this is for comparison purposes only; FC does not actually change your files.) If you use the /T option, FC will not make such substitutions. Each tab character will be treated as single, distinct character.

A complimentary option is /W. This tells FC to treat consecutive tab or space characters as a single space. When you use /W, FC will ignore any tab or space characters that come at the beginning of a line. The name /W stands for "white space," a term that is sometimes used to collectively describe tabs and spaces.

As FC works, it needs to keep differing lines in a temporary storage area called a "line buffer." Be default, the line buffer can hold up to 100 pairs of lines. If you compare two files that differ in more than 100 consecutive lines, FC will cancel the operation. If you know in advance that this may occur, you can use the /LB option to ask for a longer line buffer. Just follow /LB directly with the size you want. For example, to specify a line buffer of size 200, you could use:

```
FC OLDFILE NEWFILE /LB200
```

As we mentioned earlier, FC assumes by default that you are comparing files that contain data in the form of characters. Occasionally, you may want to compare files that contain any type of data, byte by byte. We say that this is a "binary" comparison and the option that specifies it is /B. Whenever you compare files that have extensions of EXE, COM, SYS, OBJ, LIB or BIN, FC will automatically perform a binary comparison. For example, the following two commands are equivalent:

```
FC PROG1.COM PROG2.COM
FC PROG1.COM PROG2.COM /B
```

If you are comparing files with such extensions and you want to force a character comparison, you can always use the /L option. For example:

```
FC C: CONFIG.SYS D: CONFIG.SYS /L
```

To end this chapter, let us consider the question, which command is better to use, COMP or FC?

If you have DOS 5.0 or later, both commands are powerful. Choose either one and become familiar with it. If you have an earlier version of MS DOS, the FC command is the better choice, as COMP did not receive its many options until DOS 5.0. However, if you have an earlier version of IBM DOS, you would have to use COMP since FC will not be available.

9

BASIC DISK COMMANDS

Introduction

In the last chapter, we introduced ourselves to the most basic and useful commands DOS has to work with our files. Now it's time to do the same thing for the commands that are most helpful in working with entire disks.

Checking Out Your Disks

DOS has two commands that let you find out what's on your disks. They're called DIR and CHKDSK. DIR gives you a listing, called a directory, of the files stored on a disk. CHKDSK gives you a status report on the disk itself. Let's look at DIR first, since it's a command you'll probably use quite often.

What Is a Directory?

Like a telephone directory, a disk directory lets you look things up. In the case of a phone book, you look up names, addresses, and phone numbers. In the case of DOS, you can use a directory to check on several things: the names of the files on a disk, the size of each file, and the date and time each file was created or updated. Here's an example of what a DOS directory looks like:

```
VOLUME IN DRIVE C IS HARLEY
VOLUME SERIAL NUMBER IS 12B4-B400
DIRECTORY OF C:\DOCUMENT

.                   <DIR>           01-11-91 9:18P
..                  <DIR>           01-11-91 9:18P
MEMO        DOC      4608           01-11-91 6:17P
DRAFT       DOC     11776           10-11-90 5:13P
FINAL       DOC     12288           02-23-90 1:12P
EXTRAS              <DIR>           05-30-90 4:01P
            7 FILE(S)      28672    BYTES
                         9840640    BYTES FREE
```

The first three lines are DOS's way of identifying the disk drive and directory you're looking at. As you can see, DIR reports both the volume label and the volume serial number. (These are both explained in Chapter 3).

The volume label is an internal label that you put on a disk when you format it. You can change it any time you want. Later in this chapter, I'll show you how.

The volume serial number is a unique identification number that FORMAT automatically puts on every disk (starting with DOS 4.0).

The third line of the directory listing shows that our default drive is Drive C—the hard disk—and that we are in subdirectory DOCUMENT. (I'll explain subdirectories in Chapter 14. For now, it is enough to say that you collect your files in various subdirectories so that you won't have to keep everything in one massive directory.)

The listing of the actual directory entries begins below the Volume and Directory lines. It tells us that there are six files in this subdirectory. The first two, "." and "..", have to do with subdirectories. We will explain these subdirectories in Chapter 15. The next few lines show us that we have three files. These files all have the same extension, DOC, but have different filenames, MEMO, DRAFT, and FINAL. The following line shows us that this directory contains a subdirectory of its own named EXTRAS. The second last line shows us that there are six files in this directory (subdirectories count as files) and that these six files take up 28672 bytes. Finally, the last line shows us how much room we have on the disk for storing more files.

DIR

There are several ways you can use DIR. The most common way is to type in the command DIR with or without a drive specification. If you just type DIR, you see a directory of files on the disk in the default drive. For example, if the default drive is Drive C, and you type:

```
DIR
```

you will see a directory listing of Drive C. However, if you type DIR with a drive specification, like this:

```
DIR A:
```

you see a directory of files on the disk in the drive you specified.

In either case, this form of the command will ask DIR to list all of the files. As you saw in the earlier example, the list will include the filename, the filename extension, the size of the file in bytes (roughly, characters), and the date and time the file was created or last changed. Remember that, in the coverage of the DATE and TIME commands, I mentioned that files are marked with time stamps, and that is one good reason for giving DOS the date and time whenever you start up. The DIR command is your way to see the time stamp, as well as the size of each file on your disk, and the amount of space you have left for storing new files.

If you don't want to see a list of all of the files—if all you want is information on one—you can type that file's name as part of the DIR command, and DIR will report only on it. For example, if you just wanted to know when you wrote DRAFT.DOC, this command:

```
DIR DRAFT.DOC
```

would tell you.

Similarly, you can use wildcards to get information on more than one, but still not all files. For example, the command:

```
DIR *.BAK
```

would get directory information on all files that have an extension of BAK, in this case, DRAFT.BAK and FINAL.BAK.

One of the things that DIR reports is the amount of space left free on a disk. So you may want to use the DIR command simply to find out how much space is available for use on a disk.

Specifics About DIR

A disk can have "hidden" files on it; usually if it does, they are secret parts of the DOS operating system (you'll learn more about that in the next section and in Chapter 12). The DIR command acts as though hidden files were not there at all, but CHKDSK, which we're coming to, tells you a little about them.

There is one peculiarity of the DIR command that you need to know about. Most DOS commands work with wildcard file specifications like *.*, which means all files with any names. DIR works with wild cards as well, but it has one difference: DIR will assume a wildcard even if you didn't type one. So, if you enter the command:

```
DIR
```

it is treated just as if you had typed:

```
DIR *.*
```

And if you put in a filename, with no extension, such as:

```
DIR FILENAME
```

it will be treated as if you had typed a wild card for the extension (DIR
FILENAME.*). With our earlier sample directory, for instance, the command:

```
DIR DRAFT
```

means the same as:

```
DIR DRAFT.*
```

and would cause DIR to report on two files, DRAFT.BAK and
DRAFT.DOC.

This special feature of DIR is rather handy, but it has one real draw-
back: It is inconsistent with the rest of DOS. Most DOS commands
require you to enter extensions explicitly. Consistency is important in
anything as complex as DOS, because it reduces the number of rules you
have to learn, and it increases your confidence that DOS will do what you
think you are asking it to do. In this case, don't be worried if you find that
DIR is acting a little different than all the other DOS commands. It isn't
your misunderstanding things, it's just DIR doing things its own way.

Displaying Long Directory Listings

In Chapter 8, we saw that when you use the TYPE command to display a
long file, the lines go by so fast you do not have time to read them. We
explained that there are two ways to read such listings. First, you can use
the <Pause> key to temporarily pause the display; second, you can send
the output of the TYPE command to the MORE filter. MORE will display
the output one screenful at a time.

A similar problem can arise when you are displaying long directory
listings. If your directory has a great many files, the output of the DIR
command will not fit onto a single screen. The file names will speed by
faster than you can read them.

To read such listings, you have four choices. First, you can use enter
the DIR command and use the <Pause> key, just as we described in Chapter 8. Second, you can send the output of the DIR command to the
MORE filter. Simply type the DIR command, followed by a vertical bar,
followed by the MORE command. Here are two examples:

```
DIR | MORE
DIR A:*.BAK | MORE
```

The first example displays all the files in your current directory. The second example displays all the files on the diskette in the A: drive that have an extension of BAK. In both case, the directory listings are displayed one screenful at a time by MORE.

Using the <Pause> key or sending output to the MORE filter can be used with any DOS command. However, there are two other ways to display long directory listings can be used only with the DIR command. They involve two options, /P and /W.

The /P (pause) option tells DIR to display its output one screen at a time, just as if you had sent the output to MORE. The following two examples have the same effect as the previous examples:

```
DIR /P
DIR A:*.BAK /P
```

The second option, /W, produces a wide listing in which five file names are displayed on each line. The following two examples display the same directories as before, only with a wide listing:

```
DIR /W
DIR A:*.BAK /W
```

As an example of a wide listing, here is the same directory that we looked at earlier. This time, the directory is displayed using the command:

```
DIR /W:
```

The listing is:

```
VOLUME IN DRIVE C IS HARLEY
VOLUME SERIAL NUMBER IS 12B4-B400
DIRECTORY OF C:\DOCUMENT

[.]       [..]      MEMO.DOC        DRAFT.DOC    FINAL.DOC
[EXTRAS]
          6 FILE(S0)          28672  BYTES
                            9840640  BYTES FREE
```

Notice that there are five file names (including subdirectories) displayed on each line. However, as you can see, in order to squeeze so many names on a line DOS had to leave out the size of the file, the date, and the time. So, you have a choice. If you have a large directory and you

are interested only in the file names, you can use DIR /W. If you want to
see the sizes, dates, and times, you will have to use DIR /P.

On occasion, it may happen that your directory contains so many files
that the listing may not fit on the screen, even when you use /W. In this
case, you can combine /P with /W. For example:

```
DIR /P /W
DIR A:*.BAK /P /W
```

You will get a wide listing, displayed one screenful at a time.

Specifying the Order in Which File Names Are Listed

If your DOS is version 4.0 or older, you can use only the /P and /W
options with DIR. However, if you have DOS 5.0 or later, there is a whole
set of options that you can use to control the format of a directory listing.
In the next few sections we will cover all these options.

Let us start with the option that allows you to specify the order in
which the file names will appear. This option is /O (which stands for
order). Without the /O option, DIR displays the names of files and
subdirectories in the order that they are stored in the directory. When
you use /O, DIR sorts the names in alphabetical order by filename.
Moreover, subdirectories are grouped before files.

As an example, here is the directory that we looked at earlier. The
original listing was:

```
VOLUME IN DRIVE C IS HARLEY
VOLUME SERIAL NUMBER IS 12B4-B400
DIRECTORY OF C:\DOCUMENT

.                   <DIR>         01-11-91 8:49P
..                  <DIR>         01-11-91 8:49P
MEMO      DOC          4608       01-11-91 8:31P
DRAFT     DOC         11776       12-15-90 3:05P
FINAL     DOC         12288       12-19-90 3:01P
EXTRAS              <DIR>         01-11-91 8:51P
        6 FILE(S)            28672 BYTES
                          9840640 BYTES FREE
```

If we display this same directory, but with the /O option,

```
DIR /O
```

we see:

```
VOLUME IN DRIVE C IS HARLEY
VOLUME SERIAL NUMBER IS 12B4-B400
DIRECTORY OF C:\DOCUMENT

.                    <DIR>          01-11-91 8:49P
..                   <DIR>          01-11-91 8:49P
EXTRAS               <DIR>          01-11-91 8:51P
DRAFT    DOC          11776         12-15-90 3:05P
FINAL    DOC          12288         12-19-90 3:01P
MEMO     DOC           4608         01-11-91 8:31P
    6 FILE(S)                       28672 BYTES
                                  9840640 BYTES FREE
```

By default, the /O option sorts by filename and groups subdirectories before files. If you want a different order, you can follow the /O with a colon and one or more letters from the following list.

```
D     sort by date and time, earliest first
-D    sort by date and time, latest first
E     sort by extension, in alphabetical order
-E    sort by extension, in reverse alphabetical order (Z to A)
G     group subdirectories before files
-G    group subdirectories after files
N     sort by filename, in alphabetical order
-N    sort by filename, in reverse alphabetical order (Z to A)
S     sort by size, smallest first
-S    sort by size, largest first
```

Here is an example using our sample directory. To list the directory entries from largest to smallest, use:

```
DIR /O:-S
```

The listing looks like:

```
VOLUME IN DRIVE C IS HARLEY
VOLUME SERIAL NUMBER IS 12B4-B400
DIRECTORY OF C:\DOCUMENT

FINAL    DOC          12288         12-19-90 3:01P
DRAFT    DOC          11776         12-15-90 3:05P
MEMO     DOC           4608         01-11-91 8:31P
.                    <DIR>          01-11-91 8:49P
..                   <DIR>          01-11-91 8:49P
EXTRAS               <DIR>          01-11-91 8:51P
          6 FILE(S)                 28672 BYTES
                                  9840640 BYTES FREE
```

If it makes sense to do so, you can use more than one specification after the /O. For example, consider the following command:

```
DIR /O:-GS
```

DIR acts as follows: First, the subdirectories are grouped after the files (-G). Next, the files are sorted by size from smallest to largest (S). If we use this command to display our sample directory the result is:

```
VOLUME IN DRIVE C IS HARLEY
VOLUME SERIAL NUMBER IS 12B4-B400
DIRECTORY OF C:\DOCUMENT

MEMO      DOC          4608   01-11-91 8:31P
DRAFT     DOC         11776   12-15-90 3:05P
FINAL     DOC         12288   12-19-90 3:01P
.                  <DIR>      01-11-91 8:49P
..                 <DIR>      01-11-91 8:49P
EXTRAS             <DIR>      01-11-91 8:51P
         6 FILE(S)          28672 BYTES
                           840640 BYTES FREE
```

As we mentioned, when you use /O by itself, DIR displays subdirectories before files and sorts alphabetically by filename. Thus, the following two commands are equivalent:

```
DIR /O
DIR /O:GN
```

By the way, the colon is optional. We suggest that you use it as it makes the command easier to understand. However, you can leave it out if you want. For example, the following two commands are equivalent:

```
DIR /O:GN
DIR /OGN
```

Aside from /O, there are other important options that DOS version 5.0 has made available to use with the DIR command. However, before we can get to them, we need to take a short detour and discuss what are known as file attributes.

File Attributes

Within the DOS file system, each directory entry has several attributes that are stored along with the entry. We can think of an attribute as the answer to a yes-or-no question:

Does the entry represent a subdirectory? (If not, it is a file.)

Is this a hidden file?

Is this a system file?

Is this a read-only file?

Has the file been backed up (archived)?

The first attribute tells DOS whether or not the directory entry is a subdirectory or a file. This attribute is set whenever you create a file or subdirectory and cannot be changed.

The second attribute tells DOS whether or not a file is a *hidden file.* A hidden file is the same as a regular file except that a hidden file does not usually show up in directory listings. Moreover, hidden files cannot be erased. As you might imagine, very few files are hidden.

In most cases, there are only two types of hidden files that you might run into. First, there are the DOS system files that we discussed in Chapter 5, IBMBIO.COM and IBMDOS.COM. (If you are using MS-DOS rather than IBM DOS, these files are called IO.SYS and MSDOS.SYS.) These files are stored in the main directory of the disk from which you start DOS—your boot disk. The reason they are hidden is so that you cannot accidentally erase them.

The second type of hidden file is one that was created for a special purpose by one of your programs. For example, if you use the format recovery program that comes with the Norton Utilities you will see that it keeps a hidden file in the main directory. This file contains data that can be used to recover your disk should you format it accidentally. Since such information is crucial to the integrity of your system, it is kept in a hidden file that cannot be erased. If you are using the format recovery program that comes with DOS 5.0 or later (see Chapter 18), you will see that it stores a similar file, also in the main directory.

It used to be common for programs to use a *copy protection* scheme to keep people from illegally copying software. Such schemes often used hidden files, usually in the main directory. Indeed, some software even used hidden directories! Today, copy protection is pretty much extinct and such hidden files are rare.

The third file attribute tells DOS whether or not a file is a *system file.* This type of file is a holdover from the CP/M operating system, one of the ancestors of DOS. When DOS was first designed, this feature was copied from CP/M. The intention was that system files would be special files used by the operating system. Indeed, the two DOS hidden files we mentioned above are also system files. However, the idea of system files has never really been used with DOS. For our purposes, we can consider system files to be another type of hidden file. Beyond that, it is safe to ignore them.

The next DOS attribute, the *read-only* attribute, is much more useful. It tells DOS that a file cannot be erased. Read-only files do show up in directory listings, but they are safe from accidental deletion. In Chapter 17, we will show you how to use the ATTRIB command to mark files as read-only.

The final DOS attribute is the *archive* attribute. From time to time, you will want to make copies of your files for safekeeping. Usually, this involves copying files from your hard disk to diskettes. Such copies are called backups or archives and we will discuss them in Chapter 14. Usually, you will use the BACKUP command (and sometimes the XCOPY command) to make backups. When you do, DOS will set the archive attribute for each file that has been copied.

With BACKUP and XCOPY, you have a way to specify that only those files that have not yet been backed up are to be copied. BACKUP and XCOPY identify such files by checking the archive attribute. Whenever you create or modify a file, DOS automatically changes the archive attribute to indicate that the file has not yet been backed up. And whenever you use BACKUP or XCOPY to copy a file, DOS changes the attribute to show that the file has been backed up. All in all, it makes for an easy-to-use system.

So there you have it, the five file attributes: subdirectory, hidden, system, read-only, and archive. Most of the time you leave the attributes alone, letting DOS take care of them. However, there may be times when you want to change an attribute. If so, you can use the ATTRIB command that we will discuss in Chapter 17. With older versions of DOS, you can change only the read-only and archive attributes. Starting with DOS 5.0, you can also change the hidden and system attributes.

Using Attributes to Specify Which File Names Should Be Listed

Most of the time you are interested in all your files and subdirectories, except those that are hidden or system files. Thus, by default, the DIR command displays the names of directory entries except those whose attributes mark them as hidden or system.

However, there may be times when you want to look at only those directory entries that have, or do not have, certain attributes. To do this, you use the /A (attribute) option. Like the /O option, /A is available only with DOS 5.0 or later.

By itself, the /A option displays all files, including hidden and system files. Thus, to display all of your files, use:

```
DIR /A
```

Like the /O option, you can add a colon followed by one or more letters to specify more about how the /A option is to operate. The choices are as follows:

```
  A     display files that have not yet been backed up (archived)
 -A     display files that have been backed up (archived)
  D     display subdirectories only
 -D     display files only
  H     display only hidden files
 -H     display only non-hidden files
  R     display read-only files
 -R     display files that are not read-only
  S     display system files
 -S     display only non-system files
```

For example, to display the names of hidden files only, use:

```
DIR /A:H
```

Where it makes sense, you can combine more than one specification. For example, to display the names of files only (not directories) that are not read-only, use:

```
DIR /A:-D-R
```

If you want, you can combine the /A option with the /O option. Thus, to display all of your file that are read-only, sorted by size from smallest to largest, enter:

```
DIR /A:-D-R /O:S
```

As with the /O option, the colon is optional (although it does make your command more readable). Thus, the following two commands are equivalent:

```
DIR /A:-D-R /O:S
DIR /A-D-R /OS
```

The Last Few Options to Use with DIR

As we mentioned, DOS 5.0 brought new options to the DIR command: /O to specify the order in which names are to be displayed, and /A to specify which names are to be displayed. Aside from /O and /A, there are three other options that you can use with DOS 5.0 or later. They are /B, /L, and /S.

The /B (brief) option tells DIR to display only the names of sub-directories and files, no auxiliary information. The names are displayed, one per line, in the format FILENAME.EXT.

Here is an example. Earlier, we displayed a sample directory using the command:

```
DIR
```

The output was:

```
VOLUME IN DRIVE C IS HARLEY
VOLUME SERIAL NUMBER IS 12B4-B400
DIRECTORY OF C:\DOCUMENT

.                    <DIR>            01-11-91 8:49P
..                   <DIR>            01-11-91 8:49P
MEMO     DOC             4608         01-11-91 8:31P
DRAFT    DOC            11776         12-15-90 3:05P
FINAL    DOC            12288         12-19-90 3:01P
EXTRAS              <DIR>             01-11-91 8:51P
         6 FILE(S)              28672 BYTES
                            9840640 BYTES FREE
```

If we use DIR with the /B option, we get the following brief listing:

```
MEMO.DOC
DRAFT.DOC
FINAL.DOC
EXTRAS
```

The /L option displays the names in lowercase. For example, the command:

```
DIR /L
```

produces output like this:

```
VOLUME IN DRIVE C IS HARLEY
VOLUME SERIAL NUMBER IS 12B4-B400
DIRECTORY OF C:\DOCUMENT
    .                <DIR>            01-11-91  8:49P
    ..               <DIR>            01-11-91  8:49P
    memo      doc          4608       01-11-91  8:31P
    draft     doc         11776       12-15-90  3:05P
    final     doc         12288       12-19-90  3:01P
    extras           <DIR>            01-11-91  8:51P
            6 FILE(S)                    28672 BYTES
                                      9840640 BYTES FREE
```

If you combine the /B and /L options:

```
DIR /B /L
```

the output will be brief and in lowercase:

```
memo.doc
draft.doc
final.doc
extras
```

If you are a Unix user, you may want to mimic the Unix directory command (ls). This command displays names one per line in alphabetical order. You can use:

```
DIR /B /L /O:N
```

The output looks like this:

```
draft.doc
extras
final.doc
memo.doc
```

The final DIR option is /S. This tells DIR to display information about not only the current directory, but all subdirectories, sub-subdirectories, and so on. (We will discuss subdirectories in detail in Chapter 15.) In our example, we have one subdirectory named EXTRAS. Within this subdirectory, we have stored extra copies of two files. We can see all these files by using:

```
DIR /S
```

The output is:

```
VOLUME IN DRIVE C IS HARLEY
VOLUME SERIAL NUMBER IS 12B4-B400
DIRECTORY OF C:\DOCUMENT

.                       <DIR>           01-11-91 8:49P
..                      <DIR>           01-11-91 8:49P
MEMO      DOC              4608         01-11-91 8:31P
DRAFT     DOC             11776         12-15-90 3:05P
FINAL     DOC             12288         12-19-90 3:01P
EXTRAS                  <DIR>           01-11-91 8:51P
          6 FILE(S)                     28672 BYTES

DIRECTORY OF C:\DOCUMENT\EXTRAS

.                       <DIR>           01-11-91 8:51P
..                      <DIR>           01-11-91 8:51P
MEMO      BAK              4608         01-11-91 8:31P
FINAL     BAK             12288         12-19-90 3:01P
          4 FILE(S)                     16896 BYTES

TOTAL FILES LISTED:
          10 FILE(S)                    45568 BYTES
                                     9822208 BYTES FREE
```

Listings such as this one are useful but can be unwieldy. However, we can combine /S with other options to make for more manageable output:

```
DIR /B /L /O:N /S
```

The result is:

```
c:\document\draft.doc
c:\document\extras
c:\document\final.doc
c:\document\memo.doc
c:\document\extras\final.bak
c:\document\extras\memo.bak
```

A Summary of the DIR Command

The DIR command is one of the most useful of all the DOS commands. Since DIR has many options, let's take a moment now to summarize them before we move on.

In general, DIR will display the names of files and subdirectories in the order that they are stored. You can use the following options to control the operation of DIR:

```
/A    control the output based on file attributes
/B    display a brief listing
/L    display the names in lowercase
/O    control the order in which names are displayed
/P    display output one screenful (page) at a time
/S    display information about all subdirectories
/W    display a wide listing
```

The /P and /W options can be used with all versions of DOS. The /A, /B, /L, /O, and /S options can be used only with DOS 5.0 or later.

By itself, /A displays the names of all files and subdirectories. You can use /A followed by one or more letters to specify exactly which names you want to see. You can use:

```
 A    display files that have not yet been backed up (archived)
-A    display files that have been backed up (archived)
 D    display subdirectories only
-D    display files only
 H    display only hidden files
-H    display only non-hidden files
 R    display read-only files
-R    display files that are not read-only
 S    display system files
-S    display only non-system files
```

The /O option will display subdirectories before files, the output being sorted alphabetically by filename. You can use /O: followed by one or more letters to specify exactly how the output is to be sorted. You can use:

```
 D    sort by date and time, earliest first
-D    sort by date and time, latest first
 E    sort by extension, in alphabetical order
-E    sort by extension, in reverse alphabetical order (Z to A)
 G    group subdirectories before files
-G    group subdirectories after files
 N    sort by filename, in alphabetical order
-N    sort by filename, in reverse alphabetical order (Z to A)
 S    sort by size, smallest first
-S    sort by size, largest first
```

CHKDSK

While the DIR command shows us a list of the files on a disk, the CHKDSK, or check disk, command is intended to give us a status report on our disks. CHKDSK does two main things: First, it checks the disk over to see how much space there is and how much is in use, and to see if there is any discrepancy in the space usage. It then reports the total space on the disk, the amount of space in use, the number of files, and, incidentally, whether there are any hidden files.

CHKDSK also does something else nice that is completely unrelated to its check-your-disk function: It reports on the amount of memory available in your system. Just as you might use DIR just to find out about available space on disk, you could use CHKDSK just to see how much memory you have.

Of course, the best way to check memory is with the MEM command (see Chapter 7). However, the MEM command is not available in early versions of DOS. Follow this rule of thumb: To check memory with DOS 4.0 or later, use MEM. With earlier versions, use CHKDSK.

To use CHKDSK, enter the command followed by the name of the disk you want to check. For example:

```
CHKDSK C:
```

If you use the command by itself without specifying a disk:

```
CHKDSK
```

Here is an example of the type of report CHKDSK gives you (notice that like DIR, CHKDSK includes the disk's volume ID label):

```
VOLUME NORTON          CREATED 03-10-1991 8:53P
VOLUME SERIAL NUMBER IS 0868-1BFA

32407552    BYTES TOTAL DISK SPACE
   77824    BYTES IN 2 HIDDEN FILES
   61440    BYTES IN 25 DIRECTORIES
22384640    BYTES IN 798 USER FILES
 9883648    BYTES AVAILABLE ON DISK

    2048    BYTES IN EACH ALLOCATION UNIT
   15824    TOTAL ALLOCATION UNITS ON DISK
    4826    AVAILABLE ALLOCATION UNITS ON DISK

  656368    TOTAL BYTES MEMORY
  623504    BYTES FREE
```

Let's take a look at all the information CHKDSK gives us. On the first line we see the volume label of the disk. This is the label that we specify when we format the disk and that can be changed with the LABEL command. Following the volume label we see the date and time that the volume was created—that is, when the disk was formatted. The second line shows the volume serial number that was assigned by the FORMAT program. (Volume serial numbers are not created for versions of DOS before 4.0.)

Next, we see the total amount of space on the disk and a breakdown of how this space is being used. As you can see, CHKDSK is a good command to use when you want to see how much space you have used up. Notice that CHKDSK makes special mention of hidden files.

By the way, there is one hidden file that is not really a file. DOS stores the volume label as the name of an empty hidden file in the main directory. Some versions of DOS mention this file in the CHKDSK report. Thus, if your disk has no hidden files, don't worry if your CHKDSK report says:

```
0 BYTES IN 1 HIDDEN FILE
```

It's just the volume label.

After the summary of file use, we see three lines of technical information about allocation units.

Using CHKDSK to Fix Your Disk

As the name implies, CHKDSK checks over your disk, looking for certain types of discrepancies. Fortunately, these type of problems are rare and you may never encounter one. Such discrepancies come up when things go wrong with the space allocation on the disk and, although it is a very interesting subject, it is one that is too technical for this book. If you do encounter such problems, you may want to use the disk testing and fixing tools that come with the Norton Utilities.

In addition to reporting on any discrepancies that it might find, CHKDSK will also try to repair certain types of mistakes that have to do with how the disk space is used. Most of the time, you will enter the CHKDSK command without any options:

```
CHKDSK
```

In most cases, things will go well and you will see the usual report. However, if it happens that CHKDSK does find a problem, you will see an appropriate message. Here are the first few lines of such a report:

```
VOLUME HARLEY         CREATED 01-11-1991 8:50P
VOLUME SERIAL NUMBER IS 12B4-B400
ERRORS FOUND, F PARAMETER NOT SPECIFIED
CORRECTIONS WILL NOT BE WRITTEN TO DISK

C:\DOCUMENT\DRAFT.DOC
    FIRST ALLOCATION UNIT IS INVALID, ENTRY TRUNCATED
```

(These lines are followed by the rest of the report which contains the usual statistics.)

What is happening here is that CHKDSK is telling you that there is a problem (an invalid file allocation unit). CHKDSK is capable of solving such problems but, as a safeguard, it will not do so until you give it permission. To give CHKDSK permission to fix problems, you retype the command with the /F (fix) option. In this case, if you want CHKDSK to fix the problem, you must enter:

```
CHKDSK /F
```

This time, CHKDSK will not only check over the disk but will fix any problems it finds.

Note: When you look at the original message that flagged the error, it looks as if CHKDSK had already gone ahead and fixed the problem. Rest assured, no matter what the messages look like, CHKDSK will not fix any problem until you specify the /F option.

Another type of error that you may run into occurs when space on the disk seems to be allocated even though it does not belong to a file. This might happen if you turn off the power of your computer before stopping the program you are using. The software may have opened temporary files. When you turn off the power abruptly, the program aborts before it can close the files. This results in lost allocation units. (For this reason, it is always a good idea to exit your programs before you turn off the computer.)

Most of the time, this problem is not serious. Occasionally, you may lose actual data. However, in any event, you need CHKDSK to clean things up. Under such circumstances, the beginning CHKDSK report will look something like this:

```
VOLUME HARLEY           CREATED 01-11-1991 8:50P
VOLUME SERIAL NUMBER IS 12B4-B400
ERRORS FOUND, F PARAMETER NOT SPECIFIED
CORRECTIONS WILL NOT BE WRITTEN TO DISK

    2 LOST ALLOCATION UNITS FOUND IN 2 CHAINS.
       4096 BYTES DISK SPACE FREED
```

(These lines are followed by the rest of the report which contains the usual statistics.)

In this case, CHKDSK has found two allocation units of disk space that seem to be used but are not accounted for by any file. If this space were recycled it would free up 4096 bytes. However, until you use the /F option, CHKDSK will not actually do anything. Once you enter:

```
CHKDSK /F
```

you will see:

```
VOLUME HARLEY           CREATED 01-11-1991 8:50P
VOLUME SERIAL NUMBER IS 12B4-B400

     2 LOST ALLOCATION UNITS FOUND IN 2 CHAINS.
CONVERT LOST CHAINS TO FILES (Y/N)?
```

At this point CHKDSK is ready to fix the problem. You have a choice. If you think that the lost space contains useful data, you can ask CHKDSK to create a new file for each chain (of continuous disk space). You can then check these files. If they do contain important data you can save them; otherwise you can delete them. Most of the time, however, such lost space just contains gibberish. If you suspect that this is the case, you can tell CHKDSK to recycle the space without saving the data.

As you can see, CHKDSK is asking what you want to do:

```
CONVERT LOST CHAINS TO FILES (Y/N)?
```

If you want to save the data, type <Y> and press <Enter>. Otherwise, type <N> and press <Enter>.

If you choose <Y>, CHKDSK fill create files in your main directory. The files will be named FILE0000.CHK, FILE0001.CHK, FILE0002.CHK, and so on. In this case, there are two lost allocation chains that will be saved in FILE0000.CHK and FILE0001.CHK.

Once CHKDSK is finished, it is a simple matter to use the TYPE command to examine the files. If the files do not contain anything useful, as is usually the case, you can delete them by using the DEL command. (The TYPE and DEL commands are described in Chapter 8.)

As you can see, the checking and repair operations performed by CHKDSK are important. It is a good idea to do a routine CHKDSK on all your disks, just to make sure that there are no silent problems that might cause trouble at an inopportune time.

Using CHKDSK to List All Your Files

As CHKDSK does it work, it scans every file on your disk. If you use the /V (verify) option, CHKDSK will list the name of each file as it is scanned, including hidden files.

Earlier in this chapter, we showed you how to use the DIR command with the /A option to list the names of hidden files. However, this only works if you have DOS 5.0 or later. With earlier versions of DOS, the only way to find hidden files is to use:

```
CHKDSK /V
```

If you use this command, the output is usually quite long. You will have to either be ready with the <Pause> key, or send the output of CHKDSK to the MORE filter:

```
CHKDSK /V | MORE
```

(We discuss how to use the <Pause> key and the MORE filter in Chapter 8.)

Volume Labels for Disk Identification

You've seen a few examples of DOS's reports on volume labels, so let's find out a little more about them.

VOL

If you just want to display the ID label on a disk volume, you don't need to go through the often time-consuming DIR or CHKDSK operation. There is a special command that does nothing but report the volume label on a disk. It's the VOL command, and you use it like this (include the drive specification if the disk is not in the current default drive):

```
VOL C:
```

The report it gives you is like the ones you've already seen:

```
VOLUME IN DRIVE C IS NORTON
VOLUME SERIAL NUMBER IS 0868-1BFA
```

Of course, if you are using an old version of DOS that does not have volume serial numbers (DOS 3.0 or older) only the volume label will be displayed.

How do you go about putting a label on a disk in the first place? There are actually two ways to do it.

When you are preparing a disk for use, the FORMAT command (which we discussed in Chapters 3 and 4) will prompt you to enter a volume label, or you can specify one by using /v:label. For example:

```
FORMAT A: /V:EXTRADISK
```

(In older versions of DOS, you must use /V to get a label. Check your DOS manual for the details of your particular version.)

Once a disk is formatted, you can use the LABEL command (see below) to add or change a volume label.

With either command, when DOS wants you to enter the label you will see:

```
VOLUME LABEL (11 CHARACTERS, ENTER FOR NONE)?
```

This, in DOS's terse language, means: "Type a volume label of up to 11 characters; if you've decided not to give this disk a label, press ENTER."

By the way, you might be wondering why volume labels can be up to 11 characters. As I mentioned earlier, DOS stores a volume label as the name of an empty hidden file in the main directory. The volume label is stored as a directory entry and each entry can have up to 11 characters: 8 for the filename, 3 for the extension. Thus, when DOS stores a volume label, it can make use of up to 11 characters.

LABEL

Imagine you have a formatted disk which does not have a volume label. You can't use the FORMAT command to give it a volume label, because formatting would destroy your data. In this case, you use the LABEL command, including a drive specification if necessary. The command looks like this:

```
LABEL A:
```

and LABEL's response looks like this:

```
VOLUME IN DRIVE A HAS NO LABEL
VOLUME SERIAL NUMBER IS 1848-1C21
VOLUME LABEL (11 CHARACTERS, ENTER FOR NONE)?
```

Suppose you have a diskette that already has a volume label called REPORT. You decide that you do not need the data any longer. To mark this diskette as being available you want to change the volume label to EMPTY. You place the diskette in drive A and enter:

```
LABEL A:
```

The command responds:

```
VOLUME IN DRIVE A IS REPORT
VOLUME SERIAL NUMBER IS 0B60-14ED
VOLUME LABEL (11 CHARACTERS, ENTER FOR NONE)?
```

You can now type the name EMPTY and press <Enter>. The diskette now has a new volume label. If you want to check it, enter:

```
VOL A:
```

You will see:

```
VOLUME IN DRIVE A IS EMPTY
VOLUME SERIAL NUMBER IS 0B60-14ED
```

Finally, if you want to remove a disk's volume label, replacing it with nothing, you again type LABEL A: and see the same display as before. This time, though, you press ENTER to signify that you don't want a volume label, and the command responds:

```
DELETE CURRENT VOLUME LABEL (Y/N)?
```

If you press Y, the volume label is removed.

Basically, you use the VOL command to report on a volume label, and you use the LABEL command to set one on a formatted disk. Unfortunately, the command names themselves don't tell you which does which. There's no simple way to know that VOL just shows the volume label, while LABEL actually puts it on the disk—you'll just have to remember.

Now, on to the very important subject of preparing diskettes for use.

The Diskette Preparation Commands

In Chapters 3 and 4, we learned about using FORMAT to prepare diskettes, and using FDISK and FORMAT to prepare hard disk partitions. Let's take a closer look now at FORMAT and at another disk preparation command SYS.

Keep in mind: Although you use FORMAT to prepare a hard disk for use, it is unlikely that you'll need to format a hard disk more than once. In fact, unless you're willing to lose everything on your hard disk, you would be wise to think of the FORMAT command in terms of diskettes only.

Fortunately, before you can format a hard disk, FORMAT now requires you to type in the volume label. However, older versions of DOS make no such requirement. If your DOS is like this, you must be sure that you do not unwittingly tell FORMAT to format your hard disk (probably C:) instead of a diskette.

Format

As you saw in Chapter 2, the FORMAT command is used to do the most basic preparation of a diskette for use. It is the equivalent of drawing lines on a blank sheet of paper, to make it possible to later write evenly on the paper.

FORMAT actually does two important things with a diskette: It draws the electronic "lines" that make it possible for DOS to work with the diskette and it checks for any defects in the diskette. Because diskettes are so vulnerable, they may have damaged patches on them. But a diskette with a bad patch can still be used—the FORMAT command knows how to recognize these bad patches and put up a safety fence around them. When FORMAT finds bad patches, it reports them to you, indicating their size as well as the size of the usable part of the diskette. Once this is done, the rest of the diskette is ready to use.

Whether or not you want to use a diskette with a bad patch is up to you. Whenever I encounter such a diskette, it makes me wonder if it is defective. Nowadays, diskettes are so cheap that I recommend discarding any that do not format 100% correctly. Your data is worth more than the price of a diskette.

Usually, diskettes format without any bad patches. If you encounter a lot of diskettes with bad areas, it is a sign of one of two things: Either you have a bad batch of diskettes, or there is something wrong with your diskette drive.

If you suspect that your drive is bad, have your computer serviced by a qualified technician. Unlike the tape deck that is part of your stereo system, modern disk drives do not need regular maintenance, such as cleaning the heads. If there is something wrong with one of your disk drives, there is usually nothing that you can do about it yourself.

A Word of Warning

FORMAT is one of the most dangerous of all the commands in DOS because it can wipe out an entire diskette's worth of data at one go. Be very careful when you format diskettes—check that the diskette doesn't have something important on it before you wipe it off the face of the disk with FORMAT. On the other hand, if you have to destroy some confidential data and need to be sure that it can't be reconstructed, FORMAT is the right tool to use.

Transferring DOS with SYS

Under certain unusual circumstances, you may want to copy the DOS operating system to a disk that has already been formatted. For example, you may want to copy DOS to a diskette in order to be able to boot your version of DOS on somebody else's computer. Of course, you can always reformat using /S, but that would wipe out all the data on the disk.

As I explained in Chapter 5, copying the main part of DOS involves copying the three main DOS files, IBMBIO.COM, IBMDOS.COM, and COMMAND.COM. (With MS-DOS, these files are named IO.SYS, MSDOS.SYS, and COMMAND.COM.) Since COMMAND.COM is an ordinary file, you can copy it in the usual manner by using the COPY command. However, the other files are hidden and you cannot copy them directly. Instead, you must use the SYS (system) command.

There are two forms of the SYS command. First, all you specify is the destination disk. SYS will copy from the current drive. For example, to copy the two hidden DOS files to a diskette in drive A, enter:

```
SYS A:
```

The second way to use SYS is to specify the source of the files before the name of the target drive:

```
SYS C:\DOS A:
```

In this case, SYS copies the files from the DOS subdirectory of drive C to the diskette in drive A.

Note: With older versions of DOS, before version 4.00, SYS could not copy the two hidden files to a disk unless it had been previously format- ted with /S. The reason is that these files must be in a particular place near the beginning of the disk and, with older verions of DOS, unless this space was set aside during formatting, there would be no room. Start- ing with DOS 4.00, this limitation was removed; SYS will make room if necessary.

Remember, SYS will only copy the two hidden files. If you want to make a working copy of DOS, you must use COPY to copy COMMAND.COM as well.

Copying and Comparing Disks

There is another way to set up a diskette for use besides the FORMAT command, and that is the DISKCOPY command.

DISKCOPY

DISKCOPY is a command that reads all the formatting and data from one diskette and copies it to another diskette, making a literal duplicate of the original in the process. Every file—indeed, every character in every file—will occupy exactly the same position on the copy that it occupies on the source diskette. To use DISKCOPY, you type the command name, followed by the drive specifications for the diskette you are copying from, then the diskette you are copying to. For example, if you have a data diskette in drive A and you want to make an exact duplicate of it in drive B, the command is:

```
DISKCOPY A: B:
```

If you have only one diskette drive you can still use both A: and B: and switch diskettes back and forth. DOS will use your single drive to simulate two drives and will tell you when to switch the diskettes.

DISKCOPY is a quick and efficient way to make copies of diskettes. It is so quick and efficient that you will find its use recommended to you over and over again. But there are some important problems with DISKCOPY, and so I recommend that you be very careful about using it. The preferred way to copy disk data is with the COPY command you've already learned about.

The major disadvantage of using DISKCOPY is that it does not allow for bad areas on your diskettes. If either the diskette you are copying from or the one you are copying to have unusable bad areas on them (the type of bad areas I mentioned that FORMAT detects), then DISKCOPY will not work properly. On the other hand, the COPY command, the preferred way to copy data, works nicely with bad patches on the diskettes.

Another advantage of COPY over DISKCOPY is that COPY can improve the use of space on a diskette, while DISKCOPY can't. This is an incidental and beneficial side-effect of how COPY happens to work.

Finally, DISKCOPY will wipe out anything that is on the target diskette, while COPY will merge new files with old to add information to a diskette.

There are some reasons not to use DISKCOPY, but there are still some good reasons to use it, too. For one thing, DISKCOPY is faster than COPY if the diskette is full of data. However, if there is only a little data on a diskette, COPY could be faster because it would copy only the data, while DISKCOPY would also faithfully copy all the unused diskette space as well. Another reason for using DISKCOPY is to check a diskette for physical damage. If you can DISKCOPY a diskette without any error messages, then the diskette is probably not damaged. This makes DISKCOPY a quick and easy way to check for these problems.

Confirming That a DISKCOPY Is Accurate

When you make copies of files or disks, you may need to confirm that the copy is accurate. In Chapter 8 you learned about the COMP command, which lets you compare files after you've used the COPY command to duplicate one or more files on another disk. As I mentioned then, there is little reason to check a copy you have just made—the copying process is extremely reliable, and it is very unlikely that there will be any errors in copying, unless the copying procedure itself tells you there were problems.

Where the COMP command lets you compare files, the DISKCOMP command lets you compare entire diskettes to see if they match exactly. DISKCOMP is primarily useful as a means of verifying the results of a DISKCOPY, because DISKCOMP will report two diskettes as being different even if they contain the same data and are functionally equivalent but differ in some minor way, such as the order the data is stored in.

If you have the slightest worry about whether two diskettes are identical, then by all means use DISKCOMP. If all you're interested in, however, is whether two diskettes contain the same files and you want to make sure the files bear the same time stamps, either compare directory listings for the two diskettes or use the COMP command with any specific files you need to verify.

The DISKCOMP command is easy to understand and use. To use it, you enter the command name, followed by the drive specifications of the two diskettes. Both diskettes are read from front to back and compared; any differences are reported. Here is a typical example of using disk comparison:

```
DISKCOMP A: B:
```

As with the DISKCOPY command, you can use both A: and B: even if you have only one diskette drive. DOS will use your single drive to simulate two drives and will tell you when to switch the diskettes.

As DISKCOMP compares the two diskettes, it tells you the locations of any differences it finds with messages like this:

```
COMPARE ERROR ON SIDE 0, TRACK 7
COMPARE ERROR ON SIDE 1, TRACK 8
```

and so on. Like the report you get from COMP, which is in hexadecimal, the actual information may be meaningless to you, but even one such message will tell you your diskettes are not identical.

10

BATCH FILE BASICS

Introduction

Batch-processing files are one of the most useful and powerful features of DOS, and in this chapter you'll take a look at them. First, you'll discover the simple idea of what a batch file is, and then get into some of the fancier tricks of using batch files. Finally, I'll finish the chapter with some suggestions and examples to help you begin to see batch files in terms of your own work and needs.

Before we really get into the subject, let's start with some philosophy—the philosophy of the black box. Roughly speaking, there are two ways of using a personal computer: expert and you-do-it. Experts know what they are doing (or think they do), and they usually enjoy being involved in the mechanics of how work gets done. Those of us with the you-do-it approach don't really know what's going on, and probably don't care—we want the results and don't want to get involved in the mechanics of how it's done.

For the you-do-its, computer operations need to work like what is called a black box. We don't need to see how the box gets its work done, as long as we are confident that it is doing the work correctly. Basically, it is very nice to have an expert's technical knowledge, but for most computer users, the more a computer can function as a trustworthy black box, the better for all concerned.

One of the features of DOS that can help make it work like a friendly black box is batch-file commands. My reason for explaining this so elaborately is to instill in you the idea that batch files are more than just a convenient, efficient, and safe way to direct the computer's operations. Batch files are also a key way of building black boxes to help make the use of your computer less technical. When you understand this, it can guide you into making the best possible use of batch files.

Introducing Batch Processing

The basic idea of batch processing is simple and ingenious: If you need the computer to perform a standard task, why should you have to type in the details? Let the computer find out what it is supposed to do by reading its commands from a file. With a batch file, DOS doesn't perform our commands extemporaneously. Instead it reads from a script, leaving you free to do something else with your time.

There are some interesting details concerning what a batch file can do, but let's begin with the fundamentals. First of all, batch processing is always performed by a batch file, which must have the filename extension of .BAT. The file must be a plain, unformatted text file (also called an ASCII file), which means it has to be a bare-bones, standard-characters-only type of file.

If you're unfamiliar with ASCII files, we'll be covering them in Chapter 14. For now, though, here's the important part to remember: You can create an unformatted, or ASCII, file with any ordinary text editor, such as the EDLIN editor (which comes with DOS) or with the Norton Editor. If you have DOS 5.0 or later, you can use the EDIT program, which is much better than the older EDLIN. (We discuss EDIT in Chapter 26 and EDLIN in Chapter 27.) You can also use a word-processing program to create batch files, but you'll have to use your word processor's "unformatted" or "nondocument" mode, so that the file comes out as plain unformatted text. (Your word processor's manual will explain how to do that.)

Inside a batch file are ordinary DOS commands, just as you might enter them on the keyboard. There can be one or many commands in the file. You place each command on a separate line.

You put a batch file to work by giving DOS its file name as a command. This works exactly the same way as you use a program: You type in the name of the program, and DOS finds and starts the program for you. In the case of a batch file, DOS goes looking for the file and when it finds that the file has the extension BAT, it starts executing the commands held in that file.

How Batch Processing Works

The easiest way to understand this concept of batch processing is to actually see how it works. So let's take a look at a very simple batch file. Let's suppose you've created a file with the name D.BAT. Notice that the file name has the extension of BAT. Since the file name itself is D, then D is all that you need to type to invoke this batch-processing command. To start out on the right foot, let's make the contents of this batch file something very simple: a single line that contains DIR (which, remember, is the name of the directory command that lists the contents of a disk). This is what your batch-processing file would look like. Here's the file name:

```
D.BAT
```

and this is what it contains:

```
DIR
```

Now, with this batch file set up, what would happen if you typed the file name (the letter D) and pressed the <Enter> key? DOS would first search for a file named D. When it found D, it would also find out that the file name's extension is BAT. Since BAT tells DOS to carry out the commands in the file, DOS would then start executing whatever DOS commands it finds in D. Since it would find only the command DIR, it would give you a directory listing.

This example is about as short and silly as you could imagine, and you might be thinking that it is a completely artificial example, with no practical value. Surprisingly it is not: There is a use for batch-processing commands like this.

What this command does, in effect, is let you use D as an abbreviation for DIR. At first glance, that may not seem like a big deal, yet it cuts the keystrokes you have to type in half, from four to two (counting the <Enter> key). This is one of the main purposes of batch files: to simplify the typing you have to do to get your computer to do some work for you. One of the best uses of batch files, then, is simply to provide convenient abbreviations of commands.

(In Chapter 25, we will cover an alternate way to abbreviate commands —macros. However, you can use macros only with DOS 5.0 or later. If you have an older version of DOS batch files are still the best way to create short convenient abbreviations.)

Let's expand our small batch file a little. Suppose you want DOS to check the disk before it shows the directory listing. D.BAT would have to contain two DOS commands: one to check the disk, and another to display the directory. The file would look like this:

```
CHKDSK
DIR
```

Now we come to one of the rather clever things that DOS does when it works with batch files. It keeps track of where it is working in the file. So when the file has more than one command, DOS knows how to carry on. As it finishes carrying out each command, DOS returns to the batch file, reads past the commands it has already processed, then starts the next command. Thus, in our two-line batch file, DOS would read the first command, CHKDSK, carry it out, return to the batch file, bypass the first command, and carry out the second command, DIR.

You can see the most important reason why you would want to have batch files. Even before we get into the advanced material, you know from this example that these files not only let you create an abbreviation for a command name—they let you group several commands into one functional unit.

If often happens that you need to do several things to carry out one task. For example, when I write I routinely stop to make backup copies of my files for safekeeping. (We will discuss backups later, in Chapter 14.) For this task. I use a batch file called SAVE.BAT that has five steps.

First, SAVE looks for and deletes any files that have a filename of TEMP—such as TEMP, TEMP.DOC, or TEMP.TXT. I use such names when I want a temporary file that I do not want to save. Second, SAVE uses a program from the Norton Utilities to sort the file names within my directory. Third, SAVE copies to a diskette all the files that have changed since the last backup. (For this, I use the XCOPY command which we will meet in Chapter 17.) Next, that batch file sorts the directory on the diskette. Finally, SAVE displays a wide listing of the files on the diskette so that I can check that everything looks okay. (To display a wide listing I use the DIR /W command which we met in Chapter 9.)

I could do each of these five steps separately every time I want to save my files, but I chose to put them into one batch file. That's done two very useful things for me. First, it has saved me the trouble of invoking each step by itself by having to type in the same five commands, time after time. Second, and more important, this batch file has established a standard operating discipline for me. Because it is so easy to back up my work files, neither laziness nor lack of time will keep me from performing this important task.

People often ask me, How often should I stop and back up my files? The answer depends on how much work you are willing to lose if something goes wrong. If you are willing to lose a whole day's work, then save your files once a day. If you are willing to lose only 15 or 20 minutes of work—as I am—you must stop and save your files more often. Because I have automated the backup process, via SAVE.BAT, it is not an imposition for me to stop the word processor for a few moments, enter the command SAVE, and let the batch file do its work. In fact, while SAVE is carrying out its job, I use the time for a quick stretch (which accounts for my slim youthful figure).

The most important reason, then, for using batch files is to gather together, under one name, all the separate steps needed to perform a task, and the reason for doing that is as much for uniformity and completeness as it is for convenience and ease.

Using Batch Files to Protect Data

There is one more key reason for using batch files, and that reason is safety. There are some maddeningly dangerous commands available to us in DOS, commands that can wipe out data in the blink of an eye. There are four such commands: DEL (ERASE), which discards data, COPY and XCOPY, which can overwrite good data with bad, and FORMAT, which can wipe out the entire contents of a disk beyond all hope of recovery. Batch files can reduce the danger of misusing these commands, not intentionally, of course, but everyone has one of those days—in a rush, perhaps your mind is half on something else.

Here's an example. Let's suppose you routinely delete a file called DATA.OLD, while preserving the file DATA.NEW. If you type in the command:

```
DEL DATA.OLD
```

each time, there is just a chance that one day, absent-mindedly, you will type NEW, rather than OLD. Wouldn't that put you in a pickle? But if you had a batch file with the DEL command in it, you won't have to worry about this kind of mistake. In fact, you might have a batch file that safely and reliably erased all sorts of files without a worry, because if you built the batch file correctly, then the commands would go right, each time; never a slip. You might even name the batch file something evocative and easy to remember, like

```
KILL-OLD.BAT
```

A Special Batch File—AUTOEXEC.BAT

In the rest of this chapter you'll be looking at some DOS commands that are specially made for use in batch files. But before you get to them, let's pause to meet a special batch file, called AUTOEXEC.BAT.

When DOS starts up its operation, it's prepared to perform any start-up commands we want it to do. That can be very handy—those commands can be used to get DOS off to a running start. The mechanics of how this is done are very simple: When DOS starts up, it always checks to see if there is a batch file named AUTOEXEC.BAT on the boot disk—that is, the disk from which DOS is starting. If there is an AUTOEXEC.BAT file available, DOS starts carrying out the commands in this file, just as if you had entered the command AUTOEXEC as your first instructions to DOS.

When you install DOS (see Chapter 5), the installation program will create an AUTOEXEC.BAT file for you and place it in the main directory on your boot disk (usually drive C). You can use this AUTOEXEC.BAT the way it is, or edit it to your taste.

You can also enter the command AUTOEXEC, just like any other batch command, any time you want to. The one special thing about the AUTOEXEC.BAT file is that DOS will, if it finds such a file, automatically perform the commands in that file. This can be very helpful if there are any start-up operations you want to perform when you fire up your computer.

You can use AUTOEXEC.BAT to perform any beginning commands that you want, and it doesn't have to be long or involved. You can, for example, create an AUTOEXEC.BAT file just to start up the program you use the most. There are also more exotic uses for the AUTOEXEC command, but you'll see those in Chapter 20.

The First Two Commands—REM and PAUSE

Some commands built into DOS exist just to make batch-file processing better. Two of these are the REMark and PAUSE commands. REMark, as its name implies, is intended to let you put comments into a batch file. Such comments can be useful reminders of what is going on; they can say to anyone who reads them, "This is what I'm doing." When you include a remark, the line must begin with REM. If the remark is longer than one line, each succeeding line must also begin with REM. Here's a simple example:

```
REM DISPLAY THE CURRENT DIRECTORY ON THE HARD DISK
DIR C:
```

Whenever DOS encounters REM in a batch file, it skips over the words in the remark and moves on to the next command it can carry out. (There's also another, clearer way to include remarks that DOS will display on screen; it's called the ECHO command, and we'll get to it in the next section.)

In the example, REM was followed by a DIR command. The DIR command might show us so many files in the directory that the REM-remark rolls right off the top of the screen. That could be a problem. Not in our example here, but if the REM-remark was something more important we wanted to make sure we could see on the screen, we would need a way of stopping things so that these comments can be seen. That is done with the PAUSE command, something like this:

```
REM DISPLAY THE CURRENT DIRECTORY ON THE HARD DISK
PAUSE
DIR C:
```

Using Pause

What's this PAUSE command you see here? Technically speaking, PAUSE is just another form of the REM command. Instead of commenting on what's happening, however, it suspends the operation of the batch file until you press a key—any key—on the keyboard. You saw a type of PAUSE command in the /P switch of the DIR command, the switch that stops a directory listing after each screenfull and waits for you to press a key to continue.

The PAUSE command is good for two purposes. As in this example and the DIR command, it is helpful in keeping useful information from rolling off the screen. With a PAUSE command in a batch file, you have a chance to look at what is on the screen for as long as you want before the computer carries on its work.

The other use for this command is safety. If a command in a batch file can potentially do something that might endanger some of your data, a PAUSE to check that everything is in order is a very good idea. This can be particularly valuable before a command that might ERASE or COPY over your data.

But if you use the PAUSE command in this way, what if you decide that you don't want things to carry on; how do you stop them? Simple: Press <Break> on your keyboard or type the equivalent, the <C> key combination. Either way, <Break> or <C > will stop the operation of the batch file; it will not carry out whatever command it was going to. The PAUSE command gives you the opportunity to press the key at the right moments. You'll know that DOS is waiting because PAUSE will display the message:

```
Press any key to continue . . .
```

Older versions of DOS will display a similar but more awkward message:

```
Strike a key when ready . . .
```

Here is a dummy example of how PAUSE might be used for safety. (Beside each line of the batch file we have put an explanation of what the command is doing. These comments would not appear in the actual batch file).

```
COPY DATA.NEW DATA.OLD        make a safe-copy of the old data
PROCESS DATA.NEW              use a program that creates new data
DIR DATA.NEW                  check directory for info on DATA.NEW
PAUSE                         you can press <Ctrl-Break> to stop
DEL DATA.OLD                  discard old data
```

This example is a little artificial, but the ideas are ones that you will probably want to use. Notice that DIR is used to take a quick look at the new data. It will show both the size and the time-stamp on the new data file, both of which ought to be enough to tell if the PROCESS program was successful in creating the new data. If everything looks good, we proceed from the PAUSE statement to clean things up by deleting the copy of the old data. If things aren't all well, then we break at the PAUSE, so that the old data isn't deleted, and we can try to fix whatever went wrong.

What you've seen so far makes batch files look very useful, but what you can do with them is even richer and more useful, as you'll see in the next section.

Making Batch Files More Attractive

Before we leave the subject of remarks, here's a handy and rather elegant tip to remember if you include a multiple-line remark in a batch file: Instead of beginning each line with REM, put the entire remark in a separate file and use the TYPE command to fetch and display it. Here is the kind of situation I mean. Suppose you have a remark like this (it's unlikely you'd include such a wordy one, but the idea should be clear):

```
REM This batch file copies files with extensions "NEW"
REM and gives them the extension "OLD"
REM when the copy is finished it displays a
REM directory of the copies. . .
```

Rather than clutter up your batch file with these lines, you could put the entire remark in a file named, say, NOTES.REM and replace it with this in the main batch file:

```
TYPE NOTES.REM
PAUSE
```

Note: There are certain DOS characters that have special meanings when they appear in commands and within batch files. These characters are the greater-than sign, the less-than sign, and the vertical bar:

```
<    >    |
```

These are explained in Chapter 19.

If you use these characters in a REM remark you must enclose them with double quotes to tell DOS that they are not special. For example:

```
REM HERE IS A LESS-THAN SIGN "<"
```

Using TYPE

The TYPE command, as we saw in Chapter 8, simply copies (or types out) onto the display screen the contents of any file you specify. That can be a very handy way of putting a series of comments on the screen. Using TYPE has two advantages over using a series of REMs: One is that REMs include the DOS prompt along with the comments they display and they also put a blank line between comments, which just uses up space on the screen; the other is that TYPE is usually faster, displaying the comments more briskly. On the other hand, there's a disadvantage to the TYPE approach as well: with TYPE you have another file (the one with the comments in it) to look after as well as the batch file.

CLS Command

Suppose you create a batch file that shows a directory listing. As long as your batch file is properly constructed, DOS will display a directory, regardless of what else is on the screen at the time. With a short directory and an already cluttered screen, that could mean a lot of extraneous information to look at. But there's a way to make sure the screen is nice and clean before the DIR command is carried out: It's the CLS command. Here, for instance, is how you would use CLS in our earlier PAUSE example:

`COPY DATA.NEW DATA.OLD`	*make a safe copy of the old data*
`PROCESS DATA.NEW`	*use a program that creates new data*
`CLS`	*get the screen ready*
`DIR DATA.NEW`	*check directory for info on DATA.NEW*
`PAUSE`	*you can press <Ctrl-Break> to stop.*
`DEL DATA.OLD`	*discard old data.*

Now the directory would appear on a blank screen for easier reading.

Here's another point about batch files and your screen. When DOS is working its way through a batch file, it displays the commands it is executing, just as if you had typed them in. This is good and bad. It's good because it shows you exactly what is being done, bad because it clutters the screen with extraneous information. After all, one of the points of a batch file is to turn several commands into one unified operation. When you run a program, a listing of the program doesn't appear on your screen, so why should a listing of a batch file get displayed?

ECHO

It's nice to have these two ways of showing comments, so you can make an intelligent choice between them. Shortly we'll see yet another way to make comments appear on the screen. First, though, we'll look at a way of improving the appearance of the screen when we're using batch files.

This conflict is resolved by the ECHO command. ECHO is used to tell DOS to display (echo to the screen), or not display, each batch file command as it is executed. The ECHO command itself controls command echoing, like this:

ECHO ON   *displays each command as DOS processes it*

ECHO OFF   *does not display each command*

DOS's default is ECHO ON, so it displays each command it carries out. You can turn it off and on like this:

```
ECHO OFF
COPY DATA.NEW DATA.OLD
PROCESS DATA.NEW
CLS
DIR DATA.NEW
ECHO ON
PAUSE
DEL DATA.OLD
```

Any commands performed between the OFF and ON will not appear on the screen. That is, the command itself won't appear. If the command program generates any display output, as the DIR command does, that will continue to show on the screen.

One of the things that ECHO OFF will suppress is the display of comments from the ordinary batch file commands REM and PAUSE, but we might want some comments to appear on the screen. To make that possible, there is a third option to the ECHO command, besides ON and OFF. If the command name ECHO is followed by anything other than ON or OFF, then what follows ECHO is displayed as a comment on the screen. The command is entered like this:

```
ECHO MESSAGE
```

and it works with any message that is not the word ON or the word OFF. (Of course, like all DOS commands, the words ON and OFF can be upper- or lowercase.) In our preceding example, for instance, it would help to remind people that pressing the <Ctrl-Break> key will stop the DATA.NEW files from being erased. You can do it like this:

```
ECHO OFF
COPY DATA.NEW DATA.OLD
PROCESS DATA.NEW
CLS
DIR DATA.NEW
ECHO Press Ctrl-Break to cancel deletion of DATA.OLD or
PAUSE
DEL DATA.OLD
```

The word or at the end of the ECHO message is there to work with DOS's PAUSE message. The display will look like this:

```
Press Ctrl-Break to cancel deletion of DATA.OLD or
Press any key to continue...
```

ECHO's messages appear whether command echoing is on or off, and it has one real advantage over the REM command. When we use the REM command, the word REM itself appears on the screen, which doesn't do anything to clarify the message. With the ECHO message command, only the message appears, which is cleaner and clearer.

Keeping Batch Commands from Being Displayed

Within a batch file, any line that starts with an @ sign will not be displayed when the file executes. Here is how this is useful:

As I mentioned in the last section, DOS displays the batch commands, one by one, as they are executed, unless you use an ECHO OFF command. For this reason, many people place an ECHO OFF command at the beginning of each batch file. (Of course, don't put this in until you have debugged the batch file, or you won't be able to see what is happening.)

However, even with ECHO OFF, there is one statement that you will be able to see: namely, the ECHO OFF command itself. To prevent this, just put @ before the ECHO. Here is an example:

```
@ECHO OFF
REM Batch file to check two hard disks
CHKDSK C:
CHKDSK D:
```

When this batch file is executed, all you will see is the OUTPUT from the CHKDSK commands.

Since this file is so short, another alternative is to omit the ECHO command and simply insert a @ before each command:

```
@REM Batch file to check two hard disks
@CHKDSK C:
@CHKDSK D:
```

Again, all you will see is the out put from the CHKDSK commands.

Here is a hint: Let's say you have a long batch file that is acting strange and you want to see exactly what is happening. If you have an @ECHO OFF command at the beginning, you won't see any of the commands. So, until you have solved the problem, make the command into a remark:

```
REM @ECHO OFF
```

After you get things working, simply remove the REM.

When I write new batch files, I like to start each one with a command like the one above. Then, after I am satisfied that the batch file works the way I want it to work, I remove the REM. If something goes wrong, or if I need to modify the batch file, I put the REM back in temporarily.

Using Parameters for Flexibility

Earlier, I mentioned how it was a good idea to save your work every 15 or 20 minutes. Here is a sample batch file that you might use to edit a file and then make a backup copy of your work. The file is called ED.BAT:

```
@ECHO OFF
EDIT CHAPTER.11
COPY CHAPTER.11 A:
DIR A:CHAPTER.11
```

The first line tells DOS not to display each command as it is processed. The @ at the beginning of the line prevents the ECHO command itself from being displayed. The second line starts the EDIT program to edit the file. (We will discuss EDIT in Chapter 26.) The next line copies the edited file from the hard disk to the diskette in drive A. The final line displays the statistics for the file as it is stored on the diskette, so we can check that everything looks okay.

As you can see, this batch file is used to edit a file named CHAPTER.11, presumably part of a book. But there is something drastically wrong with this batch file: It only works for one particular file. If we need to work on another file we would have to change the batch file, which would be a remarkable waste of time.

The solution is to use *parameters*. A parameter is a word or a value that you type on the command line, after the name of the command. In this case, we would want to be able to enter:

```
ED 11
```

to edit Chapter 11. Or,

```
ED 17
```

to edit Chapter 17.

Inside the batch file ED.BAT, we use a special symbol everywhere the chapter number is needed. This symbol is %1. This tells DOS to substitute the parameter that we enter for every occurrence of %1 within the batch file. So, the new batch file looks like this:

```
@ECHO OFF
EDIT CHAPTER.%1
COPY CHAPTER.%1 A:
DIR A:CHAPTER.%1
```

Now, when we execute the batch file by entering the command name followed by a number, the number, acting as a parameter, is substituted for us automatically. For example, when we enter:

```
ED 17
```

DOS treats the batch file as if it contained:

```
@ECHO OFF
EDIT CHAPTER.17
COPY CHAPTER.17 A:
DIR A:CHAPTER.17
```

There can be more than one parameter, so a single digit is used after the percent sign (%) to indicate a specific parameter. The symbol %1 is used for the first parameter after the command name, %2 for the second, and so on, up to %9. (If you need anywhere near that many you are probably making things much too complicated.)

Parameter number zero, %0, is used to get the filename of the batch file itself. Thus, if we added the line:

```
ECHO THIS IS THE %0 BATCH FILE.
```

to ED.BAT, it would display the output:

```
THIS IS THE ED BATCH FILE.
```

Before we move on to the end of this chapter, let's take one more look at our sample batch file. We were able to make it more flexible by using a parameter instead of a file extension. This allowed us to edit any file whose name is of the form CHAPTER.something. However, there is one more change that we can make to allow ED.BAT to edit any file whatsoever. We can use a parameter to stand for the entire file name, not just the extension:

```
@ECHO OFF
EDIT %1
COPY %1 A:
DIR A:%1
```

Now, we can use ED.BAT to edit any file we want:

```
ED CHAPTER.11
ED DATA.DOC
ED NAMES.TXT
```

However, if we were planning to do a lot of editing with files whose filenames were all CHAPTER, the first form of the batch file is probably better.

Other Features of Batch Processing

There are additional things to know about batch files in general, before we go on to the extra features of DOS's batch processing. Inside a batch file are commands, which can be program names, or the names of other batch files. If the command is a program, then when that program is finished, we can carry on with the batch file. But if the command is the name of another batch file, then control never comes back to the original batch file. In technical terms this means that batch files are chained but not nested. If batch file A invokes batch file B, when B is done, things stop; they don't carry on where A left off. (However, there is a way to nest batch files, using the CALL command. We'll learn about it in the next chapter.)

One of the batch commands that could be in a batch file is the file's own name. A batch file can invoke itself, starting an endless repetition of the same work done over and over again. This can be very useful when you have to repeat some operation. Pressing <Ctrl-Break> can be used to break out of this endless repetition. Putting a PAUSE command just before the repetition starts can be a good idea.

It is also possible for a program to control its own destiny, by writing out the contents of a batch file that will be executed when the program is done. This is a very clever mechanism that makes it possible to use the full rich logical capabilities of a programming language to decide what commands are to be carried out next. The way this is done is like this: We create a batch file, let's call it A, which runs our program; following the program, our A batch file tells DOS to carry out a batch file named B. But the program that is run by the A batch file itself creates the file B.BAT, thus the program decides what is to be done when it finishes. The program in the A batch file creates whatever exact instructions are to be performed in the B batch file.

If you go in for this sort of trick, test your work carefully, and beware of certain traps. For example, it is much safer for a program to create the next batch file that will be executed than to try to change the batch file currently being performed.

That gives us basics of batch files. Now we're ready to investigate some of the more advanced features and also explore some batch file tricks—both in the next chapter.

11

MORE ON BATCH FILES

Introduction

So far you've seen examples of batch files that proceed in an orderly, linear way: step to step to step. But at the end of Chapter 10, I also mentioned that you can control the way batch files are carried out—have them repeat sets of commands, and so on. Now, let's find out how to open the door to more batch-file magic—in a sense, teaching batch files how to make decisions.

Advanced Batch Commands

One of the enrichments DOS provides is a logical capability within batch commands. This means that batch files can react to developing situations, in a scaled-down version of the kind of logic that can be used in a computer program. Four batch commands are related to this logic capability: SHIFT, GOTO, IF, and FOR. The full scope of these commands is really an advanced topic beyond the range of this book, but I'll give you a sketch of what these commands can do.

The SHIFT Command

Let's start with the SHIFT command. If you have a batch file that uses several of the % replacement parameters, the SHIFT command lets you move the parameters over, one by one, to make it easier to process them. When a SHIFT is done, all the values have been moved over one place, so that the parameter symbol %1 has the value that had been %2, and %2 has the value that used to belong to %3.

The advantage of the SHIFT command is that one batch file can be used to work with a number of files fairly easily. The process first works with one file name taken from the %1 parameter, and then SHIFTs the list over to deal with the next filename, and SHIFTs again if there is a third file name. The real use of the SHIFT command comes when you use it with the GOTO and IF commands, which we'll get to next. But to help you understand what SHIFT does, let's create an artificial example.

Suppose you want to create a batch file that will COPY a list of files; let's say, for simplicity, that you want to be able to give it a list of any three file names, and have it copy them from drive A to drive B. If the name of the batch file is 3COPY, and your file names are X, Y, and Z, you can copy the files by just entering the name of the batch file, followed by the three file names as parameters, like this:

```
3COPY X Y Z
```

Here is what your 3COPY batch file might look like, using the SHIFT command. (Note that the comments at the right are not part of the batch file.)

```
COPY A:%1 B:        this copies the first file, X
SHIFT               this shifts Y into position as %1
COPY A:%1 B:        this copies Y
SHIFT               this shifts Z into position as %1
COPY A:%1 B:        this copies Z
```

Since each shift command moves the parameters over, the second and third COPY commands find the file names Y and Z in the first parameter, or %1, location.

Obviously, this example is a little artificial, since you could have just used %2 and %3 in the second and third COPY commands. But this example sets the stage for something more complex, where the SHIFT makes more sense.

GOTO

Our 3COPY batch file will copy exactly three files, no more. What if you would like it to copy more files, without limit? In that case, you can set up a loop that will SHIFT and COPY forever. To do that, you use the GOTO command, which makes the batch command loop around in circles. This time, let's look at an example before the explanation:

```
:ONWARD
COPY A:%1 B:
SHIFT
GOTO ONWARD
```

The first line you see here, :ONWARD is a label, which is needed so that the command can loop around in circles. The label begins with a colon to identify it, and it can have any symbolic name you want to use. I chose ONWARD, but you could have used any other short name, such as LOOP, or CYCLE. The label, by the way, must be on a line by itself, just as you see it here.

Following the ONWARD label are our familiar COPY and SHIFT commands; the COPY does the work, and the SHIFT command moves the % parameters over one place, ready for the next COPY command, then comes a new command, GOTO. The GOTO command tells DOS to find the label that follows the GOTO command name, and to pick up process-ing from there. Since the line says GOTO ONWARD, DOS will go back up to the ONWARD label and continue through the COPY and SHIFT commands again.

What you have here is a loop, something that will make DOS go around in circles. Each time around, another file will be copied, and then the parameter list will be shifted over one. As it's done in this ex-ample, this looping could go on forever—there's nothing to stop it. Nat-urally, at some point you would run out of filenames to copy, but the batch file would continue looping forever—with the COPY command complaining that you weren't giving it any names to copy.

Labels and Comments

There are only four rules for using labels:

1. All labels must start with a colon.
2. A label can be up to 8 characters. If you specify a longer label, DOS will only use the first 8 characters.
3. A label must be on a line by itself.
4. Like all DOS commands, a label can be in upper- or lower case.

Whenever DOS encounters a line that begins with a colon, it treats it as a label but does not try to execute it. This means that you can use such lines to hold descriptive comments. For example, you could use the line:

```
:EXECUTE THE NEXT PROGRAM
```

in the middle of a batch file as a comment. However, technically, this line is still a label and you might inadvertently get into trouble if you happen to have a label named:

```
:EXECUTE
```

Since DOS only looks at the first 8 characters, you will get an error be-cause DOS will think that you have two identical labels. (And remember, DOS does not distinguish between upper- and lowercase.)

What I suggest is that you start each comment with :*, for example:

```
:* EXECUTE THE NEXT PROGRAM
```

As long as you don't start any legitimate labels with :*, (which is un-likely) you won't have any problems.

Aside from understanding comments, you should know that DOS will ignore empty lines and spaces at the beginning of a line. Putting these devices together, you can create batch files that are easy to read and understand. This is especially important with large batch files.

Here is our previous example, rewritten as a complete, well-commented batch file. Although you will develop your own personal style, this example shows what can be done with a judicious use of empty space and comments.

```
:* =======================================================
:* 3COPY.BAT - BATCH FILE TO COPY 3 FILES FROM A: TO B:
   @ECHO OFF
:* Parameters:
:*    %1 = first file, %2 = second file, %3 = third file
:*    copy the first file
      copy a:%1 b:
:*    copy the second file
      copy a:%2 b:
:*    copy the third file
      copy a:%3 b:
:* =======================================================
```

The IF Command

To keep the batch file loop from going on forever, you can use the IF command. The IF command will test some logical condition, and then if the condition is true, it will carry out one command. One of the things you can have the IF statement test for is whether a file name exists. So, in our earlier example, we might replace the GOTO ONWARD command with the test:

```
IF EXIST A:%1 GOTO ONWARD
```

The new batch file looks like this:

```
:ONWARD
COPY A:%1 B:
SHIFT
IF EXIST A:%1 GOTO ONWARD
```

This IF statement will test whether there is a file with the name given by the parameter %1. If there is such a file, everything will loop around to the ONWARD label, and you'll continue merrily along. But, if you've run out of file names, then the IF won't loop back, and the batch file will end.

More About GOTO and IF

There is more to the GOTO and the IF than you have seen so far. For example, our GOTO skipped to a label that came before it in the batch file, but it could just as easily have gone to a label that came after the GOTO statement. There's a big difference in what happens: Skipping to an earlier point in the file will set up a loop, while skipping forward to a later point in the file will bypass any commands in between. Depending upon your needs, either direction of GOTO will work.

The IF statement can test for two conditions other than the existence of a file. One is to check whether any program has reported trouble by signaling an error code to DOS. We test for these like this:

```
IF ERRORLEVEL 1 GOTO SOMEWHERE
```

There are, by the way, nine DOS commands that set the AIRLEVEL code. These commands are: BACKUP, DISCOMP, DISCOPY, FORMAT, GRAFTABL, REPLACE, RESTORE, SETVER, and XCOPY.

The other kind of condition is a string comparison, which we can use to test for some particular parameter value. For example:

```
IF %1==FINISH GOTO SOMEWHERE
```

For all three kinds of IF conditions, there is a corresponding IF NOT condition.

In order to illustrate these new ideas about GOTO and IF, let's take another look at our last example. Do you notice that it has a bug (mistake)? What happens if the first file does not exist? Since the COPY command comes before the test, it will always try to copy the first file.

The solution is to make sure that the %1 file exists before we copy. If the file is not found, we can stop the batch file. To do this, we need to use an IF NOT command, add a new label :STOP, and add an extra GOTO command:

```
:ONWARD
IF NOT EXIST A:%1 GOTO STOP
COPY A:%1 B:
SHIFT
GOTO ONWARD
:STOP
```

There are more complicated details to the IF command than I can go into here—it becomes a quite advanced subject, to look at everything that IF can do. When you are ready for all the variations, check your computer's DOS manual for the details.

There is one more advanced batch command that gives you another way to repeat commands: the FOR statement.

FOR

FOR lets you create a list, for example, a list of file names, and then repeat a command with each of the names in the list. It involves a symbolic variable, which must be a single letter, marked with two percent signs like this: %%. That variable is then set to each of the items in the list, in turn. Here is an example:

```
FOR %%N IN (A B C D E) DO COPY A:%%N B:
```

In the example, the COPY statement will be repeated, with each of the names in the list—A,B,C,D,E—substituted for the symbolic variable %%N. In effect, this FOR command is translated into five separate COPY commands:

```
COPY A:A B:
COPY A:B B:
COPY A:C B:
COPY A:D B:
COPY A:E B:
```

If you are ingenious, you can create some very clever batch-processing files using the FOR command. It is also quite easy to create a mess with it, since the whole process is rather tricky.

All of the advanced batch commands you have seen here have their uses, but they certainly aren't for beginners. There is also some question about how really useful they might be for advanced users, when everything is considered. A lot depends upon how much taste you have for trying complicated tricks. If it suits you, don't let me discourage you at all from trying it—just be careful.

By the way, you can use the FOR command as a regular command that you type in at the DOS prompt. The only difference is that you use only one % character. For example, say that you want to copy the same five files we used in the last example. Within a batch file you use %%. As a single command from the DOS prompt, you type:

```
FOR %N IN (A B C D E) DO COPY A:%N B:
```

Take care—it is easy to make mistakes when you are typing a command directly. Be especially careful when you are using the DEL (delete) command within a FOR command. One consultant managed to erase many tens of important spreadsheet files all at once by mistyping "DEL" for "DIR" within a FOR command. (Fortunately, he was able to recover the files using the unerase program from the Norton Utilities.)

Nesting Batch Files with CALL

Now's the time for you to learn one of the most interesting and useful tricks that you can perform with batch files: nesting.

Although many of us make rather casual use of batch files, if you become a dedicated batch file user, you may get to the point where you find that practically everything you do with your computer is wrapped up in a batch file. Since batch files are designed to combine several commands into one unit, you may get to the point where the operations you want to combine together are also batch files. At that point, we're *nesting*, invoking one batch file inside of another one.

Consider an example in which you want to execute a program, followed by a batch file, followed by another program. Let's say that the programs are named PROGRAM1 and PROGRAM2, and the batch file is named BFILE.BAT. You might use the following batch file, called TRIPLE.BAT:

```
:* ======================================================
:* TRIPLE.BAT : batch files to execute PROGRAM1, followed
:*                by BFILE.BAT, followed by PROGRAM2
   program1
   bfile
   program2
:* ======================================================
```

The problem is that when DOS encounters the line bfile, it will branch to BFILE.BAT, never to return to TRIPLE.BAT. This is called *chaining* and it is useful, but only if you really want to jump to a batch file without returning.

In this case, we do want to return (in order to execute PROGRAM2). The solution is to use the CALL command. This tells DOS to start a second batch file and, when it is finished, return to the next line of the original batch file. The modified batch file looks like this:

```
:* =======================================================
:* TRIPLE.BAT : batch files to execute PROGRAM1, followed
:*                  by BFILE.BAT, followed by PROGRAM2
   program1
   call bfile
   program2
:* =======================================================
```

This time, after DOS finished with BFILE.BAT, it will return to ex-ecute PROGRAM2.

Suggestions and Examples of Batch File Tricks

In this section, I'm going to show you some examples and tricks in using batch files. Let me warn you right away that some of the examples are a bit complicated, and it's possible you might get lost as you go over them. Don't worry if that happens. Just back off from them for a while, and keep your own use of batch files simple and straightforward. Later, when you are ready and willing to tackle some of the messier tricks, you can come back here.

At the beginning of Chapter 10, I mentioned the philosophy of using batch files to make computers function like friendly black boxes. The key element in making batch files work this way is to write them in a style that makes them work as smoothly and as unobtrusively as possible.

Using ECHO and PAUSE with Batch Files

Two of the most useful things you can put into batch files are remarks and pauses, using the ECHO and PAUSE commands. It is surprisingly easy to lose track of exactly what you are doing. That sounds really dumb, but it's true—especially if you are doing the same thing over and over again. If you are working your way through a list of files, it's quite easy to lose your place in the list. This problem can be solved by using the ECHO command to show you the parameters your batch file is working with. Example? All my batch files that run my text editor end with this command:

```
REM FINISHED EDITING THE FILE NAMED %1
```

And, of course, the parameter %1 shows me the file name.

The same thing can be done with the PAUSE command, but PAUSE has some extra advantages. If you are running something lengthy and automatic through a batch file, PAUSE can be used to suspend the operation, so you can see the current screen display and decide whether or not to proceed with the rest of the batch file. If you don't want things to proceed, remember that pressing <Ctrl-Break> will stop the batch file.

Pausing for approval to continue is a very important part of any batch file that does anything potentially dangerous. For example, you might have a series of programs that deliberately leave their work files on disk, so that you can recover the data if anything goes wrong. In a batch file like this, you could end by using DEL to delete the work files. You could put a PAUSE command just before the DEL command to give yourself a chance to check that everything was all right before the files were destroyed.

A nice trick is to use an ECHO command, followed by a PAUSE command without its output. How is this done? In Chapter 19, we will explain how to send the output of a command to a file. This is called redirection As you will see, DOS allows you to throw away the output of a command by redirecting it to a special "file" named NUL:—in effect, NUL: acts as a built-in garbage can. In this case however, we can dispense with the output from PAUSE by using:

```
PAUSE > NUL:
```

(The greater-than sign tells DOS to redirect the output.)

Here is a sample batch file, DELBAK.BAT, that uses the same technique to display a warning. This batch file deletes all the files that have an extension of BAK. Within the batch file, we use the technique that we described earlier: having the DIR command list the names of all files that will be deleted prior to the actual deletion.

```
:* ========================================================
:* DELBAK: batch file to delete backup files
   @echo off

:* display the names of the files that will be deleted
   dir *.bak

:* warn the user
   echo If you want to delete all of these files
   echo press any key to continue.
   echo If not, press Ctrl-Break to stop...
   pause > nul:

:* delete the files
   del *.bak
:* ========================================================
```

Using CHKDSK and DIR

There are some commands in DOS that are very useful, but are a nuisance to type in. With batch files, you can use them liberally with no effort at all, since the batch file does all the work for you. One of the most important is the check disk command, CHKDSK. CHKDSK is useful to put in your batch commands for two reasons. First, it lets you know how much working space is left on your disk, and it is useful to see that often, so that you get early warning about running out of space. CHKDSK also inspects the disk for some logical damage (meaning scrambled data but not physical damage) on the diskette. It's a good thing to do that frequently, even though scrambling isn't a common occurrence.

It is also quite handy to add the DIR command to most of your batch files. You can put in a specific command (indicating what files you want to know about), to see things like the file size and the file's date and time stamp. Here are some examples:

```
DIR %1
DIR *.BAS
```

The first example displays information about the file whose name is the first parameter. The second specifies all the files with the extension BAS. (This extension is used for programs written in BASIC.)

In Chapter 9, we described the DIR command and the wide variety of options that is supports. When you place the DIR command within a batch file, take a few moments and choose the type of directory listing that will give the most useful type of information. For example, you might use:

```
DIR *.BAS /O:D
```

to list the names of all your BASIC programs, from earliest to latest.

RM.BAT—A Batch File to Delete Files Safely

There are many times when you want to perform a potentially dangerous operation and you have to be on your toes. An example, is using a wildcard to delete files. For example:

```
DEL *.BAK
```

One day, when you are tired, you will forget that there is one file that you want to keep that matches this pattern. The result will be lost data.

In Chapter 8, we explained how to use DEL with the /P (permission) option to force DOS to ask your permission before it deletes a file. Let's take a look at a batch file named RM.BAT that automates this procedure. (RM stands for "remove.")

```
:* ================================================
:* RM.BAT: batch to ask for permission to delete files
    @echo off
:* if the last file has been processed, stop
  :loop
    if "%1" == "" goto stop
:* ask permission to delete the current file
    del %1 /p
:* process the next file
    shift
    goto loop
:* the processing is finished
    :stop
:* =================================================
```

The batch file begins with an **@ECHO OFF** command to tell DOS not to display each command as it is processed. Next, we see the label :loop. We will jump to this spot, over and over, until each file has been processed.

After the label, we test to see if we are finished. This will be the case if the first parameter, %1, is empty. If this is true, we jump to the label :stop where the batch file ends. If not, we continue on with the next command.

Notice the tricky way in which we specified the IF command:

```
IF "%1" == "" GOTO STOP
```

We used quotes to handle the case in which %1 is empty. When this happens, the IF command becomes:

```
IF "" == "" GOTO STOP
```

and we jump to the correct place.

If we had not used quotes, the IF command within the batch file would be:

```
IF %1 ==  GOTO STOP
```

This would cause a mistake as DOS requires something on each side of the == operator.

To continue, after we have made sure that there is a file left to process, we use the DEL /P command to tell DOS to ask our permission to delete the file. Finally, we SHIFT, to send the next file name into %1, and return to the beginning of the loop.

The RM batch file is a lot more useful than you might think at first. You can use it routinely to replace your DEL command, even when you want to delete a single file. For instance, say that you want to delete TEMP.BAT but you are tired and you type:

```
RM TEST.BAT
```

RM will display the name of the file before it deletes it, giving you a change to correct your error.

RM is even more handy when you have a directory full of files, some of which you want and some of which you need to delete. You can enter:

```
RM *.*
```

As RM shows you each file in turn, you can press the <Y> key to delete it or the <N> key to keep it.

The A-B-C Trick

Besides all the handy things that you can do inside of batch files, there are some very useful things you can do outside of them—that is, how you name and organize them. One of the handiest of these things is what I call the A-B-C trick. Many of the things you do with your computer follow a logical series of steps. For example, if you are writing programs, the first step might be to use your text editor to do the writing, while the second and third steps would be compiling the program and then testing it. For each of these steps you'd set up a batch file to supervise it. You could give each of these steps meaningful names like EDIT, COMPILE, and TEST.

It is a very good idea to give batch files simple, meaningful command names. On the other hand, for convenience, we could just as easily name these steps A, B, and C, or 1, 2, and 3. There are two advantages to the A-B-C trick: The command names are shorter and quicker to key in, and it is easier to combine them and remember the names of the combinations. There is a logical progression to the steps you go through, and your batch files can simply number the steps 1, 2, 3 or letter them A, B, C. Thus, if your edit step is named A, and your compile step is named B, then a batch file to do both an edit and compile would be named AB, which can be easy to remember and key in.

There is one obvious disadvantage to the A-B-C trick: You have to remember that A means EDIT (or whatever), and so forth. This can be confusing to your co-workers, or even to yourself. But if you won't have any trouble keeping track of the meaning of the steps, then A-B-C is a good way to go.

To show you how far you can take this and how useful it can become, take a look at what I do when I write C programs. There are actually four separate steps to creating a C program: edit, compile, link, and then test the completed program.

I have separate batch files for each step (which I happen to call 1 through 4 because it suits me), and then lots of different combination batch files. Depending upon the kind of program I'm writing, it makes sense to use different combinations of the four steps. Sometimes I do step one by itself, and at other times I combine steps one and two. Other combinations are handy at other times. By having a batch file for each step by itself, and as many combinations as I find useful, I'm in full control of what is going on when I write these programs, and it's all quick and convenient for me. The same idea can be applied to any multi-step operation that you do. The more complicated the steps, the greater the advantage in setting up A-B-C type batch files to supervise them.

There is one further handy thing you can do with A-B-C, and that is to create parallel batch files for tasks that are similar in general, but different in detail. To use the example of programming again, I happen to write programs in four languages—C, Pascal, assembly language, and BASIC. For each of them, I have the same setup of batch command names. So, for me, editing a program is always done with the command named one, and the compile or assemble is always begun with the command named two. What the command "one" actually does is different in each case, but what it means to me is always the same: It means let me use my text editor to write a program.

Batch File Versions

Another handy trick with batch files is to have different versions lying around waiting. Why should you want to do that? Let me use my programming as an example again.

Sometimes I do my programming on the hard disk; other times it is handy for me to move everything onto a virtual disk. (A *virtual disk* is an area of memory that DOS uses to simulate a real disk.) So I keep two versions of my programming batch files. Now there are two ways to handle this, and I think one of them is a really nifty trick.

The first way is to have the two versions active under slightly different names. For example, my step 1 batch file could have the hard disk version named 1H.BAT, and the virtual disk version named 1V.BAT. While this puts everything on tap at once, it means that I have to remember which version I'm using and keep entering that correct form of the command name; and that's clumsy and prone to error.

The second way uses a foxy scheme to solve the problem. The trick is to keep both versions of my batch files around under the name filename, but with an alias for the extension.

My hard disk version of the first command would be in a file named 1.HAR. Now, as you know, batch files have the extension BAT; so this HAR file can't be used as it is, but it can be moved into place very easily. With a simply COPY command, all HAR files can be activated:

```
COPY *.HAR *.BAT
```

does the trick.

The versions that use the virtual disk have the extension VIR. They are activated by:

```
COPY *.VIR *.BAT
```

Thus, each set of batch files is kept with its own distinct extension. A particular version is activated by a COPY command, which makes it the current working version, and overrides whatever version was working before. I don't have to use different command names—the names stay the same, but different versions take effect. Naturally, I don't type in the COPY commands each time; another series of batch files does that for me.

Since the real magic of using batch files comes from tailoring them to our own needs, my suggestions and examples can only scratch the surface of the possibilities, and can only hint at some of the things that you can accomplish on your own through the creative use of batch files. There is almost nothing in the use of DOS that will repay your efforts like the rewards of speed, convenience, and safety you gain by making full use of batch files.

In the next chapter, we'll visit the most important batch file of all: the one that you use to start each session with DOS.

12

STARTING WITH AUTOEXEC.BAT

Introduction

As you saw earlier, batch files are the most useful and powerful instruments in our DOS toolbox. In this chapter, we are going to meet the most powerful batch file of all, DOS's own automatic startup file: AUTOEXEC.BAT.

There's no particular magic to an AUTOEXEC.BAT file. It works like any other batch file and can be as simple or as elaborate as you want it to be. The only thing special about AUTOEXEC.BAT is that DOS carries out its commands automatically, which can be a big help in getting your computer going just the way you want it. How you can take advantage of that help is the topic of this chapter.

The Where and How of AUTOEXEC.BAT

Whenever DOS starts, it checks to see if you have any initial instructions. It does this by looking for a special batch file by the name of AUTOEXEC.BAT. This file is created for you by the DOS installation program and placed on your disk. You can leave AUTOEXEC.BAT as it is, or you can make your own changes and additions. Most people end up modifying the standard AUTOEXEC.BAT to reflect their own needs.

Like any other batch file, AUTOEXEC.BAT must be a plain ASCII text file. There are several choices as to what program you can use to do your editing. If you have DOS 5.0 or later, the best bet is to use the built-in editor, EDIT, to maintain your batch files. (We will discuss EDIT in Chapter 26.) If you have an older version of DOS, you can use EDLIN, the older DOS editor (Chapter 27). Some people, who do a lot of programming, prefer to buy a more powerful editor like the Norton Editor. A final alternative is to use a word processor, making sure to save the batch file as plain ASCII text. However, this technique is slow and awkward if you do much editing.

Regardless of what editor you use, it is simple to make AUTOEXEC.BAT work. All you have to do is make sure that it is located where DOS will go looking for it: in the root directory of your boot disk.

Before we go on, let's take a moment to explain two of the terms we just used. The *root directory* is the main directory of a disk. (In Chapter 15 we will see where this name comes from.) The *boot disk* is the disk from which DOS starts, usually your hard disk, drive C. Thus, DOS expects your AUTOEXEC.BAT file to reside in the main directory of drive C. If you start DOS from a diskette, DOS will look for AUTOEXEC.BAT in the main directory of the diskette in drive A.

Using AUTOEXEC.BAT to Set Up the DOS Environment

Basically, your AUTOEXEC.BAT file performs two main tasks: First, it prepares what is known as the DOS environment; second it customizes your working conditions. Let's start with the first task.

The environment is a small section of memory that DOS sets aside to hold certain information. This information is accessible to all programs, including DOS itself. There are four commands that you can use to place information in the environment. These commands are SET, PATH, PROMPT, and APPEND.

The SET command has the form:

```
SET name=information
```

(Notice that there are no spaces on either side of the equals sign).

The SET command tells DOS to store the specified name in the environment. Along with that name, the associated information is kept so that it can be referenced at any time. Sometimes the name is called a *variable* and the information is called the *value* of the variable.

Here is an important example. The DOS environment always contains the name COMSPEC, which stands for "command processor specification." As we explained in Chapter 8, the command processor is the program that reads and interprets your commands. Occasionally, a program that needs a lot of memory may free up space by removing part of the command processor. Later, of course, DOS must be able to restore the command processor by reading in a fresh copy from disk. In such cases, DOS checks the COMSPEC variable to find out where the command processor is stored.

So, within an AUTOEXEC.BAT file, you might see the command:

```
SET COMSPEC=C:\DOS\COMMAND.COM
```

The command associates the characters "C:\DOS\COMMAND.COM" with the name COMSPEC. At any time, any program can check the environment, under the name COMSPEC, and find this information. (Later in this chapter, we'll go into a bit of interesting history and find out exactly why the COMSPEC variable is used.)

In this particular example, the SET command shows that the command processor is stored in a file named COMMAND.COM, which is on the C disk, within a subdirectory named DOS. (We will discuss directories in detail in Chapter 15.)

Occasionally, you might install software that requires you to set an environment variable. For instance, when you install a programming system, it is a common requirement that you set a variable named LIB to point to where certain libraries of programs are kept. In such cases, your documentation will tell you what SET commands are required and you can add them to your AUTOEXEC.BAT. Sometimes, the software installation program will actually modify your AUTOEXEC.BAT file for you.

If you would like to see what's in your environment, enter the SET command by itself:

```
SET
```

DOS will respond by displaying the name of each variable and its value.

The second command that sets an environment variable is PATH. Here is why it is important. In Chapter 6, we explained what happens when you enter a command. DOS checks to see if it is an internal command. If it is, DOS executes the command directly. Otherwise, DOS searches for a program of the same name and executes that program. For instance, when you enter the FORMAT command, DOS looks for a program named FORMAT.

The role of the PATH command is to tell DOS where to search. We will discuss the PATH command in detail in Chapter 16. For now, let's just look at a typical example:

```
PATH=C:\BATCH;C:\DOS;C:\NORTON;C:\UTILITY
```

This command tells DOS that when it looks for a program it should look on the C drive, first in the BATCH subdirectory, then in the DOS subdirectory, then in the NORTON subdirectory, and finally, in the UTILITY subdirectory.

The third command that sets an environment variable is PROMPT. As you know, whenever DOS is ready for you to enter a command, it displays a prompt. The PROMPT command allows you to customize the prompt to your own specifications. Here is a typical PROMPT command:

```
PROMPT $P$G
```

This command tells DOS that the prompt should consist of the path name of the current directory ($P) followed by a greater-than sign ($G). But don't worry about the details—we'll get to them later, in Chapter 15.

Actually, the PATH and PROMPT commands are really special-purpose variations of SET. What they do is to create environment variables named PATH and PROMPT. In fact, the examples we have just looked at could just as easily have been SET commands:

```
SET PATH=C:\BATCH;C:\DOS;C:\NORTON;C:\UTILITY
SET PROMPT=$P$G
```

The final command that can set an environment variable is APPEND, a cousin to PATH. Where PATH tells DOS where to search for executable programs, APPEND tells DOS where to search for data files. Here is how it works.

Let's say that the files used by your word processor are on your hard disk (drive C) within a subdirectory named WORD. Your word processor needs certain data files—such as a dictionary—in order to operate properly. The first time you initiate a spelling check operation, the word processor will call upon DOS to open the dictionary file. However, the current directory will probably not be the WORD directory. Most likely, the current directory will be the one in which you store your documents. So, in order to tell DOS where to search for the dictionary file you can use the following command:

```
APPEND C:\WORD
```

This sets a variable named APPEND to have the value C:\WORD. In effect, we have "appended" the WORD subdirectory to the list of places for DOS to search for data files.

If you don't understand this completely, don't worry. We have yet to talk about how directories are organized and we will not cover the APPEND command until Chapter 16. The important thing to appreciate now is that the APPEND information has to be stored somewhere. Left to its own, DOS will store it internally. However, if your first APPEND command uses the /E option, DOS will store all subsequent APPEND information in the environment.

Many people include such a command in their AUTOEXEC.BAT file. For instance:

```
APPEND /E
APPEND C:\WORD
```

The first command tells DOS to store APPEND information in the environment. The second command actually sets the APPEND variable. Why tell DOS to store the APPEND variable in the environment? So, like other variables, you can look at it with the SET command. However, the

APPEND command itself will let you examine this information, so being able to place it in the environment is not really necessary.

Thus we have four commands to set variables in the DOS environment: SET, PATH, PROMPT, and sometimes APPEND. The environment is a very important facility and virtually every AUTOEXEC.BAT file uses these commands, usually near the beginning of the file.

Why DOS Uses a COMSPEC Variable

We mentioned earlier that the DOS environment contains a variable named COMSPEC that points to the location of the command processor program. However, most people are unaware of why the COMSPEC variable exists in the first place. Let's take a moment and see exactly how COMSPEC came to be.

When DOS was first developed it was decided to divide the main part of DOS into three programs. The first two programs—IBMBIO.COM and IBMDOS.COM—handle the fundamental tasks of the operating system. (Within MS-DOS, these programs are called IO.SYS and MSDOS.SYS.) The third program, COMMAND.COM, is the command processor.

At the time, it was thought that some users might want to create alternate command processors—this being common with other operating systems, such as Unix—so the developers organized things so that people could use most of DOS but substitute their own command processor if they wished.

According to this plan, the first two DOS programs are stored as hidden files (see Chapter 9) so that nobody can alter them. The third file, the command processor, is a regular file. In principle, anyone can write his own command processor and use it instead of the one that comes with DOS.

In order to implement such a flexible system, the designers of DOS decided that the environment would contain a variable named COMSPEC. The purpose of COMSPEC is to point to the file that contains the command processor. If someone wants to use his own command processor, one of the things he has to do is reset the COMSPEC variable. For example, if you have your own command processor called MYCOM.COM, stored in a subdirectory called MYSTUFF on the hard disk, you can put the following command in your AUTOEXEC.BAT file:

```
SET COMSPEC=C:\MYSTUFF\MYCOM.COM
```

This tells DOS to use your command processor instead of its own.

So how does this plan work in practice? Not very well. It is true that various new user interfaces have been developed—such as Microsoft Windows, the DOS Shell, and the Norton Commander. But all of these programs have been designed to work with COMMAND.COM. So far, no one has written an outright replacement for COMMAND.COM and it looks as if no one ever will.

In retrospect, we can see that COMMAND.COM might just as well have been a third hidden file and that the COMSPEC environment variable was never actually necessary.

Using AUTOEXEC.BAT to Set Up Your Working Conditions

Once the DOS environment is prepared, your AUTOEXEC.BAT file is ready to handle its second main task: to customize your working conditions. This may involve up to five different chores, all of which are optional:

- Preparing DOS to use your hardware
- Copying files to a virtual disk
- Initializing memory resident programs
- Setting your current directory and default drive
- Starting a program

Most of these operations involve concepts that we have not yet covered. We'll describe them briefly, just to give you an idea of how they fit into AUTOEXEC.BAT, and defer the detailed discussions until later in the book.

To start with, there are certain commands that you may need to set up your hardware. A common example is to prepare DOS to use a serial printer. (That is, a printer that plugs into the serial port of your PC, rather than the parallel port.)

One of the most useful commands to set up your hardware is MODE. You use MODE to prepare DOS for serial printers as well as a variety of other tasks: to control your display, your keyboard, and so on. We won't go into the MODE command in detail here. We'll just mention it as an example of a command that often finds its way into the AUTOEXEC.BAT file.

Next, you may want to copy files to a virtual disk. This is a simulated disk that DOS creates using regular memory. Virtual disks are faster than real disks—after all, they reside in memory. However, because memory is cleared whenever you turn on your PC, a virtual disk must be re-initialized each time you start DOS. Usually, this involves using the COPY command to copy certain files from a real disk to the newly created virtual disk. The AUTOEXEC.BAT file is a good place to perform this task.

The next task involves *memory-resident* programs. These are special programs that stay in memory to be instantly available whenever you press a specific combination of keys, usually referred to as a "hot key." For example, by pressing certain keys you may be able to pop up a calendar program on top of your current work. When you have finished with the calendar, you can tell it to disappear so that you can return to your work.

There is also a second kind of memory-resident program, typified by the DOS GRAPHICS and PRINT programs. Programs like this stay in memory, not so you can pop them up, but to lurk in the background, waiting to perform a particular service.

One of the most important functions of the AUTOEXEC.BAT file is to start up memory-resident programs. Performing this task from AUTOEXEC.BAT has two advantages. First, you can set things up the same every time you start work. Second, it is sometimes necessary to start up memory-resident programs in a certain order. Putting the requisite commands in AUTOEXEC.BAT guarantees that they will always be executed in the same order.

As you gain experience with such programs, you may find that they work better when some of their files reside on a virtual disk. That is why we recommend that you prepare a virtual disk before you initialize the memory-resident programs.

The next task for AUTOEXEC.BAT is to ensure that when you start work you will be using the disk and the directory you want. For example, let's say that you always want to start work with your default drive set to D: and your current directory set to \DOCUMENT. The following two commands, placed in your AUTOEXEC.BAT file, will do the job:

```
D:
CD \DOCUMENT
```

Finally, you may want to work with the same program each time you turn on your computer. If so, you can end your AUTOEXEC.BAT file with a command to start this program.

There are two cases in which this is a good idea. First, you may want to use a PC for only one main program. In this case, it makes sense to start that program automatically. For instance, if you are setting up a computer for someone who will use it only for word processing, it may be easier for them if the AUTOEXEC.BAT file automatically starts the word processor each time they turn on the computer.

Second, you may prefer to work with a special user interface program rather than directly with DOS. (Sometimes such programs are called "shells.") Examples of such programs are Microsoft Windows, the DOS Shell, and the Norton Commander. If you use such a program, you will probably want to start it from the very end of your AUTOEXEC.BAT file.

A Summary of What to Put in Your AUTOEXEC.BAT File

So there you have it, a quick tour of how what your AUTOEXEC.BAT file can do for you. For reference, here is a summary. The tasks that are marked with a * are standard for any system. The others are necessary only if you need them for your particular situation.

1. Use SET to create required variables
2. Use PATH to set the search path
3.* Use PROMPT to set the DOS prompt
4.* Use APPEND to set the alternate search path
5. Prepare DOS to use your hardware (possibly using MODE)
6. Copy files to a virtual disk
7. Initialize memory resident programs
8. Set your default drive and current directory
9. Start a program (possibly a shell)

A Typical DOS-Generated AUTOEXEC.BAT File

As you know, DOS will automatically create your AUTOEXEC.BAT file as part of the installation procedure. If you are updating to a newer version of DOS, the installation program will update your current AUTOEXEC.BAT file if necessary.

Your actual AUTOEXEC.BAT file depends on your version of DOS and how you answer certain questions during the installation. Let's take a look at a representative example of such a file. We will see that what DOS generates is not always up to our standards. However, in the next section, we'll show you how take what DOS gives you and create a high-quality AUTOEXEC.BAT file of your own.

Here is a typical AUTOEXEC.BAT that might be generated as part of the DOS installation process. To make it easier to follow the discussion, we have added line numbers which, of course, are not part of the actual file.

```
 1)    @ECHO OFF
 2)    SET COMSPEC=C:\DOS\COMMAND.COM
 3)    VERIFY OFF
 4)    PATH C:\DOS
 5)    APPEND /E
 6)    APPEND C:\DOS
 7)    PROMPT $P$G
 8)    C:\DOS\GRAPHICS
 9)    VER
10)    DOSSHELL
```

Line 1 tells DOS not to display each batch file command as it is executed. The @ keeps the ECHO command itself from being displayed.

Line 2 sets the COMSPEC variable to point to the command processor, COMMAND.COM. If for some reason you do not have this command, DOS will assume that the command processor is in the main (root) directory of your boot disk. If DOS ever looks for COMMAND.COM and can't find it, you will see a message like:

```
INVALID COMMAND.COM
CANNOT LOAD COMMAND, SYSTEM HALTED
```

If this happens, you will have to press <Ctrl-Alt-Delete> to restart. Be sure to fix the problem right away or it will reccur.

Line 3 turns off an option called VERIFY. When VERIFY is on, DOS makes an extra check whenever it writes to a disk. This is rarely necessary and, since it slows things down, it is best to turn VERIFY off. However, this happens to be the default, so line 3 is not really necessary.

Line 4 sets the search path. Right now, the path references only a single directory, the one that holds the DOS files. This search path will have to be augmented with some of our own directories.

Lines 5 and 6 set up the APPEND search path. The first command tells DOS to keep the APPEND variable in the environment. The second command sets the path to point to the DOS directory. However, unless you have a particular reason for wanting these commands you do not really need them.

Line 7 sets the DOS prompt.

Line 8 initializes a memory resident program named GRAPHICS, which allows your printer to work with graphic images. Notice that this line specifies a path name (C:\DOS) in front of the command name. This tells DOS where to find the command. Strictly speaking, this is not necessary because the preceding PATH command has placed the DOS subdirectory on the search path. However, specifying full path names in the AUTOEXEC.BAT file is always a good habit.

Line 9 issues the VER command to display the DOS version number. Again, this isn't necessary, although some people like to see it.

Line 10 finishes up by starting the DOS Shell (which we will discuss in Chapter 25). COMMAND.COM is still present, but the shell sits on top of it, so to speak, presenting a completely different face to the user. Most of the time, shells are easier to use than the regular DOS interface.

Starting with DOS 4.0, a DOS Shell is included as a part of DOS. (And for DOS 5.0, the shell was completely rewritten.) During the DOS installation, you can specify whether or not you plan to use the shell. If you do, DOS will place the DOSSHELL command at the end of your AUTOEXEC.BAT file. This will automatically start the DOS Shell every time you turn on your computer—the DOS Shell will then become your primary means of interacting with DOS. If you get tired of it, all you need to do is remove the DOSSHELL command from your AUTOEXEC.BAT file.

Customizing Your Own AUTOEXEC.BAT File

Turning your AUTOEXEC.BAT file into a paragon of batch file programming is simple. All you need to do is remove any unnecessary commands and follow the guidelines we have already covered. In particular, place the commands in the order we discussed and remember the hints on programming style that we explained in Chapter 11.

Here is an example of a well-written AUTOEXEC.BAT file, based on the example from the previous section. Notice that we have put the date at the beginning of the file. From time to time, you may make changes. Keeping the date reminds you of what version of your AUTOEXEC.BAT you are working with.

Notice also that we have added two new memory resident programs, DOSKEY and FASTOPEN. Both of these will be discussed later in the book.

```
:* =========================================
:* AUTOEXEC.BAT:   December 21, 1990
   @echo off

:* set the environment variables
   set comspec=c:\dos\command.com
   path=c:\batch;c:\dos;c:\norton;c:\utility
   prompt $p$g

:* initialize memory resident programs
   c:\dos\doskey
   c:\dos\fastopen c:
   c:\dos\graphics

:* start the DOS Shell
   c:\dos\dosshell
:* =========================================
```

Of course, you will want to customize your own AUTOEXEC.BAT file to suit your needs. You may want to use the example here as a starting point and add new commands as necessary. Whatever you do, remember that AUTOEXEC.BAT is your most important batch file. Take a few extra minutes and keep things as readable as possible.

13

MORE ABOUT DISKS
AND FILES

Introduction

Now that you've gotten a handful of the most useful DOS commands under your belt, it's time to look inside the workings of your disks. Understanding them is the key to knowing the whys, hows, and wherefores of the DOS commands, particularly the more advanced disk commands you'll encounter in this part of the book. This chapter is mostly about understanding disks, but you will learn about one special command, called RECOVER, that deals with scrambled disks.

What's on a Disk

Let's begin by briefly pulling together everything we've covered about disks. A storage disk is used to hold data that you need to preserve. Like a filing cabinet, a disk is a safe place to keep information, and it has a large, but limited, capacity. And, just as a filing cabinet has its contents organized into file folders, a disk has its data organized into files.

The files on a diskette are distinct, and each file contains its own particular data. The files are identified by their file names. On any one disk, each file name must be unique, but on two separate disks you can have separate files with the same name. Since files are identified by their file names, it is a very good idea to make sure that every file on every disk has a completely unique name, except when there is some good reason to reuse the same name. For example, if a file on one disk exists solely as a safeguarded copy of a file on another disk, that is a good reason for having a duplicate file name. Even then, it could be a good idea to give the files different names in order to distinguish the original from the copy.

Most of the space on a disk is devoted to storing data, but some of the space is used by DOS for bookkeeping purposes, such as maintaining a directory of the files on a disk. In the directory, DOS keeps its record of everything that it needs to know about the disk's files, including notes to itself about how to find their contents. Most of this information is of little use to us, but there are four things about a file that DOS will let us know.

The first is the name of the file, including the file name and extension; the second is the size of the file; the third is the time stamp that shows the date and time when the file was most recently changed. If a file has not been changed, the time stamp shows when it was created. Finally, DOS can show us the attributes of a file (see Chapter 9). The attributes tell us whether or not a file is hidden, system, read-only, or archived.

Time Stamps

There are several special things to know about time stamps. First, if a copy is made of a file, the copy gets the same time stamp as the original. Second, there is no way to tell if a time stamp is the original time the file was created, or the time the file was later changed. Third, although time stamps are displayed to the minute, they are actually calculated to within two seconds of the exact time. When necessary, advanced programming techniques can be used to find the complete time stamp.

These time stamps on files can be very useful in safely controlling your data. Looking at the time stamp can answer such questions as:

- Which of these files was I working on yesterday?
- Is my backup copy up-to-date with my master copy?

Because of this, it is important to make sure that your system always knows the correct date and time. Most personal computers automatically keep track of the date and time. However, if you have an older computer which needs to have this information entered when it is turned on, I urge you to never be too lazy to key in the right date and time. The benefit of having the right time stamps on your files can be enormous. Sometimes it can be as valuable as an insurance policy.

Other Parts of Disk Storage

Including the directory, there are actually three parts of overhead (un-available storage space) on a disk. Since you may occasionally come across mention of them, it is worth knowing what they are.

The first is called the boot record, and it contains a very short program used to help start up the DOS operating system from the disk. Each disk has a boot record on it, whether or not the disk contains the rest of DOS.

After the boot record, the next bit of overhead on the disk is a table DOS uses to keep track of the available space on the disk; this table is called the *File Allocation Table*, or just FAT for short. The FAT records where each file is located, so it is something like an index to the disk. It also keeps a record of the part of the disk's space that isn't in use. When the CHKDSK command reports on how much space is available on a disk, the information comes from the disk's FAT.

The third and last part of the overhead on a disk is the directory, which lists all of the files on the disk. We've already discussed the directory since its contents are so important to us.

Altogether, the three overhead parts of a disk, the boot record, the FAT, and the directory, take up very little of the space on a disk. The rest of the space is used to store data.

All About File Names

Files have file names, and the better you understand them, the less likely you are to make a mess of them. First, the simple mechanics. File names have two parts, the file name itself and the file-name extension. A file name can be up to eight characters long. Some examples are:

```
A
LONGNAME
1234
AB_34
```

The file-name extension is just that—an extension to the file name. An extension can be up to three characters long. While a file name must have at least one character in it, the extension can be nothing at all. When a file name has an extension, the two parts are connected by a period between them. Here are some sample file names with extensions:

```
JANUARY.85
PROGRAM.BAS
CHAPTER.2-3
1985-12.25
```

There are some rules about what is a proper file name. The file name and the extension can be made up from any combination of the allowed characters, which consist of:

- the letters of the alphabet, A through Z
- the digits 0 through 9
- the punctuation characters:

  $ dollar sign

  !   exclamation point

  ^   circumflex (caret)

  #   pound (number) sign

  %   percent sign

  -   hyphen

& ampersand

~ tilde

{ } braces

( ) parentheses

_ underscore

You can use any of these symbols in any combination, but you can't use blanks. It seems like a terrible idea to use the more exotic symbols, but some of these symbols work very nicely as a form of punctuation in a file name. For example: JAN_MAY

You'll notice that a few common (and some uncommon) symbols aren't allowed in file names and extensions. They're reserved for other uses. Table 13.1 shows the symbols and their uses.

Table 13.1 *Symbols and Their Uses*

Symbol	*Use*
* and ?	reserved for wildcards
.	used to separate file name and extension
:	used to identify drives and devices
\	used for paths
/	used for options (switches)
< and >	used for data redirection
, and ;	used to punctuate parameter lists
=	used to punctuate parameter lists
+	used to punctuate parameter lists
|	used for piping
[and]	reserved
"	reserved

Only capital letters are actually used in file names. DOS, in a friendly way, lets us type file names in lowercase if we want, but it automatically converts lowercase to upper. This is why you'll find that DOS always lists files with their names all in uppercase letters (unless you use the DIR command with the /L—lowercase—option).

You may discover that there are some trick ways to sneak illegal file names past DOS. For example, it is possible to create a file that has a blank space in the middle of its name (like "AA BB.CCC"), or to create a file that has a lowercase name. Don't play that dangerous game; you are almost certain to regret it.

Names for Devices

One of the nice things DOS does to make life convenient and easy is that it lets us refer to parts of the computer, such as the printer, with simple names that are the same as file names. These are called *device names*, because they refer to devices, or parts, of the computer. In order to be able to do this DOS has to reserve these names for their special uses, so there is a short list of names you can't use as your own file names. The usual list of names with what they are used for is shown in Table 13.2.

Table 13.2   *Device Names*

Name	*Meaning*
COM1	the first serial communications line
COM2	the second serial communications line
COM3	the third serial communications line
COM4	the fourth serial communications line
AUX	another name for COM1
LPT1	the first printer (LPT = "line printer")
LPT2	the second printer
LPT3	the third printer
PRN	another name for LPT1
CON	the console: the keyboard and the screen
NUL	empty file; data sent to NUL is thrown away
CLOCK$	the system clock device driver

When you use one of these names in a command, you put a colon at the end of the name, just as you do when you use the name of a disk. For example:

```
COPY CON: A:DATA.TXT
```

Warning: Do not do anything with the CLOCK$ device. If you send data to it, you will change your system's time and date.

With the exception of these special device names, you are free to give your files any names you wish, within the grammatical rules for file names (one to eight characters, and so forth). It is almost the same with file-name extensions, but not quite. We'll cover that in the next section.

There are two more things you need to known about file names which we'll cover in the next two sections: what file-name extensions are really about and how global file-name characters are used.

The Importance of File-name Extensions

You can give your files extensions as freely and arbitrarily as you can give them file names. In fact more freely, since there are reserved filenames, but there are no reserved file Name extensions. Extensions like COM and BAT are reserved in the sense that they represent certain types of files, but you can use them—if you know when it's appropriate.

There is, then, a distinct purpose for file-name extensions: They indicate the category and classification of files. Unfortunately, the importance and usefulness of file-name extensions isn't emphasized much, and many users of DOS don't fully understand them. In this section, let's see what file-name extensions are all about.

File-name extensions are intended to classify and categorize files so that their purpose can be quickly and simply identified. The assignment of standard file-name extensions is rather casual, and it is not explained fully anywhere that I know of, which leads to confusion about them.

There are two basic types of file-name extensions: those that you assign and those that are used by programs—all sorts of programs, from DOS to applications to programming languages. In DOS, the common extensions you'll encounter are EXE and COM, which refer to executable programs and commands, BAT, which refers to batch files, and SYS, which refers to system files that contain special hardware programs or data.

In the applications arena, there are many different extensions you may encounter, because these programs use extensions of their own for identifying their support files. Here are a few examples of common programs and some of the extensions they use.

- Ashton-Tate dBASE:
  DBF   (database file),
  DBT   (database text file for memos)
  FMO   (screen form: object code)

FMT	(screen form: generated source code)
FRG	(report: generated source code)
FRM	(report: format design)
FRO	(report: object code)
LBL	(label: format file)
LBT	(label: generated source code)
LBO	(label: object code)
MEM	(memory variables)
NDX	(single index)
MDX	(multiple index)
PRG	(dBASE source program)
SCR	(screen form: format design)
TXT	(ASCII text output)

- Microsoft Excel

XLS	(spreadsheet)
XLM	(macro)
XLC	(chart)
XLW	(workspace)

- Norton Utilities

BAK	(backup data)
DAT	(data)
DBD	(database for demo)
FI	(file-info comments)
HLP	(help data)
IDX	(index)
INI	(initialization data)
NCD	(directory information)

- Lotus 1-2-3

FNT	(font)
HLP	(help text)
PIC	(graph)
PRN	(ASCII print file)
WKS	(worksheet, version 1, 1A)
WK1	(worksheet, version 2, 2.01, 2.2)
WK3	(worksheet, version 3)
XLT	(translation file)

Here are the main standard uses of file-name extensions:

- Executable program files have extensions of EXE or COM; there are two formats for program files, (which we'll go into in the next section), so that there are two file-name extensions to distinguish them.

- Batch execution files have the extension BAT.

- Certain system programs and data files are denoted by an extension of SYS.

- When a program creates printer-type output that is to be stored in a file, the extensions that are commonly used are PRN and LST.

- Editors and word processors use some standard extensions. When the old version of an edited file is preserved for safety reasons, it is given the extension BAK (for BAcK-up copy). DOC is very commonly used by word processors for text files. Some word processors prefer to use TXT as the extension for the edited data. The DOS EDIT program, which we will discuss in Chapter 26, uses the extension TXT by default.

- When a program uses a data file in its own format, DAT is often the extension.

- When a program needs a temporary work file, a file that begins with "$" is most often used as the extension; occasionally TMP is used instead. The program fully intends to delete these temporary work files before finishing. If you ever find a file lying around with an extension of $xx or TMP, that's a very good sign that something has gone wrong—you ought to take the time to figure out what it was.

- Programming languages make use of several standard file names. For source code, a different extension is used for each language: ASM for assembly, BAS for BASIC, C for C-language, COB for COBOL, FOR for FORTRAN and PAS for Pascal. For object code, in any language, OBJ is the extension. For library routines, the extension is LIB. When BASIC uses BLOAD-format files, BLD is the customary extension.

The more closely you follow the pattern of these extension names, the more easily your files will smoothly fit into the broad use of your computer. This is one of the many ways that you can safeguard the effective operation of your computer.

Global File-name Characters (Wildcards) and Their Uses

Connected with the subject of filenames is the use of *global file-name characters*, often called *wildcards*, which are used as generic file names. A wildcard is a nonspecific part of a file specification that can be used to match more than one particular file.

Every file has a specific, unambiguous file name (and extension), but you can often refer to more than one file at a time by using wildcards in a file specification.

There are two forms of wildcard—the question mark (?) and the asterisk (*). When a question mark is used in a file specification, for example:

```
THISNAM?
```

then it will match with any letter in that one particular position of the file name. So THISNAM? would match with any of these files:

```
THISNAME
THISNAM1
THISNAM$
THISNAM
```

This works as long as all of the rest of the positions of the file name match exactly. Wildcards, as you might expect, can be used in both the file name and extension parts of the complete name.

The asterisk form of the wildcard is just a shorthand for several question marks. While a question mark is wild for the single character position that it occupies in a file name, an asterisk is wild from that position to the end of the file name, or the end of the extension. An asterisk acts as if there were as many question marks as there are positions left in the file name or in the extension. An asterisk in the file name "stops" at the end of the file name, not at the end of the extension. If you use the question mark form, then you can be specific about the following positions in the name; with an asterisk, you can't; if you try it, anything after the asterisk will be ignored, without warning.

Either of these uses of wildcards:

```
*.*
????????.???
```

would match any file name and extension. Note that they mean exactly the same thing, since an asterisk (*) is just shorthand for a series of question marks.

These wildcard specifications are mainly used with five commands, the DIR directory listing, the DEL/ERASE file erase command, the REN/RENAME file name change command, and the COPY and XCOPY command. They also have a special copy-and-concatenate use with the COPY command, as I mentioned in the section on combining files with COPY in Chapter 8. (If *concatenate* is a new word to you, it means to join the two files together into one.)

Other than the commands just mentioned (DIR, DEL/ERASE, REN/ RENAME and COPY), most programs that require a file specification will not successfully use a name with a wildcard, even if the wildcard specification ends up matching only one single file.

There are advanced programming techniques that make it easy for a program to make good use of wildcards, and DOS provides some special services to programs just for that purpose. It's a good thing for programs to make use of these services, so that they can accept file names with wildcard specification. But not all programs do so, and you shouldn't be disappointed if one of yours doesn't recognize wild cards. Finally, before we leave this discussion, here's a one-word piece of advice: Beware.

The use of wildcards can be very dangerous. Many a DOS user has accidentally misused wildcards and erased files that weren't supposed to be erased; and giving a wildcard to a program that doesn't expect it can lead to other mishaps.

Disk File Formats and What They Mean to You

It can help to understand what your disk data is like—how it is structured, what it looks like, and how it is stored. In this section, we'll take a look at disk file formats.

First, how is data stored on disks? The scheme is simple and efficient. As DOS sees it, the storage space for data on a disk is made up of fixed-size chunks of space, called *sectors*. The size of the sectors may vary from one type of disk to another, but within one disk, the sectors are all the same size—typically 512 bytes.

In order to manage disk storage effectively, DOS allocates space in *clusters*, one at a time as needed. The size of a cluster is fitted to the size of the disk. For example, for a 120 MB hard disk, DOS uses 8 sectors per cluster, but for a 1.44 megabyte 3 $\frac{1}{2}$ inch diskette, DOS uses only 1 sector per cluster.

Actually, while this is interesting to learn about, you don't need to know this information at all, which is one of the beauties of DOS's way of storing data on disks. DOS reads and writes disk data in fixed-size sectors, and allocates this space one or more sectors at a time. We and our programs don't see these fixed-size sectors at all; instead, DOS lets us store our data in any size that is convenient to us.

DOS worries about fitting our data into the fixed-size sectors, and does it so efficiently and so quietly that we never have to concern ourselves about the mechanics of how the data is stored. Shoehorning our data into fixed-size sectors is work for DOS and not for us, nor our programs. This is a very good thing, because it makes a clean division of labor: DOS worries about where and how to store our data, and all our programs have to worry about is how to use the data.

There are usually four file formats that are used to store our data on disks—three special formats and one sort of a catch-all format.

COM and EXE Formats

Two of the three special formats are used to store executable programs. The formats are known by their standard file name extensions—COM and EXE. COM files are used to hold programs that are completely ready-to-execute; this is a memory-image format, which means that what's on disk is identical to what is in the computer's memory when the program is executed. The EXE format is more sophisticated; EXE programs require some last minute fix-up work to be done as they are loaded from disk into memory. This fix-up mostly involves placing the program into the right part of memory, and letting the program know where it has been placed. The EXE format is mostly used for the more complicated type of program that is produced by compilers. Because of the extra overhead, EXE format programs are bulkier when they are stored on disk; but inside the computer's memory, they can be just as compact as COM-type programs.

There is nothing about these two special program file formats that is of much practical consequence to you. In fact, the main thing worth knowing about COM and EXE program files is just their file-name extensions. By looking for COM and EXE files, you can see which are the executable programs on a disk.

BASIC Formats

The BASIC programming language is an exception to many rules, and that's also true when it comes to program files. There are two BASIC interpreters that you might use with DOS: the old one, named BASICA, or the new one, QBASIC, that comes with DOS 5.0 or later. If you have programs that run with either of these interpreters, they are stored in files that have an extension of BAS. You may think of these as executable programs and from your point of view, they are; but from DOS's point of view, a BASIC program in a BAS file is just data that the BASIC interpreter reads in order to find out what to do. This is a technical point, but one worth knowing. As DOS and the computer see it, the BASIC interpreter is a true program, and a BASIC BAS file is just data. That is why the BASIC interpreters are stored in files named BASICA.COM and QBASIC.EXE.

ASCII Format

The other special file format—one that will be of particular interest to you—is the ASCII text file format. This is the format that is used to store your text data, such as correspondence, reports, and the source code form of programs.

There are various terms used to talk about this file format—sometimes it is called a "text file," or an "ASCII file." I usually call it an "ASCII text file." ASCII text files use a format that is very flexible and is adapted to serve many purposes. It is probably the most widely used format for computer data; it is certainly universal to personal computers and workstations.

The acronym ASCII refers to the code scheme computers use to recognize the letters, numbers, and symbols that make up a file of written text. ASCII is short for the American Standard Code for Information Interchange, and it's the standard code used for computer characters. In lay terms, the letters ASCII mean written material, as the computer sees it.

An ASCII text file consists mostly of a stream of written information: the alphabet letters, numbers, and punctuation that make up the types of things we write. What you are reading in this book is typical of the contents of an ASCII text file and, in fact, these very words are stored on a disk in an ASCII text file on my computer.

Besides the words, or text, an ASCII text file also contains some formatting information that helps make the text more useful. At the end of an ASCII text file is an end-of-file format marker. (This is the ASCII character number 26, which is sometimes called Control-Z.)

Within an ASCII text file itself, the text is broken into lines by two formatting characters at the end of each line; these two characters are known as "carriage-return" (ASCII character 13) and "line feed" (ASCII 10). This is all the formatting that is normally placed in an ASCII text file—carriage return and line feed at the end of each line, and end-of-file at, naturally, the end of the file. ASCII text files don't normally have any more format punctuation in them. There aren't normally paragraph or page markings. But in the definition of ASCII there are formatting characters, which can be used for this kind of marking, and more besides.

I've been mentioning some special characters by their ASCII codes—for example, ASCII 13 is the carriage return character. Everything inside a computer works like a number, and so every character has a numeric code, whether it's a letter of the alphabet, like capital A, which is ASCII 65, or it's a special character, like end-of-file, which is ASCII 26. If you know, or will be learning, the BASIC language, BASIC refers to these numeric character codes like this: CHR$(26).

The type of programs that are known as editors or text editors all work with ASCII text files. DOS itself comes with two simple but powerful text editors: EDIT (with DOS 5.0 or later) and the older EDLIN (with all versions of DOS). We will discuss these editors in Chapters 26 and 27. Another editor designed for simple editing or for programming is the Norton Editor. Word processors, too, usually work with ordinary ASCII text files. However, sophisticated word processors, such as WordPerfect, and Microsoft Word, need more complex formatting information than ordinary ASCII can easily accommodate; therefore, they augment some, and bend the rules some, to get the kind of data that they need. As a consequence, word-processing text files are a little different from ordinary vanilla-flavored ASCII text files. Yet, underneath the trappings of a word-processing file, there is a simple ASCII text file.

What's particularly interesting and important about ASCII text files is that they are the most common and interchangeable of all file formats. This means that if you have one program tool using ASCII text files, then you can expect to be able to move data from it to other programs using ASCII, with a minimum of fuss and difficulty. This transportability can be a tremendous advantage in flexibility. Because of this, it can work greatly to your advantage to have as much data in ASCII format as possible—or to have the ability to convert files to and from ASCII format, as many word processors do.

The upshot is, if you are programming, or having programs designed for you, consider using the ASCII text file format, even if it is not the most convenient for your programs. In the long run, the benefits can be considerable.

General Data Files

After these three special file formats—COM program files, EXE program files, and ASCII text files—we come to the catch-all format of the general data file. Unless a file has a special format, it consists simply of data stored on a disk. Usually data files are made up of fixed-length parts called *records*. The records can be as short as a single byte, or as long as you like. To read or write such a data file, a program tells DOS the basic information about the file, such as what the record size is; and DOS does the work of finding where each record is, in what part of what disk sector.

There is one special thing worth knowing about files that are made up of fixed-length records. Since the records are all of the same size, a simple arithmetic formula can be used to calculate where each record is stored. This means that it is possible for a fixed-length record file to be accessed randomly, skipping arbitrarily from one record to another. A fixed-length record file can be processed either sequentially, one record in order after another, or by random skips. This is one tremendous advantage over an ASCII text file, which must be read and written sequentially, from beginning to end in proper order.

When you think about files, and consider what can be done with them, you should keep in mind the special random access capability that a fixed-length record file has.

Risky File Recovery Using RECOVER

Now we come back to DOS, and to a powerful, but dangerous, file-recovery program called RECOVER.

There are many ways that your disk data can be lost or damaged and the whole subject of data recovery is an important one. Starting with version 5.0, DOS provides a family of commands to help you protect your data and to recover lost files. We will discuss these commands in detail in Chapter 18.

However, if you are using an older version of DOS, there are only two data recovery commands available. First, CHKDSK, which we discussed in Chapter 9, and second, RECOVER which provides two limited kinds of data recovery.

If part of a disk has been damaged so that a file can be partially read and partially not, the RECOVER command will remove the unreadable part so that you can use the rest. Depending upon the kind of file it is, the recovered portion may or may not be usable. Generally, this kind of file recovery only works with ASCII text files, which contain written material. To use RECOVER in this way, you enter the command followed by the name of the file it is to check for readable and unreadable parts.

The other kind of file recovery done by RECOVER is completely different. Unfortunately, it is easy to confuse the two, and this is where the danger lies. In this second kind of file recovery, RECOVER assumes that the entire directory of the disk is damaged and nonsensical. It throws away the entire directory and replaces it with a new one, which contains the data it found on the disk, organized into files as well as possible. But the new directory contains files with strange new names that RECOVER gives them—it is then your job to figure out what is what, as best you can.

To use RECOVER in this way, you enter the command without specifying any file name. But remember that this form of RECOVER wipes out your entire directory. Be careful—and attentive—if you use it. It can be extremely dangerous, as too many sad folks have discovered. In fact, you might want to completely avoid the use of the RECOVER command, for safety's sake.

Actually, the best way to handle damaged files is to use special utility programs that have been written for that purpose. This is the reason that I developed the Norton Utilities. They contain several such programs, to restore lost files and directories, to unformat formatted disks, and even to recover from the DOS RECOVER command. With DOS 5.0 or later, you can use new data recovery commands which provide similar, but less powerful, protection.

14

HARD DISK SETUP

Introduction

The first computers had only diskette drives. Today, however, most computers have hard disks. As a matter of fact, unless you need a special-purpose machine (say, a workstation on a network) I strongly recommend that you buy only computers that have hard disks. In this chapter, you'll find out about the special needs of hard-disk storage; but, before we get into the details, let's cover a little background information.

First of all, the practical use of a computer centers around its storage. That may not seem sensible—after all, computing power is what you use a computer for. Besides, the features most people are most interested in are more likely to concern the quality of the display screen (can it do high-resolution graphics? is it easy to read?) or the printer (how fast is it? can it print italics?). But while we may think most about our machine's computing speed, or its display formats and printing quality, storage is the element that the entire use of the computer centers around.

Initially, the widespread use of personal computers and their operating systems, such as DOS, was based upon the floppy diskette—and for good reason. Diskettes are cheap, reliable, and flexible in more ways than one. Their technical flexibility made it easy for all sorts of computers to use them. Their flexibility of use, easy for put in and take out, easy to store, easy to mail, greatly enhanced how practical it was to get things done with a small computer. But floppy diskettes have two severe disadvantages: slow speed and small storage capacity. Let's look a little at each.

Computing Speed

A computer consists of a collection of components all working together. Each part has a particular speed at which it can accomplish its own task. In a rough sort of way, the separate speeds of the different parts can be compared, so that we can get an idea of whether they are appropriately balanced. If the parts of the computer are well matched, all is well. Let's consider what happens if one part is made much faster or much slower.

Suppose that one part of our computer takes up exactly 10% of the total time needed to get some work done. If we replace that part with one that is ten times faster, then the new part will get the same job done in only 1% of the old time—and our whole computer will run 9% faster. One part is improved 10 times, but the whole is improved less than 10%. If we now replace that part with one that's 10 times slower than the original, the one part now takes 100% of the original time just to do that one part of the work. The whole computer now runs 90% slower, almost halving its effective speed, thanks to just one slow component.

The moral here is that there is little advantage in having one part of the computer that's disproportionately fast, but there is a huge disadvantage in having one part that's disproportionately slow. The question is one of balance, and of bottlenecks. If one part is slow relative to the rest of the computer, it becomes a bottleneck that can cripple the entire computer.

Time Trials

If you were to use a computer without a hard disk, you would find the diskette drives to be the greatest bottleneck in overall performance. This statement is not absolutely true, but is generally true. How true it might be for you depends upon two things: first, the relative balance of speed in the parts of your computer and second, the relative balance of how your work utilizes the computer's parts. If you and I had identical computers, but you used your disks hardly at all, they wouldn't be a bottleneck for you. But if I use mine very heavily, mine are certain to be a bottleneck for me, so there are no absolutes here. For most users of most personal computers, though, the disks are clearly the bottleneck, the limiting factor in the entire computer's working speed.

Let's look at some representative numbers, so that you can see what I'm talking about. The computer this book was written on uses both diskettes and a hard disk for storage. In my own practical speed trials, I found that the hard disk was five to ten times faster than the diskettes. But these speed tests were for purely disk operations, not for the whole computer. What did they mean in practice? Is there a bottleneck? To find out, I tested one of the most time-consuming things I do with my computer: I checked something that I wrote for spelling errors.

I knew that my spelling checker did lots of computing and a fair amount of disk work, but I didn't know about balance; I didn't know where the bottlenecks were for that particular computer task. I chose a large chunk of text for the spelling check, and used each of the three possible storage media: diskette, hard disk, and virtual disk.

Using the diskette, the operation took about three minutes. Then I tried the hard disk, which, for disk work alone, is five times faster. When I used the hard disk for checking spelling the time was down to about two minutes. A dramatic improvement—a full third off the time. Then I tested further to see if, even with a hard disk, the disk speed was still a bottleneck. I did that with a virtual disk, using the computer's electronic memory (RAM) as a storage disk. But even though a virtual disk works many times faster than a hard disk, using it to check spelling only saved another six seconds; proof that my hard disk was fast enough for this job, and no bottleneck at this task.

My own speed trials dramatically demonstrated both sides of the speed question. Up to a certain point, a faster disk can help you, but beyond that, speed is not the problem. Your own speed needs or problems are uniquely yours, but typically they will be similar to mine. For most users of personal computers, ordinary diskettes are somewhat of a bottleneck, and anything that promises to be several times faster will eliminate that bottleneck.

Holding Capacity

Let's look at the other side of storage: capacity. There are many formats used in disk storage; there are many different storage capacities for different disks. As we explained in Chapter 3, the diskettes used in personal computers range in capacity from a low of about 360 thousand bytes (for the oldest $5\frac{1}{4}$ inch diskettes) to a high of 2.88 million bytes (for the newest $3\frac{1}{2}$ inch diskettes).

There are three problems you encounter when you use diskettes that won't hold all of your data. First, there is the nuisance of shuffling diskettes, putting in one set for one kind of work, and another set for other work. Not only is this inconvenient, but the physical handling of the diskettes increases the danger of damage to your data. Second, you may want to have more data on tap than will fit into your diskette drives at one time—it is hard to correlate the information on three diskettes, when you have only two diskette drives. Third, diskettes set a low limit on how big your biggest single file can be, since no file can be bigger than the disk that holds it.

Hard Disks

Hard-disk systems solve all three problems. They eliminate diskette shuffling, allow the simultaneous use of large amounts of data, and they allow single files to grow quite large, indeed.

If you don't have a hard disk, you may be wondering how much you might need one, or what size you should get. (After all, if you get one that is too small, you again have the problems you faced in the diskette world.) If you can estimate your data storage needs, fine; if not, my suggested rule of thumb follows.

For a computer in personal use, or in professional use without large amounts of data, a hard disk with a storage capacity of 40 million bytes capacity is likely to be enough. For a professional user, or for a business with moderate amounts of records, 100 million bytes might be right. For extensive business records, a large research data base, or anything similar, several hundred might be needed. (I have a 120-megabyte disk in mine, and I've never regretted having so much.) If you are choosing a hard disk, it is safer to get larger, rather than smaller. If you know that you can add more later, then you can safely start small.

Organizing Your Hard Disk

Whether your hard disk holds 10 million bytes or 500 million, basically what you have is a whole lot of storage space into which you can toss programs and data with gay abandon. The problem is, if you don't do anything to organize those millions of bytes' worth of files, you might as well have tossed all that information into a black hole. How are you going to find it again?

We'll leave the details of organizing your files to the next chapter, because that's where you'll find out about some commands that help you treat a hard disk like a giant filing cabinet. But right now, in terms of the things we'll look at in this chapter, a small introduction is needed.

Basically, you can treat a hard disk as if it were a huge warehouse with movable dividers inside: You divide and subdivide, until all your files (things in storage) are neatly organized and easily accessible. This analogy of a warehouse is fairly useful, in fact (and a little different from the traditional hard disk equals file cabinet analogy).

Overall, think of your hard disk as the warehouse building. Big and roomy, but potentially chaotic if things aren't organized correctly. In your warehouse, you have one main area—let's call it receiving—where everything gets checked in and out. On your hard disk, this "receiving area" is a special directory called the *root* directory.

Moving out from the receiving area, you can separate this from that in your warehouse by putting up dividers; on your hard disk, you can do that same thing by creating electronic dividers called *directories*. Likewise, in your warehouse, you can separate a divided area into smaller areas holding related goods. Same with your hard disk, only the smaller dividers are called *subdirectories*. And, warehouse or directory, you can divide and divide again, until things (files) are stored just where you want them.

Finally, to finish up our warehouse analogy, when you don't need a divided area anymore, you can remove the walls or shelves and stick new things in the same storage space—again, the same with hard disks.

That is the idea behind organizing a hard disk. You, instead of DOS, decide which directories need to be created and what they should be named, you divide directories into smaller units, or subdirectories, and you tell DOS which directory/subdirectory to store your files in.

Now that we've finished this general introduction to the needs for, and uses of, hard disks (and virtual disks, since a lot of what I've discussed about speed and storage capacity applies to them, too), let's move on to the special things you need to know about each.

Key Hard-Disk Commands

Having a high-capacity hard-disk system on your computer adds extra power and capabilities to your system. It also calls for some special servicing, and to meet that need, DOS provides four special programs tailored to the needs of hard disks (although, except for FDISK, they work on diskettes as well). The programs are FDISK, BACKUP, RESTORE, and ATTRIB.

I discussed the FDISK command and DOS partitions in Chapter 4. Aside from that discussion, here are a few more observations:

To continue our analogy of a hard disk being like a warehouse, partitioning a disk is like dividing it into more than one smaller warehouse. As I explained in Chapter 4, there are three reasons why you might partition a hard disk: to put more than one operating system on your computer, to organize your data into separate file systems, and to get around the 32 megabyte limitation of early versions of DOS.

The important thing to realize is that each partition, each separate warehouse, holds its own file system. If you have more than one DOS partition, you can access them as drives C, D, and so on. If you have more than one operating system, each will store its files in a different way. As a general rule, Unix systems (Unix, AIX, Xenix) have special commands to read and write files in DOS partitions. However, DOS will not be able to access files in a Unix partition.

If you will be using more than one operating system, you will probably have to install the non-DOS one first. If you already have DOS installed on your computer, you will have to *back up* (save on diskettes; see below) all the files on your hard disk, remove all the partitions, install the non-DOS system (leaving some room for DOS), reinstall DOS, and restore the files that you saved.

How you store files for safekeeping is the topic of the next section.

Protecting Your Data

Once you start using a hard disk system, you're sure to load it up with lots and lots of data—that's what a hard disk is for. How do you safeguard that data? For one thing, you should make periodic backup copies of the data on your hard disk, and that's where the commands BACKUP and RESTORE come in.

BACKUP

BACKUP is designed to copy your data from a hard disk to as many diskettes as are needed to hold them. You can use BACKUP to copy from any type of disk to any other and you can even back up your diskettes onto a hard disk. In fact, if you have more than one partition or hard disk, you can back up one hard disk drive to another. While it's nice to be able to transfer data in any direction, the main use for the BACKUP command is to put copies of your hard disk data onto floppy diskettes for safekeeping.

BACKUP provides you with several options that make it easier to control how you copy your data and what data you copy. We will discuss the most important of these options. Starting with the big picture, if you want to copy the entire contents of a hard disk (we'll assume it's drive C) onto diskettes (assume they're placed in drive A), then you use the BACKUP command like this:

```
BACKUP C:\ A: /S
```

Here are the key ingredients of that command: the parameter C:\ instructs BACKUP to start from the root directory (that's the main directory—the receiving area in our warehouse analogy) of drive C. The /S switch tells BACKUP to copy all the subdirectories as well as what's in the root directory. By starting at the root directory, and including any subdirectories, you've told BACKUP to copy everything that's on the disk.

As you remember from our discussion in Chapter 13, the wildcard name *.* matches all files. Thus, the command:

```
BACKUP C:\*.* A: /S
```

is equivalent to the previous example. All it does is specify explicitly that all files must be processed. The reason we mention it is that you will often see the BACKUP command written in this way even though, strictly speaking, the *.* is not necessary.

If you wanted to, you could back up just the contents of a particular directory or subdirectory. You would do this by telling DOS how to get to the directory you want to back up. This route you specify is called the directory pathname, and it's your way of telling DOS, "Go to directory Document, then find subdirectory Extras, and back up all the files you find there." Using this form of the command, you would specify a sub-directory this way:

```
BACKUP C:\DOCUMENT\EXTRAS A:
```

If you also included the /S option:

```
BACKUP C:\DOCUMENT\EXTRAS A: /S
```

you would include any additional subdirectories within the directory you chose.

BACKUP is clever enough to work with as many floppy diskettes as are needed to copy the files we've asked it to, and even to spread files across more than one diskette when it's necessary. This is one of the important advantages offered by the BACKUP command over other forms of copy-ing—it allows you to store a file that is larger than a single diskette.

You'll find when you back up the contents of a hard disk that it's a time-consuming process that takes lots of diskettes. Fortunately, there are some shortcuts that can reduce the time and quantity of diskettes involved in the process.

BACKUP Shortcuts

Once you've backed up all of a disk, you really don't need to copy it all for a while; just periodically copying any files that you've added or changed should be enough. DOS keeps a record of which files have been changed and have not been backed up, and BACKUP is smart enough to recognize them if you ask it to. This is done with the /M option, which tells BACKUP to copy only the files you've changed since the last backup.

How does BACKUP know if a file needs to be backed up? It checks the archive attribute that we discussed in Chapter 9. Whenever a file is create or modified, DOS turns on the archive attribute. This means that the file has yet to be backed up (archived). After BACKUP copies the file, it sets the archive attribute off. The attribute will stay off until the next time you modify the file. If the archive attribute is still off the next time you back-up using the /M option, the file will not be copied.

What I do, and what I recommend that you do, is periodically make a complete copy of your hard disk—however often you think is wise. I think once a month is a good idea. In fact, if you are using your computer to run a business, I recommend doing a full backup once a week. Then, between these complete backups, make *incremental* backups, copying only the files that have been changed in the meantime. You should do this much more often—daily, or at the very least, weekly.

If you follow these suggestions, you'll find that your backing up proce-dures will be very practical and not that tedious.

As a reminder, here are the two commands to use to back up files:

```
BACKUP C:\ A: /S        (for a full backup)
BACKUP C:\ A: /M /S     (for an incremental backup)
```

Other Switches in BACKUP

There are several more switches in BACKUP you ought to know about. One is the Date option, /D. Like the /M (meaning back up only Modi-fied files) option, the Date option lets you select which files will be backed up, but the selection is based on the date (the date stamp that indicates when they were last changed) on or after a date you give to BACKUP. This lets us choose to back up recent materials, without regard to whether they have been backed up before or not (which the /M op-tion uses). That's a handy alternative. Here's the command form using the /D switch:

```
BACKUP C:\ A: /D:mm-dd-yy /S
```

You specify the date as shown: month-day-year. For example, to back up all the files on you hard disk that have changed since December 21, 1990, use:

```
BACKUP C:\ A: /D:12-21-90 /S
```

Similarly, there is a /T option that let's you specify a time. The form of the basic command looks like this:

```
BACKUP C:\ A: /T:hh:mm /S
```

You specify the time as hours:minutes. You can add "a" or "p" to specify AM and PM, or, you can use a 24-hour clock. For example, to back up all the files that have changed since 3:00 PM, use either of the following commands:

```
BACKUP C:\ A: /T:3:00p /S
BACKUP C:\ A: /T:15:00 /S
```

The other thing that you need to know about BACKUP is that it will completely take over a diskette and wipe out any existing files on the target diskette, unless you tell it to be more civilized. This is done with the /A switch, which tells BACKUP to add its backup files to whatever else is on the target diskette. Without the /A option, BACKUP will clear out whatever is already on the target disk. Here's that command form:

```
BACKUP C:\ A: /A /S
```

Restoring Data to the Hard Disk

Naturally, there is a RESTORE command to match BACKUP. RESTORE reverses the backup operation, and has the same sort of features. There is one practical inconvenience that you should be aware of. More often than you might think, an occasion arises when you want to restore a copy of a file that's been backed up, but you want to place in a different directory—probably so you can work on it separately from the original copy. Unfortunately, RESTORE will only restore files to exactly the same directories from which they were backed up. Keep this in mind when you selectively restore files.

If you do need to put a file into a different directory, about the only way to do so is by using the COPY command.

Note: As a general rule, when you save files using BACKUP, you should use the RESTORE program from the same version of DOS.

The plain vanilla RESTORE command looks like this:

```
RESTORE A: C:\*.*
```

You tell DOS what disk holds the backup file and which files you want to restore. In this case, we have told DOS to restore files from the diskette in drive A. We have also specified that we want to restore all the files that originally came from the root (main) directory of hard disk C. (Remember, the wildcard specification *.* matches all files.)

Of course, it is a lot more useful to restore every file, including those that came from the subdirectories. Like BACKUP, RESTORE has a /S option to do the job:

```
RESTORE A: C:\*.* /S
```

This command tells DOS to restore everything that was backed up from the root directory and all subdirectories—that is, everything that was on the hard disk. RESTORE will automatically place each file in its proper subdirectory.

If you want, you can specify that only certain files are to be restored. For example, the following command restores the file BILLG.DOC that had previously been backed up from the \DOCUMENT directory on the D disk.

```
RESTORE A: D:\DOCUMENT\BILLG.DOC
```

Similarly, the following command restores all the files with the extension BAS that were in the \BASIC directory on hard disk C:

```
RESTORE A: C:\BASIC\*.BAS
```

When you restore, DOS copies files from one place to another. If the target already contains a file of the same name, it will be replaced by the restored file. On occasion, you may want to make extra sure that you are not replacing an important file. You can do this by using the /P option. The /P (permission) option tells DOS to ask you before replacing any file that has changed since it was last backed up, or any file that is marked as being read-only. Here is an example:

```
RESTORE A: C:\BASIC\*.BAS /P
```

Finally, there are a number of options that let you decide, by category, which files are to be restored. These options are:

```
/M restore only those files that have been modified or
     deleted since the last backup
/N restore only those files that no longer exist
```

In addition, by specifying a date or time, you can restore only those files that have been changed before or after a certain time:

```
/B:date   on or before the specified date
/A:date   on or after the specified date
```

```
/E:time   at or before (earlier than) the specified time
/L:time   at or after (later than) the specified time
```

These dates and times apply to the files that would be replaced by the backup.

Here is how you might use these options. Say that your last backup was December 21, 1990. Since then, you have changed a few files but you wish you hadn't. Using your backup, you want to restore only those files that you have changed since December 21, 1990. Enter:

```
RESTORE A: C:\*.* /A:12-21-90 /S
```

Backing Up Large Systems

These days, many hard disks are so large that it would be far too much trouble and too laborious to back them up on diskettes. This is especially true for computer networks that have enormous disk storage facilities.

The usual solution is to use a tape backup system. Unfortunately, there is no standard for tape drives. Although there is only a handful of tape sizes that are used, each different system stores data in its own way. This means that you can only restore data from a tape by using the same system that backed it up.

Tape backup systems consist of several components: a tape drive, an adaptor board for your computer (into which you plug the tape drive), and special software.

When you use a tape system, you will not be able to use the regular BACKUP and RESTORE commands; rather, you use the programs that are supplied with the tape drive. I recommend that you look very carefully at these programs and the documentation before you select a tape system. Don't make a choice based on hardware considerations alone.

If you have a medium-sized hard disk, an alternative to tape systems (which you might find expensive) is to use diskettes but to buy a third-party program to use instead of BACKUP and RESTORE. Such programs usually offer increased speed and more flexibility than the DOS commands. However, there are two major advantages to BACKUP and RESTORE: First, they do not cost extra; second, everyone will have them on his or her computer. These commands are a handy way to move large amounts of data from one computer to another.

15

WORKING WITH SUBDIRECTORIES

Introduction

Disks, especially hard disks, can be used in a rich and complex way in DOS, thanks to the concept of subdirectories and paths, which you encountered briefly in the last chapter. Let's take a closer look at directories and see them in relation to what you now know about disks.

All disks—whether diskettes, hard disks, optical disks, or virtual disks—have a fixed-size directory of files. This is called the *root* or *main directory*. This isn't the only directory a disk can have, though. The disk's root directory can have subdirectories under it, and each of those can also have any mixture of files and subdirectories under it. Logically speaking, all directories are subdirectories except for the root directory. However, the custom is to use the terms "directory" and "subdirectory" more or less interchangeably.

As they are stored on the disk, subdirectories are files, just like any other you keep on the disk. But DOS marks subdirectories specially, so that it can treat them as part of the directory structure. Thus, subdirectories are unique hybrids—plain files in the way they are stored on disk, but very special files in terms of what they are and what they contain. This has some interesting and important consequences for us.

First, a subdirectory can grow in size, just as any file is allowed to grow. This is a major difference between the root directory and a subdirectory. The root directory is fixed in its location and size; thus there is a definite upper limit to the number of entries it can hold. A subdirectory, on the other hand, is limited only by the space on the disk and there is no predetermined limit to the number of entries it can hold.

The second practical consequence of a subdirectory being stored in the same way as any other file is not as advantageous. DOS has to hunt around the disk for a subdirectory, and it takes longer to get to it. A disk's root directory is always located at the very beginning of the disk, next to the table (FAT) that keeps track of the available and used space on the disk. When you tell DOS to process a file with an entry in the root directory, all the information DOS needs to find the file—the directory entry and the storage location where it can find the file itself—is placed close together, where DOS can find it quickly.

With a subdirectory, it's another matter. Suppose you have a set of subdirectories like this (we always begin with the root directory, because everything else comes under it):

```
ROOT
   SUBDIRECTORY AA
        SUBDIRECTORY BB
           MYFILE
```

To work with MYFILE, which is kept in subdirectory BB, DOS first has to hunt through the path of subdirectories that leads to the file. The path here is Root to AA to BB to MYFILE. Each subdirectory is stored on the disk some distance away from the space table (officially known as the FAT, for File Allocation Table). Tracing through the directory path, and going back and forth from each directory to the table and back again adds a lot of overhead to the work that DOS must do. If a disk is fast (as are modern hard disks and virtual disks), then there isn't much problem. However, with diskette drives, or with old, slow hard disks, the extra work can slow your computer down considerably. In some cases, long, complex directory paths can make matters even worse.

Tree-Structured Directories

As I've mentioned, each of your disks has a root directory, to which you can add other directories. Each new directory branches out from its parent directory, and each one in turn can have any number of other subdirectories under it. This type of branching is referred to as a hierarchical, or *tree-structured,* directory system.

It is possible to have directories branching out from directories without limit, creating a complex tree structure. You may be tempted to make use of this capability to give a thoroughly logical structure to your files. The idea is appealing: You create master directories for a major subject area, and subdirectories under it for more details. For example, you might want to create a directory for all accounting data, with subdirectories for each accounting year. Or you might want to create a master directory for each person who uses the computer, with subject-matter directories under them. There are all sorts of possibilities.

As you can see, there are many ways to organize your tree structures. Because this is such an important subject I will discuss it in more detail in the next chapter. For now, let's move on and learn more about directories and the commands you need to maintain them.

When Do You Need a Subdirectory?

Subdirectories are really only intended for use with the fast speed and huge capacity of a hard disk system. Unless you have a lot of files on a disk, there is little need for organizing them into isolated groups by putting them in subdirectories. More important, the extra overhead of work that subdirectories require can retard the operation of slower, diskette-type storage. Subdirectories are practical only with the fast speed of a hard disk system, which works about five or ten times faster than an ordinary diskette system.

As a general rule, you only need subdirectories if you have a multimillion-byte-capacity hard disk system. Also, you can only afford the extra overhead of subdirectories if you have a hard disk. Otherwise, you should not use them.

From my own practical experience, I would recommend that you create as many subdirectories as you need, but make your tree structure the simplest possible: Place most of your subdirectories within the disk's root directory. Unless you have a really good reason to do so, don't create branches more than two levels from the root.

Judging when you should create a directory at all is another question. There are advantages and disadvantages to creating lots of small directories. With many directories containing only a few files each, it is easier to keep track of the files that belong in one particular category. But it is more difficult to use files in different directories at the same time, so it can become inconvenient if you have your files split into lots of directories. Also, the more subdirectories you have, the harder it becomes to manage the totality of your files.

The way you create and use your subdirectories will depend upon your needs and your own taste. Please resist the temptation to dump everything into one large root directory. Except for a few key files, the root directory should contain only subdirectories. Actually, this whole issue of how to design your directory structure is so important that we have devoted the entire next chapter to it. So let's put design considerations aside for a moment and move on to the commands and techniques that you will need to maintain your subdirectories.

Paths to a Directory

With the potential complexity of a branching tree-structured directory, you need a way to find and control where you are, and you need a way to indicate what part of the tree you are interested in. You need a notation, a way of specifying a location in the tree.

How you (and DOS) find your way to a particular subdirectory on a disk is referred to as a *path*. A path is the route that traces the way from a disk's root directory, out to some point in the branching directory tree. The description of the path is called the *path name.*

Let's take our earlier example, in which we have the subdirectories AA and BB leading to a file named MYFILE. At the top of the heap is the disk which, of course, has a root directory. The root directory has a subdirectory named AA, and it in turn has a subdirectory named BB. Finally, in subdirectory BB is the file we want to refer to, MYFILE. To find the way to MYFILE, we need to describe the path something like this.

- Starting with the ROOT, find its subdirectory named AA;
- next find AA's subdirectory named BB;
- then find BB's file named MYFILE.

Path names can be written like this, but all the lengthy words can be replaced with a short and simple backslash (\) so that our verbose path description shortens down to this:

```
\AA\BB\MYFILE
```

Notice you don't have to say anything about starting from the root—the first backslash indicates that. If a path name begins with a backslash, that tells DOS, "start the path from the root."

With this way of writing a path name, we can tell DOS where—in any disk's directory tree—we want to work. And vice-versa: DOS can tell us where things are.

With the "hooks" on which we can hang subdirectories and path-names out of the way, let's see how to go about setting up and managing directories.

Creating a Directory with MKDIR

To create a new directory, you use the Make Directory command, which is typed either as MKDIR or as MD. For example, you would add a directory named LETTERS to the root directory with this command:

```
MD LETTERS
```

When a directory is created, it is empty except for two terse reference entries, a single dot (.) and a double dot (..), which DOS uses as markers to tell it where it is and where it came from. For example, a directory listing of our LETTERS example would show entries like these:

```
VOLUME IN DRIVE C IS HARLEY
VOLUME SERIAL NUMBER IS 12B4-B400
DIRECTORY OF C:\LETTERS

   .            <DIR>      12-20-90      6:52P
   ..           <DIR>      12-20-90      6:52P
        2 FILE(S)              0 BYTES
                        2430976 BYTES FREE
```

After a directory has been created, then files (or other directories) can be placed in it. Within a particular disk or partition, all of the names in one directory—names of files, or names of subdirectories—must be unique within that directory, but the same names can be used in other directories.

If you want to add a subdirectory to another directory, include the path to the new directory in your command. For example, you would create the subdirectory STEVIE under LETTERS with this command (you'll see another way to do this when we get to the Change Directory command):

```
MD \LETTERS\STEVIE
```

and if you requested a directory listing, DOS would show you something like this:

```
VOLUME IN DRIVE C IS HARLEY
VOLUME SERIAL NUMBER IS 12B4-B400
DIRECTORY OF C:\LETTERS

   .            <DIR>      12-20-90      6:52P
   ..           <DIR>      12-20-90      6:52P
STEVIE          <DIR>      12-20-90      6:54P
        3 FILE(S)              0 BYTES
                        2428928 BYTES FREE
```

Using RMDIR to Remove a Directory

If you can make directories, you should be able to remove them as well, and this is what the RMDIR, or RD, command is for. It's as easy to use as MKDIR, but to avoid leaving any files or subdirectories without a home, RMDIR will not work unless the directory is empty. If you try to delete a directory that contains any files or subdirectories, DOS displays the informative message:

```
INVALID PATH, NOT DIRECTORY,
OR DIRECTORY NOT EMPTY
```

If you see this message, take a look (with the DIR command) at the files in the directory. If you want to keep what's there, use the COPY and DELETE commands to move the files to another directory. If you want to keep a subdirectory, think twice about whether you really want to remove the directory at all.

Another restriction on RMDIR is that you cannot remove the directory you are in or a directory that is between you and the root. If you were sitting on a real branch in a real tree, this rule would be like saying that you couldn't cut off a branch that is supporting you.

For instance, if \LETTERS\STEVIE is the current directory and you want to remove it, you must first move to either \LETTERS or to \ (the root directory).

If you do try to remove your current directory, DOS will display:

```
ATTEMPT TO REMOVE CURRENT DIRECTORY - .
```

Note: This error message will be displayed by versions of DOS that are 4.0 or later. If you have an older DOS, you will get the same "Invalid Path" message that we showed above.

Changing Direction with CHDIR

If you are going to be working with various files in a subdirectory, such as our sample \AA\BB directory, it would be a nuisance to have to keep typing \AA\BB in front of the name of each file. More than likely, you'd make a typing error at some point. To solve this problem, DOS keeps track of what it calls the *current directory*. If you refer to just a file name, without specifying the path to get to it, DOS assumes that the file is in the current directory.

You can control which directory DOS assumes is the current directory, and you do it with the Change Current Directory command, CHDIR (which can be abbreviated CD). For example, to make \AA\BB your current directory, you would enter the command:

```
CD \AA\BB
```

If you wanted to change back to the root directory, you would only have to type:

```
CD \
```

because the backslash is DOS's shorthand for the root directory.

Then, too, if you ever forget which directory you're in, the command:

```
CD
```

with no parameters tells DOS to let you know. For example, if you type CHDIR while you're in the BB subdirectory, DOS displays:

```
C:\AA\BB
```

to let you know where you are.

Furthermore, if you want to create a subdirectory under another directory, you can use CD to change to the first directory and then use MD to create the new one. For example, to create a subdirectory named NEWDIR under the \AA directory, use:

```
CD \AA
MD NEWDIR
```

Finally, to make things even easier, DOS keeps track of a separate current directory for each disk device it has. If you have a C: disk and a D: disk, you could set the current directories for them, independently, like this:

```
CHDIR C:\DIR1\DIR2
CHDIR D:\OTHER1
```

Then, whenever you referred to the C drive, DOS would look in the \DIR1\DIR2 directory, while for any use of drive D, DOS would look in its \OTHER1 directory; If you did a global copy command, like this:

```
COPY C:*.* D:
```

the files from the \DIR1\DIR2 directory in drive C would be copied to the directory \OTHER1 in drive D. No other files and no other directories would be affected.

Using the TREE Command to Find Branches

Since a disk can have numerous subdirectories branching out from the root directory, you need a way of finding out what all the branches of the tree are. The TREE command does this for you. TREE will display a list of all the branches of the directory tree for any disk. To use the Tree command, simply type TREE, followed by the path showing where you want to start from. For example, to display the entire tree, starting from the root directory, type:

```
TREE \
```

You will see a display like this:

```
DIRECTORY PATH LISTING FOR VOLUME NORTON
VOLUME SERIAL NUMBER IS 3746-1AF3
C:\
    |_____ACCOUNTS
    |     |_____SMALL
    |     |_____MEDIUM
    |     |_____LARGE
    |
    |_____INVOICES
    |     |_____CURRENT
    |     |_____PAST_DUE
    |
    |_____LETTERS
          |_____PERSONAL
          |_____HARLEY
```

If you want to see only part of the tree, specify the path of the directory at which you want to start. For example, if you enter:

```
TREE \ACCOUNTS
```

you will see:

```
VOLUME SERIAL NUMBER IS 3746-1AF3
C:\ACCOUNTS
    |_____SMALL
    |_____MEDIUM
    |_____LARGE
```

If you want, you can specify a specific disk as a part of the path, such as:

```
TREE D:\
```

If you do not specify a path, DOS will start from your current directory on the default drive.

There are two switches that you can use with TREE: /F will list all your files along with the directory names, and /V will draw the tree using regular characters (+, | and \) instead of the special line drawing symbols.

Pathfinding Shortcuts

If you type a path name starting with a slash, you are telling DOS to start tracing the path from the root, but there are other ways to work around directory trees. If you don't precede the path name with a slash, then the pathfinding begins right where you are, at whatever happens to be the current directory. Thus, this path name tells DOS to start with the root:

```
\AA\BB\MYFILE
```

while this path name tells DOS to start wherever the current directory is:

```
AA\BB\MYFILE
```

There are also two special trick names to help you work your way around paths. They are the single (.) and double (..) dots mentioned earlier. These special names are used to refer to the current directory (.) and the directory, called the *parent directory,* that is one level above the current directory (..), For example, if you were in the AA directory and wanted a directory listing, you could type:

```
DIR .\BB
```

instead of:

```
DIR \AA\BB
```

It might seem silly to you, at first glance, to have a . entry that just refers to the same directory that you're already in. Why have a directory name that basically means "do nothing—don't shift to another directory?" The reason emerges when you start thinking about some of the complex ways that you can use directories in batch files, which were covered in Chapters 10 and 11.

If you can specify a directory name in the middle of a path, like this: \DIRECTORY\ then you also ought to be able to substitute nothing in place of the name DIRECTORY. That's just what the period (.) will do for you, like this: \.\ Without the period, you'd have something like this: \\. And those two slashes would confuse DOS no end.

The parent-name, two periods (..), is used if you ever want to trace your way backward from the current directory. Let's switch back to our first example:

```
CD \AA\BB
```

You're now in the \AA\BB directory. But suppose you want to find a file named MEMO that's in the \AA directory—the parent of the current directory? You can find your way to it like this:

```
..\MEMO
```

This business of using .. to refer to the parent directory can be used for all kinds of sophisticated tricks. But bear in mind that they would be tricks and as such, any command that uses them is likely to be tricky and error prone. It's nice to know what the two periods mean, but you'd be well advised to steer clear of the whole business. After all, if you had a complex pathname that traced its way forward and back, like this:

```
..\..\AA\BB\..\CC\FILE
```

you'd have to think your way up and down the directory tree and very likely would misunderstand or misremember it. There's really no reason to introduce unnecessary complications.

Let's take another look at the directory listing for the LETTERS directory that we used earlier in the chapter:

```
VOLUME IN DRIVE C IS HARLEY
VOLUME SERIAL NUMBER IS 12B4-B400
DIRECTORY OF C:\LETTERS

.            <DIR>     12-20-90      6:52P
..           <DIR>     12-20-90      6:52P
     2 FILE(S)            0 BYTES
                    2430976 BYTES FREE
```

Now you can understand why every new directory will automatically have at least two entries: the current directory (.) and the parent directory (..).

The PROMPT Command

Left to itself, DOS will display a very simple prompt: the name of the current disk drive, followed by a greater-than character. For example:

```
C>
```

However, by using the PROMPT command, you can change the prompt to your liking. The command is easy to use; simply specify the prompt you want. For example, to change the prompt to "Hello, Kevin," enter:

```
PROMPT HELLO, KEVIN
```

Of course, a prompt like "Hello, Kevin" is of little use (unless your name happens to be Kevin). Where the PROMPT command comes in handy is when you use some of its built-in features. To do so, you use special 2-character codes, each of which starts with a "$". Here are the most useful of the codes:

Table 15.1 *Prompt Codes*

Code	Meaning
$B	display a | (vertical bar) character
$D	display the current date
$E	write an escape character (hex 1B) to standard output
$G	display a > (greater-than sign) character
$H	move back one space (erases previous character)
$L	display a < (less-than sign) character
$N	display the name of the default drive
$P	display the path (default drive + current directory)
$Q	display the = (equal sign) character
$T	display the current time
$V	display the DOS version number
$$	display the $ (dollar sign) character
$_	start a new line (carriage return + linefeed)

Note: The $E combination writes an escape character. You can use this to initiate special commands known as "ANSI escape sequences." The details are highly technical and, unfortunately, are beyond the scope of this book. For further information, see your DOS manual.

Here are some examples:

To display the default drive, followed by a greater-than charatcer, enter:

```
PROMPT $N$G
```

The prompt will look like this:

```
C>
```

To display the default drive followed by the current directory, enter:

```
PROMPT $P$G
```

If you are in the \LETTERS\PERSONAL directory, for example, the prompt will look like this:

```
C:\LETTERS\PERSONAL>
```

Here is an elaborate prompt that might be helpful when you are teaching someone how to use DOS:

```
PROMPT $_TIME: $T$_DATE: $D$_YOU ARE USING $V$_CURRENT PATH: $P
```

Note: There is a space at the end of this command (after the $P), even though you can't see it here.

Try this prompt for yourself. Notice how I used $_ in several places to break the prompt onto more than one line. The $_ at the beginning separates the prompt from whatever has just been displayed on the screen. The actual prompt looks like this:

```
TIME: 22:14:38:89
DATE: FRI 01-18-1991
YOU ARE USING IBM DOS VERSION 5.0
CURRENT PATH: D:\DOSBOOK\GENERAL
```

As I mentioned, unless you tell DOS otherwise, it displays a simple prompt: the default drive, followed by a greater-than character. In other words, PG.

Most people find the PG prompt to be the best one. In fact, when you install DOS, the installation program automatically places the command:

```
PROMPT $P$G
```

in your AUTOEXEC.BAT file (the batch file that is automatically executed each time you start DOS). Thus, many people already have this prompt on their systems without even having to understand the PROMPT command.

If you are using an old version of DOS (before 4.0), there is no elaborate installation program and you will have to put this command in your AUTOEXEC.BAT for yourself.

One last point: If you enter the PROMPT command by itself:

```
PROMPT
```

DOS will change it back to NG. This is handy if you are experimenting and you have somehow created an unworkable prompt that you want to eliminate. (The choice of NG as a default dates back to the early days of DOS. When the PROMPT command was first introduced, there were only diskettes, not hard disks, and there was really no need to display a pathname.)

16

ORGANIZING YOUR HARD DISK

Introduction

Your hard disk will come to hold many files—perhaps even several thousand. Organizing your files well will make an enormous difference in your ability to manage that much data on a day by day basis. Moreover, a smart organization will make it easier for you to maintain a responsible backup system.

I promise you—one day your hard disk will fail. It is not a matter of "if," but a matter of "when." Do not depend on special utility programs—even my Norton Utilities—to make up for a lack of organization and planning. Your only dependable defense against hardware failure is a well-organized directory structure and frequent backups.

In this chapter, we will explore various ways to organize a hard disk. We will then learn about the commands that you use to make your organization known to DOS so it can find the files it needs as it needs them.

Why Organize a Hard Disk?

In a nutshell, here is the problem: Our minds can deal with only a limited amount of complexity. In fact, part of the human condition is the continuing struggle to keep life simple enough for a human brain.

With older computers, we used diskettes exclusively; and diskettes can hold only a small amount of data. It was uncommon to run into problems because of too many files on a single diskette.

In those days, it was natural to divide our files into groups, and to use a separate diskette for each group. For example, you might keep each program and its associated files on its own diskette. And you might keep separate sets of diskettes for different types of data: spreadsheets on one, documents on another, and so on.

With a hard disk things change radically. The main advantage to using a large hard disk is that we can have all our files accessible all of the time, without having to swap diskettes back and forth.

However, having many, many files on a single disk requires us to impose some sort of organization. Obviously, it would be impossible to use one massive directory containing thousands of files. The solution is to divide our storage space into logically manageable subdirectories—that is, we need to develop a plan for a tree structure that we can live with.

There are two advantages to such a system: First, we can find files that we need when we need them. Second, we can find files that we don't need once they have become obsolete. This allows us to delete files that we don't use anymore, freeing up the space and keeping our tree pruned and healthy.

Guidelines for Organizing the Tree Structure

As I explained in Chapter 14, the subdirectories of a hard disk form a tree structure emanating from a single root directory. The question is: How many subdirectories do we need and where do we put them?

Since everyone's needs are different, there are no hard and fast rules. But there are two important guidelines that you should follow:

- A directory should contain either files, or other directories, but not both.

In other words, do not mix files and subdirectories together.

This one rule will go a long way towards keeping things simple and manageable. There should be only one exception to this rule: The root directory—which contains all your first-level subdirectories—must contain a small number of files as well. This is explained in the next section.

- Keep your programs separate from your data.

For example, store your word processing program separately from your documents.

Segregating programs from data has two important advantages: First, since programs do not change once they are installed, they do not have to be backed up more than once, unless you install new programs. Data files, on the other hand, must be backed up regularly, since it is the data that changes every time you work. These days, programs can be quite large and take a long time to back up. Concentrating your backup efforts where you need them—on your data—can save you a lot of time. And anything that saves time makes it more likely that you will actually do the backup.

Second, from time to time you will need to install new versions of your programs. Keeping them separate from your data allows you to upgrade your software without having to disturb your work areas.

Which Files Must Be in the Root Directory

As I mentioned in the last section, some files must be in the root directory—in fact, there are five such files.

To be precise, these files must appear in the root directory of the disk from which you boot DOS. If you have more than one hard disk partition, these files need only be on drive C. With the other drives, you should follow the rule we discussed earlier and keep only subdirectories in the root directory.

The first three files are the DOS files, IBMBIO.COM, IBMDOS.COM and COMMAND.COM. (If you have MS-DOS, these files will be called IO.SYS, MSDOS.SYS, and COMMAND.COM.) As I explained in Chapter 5, these three files comprise the main part of DOS and are placed in the root directory by FORMAT when you use the /S (system) switch.

Both IBMBIO.COM and IBMDOS.COM are hidden files. This means that, as a general rule, they do not appear in directory listings. More important, because these files are hidden, you cannot accidentally erase them or change them. In fact, there are only three ways that you can detect hidden files. First, CHKDSK /V will display all file names, hidden or not. Second, if you have DOS 5.0 or later, you can use DIR with the /A:H option. (These commands are explained in Chapter 9.) Third, you can use the ATTRIB command that we will discuss in Chapter 17. So, although IBMBIO.COM and IBMDOS.COM are in the root directory, under normal circumstances you will not see them.

The COMMAND.COM file is not hidden and will appear in the directory listing. Strictly speaking, you can keep COMMAND.COM elsewhere but this requires you to set things up in special ways and I don't recommend it.

The other two files which must appear in the root directory of your boot disk are AUTOEXEC.BAT and CONFIG.SYS.

The AUTOEXEC.BAT file, of course, is the special batch file that DOS executes each time it boots (see Chapter 10). CONFIG.SYS is a special configuration file that tells DOS how you want to set up your system. We discussed AUTOEXEC.BAT in Chapter 13, and we will will meet CONFIG.SYS in Chapter 28.

When you install DOS, the installation program (see Chapter 5) creates AUTOEXEC.BAT and CONFIG.SYS files for you automatically and places them in the root directory of your boot disk. You will, of course, change these files from time to time to suit your needs. Just make sure that they stay in the root directory or DOS won't be able to find them.

Aside from these five special files (of which two are hidden), there may be other files in your root directory, placed there by various programs. For example, some of the Norton Utility programs need to keep technical information in files which must be in the root directory.

However, in the interests of good organization, strive to keep your root directory as empty of files as possible.

Where to Put Your Programs

We have already discussed two guidelines for organizing your hard disk:

- A directory should contain either files, or other directories, but not both.
- Keep your programs separate from your data.

The question as to where to store programs brings us to a third guideline:

- Keep each program in its own directory.

For each program, use a subdirectory that is named after the program. For example, when you install the Norton Utilities, you would put them in a directory named \NORTON.

Basically, there are two ways that you might install new software: First, most software comes with an installation program. All you need to do is start this program and follow instructions.

As often as not, the installation is superintended by a batch file with a name like INSTALL.BAT. Typically, you insert the first software diskette in drive A, switch to drive A:

```
A:
```

and then start the installation by entering:

```
INSTALL
```

(Of course each program has its own installation and you will have to check the manual for specific details.)

The point is that somewhere along the way, you will have to specify where you want to install the program. As I mentioned, the best idea is to put it in its own directory. Usually, this will be a new directory which the installation program will create for you.

The second way to install software is to create the new directory yourself and then copy all the program files to it, using the COPY or XCOPY command. Usually, you do this only when your software does not come with its own installation program.

Here is an example, again using the Norton Utilities, which can be installed either way. All you do is create a program directory:

```
MD \NORTON
```

and, one by one, copy the contents of each program disk to the new directory by entering:

```
COPY A:*.* C:\NORTON
```

Some Important Program Directories

Aside from having one directory for each program, there are several other standard directories that you should create.

First, you will have a \DOS directory to hold all your DOS files. The DOS installation program will create \DOS for you. If you are using an old version of DOS that does not have the automatic installation program, you will have to create \DOS and copy the files to it yourself.

Second, you should create a \BATCH directory to hold all your batch files. These are not the batch files that may come with your software, but rather batch files that you yourself write.

Third, create a directory called \UTILITY to hold small, miscellaneous programs. For example, you might write yourself a program to time your phone calls; or a friend might give you a copy of a small public domain program that he loaded from a computer bulletin board system. When you are not sure where to put a program, put it in \UTILITY.

Here is part of a tree-structure that illustrates what I have been saying. This example is from a computer which is set up to use DisplayWrite for word processing, Microsoft Excel for spreadsheets, Ashton-Tate's dBASE for databases, and the Norton Utilities for file and disk maintenance.

```
|---BATCH
|---DBASE
|---DOS
|---DW
|---EXCEL
|---NORTON
\---UTILITY
```

Telling DOS Where Programs Are: The PATH Command

There are two ways to tell DOS where to find your programs. First, whenever you reference a program, you can preface its name with a path, or you can make sure that the program is in your current directory.

For example, let's say that you want to start DisplayWrite version 5. The name of the program is DW5PG.COM and it resides in the \DW directory. You can either specify a path:

```
C:\DW\DW5PG
```

or you can change directories before starting the program:

```
C:
CD \DW
DW5PG
```

With most programs, you will use a variation of this method, with the actual commands residing in a batch file. Later in the chapter, we will go into this in detail and I will show you how to build such batch files.

The second way to tell DOS where your programs are is by using the PATH command. There are three ways to use PATH. First, you can specify a list of directory paths separated by semicolons. For example:

```
PATH C:\BATCH;C:\DOS;C:\NORTON;C:\UTILITY
```

Notice that, except following the word PATH, there are no spaces anywhere in the command. This list of directories is called the *search path*.

This command is used to tell DOS where to look for executable programs that are not in your current directory. For example, say that you want to run the DISKEDIT program in the \NORTON directory. This is what happens if you enter:

```
DISKEDIT
```

First, DOS checks the current directory. If the program isn't there, DOS then checks each directory in the search path, in the order you specified. In this case, DOS would find the program in the third directory, C:\NORTON. If DOS can't find the program anywhere, it will display the error message:

```
Bad command or file name
```

When you use the PATH command be careful not to make a mistake. DOS does not check the paths until it actually goes to use the search path for the first time. If you specified a bad disk name, you will see the message:

```
Invalid drive in search path
```

However, if you make a simple spelling mistake, or specify a directory that does not exist, DOS will not tell you and it may take you a while to figure out why your programs can't be found.

The second way to use PATH is to enter the name of the command by itself to check the current status of your search path:

```
PATH
```

DOS will respond with something like this:

```
PATH=C:\BATCH;C:\DOS;C:\NORTON;C:\UTILITY
```

And finally, if you enter the name of the command followed only by a semicolon, DOS will erase your search path:

```
PATH;
```

Now, if you enter:

```
PATH
```

DOS will display:

```
NO PATH
```

At this point, DOS will search for programs only in your current directory.

Obviously, PATH is the type of command that you do not want to have to enter each time you start work. For one thing, it is too easy to make a spelling mistake. The best thing is to decide on a search path, and then place the appropriate PATH command in your AUTOEXEC.BAT file where it will be executed each time you boot DOS. (This is what we did in Chapter 12).

In fact, the DOS installation program creates such a command and puts it in AUTOEXEC.BAT for you. It is a simple PATH command that points only to your DOS directory:

```
PATH C:\DOS
```

(After all, the DOS installation program has no way of knowing what software you will be using.)

Searching for Executable Programs: COM, EXE, and BAT Files

As I explained in Chapter 12, DOS can execute programs (that have the extensions COM or EXE) and batch files (that have the extension BAT). However, what happens if you enter a command and DOS finds more than one executable file with that file name? For example, what if you have the files TEST.COM, TEST.EXE and TEST.BAT all in your current directory and you enter:

```
TEST
```

The rule that DOS follows is that it finds COM files, EXE files, and BAT files, in that order. In this case, the file TEST.COM would be executed and the other two would be ignored.

If you want, you can override this priority scheme by specifying an extension. For instance:

```
TEST.BAT
```

In this case, DOS would execute TEST.BAT directly. However, having to specify an extension is awkward and is seldom used.

In practice, the only time that you run into this problem is when you write a batch file that has the same file name as a program. For example, you might have a batch file named WORD.BAT that you use to start the WORD.COM program.

The way to solve this problem is to place all your batch files in their own directory and to place the directory name—\BATCH—at the beginning of your search path. This means that whenever you enter a command that is not in your current directory, DOS will check your batch files first.

Where to Put Your Data Files

I have already said that the best place to put your program files is in their own directories. You will have one directory for each program, a DOS directory, a batch file directory, and a miscellaneous \UTILITY directory. But where should you put your data files?

From our discussion above, you know that you should keep them separate from your programs. The best idea is to start with one data directory for each program and expand when necessary.

As an example, let's continue with the programs that we used in the last section: DisplayWrite, Excel, and dBASE. To store your data files, you would create three directories named DW, EXCEL, and DBASE. However, this causes a problem: We have already used these names for our program directories.

A good solution is to gather all the data directories and place them under one directory called \DATA. Thus, the data part of our tree structure would look like this:

```
\---DATA
    |---DBASE
    |---DW
    \---EXCEL
```

and the full tree would be:

```
|---BATCH
|---DBASE
|---DOS
|---EXCEL
|---NORTON
|---UTILITY
\---DATA
    |---EXCEL
    |---DW
    \---DBASE
```

When you find yourself with too many files in one of the data directories, simply split it into one or more subdirectories.

For example, let's say that you have only a few dBASE files, but a moderate amount of Excel spreadsheets and many DisplayWrite documents. You might keep the Excel files in two subdirectories, called PAY and RECEIVE, and the DisplayWrite files in three subdirectories, called LETTERS, MEMOS, and REPORTS:

```
|---BATCH
|---DBASE
|---DOS
|---DW
|---EXCEL
|---NORTON
|---UTILITY
\---DATA
    |---DBASE
    |---DW
    |    |---LETTERS
    |    |---MEMOS
    |    \---REPORTS
    \---EXCEL
        |---PAY
        \---RECEIVE
```

Telling DOS Where Data Files Are: The APPEND Command

As you know, the PATH command tells DOS where to look for files that aren't in your current directory. But PATH only works for executable files—those with the extensions COM, EXE, or BAT. The APPEND command performs the same function for all files. The idea is that DOS uses PATH to find a program to execute, and APPEND to find a file for any other reason.

The basic forms of the APPEND command are similar to those of the PATH command: To set up an APPEND search list, enter the name of the command followed by a list of directory paths, separated by semicolons. For example:

```
APPEND C:\DW\LETTERS;C:\DW\MEMOS;C:\DW\REPORTS
```

When you have a program that requests a nonexecutable file, DOS first checks your current directory. If it's not there, DOS will check each directory in the APPEND search path in the order you specified.

In this example, say that your program is looking for a file named TEST.DOC. If it is not in your current directory, DOS will then look for:

```
C:\DW\LETTERS\TEST.DOC
C:\DW\MEMOS\TEST.DOC
C:\DW\REPORTS\TEST.DOC
```

in that order.

To check what your APPEND search list is, enter the command by itself:

```
APPEND
```

DOS will display the list:

```
APPEND=C:\DW\LETTERS;C:\DW\MEMOS;C:\DW\REPORTS
```

To remove the APPEND search list, enter the command followed by a single semicolon:

```
APPEND;
```

If you now ask for the append list, DOS will display:

```
NO APPEND
```

APPEND is more complex than PATH and there are a number of different switches that you can use to have the command act in different ways. However, these options are beyond the scope of this book. For the details, check your DOS manual.

There are two common ways to use APPEND. One is to allow a program to find its system files, and two, to allow a program to find your data files. Two illustrative examples follows.

First, say that the DisplayWrite program files are stored in the \DW directory. You are starting the program from a different directory. In order that DisplayWrite should be able to find its program files, you issue the command:

```
APPEND C:\DW
```

before the program.

Second, your DisplayWrite documents are kept in the directory \DOCUMENT. You may be working in another directory but you still want the program to be able to find your documents. In this case, you issue the following command before starting the program:

```
APPEND \DOCUMENT
```

If you wanted to combine both search lists, you could use:

```
APPEND C:\DOCUMENT;C:\DW
```

In practice, you will usually embed your APPEND commands in a batch file whose job it is to start a particular program. We will go into this in detail later in the chapter. However, before we do, let's spend a few more minutes discussing an overall strategy for hard disk organization.

An Overall Strategy for Organizing Your Hard Disk

In this section we will discuss three overall strategies for organizing your hard disk. Each of these uses the guidelines I have already discussed: keeping programs and data in their own directories, and not mixing files and subdirectories together in the same directory. Each of the strategies has advantages and disadvantages. You should decide which one suits best.

The first strategy is the one that I have already described. Keep each program in its own directory and place your data files in their own directories under \DATA. Using the example from earlier in the chapter, the tree looks like this:

```
|---BATCH
|---DBASE
|---DOS
|---DW
|---EXCEL
|---NORTON
|---UTILITY
\---DATA
    |---DBASE
    |---DW
    |     |---LETTERS
    |     |---MEMOS
    |     \---REPORTS
    \---EXCEL
          |---PAY
          \---RECEIVE
```

The second way of organizing is similar; the only difference is that the program directories are now gathered into their own parent directory, named \SYSTEM. With this structure, the tree looks like this:

```
|---SYSTEM
|     |---BATCH
|     |---DBASE
|     |---DOS
|     |---DW
|     |---EXCEL
|     |---NORTON
|     \---UTILITY
\---DATA
      |---DBASE
      |---DW
      |     |---LETTERS
      |     |---MEMOS
      |     \---REPORTS
\---EXCEL
      |---PAY
      \---RECEIVE
```

This strategy has the advantage of isolating the programs into their own part of the tree which makes managing the system easier. For example, to back up all the programs, you can tell your back up program to copy everything that is stored under \SYSTEM; and to back up all your data, you can copy everything under \DATA.

The disadvantage is that search path names are longer. For example, the path that points to your DOS files is C:\SYSTEM\DOS rather than C:\DOS.

The third strategy combines the advantages of the first two: isolation of programs and data, along with short path names. So far, we have used tree-structures that are completely contained on one disk, drive C. The third strategy involves breaking up your hard disk into two partitions, drives C and D. Drive C will be used for programs, drive D will be used for data files. In order to do this, you will have to use FDISK to partition your disk into two parts (see Chapter 4). You can do this when you install DOS or you can change what is already there. If you do change your disk, make sure that you first back up all your files: repartitioning will destroy your data.

Using separate partitions for programs and data affords important advantages because the organization is simpler. However, there is a disadvantage: You will have to tell FDISK in advance how much space to allot to programs (drive C, your primary disk) and how much to allot for data (drive D, your secondary disk).

If you are an experienced computer user, take a survey of your disk and see how much space is devoted for each purpose. If you are not sure, allow two thirds of the space for programs and one third for data.

Once you have used FDISK to make the two partitions, and FORMAT to format them (using /S for drive C), you can create simple tree structures on each:

The Program Disk—Drive C:

```
C:--\
    |---BATCH
    |---DBASE
    |---DOS
    |---DW
    |---EXCEL
    |---NORTON
    \---UTILITY
```

The Data Disk—Drive D:

```
D:-\
    |---DBASE
    |---DW
    |    |---LETTERS
    |    |---MEMOS
    |    \---REPORTS
    \---EXCEL
         |---PAY
         \---RECEIVE
```

Setting Up a System for More Than One User

If more than one person is to be using the same computer, it is a good idea to give them each their own set of directories. All you have to do is create one directory per person, under which you will put all their data directories.

Here is an example of a system that will be used by six different people. Some of them will use all of the available programs, other will use only one or two. The data part of the tree looks like this:

```
\---DATA
    |---BURT
    |     \---DW
    |---ERIC
    |     \---DBASE
    |---HARLEY
    |    |---DBASE
    |    |---DW
    |    |    |---LETTERS
    |    |    |---MEMOS
    |    |    \---REPORTS
    |    \---EXCEL
    |         |---PAY
    |         \---RECEIVE
    |---KEVIN
    |    |---DBASE
    |    |    |---PROJECTS
    |    |    \---RESEARCH
    |    \---EXCEL
    |         |---PROJECTS
    |         \---RESEARCH
    |---KIM
    |    |---DBASE
    |    \---EXCEL
    \---PETER
    \---DBASE
```

As this example shows, you can make each person's part of the tree as simple or as complex as he or she requires. A handy thing to do is to create a batch file named after each person. For example, HARLEY.BAT.

When group members start work, they simply enter their own name. This invokes their own personal batch file which, among other things, can move them to their part of the tree. In this example, KIM.BAT can execute the command:

```
CD \DATA\HARLEY
```

You can use the same techniques for different departments of a large office. For example, you might have different parts of the tree for accounting, shipping, and so on.

Using Batch Files to Start Your Programs

In general, the best way to start your programs is to use batch files. This allows you to customize the environment for each program. In this section, I will explain how to use the APPEND command to set up such batch files.

A typical batch file does the following:

- Sets the APPEND search path to point to the program's directory
- Changes to your data directory
- Starts the program
- Removes the APPEND search path

Here are three examples, one for each of the three tree structure strategies described in the previous section. The examples show DW.BAT, a batch file used to start DisplayWrite. The DisplayWrite program is DW5PG.COM and is in the program directory DW. The data is in \DATA\DW\MEMOS.

First, here's what DW.BAT looks like with the first strategy:

```
:* ----------------------------------------------------------
:* DW.BAT: batch file to start DisplayWrite
:* ----------------------------------------------------------
     @echo off

:* set the APPEND search path
     append c:\dw

:* move to the data directory
     c:
     cd \data\dw\memos

:* start the program
     c:\dw\dw5pg

:* remove the APPEND search path
     append;
:* ----------------------------------------------------------
```

I want you to notice something important: I have put "C:" in front of all the paths and I have explicitly changed to drive C before changing to the data directory. The reason is that this batch file has to work under all circumstances. In particular, you can't assume that drive C will always be the default drive. For instance, you may have changed to drive A to work with a diskette.

Here is another version of DW.BAT to use with our second tree structure strategy. The only different here is that the program directories all come under \SYSTEM:

```
:* ----------------------------------------------------------
:* DW.BAT: batch file to start DisplayWrite
:* ----------------------------------------------------------
     @echo off

:* set the APPEND search path
     append c:\system\dw

:* move to the data directory
     c:
     cd \data\dw\memos

:* start the program
     c:\system\dw\dw5pg

:* remove the APPEND search path
     append;
:* ----------------------------------------------------------
```

The third version of DW.BAT show how things are simplified with the third tree structure strategy; namely, separate disk partitions for programs and data. Notice how, in this case, we must change to drive D to find the data directory:

```
:*  --------------------------------------------------------
:*  DW.BAT: batch file to start DisplayWrite
:*  --------------------------------------------------------
    @echo off

:*  set the APPEND search path
    append c:\dw

:*  move to the data directory
    d:
    cd \dw\memos

:*  start the program
    c:\dw\dw5pg

:*  remove the APPEND search path
    append;
:*  --------------------------------------------------------
```

Be forewarned that your particular software packages may have demands that call for special handling. Moreover, when you call a software company for technical support, you will find that many support people do not understand how to use APPEND.

The best advice I can give you is to read your software manual carefully. However, even the manual may not help. The software companies seldom suggest using APPEND because they realize that many people still have old versions of DOS that do not support this command.

Using APPEND to Point to Your Data Files

So far, we have used APPEND to show DOS where to find your non-executable program files. But, as I mentioned earlier, you can also use APPEND to show DOS where to find your data files.

For example, say that you are using DisplayWrite and you have three directories of data files, LETTERS, MEMOS, and REPORTS, all of which reside in the DW data directory. You want to be able to work with files in all three directories at the same time, without having to change directories from within DisplayWrite.

The way to do this is to add the three data paths into your APPEND command. Here is what the batch file, DW.BAT, would look like after making the appropriate changes. (**Note:** This is the version of DW.BAT which uses drive C for programs and drive D for data.)

```
:* -----------------------------------------------------
:* DW.BAT: batch file to start DisplayWrite
:* -----------------------------------------------------
    @echo off

:* set the APPEND search path
    append d:\dw\letters;d:\dw\memos;d:\dw\reports;c:\dw

:* move to the data directory
    d:
    cd \dw

:* start the program
    c:\dw\dw5pg

:* remove the APPEND search path
    append;
:* -----------------------------------------------------
```

This example is different in two ways: First, the APPEND search path lists the three data directories and they come before the program directory. Here is why: Remember that DOS will search the directories in the order you specify. Some programs come with sample data files. If the C:\DW directory contained such files, and some of them happened to have the same name as your files, there would be a mix-up if C:\DW came first in the list. As unlikely as this contingency might seem, think of how long it would take you to find the problem if it did arise.

The second change to the batch file is that we now move to the parent of the data directories (D:\DW) before starting work.

Placing multiple data directories in your APPEND search path works fine in most cases, but you must be careful not to use the same file name in more than one directory. You must also test each particular program carefully to make sure that it is using the APPEND search path the way you intended. In particular, you should make sure that the program is placing newly created files in the correct directory.

The Best Way to Use the PATH Command

As I explained earlier, the PATH command tells DOS where to look for executable files that are not in your current directory. The best way to use this command is to place it in your AUTOEXEC.BAT file, where it will be executed every time you boot DOS. Moreover, you should only list directories that contain programs of a general nature—programs that you want available at your fingertips at all times.

In general, your path command should look like the example we saw earlier in this chapter:

```
PATH=C:\BATCH;C:\DOS;C:\NORTON;C:\UTILITY
```

The batch file directory, followed by the DOS directory, followed by your utility directories.

Some software manuals and installation programs suggest that you add a program directory to your search path so that you can execute the program from any directory. This is not the best idea. The best idea is the keep your search path short—containing only programs of general usefulness—and to start all of your applications programs from batch files.

Summary of How to Organize a Hard Disk

To tie it all together, here is a quick summary of what we covered in this chapter. When you actually start work on your own system, use the examples I have given you as prototypes.

The steps in organizing a hard disk are as follows:

- Choose one of the three strategies for organizing your tree structure.
- If you have chosen to use separate program and data disks, back up and then partition your disk accordingly.
- Create separate program directories for batch files, DOS, utilities, and any programs of general usefulness.
- Create a separate program directory for each software product you intend to use.
- Create separate data directories, at least one for each program.
- Install each product into its own directory.
- Place the appropriate PATH command in your AUTOEXEC.BAT file.
- Create a batch file for each program you will be using. Place these files in the batch files directory.

17

ADVANCED DISK COMMANDS

Introduction

In your everyday work with disks, especially hard disks and subdirectories, you'll probably need no more than the DOS commands you've encountered so far. I would guess that somewhere in the neighborhood of 80 to 90 percent of all your work with disks will involve four basic commands: FORMAT, COPY, DIR, and DELETE. With your hard disk, you'll expand your repertoire with the commands in the last chapter, particularly APPEND, MKDIR, CHDIR, RMDIR, and PATH.

But there's more to DOS, a lot more. So in this chapter, let's finish up our work with disks by covering some of DOS's advanced disk-management commands. We'll begin with a look at a way to check up on DOS.

Double-Checking Your Disk with VERIFY

When DOS is writing information to disk, it normally accepts the disk drive's report that all went well. This is generally okay because disk drives are quite reliable. If you wish, you can ask DOS to check, or *verify*, all data that is written to disk. This is controlled with the VERIFY command, which can set verification on or off. DOS normally does not verify. If you are concerned, you can set verification on, but it will add somewhat to the time it takes to use the disks.

Because our computers and their disk drives are so reliable, I personally don't recommend using the verify option, but I'm glad it's there for anyone who feels they need it. When most people first learn about the verification option, they assume that it's something more thorough than it really is. You'd be inclined to think that verifying the data that's been written to disk means reading it back and comparing it with the original—that's not what VERIFY does. VERIFY simply has the disk drive perform a routine that tests for recording errors. Every disk has a self-check mechanism built in that can detect lost bits. So, the verify operation checks that the data is recorded correctly (i.e., no lost bits). It doesn't actually check that the correct data is there. Verification isn't quite as thorough a test as you might think, but it is a reasonably good test for errors.

You can turn verification on and off at will with the VERIFY command. Turn it on like this,

```
VERIFY ON
```

and turn it off like this,

```
VERIFY OFF
```

If you want to find out the current VERIFY status, enter the command by itself:

```
VERIFY
```

Being able to turn it on and off like that can be handy, because you may not want to have verification in action all the time, but you might want to turn it on for some critical operations. By putting these VERIFY ON and OFF commands in a batch file, you can easily control when verification is done. DOS defaults to having verification off.

As an alternative, you can use a switch, /V (verify), with both the COPY and XCOPY commands. (XCOPY is explained later in this chapter.) With this switch, DOS verifies only for the duration of the command.

Masking Your Disks

DOS includes several commands that can help you fool a program into thinking that one drive or directory is a different drive or directory. While such pretenses may strike you as electronic sophistry, they are actually both necessary and realistic in certain circumstances, as you'll see.

Pretending One Drive Is Another

Some programs have to have things their way. This causes a very special problem that arises when we try to match old-fashioned programs with new computer concepts. Here is the problem: Many older programs for personal computers were written in the days when PCs just used small-capacity floppy disks for storage. In those days, the standard way of operating a PC was to have two diskette drives, A and B, and to use them in a certain way: the program disk in drive A, and the data disk in drive B.

Now, there is nothing wrong with that style of operating. Lots of today's computers have two diskette drives, A and B, used in the way I just described. The problem is that, these days, virtually all personal computers have a hard disk which is used as drive C. But some programs were written so that they could only work in one way: with the program disk in drive A, and the data disk in drive B (or whatever). This creates a problem when you try to adapt such programs to work a hard disk. The ASSIGN command is designed to help.

The ASSIGN Command

ASSIGN instructs DOS to reroute requests for one disk drive to another, essentially "pretending" that drive X is really drive Y. For example, if you assign both drives A and B to your hard disk drive C, then any program that insists on asking for drives A and B will have DOS, in a sneaky end-run maneuver, actually refer the requests to the hard drive C. That lets DOS outfox some single-minded programs, and helps you a lot.

To have all this happen, you issue the assign command in this form:

```
ASSIGN olddrive=newdrive
```

You can assign several drives at the same time if you want to. Thus, for example, if you want to assign drives A and B to your hard drive, C, the command is:

```
ASSIGN A=C B=C
```

When you want to undo the assignment, as you certainly will, so that program references to A and B go where they were originally intended, just issue the ASSIGN command with no parameters, like this:

```
ASSIGN
```

If you want to find out if any assignments are currently in effect, use the /STATUS option:

```
ASSIGN /STATUS
```

(Notice that /STATUS is one of the few DOS options that is not a single letter.)

Now, the reason—it's an important one—that you will want to un-assign drives is this: ASSIGN can be very dangerous, because it will redirect destructive operations as well as constructive ones. Commands like DEL *.* or FORMAT can be redirected by ASSIGN, so you could end up erasing data or reformatting a disk you didn't mean to.

To avoid this problem, I strongly recommend that you follow these guidelines when, and if, you use ASSIGN:

- Use it only when you really need it; don't use it routinely.
- Use ASSIGN only in batch files, and have those batch files automatically reset the assignments as soon as you're done with them.

Following these rules should avoid most problems with ASSIGN.

Pretending a Subdirectory Is a Disk Drive

We come next to a more sophisticated variation of the ASSIGN command. It's called SUBST (for Substitute), and it lets you make a subdirectory appear to be a separate drive. Why would you want to do this?

Well, first of all, some programs refuse to admit that subdirectories are the legitimate offspring of the root directory of a disk. They will not work with a subdirectory, and that can cause problems for you if you've got your hard disk neatly organized into a bunch of different subdirectories. The solution is the SUBST command.

Then, too, there's you. If you've divided and subdivided your directories to create a many-splendored tree, your pathnames can become long and somewhat unwieldy, and unless you're a good typist, they can become prone to typing errors. Again, the solution (other than pruning your tree) is the SUBST command.

In both cases, you can tell DOS to treat a subdirectory as if it were a disk drive. The basic form of this command is:

```
SUBST Drive: \Pathname
```

For example, if your word processor won't work with your subdirectory named LETTERS, which is on your hard disk C, you can type:

```
SUBST B: C:\LETTERS
```

and make it treat the subdirectory as if it were drive B.

Likewise, if you've created a directory system with a pathname like this:

```
C:\DATA\HARLEY\DW\LETTERS
```

you can type:

```
SUBST B: C:\DATA\HARLEY\DW\LETTERS
```

and make the drive letter B act as a shorthand substitute for this lengthy pathname.

When you're finished with a substitution, you can turn it off with the /D (delete) option. For example:

```
SUBST B: /D
```

If you want to see what substitutions are currently in effect, enter the command on a line by itself:

```
SUBST
```

and DOS will display something like this:

```
B: => C:\DATA\HARLEY\DW\LETTERS
```

Don't take the SUBST command as a license to build a towering tree of directories. It isn't, and you shouldn't treat it that way. Like ASSIGN, it's best used sparingly, and only when necessary—meaning with programs that cannot work with subdirectories. There are the same types of pitfalls here as there are with ASSIGN, and you're really much better off using SUBST as a way of making a closed-minded program work for you. And, again, it's best to use SUBST as part of a batch file that turns the command on at the beginning and turns it off at the end. That way, you guard yourself and your valuable data against the forgetfulness that afflicts us all at times.

Here is an important way that you might use SUBST. In Chapter 15, I discussed how you would organize a hard disk that would be shared by several people. I suggested that each person be given his own directory, under which all his data directories and files would be stored. Here is a tree structure like the ones we looked at:

```
\---DATA
  |---BURT
  |      \---DW
  |---ERIC
  |      \---DBASE
  |---HARLEY
  |      |---DBASE
  |      |---DW
  |      |     |---LETTERS
  |      |     |---MEMOS
  |      |     \---REPORTS
  |      \---EXCEL
  |            |---PAY
  |            \---RECEIVE
  |---KEVIN
  |      |---DBASE
  |      |     |---PROJECTS
  |      |     \---RESEARCH
  |      \---EXCEL
  |      |---PROJECTS
  |      \---RESEARCH
  |---KIM
  |      \---DW
  |---PETER
  |      |---DBASE
  |      \---EXCEL
  \---SCOTT
  \        ---DBASE
```

I also mentioned that you might want to make a batch file for each person, using his or her name—for example, HARLEY.BAT. You would tell your users to start work by entering their names. This would invoke their personal batch files.

The SUBST command is something that you would want to put in such a batch file. You would use it to give the user's sub-tree its own drive name. For example, consider the following batch file, HARLEY.BAT, that you might use to set things up for a user named Harley.

```
:* =================================================
:* HARLEY.BAT: batch file to set up DOS for HARLEY
      @echo off

:*  set E: to point to the user's part of the tree
      subst e: c:\data\HARLEY

:* change to the root directory on the user's disk
      e:
      cd \

:* tell the user that the system is ready
    echo Hello HARLEY. You can start work now.
:* =================================================
```

The SUBST command sets E: to point to the part of the tree that contains all the data Harley. This command allows Harley to act as if the entire disk E: belonged to him and him alone. The next command changes to this disk. The CD command is insurance: To make sure that when Harley starts work, he will be in the "root" directory of his personal disk (which is, in reality, C:\DATA\HARLEY).

Such an arrangement allows each user to deal exclusively with his or her part of the tree and to stay away from other people's data. For example, if Harley wanted to backup his data files, he need only copy all the files on drive E:.

The beauty of this scheme is that, since only one person at a time can use the computer, each person's "startup" file (such as HARLEY.BAT) can point the same E: disk to the appropriate part of the tree. Thus, you can tell each person that they own the E: disk.

In fact, you could write a batch file, called say SAVE.BAT, to backup the files on E:. Since E: points to the current user's part of the tree, no matter who is using the computer, the same batch file can be used by everybody.

Aside from the SUBST and related commands, you can personalize the startup batch file as much as you want. For example, say that a user named Kim uses only a word processor. At the end of the startup file KIM.BAT, you can place the command to start the word processor. All Sherry has to know is that to start work she just types her name. DOS will automatically set up her E: disk and start the word processor.

Pretending a Disk Is a Subdirectory

Aside from ASSIGN and SUBST, there is one more disk-based substitution that you can do: You can pretend that an entire disk is a subdirectory of another disk. For example, You might pretend that everything on the A: drive emanates from a subdirectory on the C: drive named \CLIENTS. This is the opposite of the idea behind SUBST, and the command you use is called JOIN. There's no really compelling reason to use JOIN, although it can be convenient, especially if you want to gather several diskettes together and work with them and a subdirectory in a unified way.

To use the JOIN command, type it in the form:

```
JOIN drive: drive:\pathname
```

If, for example, you have a data disk in drive A and you want access to that data while you're working with the files in a subdirectory called CLIENTS, you would type:

```
JOIN A: C:\CLIENTS
```

When you use a command that refers to "C:\CLIENTS", DOS will automatically go to the A: drive. If you refer to a subdirectory of CLIENTS, say "C:\CLIENTS\NEW", DOS will look for that subdirectory on the A: drive (in this case, A:\NEW).

Note: During the time that a disk is JOINed, it can only be referenced by its new name. Using the example above, you can only reference your diskette as C:\CLIENTS, not as A:.

When you're finished, you undo the marriage with the command:

```
JOIN A: /D
```

(The /d stand for "disconnect," or, if you prefer, divorce.)

If you want to see what JOINs are currently in effect, enter the command on a line by itself:

```
JOIN
```

and DOS will display something like this:

```
A: => C:\CLIENTS
```

Once again, my advice is not to use this command willy-nilly. It's a special-purpose command, best left to those situations when you really need it (for example, when you're using a disk that you cannot, or should not, copy to another drive). And, like ASSIGN and SUBST, use JOIN as part of a batch file that will automatically turn off the command when you're through.

Using ASSIGN, SUBST, and JOIN

I've emphasized several times the importance of not using ASSIGN, SUBST, and JOIN as everyday commands that you think will be handy shortcuts to a little bit of disk-swapping or extra typing. These operations are all a little screwy and potentially confusing. (It's easy to forget what you've assigned, joined, or substituted—and where.) In fact, the only really strong reason to use them at all is when a program can't work with subdirectories in which case you use SUBST. But the fact is, programs that can't handle subdirectories, are quite old-fashioned now and getting more and more obsolete, so there's less and less need to find your way around such problems.

Also, these operations are intended only for alternate ways of accessing data files. They are definitely not for hard-core disk operations such as formatting or deleting files. Such operations can have frustrating, if not disastrous, results when they're carried out with these "masquerade" commands in effect. ASSIGN, SUBST, and JOIN are useful, but as I mentioned, they should be used sparingly and with a full understanding of what they do. It's also very important not to leave them active when you're finished with them. As a safeguard, you should only use them in batch files that do three things: activate them, use them, and end by deactivating them. The only exception to this should be when you are using a SUBST command to refer to a particular user's part of the tree. (See the discussion earlier in this chapter.)

Special Kinds of Copying

We've learned how to copy files with the COPY command, and we've already learned about one special file-copying command, the SYS command that will transfer DOS's two special hidden files onto a system disk. Now it's time for us to learn about two more specialized file-copying commands, REPLACE and XCOPY.

The REPLACE Command

The REPLACE command is designed to help automate a problem that you'll encounter occasionally: updating copies of files when, for some reason, you are keeping more than one copy of the files on the same disk.

REPLACE performs this task of tracking down files with matching names and copying new versions on top of them. It also performs some related tasks whose use will be obvious as we explain them.

The command form for REPLACE is like this:

```
REPLACE source-files target-path
```

"Source-files" is the specification for the *new* files that you want to put into place; it's a *file* specification, since it says what you want to install. Often enough that'll be just *.* or A:*.* to bring over all the files from a new diskette. "Target-path" says where you want the files to go; it's a *path* specification, since it says where (not what) to make the replacement. Here is an example:

```
REPLACE A:*.* C:\
```

A simple replace command will just replace the files in one directory (the target-path), but we probably want REPLACE to track down files in whatever directory they are. To do this we use the /S (subdirectory) option that tells REPLACE to hunt in all subdirectories of the path we specified. Our example probably should be like this, with the option added:

```
REPLACE A:*.* C:\ /S
```

Sometimes we may not want to actually replace any files we have: We may just want to bring in new ones we don't already have copies of. For that, REPLACE has a /A (add) option. With /A, REPLACE will copy over only those files that are completely new to the target directory. The /U (update) option replaces only those files that are older than the corresponding target files. The /A option, by the way, can't be used with the /S or /U option.

There are also some other handy switches for the REPLACE command. /P, the (permission) switch, pauses for Yes/No confirmation before copying any file. There is also a /R switch to allow replacing read-only files. Finally, the /W (wait) switch pauses before beginning to search for source files, so you can use REPLACE with a single disk drive (and two disks) if you wish to.

That's the story on REPLACE. Now we're ready for another fancy variation on copying, one that is even more powerful.

XCOPY

XCOPY, like REPLACE, is another "power copier." But what distinguishes it? Before we plunge into the details of the command, we need to know the concept behind it—so we can easily understand it's features. While REPLACE is a power copier that's oriented toward *updating*, XCOPY is oriented toward the backup and transfer of files. If you keep that in mind, then the features of XCOPY will make sense to you. (By the way, I guess we're supposed to pronounce XCOPY as "Cross Copy." At least, that helps us understand what it's about as a useful command.)

XCOPY will copy groups of files including (and here's the key part) a whole tree structure of files. Note that while REPLACE will track down multiple copies of the same file name in a *target* tree (and replace all the copies), the *source* of REPLACE's files is a single directory (typically, a disk that is being used to update a hard disk). But with XCOPY, the *source* of copying can be all the files in a directory tree and XCOPY will duplicate that directory tree on the target disk.

The basic form for XCOPY is this:

```
XCOPY source target
```

where the source and target specifications can be either file specifications indicating which files we want to cross copy or directory path specifications indicating all the files in the source directory and corresponding filenames in the target directory. All the various rules for the copy command (wildcard file names, target names different than source names, etc.) also apply here, as you might expect.

XCOPY is interesting, not its simplest basic form, but in what its options can do for us. Let's take a look at them.

Option XCOPY

The key option—the most important one—is the /S (subdirectory) option that tells XCOPY to perform its copying magic on any subdirectories under the source directory. XCOPY will make sure that there are corresponding subdirectories on the target—using them if they exist, creating them if they don't.

Note that while XCOPY will duplicate a subdirectory structure for us, the tree structure above where we're cross copying doesn't have to be the same. For example, our source could be all the directories under a directory called \ACCOUNTS\CURRENT while our target might be something called \DATA\LASTMNTH. This example should suggest one of the most important reasons for using XCOPY: It can be easily used to do things like preserving a copy of data that will be changing.

There's a supplement to the /S option that deals with the problem of empty directories. If we use XCOPY with just the /S option, it will copy only where there are files; thus it won't create any empty directories on the target area. But if we need to have an exact duplicate of our source (including empty directories, which are ready to accept files) XCOPY can do that for us, too, if we give it the /E (Empty) option. This feature—of creating copies of empty directories—can be an important one because we may be copying the data of programs that will create files in those directories and expect the directories to be here, empty or not.

Other switches for the XCOPY command echo things we've already seen with other commands. Like the BACKUP command, XCOPY can use an /M option, which copies only files that have been modified (this is noted by the file's archive attribute being set). As it is with the BACKUP command, if we use the /M option, XCOPY will reset the archive bits that it acts on. On the other hand, if we use the /A (archive) option, XCOPY will copy the same, but won't reset any archive bits, so that the fact that these files have been changed is still recorded. Likewise, the /D (date) option will only copy files dated on or after a given date.

As with the REPLACE command, there are /P (permission) and /W (wait) option to give you more control over the progress of the cross-copying. And finally, as with the COPY command, there is a /V (verify) option, in which the copies are verify checked to see if they are recorded correctly.

It might appear to you that the XCOPY command is a lot like the BACKUP command, but there are several key differences. Both commands can be used to make archival backup copies of our files, but the BACKUP command is entirely oriented to archiving. The copy it makes can't be directly used but must be copied back with the RESTORE command. Furthermore, BACKUP doesn't re-create the source's directory structure (that's done when the backed-up files are restored). But XCOPY does give us an exact copy of the files, unmodified, and it also duplicates the directory structure that the files reside in. You'd use BACKUP to make a purely archival copy—particularly one that has to fit onto smaller media, say from a big hard disk onto little diskettes. You'd use XCOPY to make a full working copy of files in the context of their directories.

Actually, XCOPY is a lot more like COPY than like BACKUP. In fact, some people like to think of the name XCOPY as standing for "extended copy."

Setting File Attributes with the ATTRIB Command

In Chapter 13, we saw how the BACKUP command could copy only those files that needed archiving by using the /M option. Earlier in this chapter, we saw that XCOPY had a similar capability, also with a /M option. Both of these commands check the archive attribute of a file to see if it should be copied. This attribute is turned on automatically whenever you change or create a file and turned off when BACKUP or XCOPY copies the file.

However, our discussions about attributes have yet to cover one important topic: Is there a way to set an attribute exactly the way you want it, whenever you want? The answer is yes, by using the ATTRIB command.

The basic form of this command is:

```
ATTRIB setting filename
```

To turn on an attribute, use a plus sign (+) followed by a single letter R, A, S or H, and specify the file you want to affect. The meanings are as follows:

```
+R   make the file read-only
+A   mark the file as needing archiving
+S   make the file a system file
+H   make the file hidden
```

For example, let's say that you have a very important file, DATA.NEW, and you want to make sure that you do not accidentally change or erase it. You can make the file read-only by using:

```
ATTRIB +R DATA.NEW
```

One important thing you should know about ATTRIB is that it was enhanced for DOS 5.0. If you are using an older version of DOS, you will only be able to set the read-only and archive attributes (R, A). With DOS 5.0 or later, you can set all the attributes.

Like many other commands, ATTRIB will recognize wildcards. For instance, to turn on the archive attribute for all the files in the \DOCUMENT subdirectory, use:

```
ATTRIB +A \DOCUMENT\*.*
```

If you do not specify a file name, ATTRIB will act on all the files in the current directory. For example, to make all the files in the current directory read-only, you can use either of the following two commands:

```
ATTRIB +R
ATTRIB +R *.*
```

If you want to turn off a particular attribute, just use a minus sign instead of a plus sign. For example, you decide to delete the file DATA.NEW but you cannot because it is read-only. To turn off the read-only attribute, use:

```
ATTRIB -R DATA.NEW
```

You can now delete the file.

Here is another example. Out of a large directory of files, you want to set all of the files to be read-only except those that have the extension TXT. First, make all the files in the directory read-only:

```
ATTRIB +R *.*
```

Next, make all the files with the extension TXT not read-only:

```
ATTRIB -R *.TXT
```

For those cases in which you want to set attributes for an entire section of the directory tree, you can use the /S (subdirectory) option. This tells ATTRIB to process all subdirectories. For example, to set all the batch files on your hard disk to be read-only, use:

```
ATTRIB +R C:\*.BAT /S
```

Another use for the /S option would be if you wanted to copy selected files, here and there, from your hard disk to a diskette. One way to do it is to start by turning the archive attribute off for all the files on the hard disk:

```
ATTRIB -A C:\*.* /S
```

Next, turn on the archive attribute for the files which you want to copy:

```
ATTRIB +A C:\DOCUMENT\MASTER.DOC
ATTRIB +A C:\ACCOUNTS\OLD.DAT
ATTRIB +A C:\MONEY\INCOMING\FRED.91
```

Finally, use XCOPY /M to copy only those files whose archive attribute is turned on:

```
XCOPY C:\*.* A: /S /M
```

If it happens that you want to make more than one copy of the files, say to send a disk to each of five people, you can use XCOPY with the /A option. This will copy the same files as /M but will not turn off the archive attribute when it is finished. Thus, you could enter the following command:

```
XCOPY C:\*.* A: /S /A
```

five times in a row (changing the disk each time) to copy the same files, over and over.

If, at any time, you want to check the attributes of a file, use the ATTRIB command with just a file name. For example, say that you have a file named MYFILE.DOC within the \DOCUMENT subdirectory. Your current directory is \DOCUMENT. To check the attributes of MYFILE.DOC, use:

```
ATTRIB MYFILE.DOC
```

DOS will display the file name, preceded by a single letter for each attribute that is turned on. For example, if the file has its archive attribute turned on, you will see:

```
A         C:\DOCUMENT\MYFILE.DOC
```

If, in addition, the file is read-only, you will see:

```
A  R      C:\DOCUMENT\MYFILE.DOC
```

If all the attributes are off, all you will see is the file name:

```
          C:\DOCUMENT\MYFILE.DOC
```

If you enter the ATTRIB command without the name of a file:

```
ATTRIB
```

DOS will show you attribute information for all the files in the current directory, the same as if you had entered:

```
ATTRIB *.*
```

Using ATTRIB to Search for Files

Aside from showing and changing attributes, ATTRIB has an important use that is not generally appreciated. You can use ATTRIB to find out where a file is on a disk; or, you can search a disk for files that match a particular pattern.

The trick is to specify the root directory as a starting place and to use the /S option. For example, to search your entire hard disk for a file called MYFILE.DOC use:

```
ATTRIB C:\MYFILE.DOC /S
```

To search for all of your batch files, use:

```
ATTRIB C:\*.BAT /S
```

With DOS 5.0 or later, ATTRIB can search for all files, even those that are marked as being hidden or system. If you have an older version of DOS, ATTRIB will not display the names of hidden or system files. In fact, unless you have DOS 5.0 or later, there is no way to hide or unhide a file unless you have a special program like the one that comes with the Norton Utilities.

So, now that we have looked at the advanced disk commands— VERIFY, ASSIGN, SUBST, JOIN, REPLACE, XCOPY, and ATTRIB—let's move on to another very important topic: DOS's built-in system to recover lost data.

18

THE DOS DATA
SECURITY SYSTEM

Introduction

It's all too easy to make a mistake and, in an instant, lose important data. You can format the wrong disk, or delete the wrong file and, all of a sudden, hours of work have disappeared.

Of course, the best strategy is to make regular backups (see Chapter 14). However, there are times when you need more than a backup. Starting with DOS 5.0, there are some new commands that can help you prepare for and recover from a data disaster.

DOS's Data Security System

DOS has a data security system that consists of three commands: UNFORMAT, UNDELETE, and MIRROR. As the names suggest, the first two commands will "unformat" a disk and "undelete" a file. This means that if you accidentally format or delete, it may be possible to get back your data. The MIRROR command creates an "image" of certain parts of the disk that can be used to assist subsequent UNFORMAT and UNDELETE commands.

The three data security commands were introduced with DOS 5.0. Unfortunately, if you have an older version of DOS there is no good way to recover lost data using DOS commands. In that case, you can use a special package (like the *Norton Utilities* which have significantly more-sophisticated capabilities).

What Happens When You Format a Disk?

Before we can discuss the DOS data security system, we need to know a little about what happens when you format a disk. Generally speaking, there are six functions that can be performed as part of a formatting process:

1. **Create a new boot record.** As we mentioned in Chapter 3, the boot record is a small program that is used to start DOS. Every disk has a boot record.

2. **Remove data by creating a new FAT (file allocation table).** The FAT is used to keep track of data storage. DOS uses the FAT to remember which space is in use and which space is available. Creating a new, empty FAT effectively erases all the data on the disk.

3. **Create a new root directory.** As you know, this is the main directory of the disk.

4. **Check the entire disk for bad spots.** If there are any bad areas on the disk, DOS will mark them and they will not be used.

5. **Destroy the data that was on the disk.** For extra security, it is possible to physically eliminate all previous data by overwriting it with new, meaningless data.

6. **Save the old boot record, FAT and root directory.** By saving the old system information to a hidden place on the disk, it is possible to unformat the disk, should this become necessary. Of course, you can only unformat a disk if it has not been reused and if the data was not destroyed by the formatting process.

Generally speaking, there are three reasons to FORMAT a disk:

*   To prepare a disk to be used for the first time.
*   To reformat a disk (usually a diskette) to use it again.
*   To wipe out all the data on a disk.

As you will see in a moment, there are certain options that you can use with the FORMAT command in order to choose the type of format that best suits the situation. If you choose a format that does not destroy the old data, it is possible, in principle, to unformat the disk, as long as you have not reused the disk for new data.

The Old and New FORMAT Commands

In the last section, we explained how the formatting process can involve up to six functions:

1. Create a new boot record
2. Remove data by creating a new FAT (file allocation table)
3. Create a new root directory
4. Check the entire disk for bad spots
5. Destroy the data that was on the disk
6. Save the old boot record, FAT and root directory

Before DOS 5.0, the FORMAT command was straightforward. With a diskette, FORMAT performed steps 1, 2, 3, 4, and 5. With a hard disk,

FORMAT skipped step 5 (destroying the old data), largely because it was just too time-consuming.

Starting with DOS 5.0, the picture became more complicated. First of all, FORMAT was enhanced to make it easier to recover from an accidental format. By default, FORMAT will now save the system information (step 6) in a hidden place on the disk.

In addition, FORMAT now has two new options, /Q (quick) and /U (unconditional). This gives us four ways to format:

```
FORMAT
FORMAT /Q
FORMAT /U
FORMAT /Q /U
```

Let's take a moment and see how each of these commands works. As we do, please remember that we are talking about DOS 5.0 or later, not the earlier versions of DOS.

The plain vanilla FORMAT command, does not use the /Q or /U options. For example:

```
FORMAT A:
```

This command performs the following steps:

1. Create a new boot record
2. Remove data by creating a new FAT (file allocation table)
3. Create a new root directory
4. Check the entire disk for bad spots
6. Save the old boot record, FAT and root directory

In other words, with no options, FORMAT does everything except destroy all the data. This type of format is sometimes called a *complete* format.

The second form of the format command uses the /Q option. For example:

```
FORMAT A: /Q
```

With /Q, DOS will neither check the disk for bad spots nor destroy the old data. In other words, FORMAT /Q will:

1. Create a new boot record
2. Remove data by creating a new FAT (file allocation table)

3 . Create a new root directory

6 . Save the old boot record, FAT and root directory

By leaving out the disk check (step 4), FORMAT can process a disk much faster than usual. This is called a *quick* format.

The next form of FORMAT uses the /U option. For example:

```
FORMAT A: /U
```

The /U option tells DOS to do whatever it can to make sure that your old data can never be recovered. This means destroying the old data and not saving a copy of the system information. That is, FORMAT /U does the following:

1. Create a new boot record
2. Remove data by creating a new FAT (file allocation table)
3. Create a new root directory
4. Check the entire disk for bad spots
5. Destroy the data that was on the disk

This type of format is called an *unconditional* format because there is no way to ever recover the old data. If you are ever formatting a disk and you get a read or write error, try formatting with the /U option before you give up.

Finally, we have the combination of /Q and /U. For example:

```
FORMAT A: /Q /U
```

You might think that this would combine the actions of /Q and /U. Actually, it doesn't. What it does is to provide a quick type of unconditional format, while performing only the minimum number of steps:

1. Create a new boot record
2. Remove data by creating a new FAT (file allocation table)
3. Create a new root directory

Thus, FORMAT /Q /U, is the fastest possible format, faster even than the quick format. We might call this the *quick unconditional* format.

FORMAT /Q /U is a pretty safe way to format a disk when you want to get rid of the data. True, it doesn't actually destroy the data, but it doesn't save the system information, either. It is possible to recover the data, but not with the UNFORMAT command. You would need a special utility program like those that are part of the *Norton Utilities.*

As we mentioned, formatting before DOS 5.0 was simple because you had no choices. Starting with DOS 5.0, you have four types of format from which to choose. To help you, Table 18-1 shows each type for format, the FORMAT command, and when to use it.

Table 18.1 *Using FORMAT With DOS 5.0 or Later*

Type of Format	Command	When to Use
Complete	FORMAT	To format a disk for the first time.
Quick	FORMAT /Q	To quickly reformat a disk that you want to use again.
Unconditional	FORMAT /U	To destroy all the old data on a disk or to format a disk that is giving read or write errors.
Quick Unconditional	FORMAT /Q /U	To very quickly reformat a disk when you are sure that you will never again need the old data.

To summarize all of this into a simple rule of thumb: Use FORMAT with no options to prepare new disks, and FORMAT /Q to reformat old disks.

What Happens When You Erase a File?

Strangely enough, when you erase a file DOS does not destroy the data. Here is what actually happens.

In order to erase a file DOS does two things. First, it changes the FAT (file allocation table) to show that all the space taken up by the file is available to be reused. Second, DOS removes the directory entry that points to the file.

In order to remove the directory entry for a particular file, DOS changes the first letter of the filename to a special character that marks the file as being officially "erased." The character that DOS uses has the value 229 (hexadecimal E5) in the ASCII code. As it happens, this character represents the symbol σ (the lower case Greek letter sigma).

Whenever DOS sees an σ at the beginning of a filename, it knows that the file has been erased.

For example, say that you have just erased a file called DATA.TXT. If you could look into your disk you would find two things. Within the FAT, the space that used to be taken up by DATA.TXT has been marked as being available. And within the directory that contained DATA.TXT, the name has been changed to σATA.TXT.

Thus, in principle, it is possible to unerase a file. To unerase the file in our example, you would have to do two things. First, change the FAT so that, once again, the original space used by DATA.TXT would be marked as being in use. Second, modify the directory, changing the name σATA.TXT back to DATA.TXT.

The actual details can be complex, especially if the file is stored in pieces across the disk. However, for us, the important thing to realize is that unerasing a file is possible if—and this is a big if—the space has not yet been reused for another file.

Preparing the DOS Security System— The MIRROR Command

DOS has two commands to restore lost data, UNFORMAT and UNDELETE. However, in order for these commands to do as good a job as possible, you must prepare by using the MIRROR command.

There are three forms of the MIRROR command. The first protects against an accidental format. All you do is type the command along with the name of the disk you want to protect. For example:

```
MIRROR C:
```

If you want to protect more than one disk, use more than one MIRROR command:

```
MIRROR C:
MIRROR D:
```

The effect of the MIRROR command is to save the information you would need to unformat the disk—the boot record, the FAT and the root directory—in a file named MIRROR.FIL. This file is stored in the root directory of the disk you are protecting. If you accidentally format your disk, you can use the UNFORMAT command to search for MIRROR.FIL and restore things—hopefully pretty close to the way they were.

If you execute MIRROR a second time, it copies the previous contents of MIRROR.FIL to another file called MIRROR.BAK. This way, you have an extra copy of the system information, just in case something goes wrong with MIRROR.FIL.

Of course, unformatting a disk can be only as accurate as the information that was saved. For this reason, you should use the MIRROR command regularly. It won't do you much good if you accidentally format your hard disk and you haven't saved the system information for six months. The best idea is to put a MIRROR command in your AUTOEXEC.BAT file. That way, each time you start DOS, MIRROR will automatically save the data that is necessary to protect your disk.

Using MIRROR to Keep Track of Deleted Files

Besides saving information for UNFORMAT, the MIRROR command has a second form that saves information for UNDELETE. This makes it easier to unerase files.

This form of the MIRROR command sets up a system called *delete tracking*. To use MIRROR in this way, specify the /T option, followed by the letter of the drive whose files you wish to protect. For example, to set up delete tracking for the hard disk C:, use:

```
MIRROR /TC
```

Notice that you do not put a colon after the "C".

When you use MIRROR /T, it initializes a small memory resident program that monitors your activities. Whenever you or one of your programs erases a file, the delete tracking system stores its location and name in a special file called PCTRACKR.DEL. If you ever need to unerase a file, UNDELETE will look for the PCTRACKR.DEL file. If it is present, UNDELETE will have a much better chance of recovering your lost data. Otherwise, UNDELETE will do the best job it can, but the results may be imperfect.

If you want to start delete tracking for more than one disk, you use /T more than once within a single command:

```
MIRROR /TC /TD
```

You cannot use more than one MIRROR /T command because a memory resident program cannot be initialized more than once.

The best idea is to place the MIRROR /T command in your AUTOEXEC.BAT file, along with your other MIRROR commands. In the next section, we will see an example of just such an AUTOEXEC.BAT.

Starting the DOS Data Security System From Your AUTOEXEC.BAT File

We mentioned that the UNFORMAT and UNDELETE commands work best when you have prepared the system by issuing the appropriate MIRROR commands. The best place to do this is within your AUTOEXEC.BAT file. Here is the AUTOEXEC.BAT file like one that we looked at in Chapter 12, to which we have added two MIRROR commands: one to save format recovery data, and one to start delete tracking.

```
:* ==============================================
:* AUTOEXEC.BAT: AUGUST 5, 1991
   @echo off

:* set the environment variables
   set comspec=c:\dos\command.com
   path=c:\batch;c:\dos;c:\norton;c:\utility
   prompt $p$g

:* save format recovery information
   mirror c:

:* start delete tracking
   mirror /tc

:* initialize memory resident programs
   c:\dos\doskey
   c:\dos\fastopen c:
   c:\dos\graphics

:* start the DOS Shell
   c:\dos\dosshell
:* ==============================================
```

Using UNFORMAT to Recover a Disk

Hopefully, you will never have to use the UNFORMAT command. However, if you do, it can be a godsend, recovering data that would otherwise be gone for good.

UNFORMAT will attempt to undo the work of a previous FORMAT command. Generally speaking, UNFORMAT will be successful as long as you did not use an unconditional format (FORMAT /U or

FORMAT Q/U). However, you will lower your chances of a successful recovery if you have used the disk to store any new data. So, if you ever find you have accidentally formatted a disk, stop whatever you are doing and run UNFORMAT immediately.

The UNFORMAT command is straightforward. Usually, all you need to do is specify the name of the disk you want to unformat:

```
UNFORMAT A:
```

Read the messages carefully and answer any questions that UNFORMAT asks.

When UNFORMAT refers to a MIRROR file it means the recovery information that was previously saved, either by a MIRROR command or by a FORMAT command.

When UNFORMAT refers to the SYSTEM area, it means the boot record, FAT and root directory. So, when you are asked if you want to update the system area of your drive, you should say yes.

Aside from the basic form of the UNFORMAT command, there are a number of options that you can use.

If you want to verify that a disk has been protected by MIRROR, you can use the /J option. For example:

```
UNFORMAT C: /J
```

No unformatting will take place. Instead, DOS will verify that the MIRROR file agrees with the system information on the disk. If it does, you are safe.

Whenever you use UNFORMAT to recover a disk, the first thing DOS will do is check to see if there is a MIRROR file. If so, DOS will use it and your chances of success are good. If there is no mirror file, which is often the case with a diskette, DOS will then check for special hidden information that may have been left by the FORMAT program. If DOS can find such information, there is still a good chance that your disk can be recovered.

However, if there is no MIRROR file and no hidden information, your chances of a total recovery are decreased. UNFORMAT will proceed, doing the best it can, but it may need to ask you some questions if it finds files that are fragmented and it can't decide what to do on its own.

If you find yourself in the position of having to unformat an unprotected disk, there are three options that you can use that may be of some help. First, the /TEST option will show you how DOS would rebuild your disk but will not actually do any unformatting. Second, when you do unformat, the /L option will list each file that is recovered, not just those for which DOS requires your help. Finally, the /P option will direct all the output to a printer so you can have a permanent record of the recovery process.

Note: You cannot use/P with the /J option.

If you use /TEST, /L, or /P, DOS will assume that you do not want to use a MIRROR file. Thus, if you do have such a file, do not use these options.

If you would like to practice unformatting, use a spare diskette that has some files on it and format it by using:

```
FORMAT A: /Q
```

When the formatting is complete, you can unformat by using:

```
UNFORMAT A:
```

Be careful not to practice on your hard disk!

Using UNDELETE to Unerase a File

To unerase a file, use the UNDELETE command, followed by the name of the file you want to recover. For example:

```
UNDELETE MYFILE.DOC
```

You will see a number of messages, explaining the status of the deleted file. When you see the word "clusters," it refers to the units in which DOS allocates space on the disk.

If it is possible to unerase the file, DOS will ask your permission. You should answer yes.

Most of the time, unerasing is straightforward. Other than specifying the name of a single file, you can specify a collection of files:

```
UNDELETE *.*
UNDELETE *.BAT
```

DOS will try to unerase all the files that match the pattern. If you specify the name of a directory:

```
UNDELETE \DOCUMENT
```

DOS will try to unerase all the deleted files in that directory. If you use UNDELETE without a file name:

```
UNDELETE
```

DOS will try to unerase all the deleted files in the current directory.
If you want to check what files can be unerased without actually commit-ting yourself, use the /LIST option.

```
UNDELETE /LIST
```

If you are interested in a particular file or pattern of files, you can specify the name:

```
UNDELETE MYFILE.DOC /LIST
UNDELETE *.BAT /LIST
```

As we explained earlier, UNDELETE works best if you are using the delete tracking system (MIRROR /T). If you aren't, UNDELETE will do the best it can by checking the directory for the names of files that have been erased. As you can imagine, this method is not as reliable as delete tracking. Also, if a file can be unerased, DOS will have replaced the first letter of the filename. UNDELETE will need you to fill in that character.

UNDELETE has three options that you can use. /DT forces DOS to use only delete tracking. /DOS ignores delete tracking and processes only those files that DOS has marked as being deleted.

Finally, /ALL will first try delete tracking, then try to look in the direc-tory. If erased files are found in the directory, /ALL will not prompt you for the first character of the filenames. Rather, it will recover the files automatically, filling in the first character with #. If this would create two files with the same name, /ALL will select another character.

Unerasing a file is one of the most important services that DOS pro-vides. However, UNDELETE has a number of significant limitations: It cannot unerase a file once the space has been used by another file. It cannot unerase a directory. And, it cannot unerase a file if its directory has been removed.

UNDELETE is handy but it cannot save you from every type of unex-pected loss. The only thing you can really depend on is a good system of regular backups.

Using MIRROR to Save a Copy of Your Partition Table

In Chapter 4, we explained that every hard disk must be partitioned before it can be formatted. Each hard disk can have up to four partitions. The information that describes the partitions is kept in a partition table at the beginning of the disk.

Most people choose to make one large partition, which they format into a single drive C:. However, there are two cases in which you would need more than one partition.

First, you may choose to divide your hard disk into two drives, C: and D:. In Chapter 16, we explained how you can use such a scheme to segregate your programs from your data.

Second, you may want to install more than one operating system on your computer, say both DOS and Unix. If so, each operating system may require its own partition.

If something goes wrong with your disk you can always restore the data using a backup. However, before you can use a backup you need to format the disk, and before you format the disk you need to partition it. If you have multiple partitions, it can be a problem to restore them to their original form. For this reason, DOS provides a way for you to make a copy of your partition table. You use the MIRROR command with the /PARTN option.

All you do is enter:

```
MIRROR /PARTN
```

DOS will ask you to insert a formatted diskette into drive A:. Then, DOS will copy the partition table from your hard disk onto the diskette. The information will be stored in a file named PARTNSAV.FIL.

If you ever need to restore the partition table, use UNFORMAT, also with the /PARTN option:

```
UNFORMAT /PARTN
```

DOS will ask you to insert the diskette that contains the partition table file. The partitions will then be restored.

You might ask, why does MIRROR insist on saving the partition table to a diskette? The reason is that if you ever get to the point where you need to restore such information, your hard disk will be inoperable. The information will have to come from a diskette.

254 *Peter Norton's DOS 5.0 Guide, Fourth Edition*

The Importance of Being Able to Start DOS From a Diskette

One of the most important things that you can do to protect yourself from disaster is to make a boot diskette—a diskette from which you can start DOS.

Most of the time you will start DOS from your hard disk. However, if something goes wrong with your hard disk, you will be locked out. In such cases, you will need to be able to start from a diskette.

Here is a common scenario. You are customizing your system by changing the CONFIG.SYS file (which we will discuss in Chapter 28) and you accidentally put in an incorrect command. Under certain circumstances, this will stop DOS in its tracks and you will not be able to boot from the hard disk.

What to do? You take control by starting from your boot diskette. Now you can fix the CONFIG.SYS file and restart from the hard disk. If it wasn't for the boot diskette, you would be in big trouble.

Here is another case. You are in the middle of working and all of a sudden you see the message:

```
INVALID DRIVE SPECIFICATION
```

You try everything you can think of, but it seems as if your hard disk has vanished into thin air. What has happened is that your partition table has become corrupted.

You start DOS from a diskette and then use UNFORMAT /PARTN to restore the partition table. You can then use UNFORMAT C: to restore the C: disk. If you hadn't saved the partition table you might have ended up losing all your data; at the very least, you would have lost a lot of time. But without a boot diskette, you would have never been able to take control of the computer in order to restore the partition table.

Making a Boot Diskette

There is no doubt that having a boot diskette can be a lifesaver. The question is, how do you make one?

There are two ways. First, you can run the DOS installation program and specify that you want to install DOS to a diskette. Just follow the instructions. When you are finished, you will have DOS installed on a set of diskettes that you can keep in a safe place. (DOS is too big to fit on one diskette.) The first diskette in the set is the one from which you can boot.

The second way is to make your own custom boot diskette. Start off by formatting a diskette using:

```
FORMAT A: /S /V:BOOTDISK
```

The /S option will copy the main part of DOS to the diskette and make it bootable. /V will set the volume label.

Next, copy your AUTOEXEC.BAT and CONFIG.SYS files to the diskette:

```
COPY C:\AUTOEXEC.BAT A:\
COPY C:\CONFIG.SYS A:\
```

Now, make a \DOS directory on the diskette:

```
MD A:\DOS
```

From the DOS directory on your hard disk, copy the DOS command files into this directory.

Unfortunately, unless you have a 2.8 MB diskette, you will not be able to fit all of the DOS files onto a single diskette. However, you will be able to get a lot of them. Use the XCOPY command with the /P (permission) option. DOS will display the name of each file and ask you if you want it copied.

```
XCOPY C:\DOS\*.* A:\DOS /P
```

Copy the files that are most important to you. At the very least, be sure to get the following commands:

ATTRIB	EDIT	MIRROR	SYS
BACKUP	FDISK	MODE	TREE
CHKDSK	FORMAT	MORE	UNDELETE
DISKCOPY	HELP	PRINT	UNFORMAT
DOSKEY	LABEL	RESTORE	XCOPY

as well as the two HELP files:

```
DOSHELP.HLP, EDIT.HLP
```

Once you have copied DOS, you might want to create one or more directories to hold some of your favorite batch files and utility programs. For example, you might make an A:\BATCH directory to hold batch files and an A:\NORTON directory to hold the Norton Utilities. Remember, what you are doing is making a toolbox to use in times of trouble.

The next step is to edit the AUTOEXEC.BAT and CONFIG.SYS files to make sure they work properly with a diskette. Be sure to change all the references of C: into A:. For instance, within your AUTOEXEC.BAT file, your search path should point only to A:

```
PATH=A:\BATCH;A:\DOS;A:\NORTON
```

Similarly, path references within the CONFIG.SYS file should point to the A: diskette.

Now, test your diskette by making sure that you can start from it. Do not assume the diskette will work just because everything looks correct.

You will find that a well tested, customized boot diskette can be used for more than disaster recovery. For instance, if you need to use someone else's computer for awhile, you can start DOS from your own diskette. Your working environment will be set up just the way you like, including all of your favorite tools. Seasoned consultants carry a copy of their boot diskette wherever they go.

Once you have a foolproof boot diskette, use the DISKCOPY command to make a copy. It will be the cheapest insurance you will ever buy.

Protecting Your Data—A Checklist of What to Do

To end this chapter, here is a checklist of what you can do to protect yourself against loss of data. We strongly recommend that you make a practice of carrying out each of these safeguards.

- **Make regular backups.** Keep one set of backup diskettes offsite, away from your computer. If your computer site is damaged and you have a safe set of backup disks, you will be back in business with a minimum of fuss.

- **Prepare for unformatting.** In your AUTOEXEC.BAT file, use a MIRROR command to prepare each of your hard disks for unformatting.

- **Prepare for unerasing.** In your AUTOEXEC.BAT file, use a MIRROR /T command to initialize delete tracking.

- **Create a boot diskette.** Don't forget to test it. Once it is tested, make a copy.

- **Save your partition table**. Use the MIRROR /PARTN command to save your partition table to a diskette. Make two copies. Keep one offsite with your extra backup set.

Losing data is no fun, as any experienced computer user will tell you. However, by planning ahead, you can minimize any loss that you might suffer. Follow these five steps and you will be able to recover completely from almost any data disaster.

19

PIPELINE TRICKS

Introduction

In this chapter you're going to learn about a pair of interesting facilities in DOS known as *redirection* and *pipes*. These two features are interrelated and allow you to do some quite useful and fascinating stunts, as you'll see. Besides, they're fun.

Introducing Redirection

The idea of redirection is one of the most interesting parts of DOS, and basically what it does is enable you to act like a railroad engineer, switching trains from one track to another. Let's start at the beginning.

First, it's easy to see that DOS directs information to certain predictable places. Leaving disk commands and whatnot aside, think of what happens when you type a DOS command. Suppose you type the command DIR. DOS takes your keystrokes and mulls over them somewhere inside your computer. But, when it carries out your DIR command, it automatically directs the results of that command to the screen. It's like a train going from station A to station B, with no switches in between. In DOS's terminology, the information moves from one of its standard input devices (here, the keyboard) to one of its standard output devices (the screen).

Suppose you didn't want to see the directory listing; you wanted to print it instead. Could you do it? Sure, by telling DOS to shunt that listing off to your printer, instead of the screen. In effect, you move your train to a different track, so that it goes somewhere else. That's the idea of redirection: Send my information someplace other than its usual destination. And, given DOS's usual linguistic economy, you redirect your information with either of two small symbols: >, meaning send data from here to there, and <, meaning send it from there to here.

The redirection symbols are used like this: If we want to change a program's routine output (which would normally appear on the screen) so that instead of going to the screen, it goes into a file (which we'll name OUTFILE), we'd do it like this:

```
PROG >OUTFILE
```

On the other hand, if we wanted to change a program's input, so that instead of coming from the keyboard it comes from a file (for example, INFILE), we'd do that like this:

```
PROG <INFILE
```

And, as you might expect, we can do both at the same time:

```
PROG <INFILE >OUTFILE
```

Before you get too excited about the prospects of using a command like this, it's important for you to know that it only works for a limited variety of information. We can only redirect a program's output when its very garden-variety line-by-line output that would normally appear on the screen. This means that we can't redirect file data (that's not screen output) and we can't redirect, say, the screen display for a spreadsheet program (that's not garden-variety line-by-line output). Likewise, for input we can only redirect input that would be coming from the keyboard and used by the program in a standard way. In short, only certain kinds of very plain input and output can be redirected, and then only if the program that's working with them is designed to allow DOS to do this redirection. You can't necessarily tell in advance when redirection will work for you—when you want to do it, you have to experiment with the programs you want to use it on to see if it will work or not.

When a program writes its output in such a way that it can be redirected, we say that it writes to *standard output.* Similarly, a program that accepts input from the keyboard in the usual way is reading from *standard input.* Thus, we might talk about redirecting the standard output of some program to the printer (to print the output), or redirecting the standard input of some program to a file (to read commands from a file).

Redirection is a powerful tool but remember, you can use it only with programs that read and write to standard input/output. Fortunately, just about all of the DOS commands fall into this category.

For example, I mentioned that you can send a directory listing to your printer instead of to the screen. The command is simple:

```
DIR>PRN:
```

(PRN: is DOS's name for your printer.) The result is that nothing appears on your screen, but your printer immediately begins spewing out the directory listing you requested. However, before you enter this command, make sure that your printer is connected and ready. If it isn't, DOS will stop and wait for it.

You can also send a directory to a disk file with the command:

```
DIR > FILENAME
```

Getting Rid of Output

DOS has an interesting way to let you get rid of output that you don't like: you can redirect it to a device that doesn't exist. The idea may sound strange, but the way it works is easy.

Whenever you have a program that writes to standard output you can redirect its output to the null device, whose name is NUL:. Any output that is sent to NUL: is automatically discarded.

Here is an example. Enter:

```
DIR >NUL:
```

The DIR command will execute but the output will be thrown away and you won't see it.

You might ask, what good is throwing away output? True, most of the time you do want to see the output. But on occasion, what a command writes only gets in the way of what you are trying to do. Usually this happens when you are automating some procedure in a batch file.

Here is an example. As we discussed in Chapter 10, the PAUSE command will display the following message

```
Press any key to continue . . .
```

and then wait for you to press a key.

In some cases, this message may not be adequate. You can supplement it by inserting an ECHO command before the PAUSE. For example:

```
ECHO to start copying the files
PAUSE
```

The output of these two commands would be:

```
To start copying the files
Press any key to continue . . .
```

However, the wording of this message is stilted. You would be better off making up your own complete message and throwing away the PAUSE message. You can do this by redirecting the standard output of PAUSE to NUL:. For example:

```
ECHO Press any key to start copying the files . . .
PAUSE >NUL:
```

The output of these commands is:

```
Press any key to start copying the files . . .
```

The result is that, by throwing away the output of a command, you have complete control over what appears on the screen.

Standard Output and Standard Error

The designers of DOS recognized that you might discard the output of any command. However, there are certain messages that are too important to be missed. For instance, if DOS runs into a problem, you certainly want to see the error message.

For this reason, DOS provides two standard targets to which programs can send their data. The first is standard output, the second is standard error. Normally, both types of output are displayed on your screen. The big difference is that *standard error* cannot be redirected. Since standard error is a sure way of getting a message to you, DOS uses it for all crucial messages, including error messages.

For example, here is a COPY command that you might use from within a batch file. This command makes a backup copy on diskette of an important file named INFO.DOC.

```
COPY INFO.DOC A:INFO.BAK
```

Normally, you would see the message

```
1 FILE(S) COPIED
```

every time the command executed.

However, you have decided that this message just clutters up the output of the batch file. To suppress the message, you edit the batch file so the command now reads:

```
COPY INFO.DOC A:INFO.BAK >NUL:
```

However, one day, the diskette is full. Normally, you would get the message

```
INSUFFICIENT DISK SPACE

        0 FILE(S) COPIED
```

which would warn you that something has gone wrong and your backup was not made. But, you have redirected the output of the command to NUL:. What happens now?

Although DOS sends most of its output to the standard output, the error message is sent to the standard error. The line showing how many files are copied is sent to standard output and, per your instructions, is thrown away. Fortunately, though, the error message is written to standard error and cannot be redirected. You will see the single line:

```
INSUFFICIENT DISK SPACE
```

Thus, by not letting you redirect the standard error, DOS has preserved a way to send you important messages.

The Case of the Phantom Directory

It is not generally known, but there are two ways to tell DOS to send output to a null device. First, as we have already discussed, you can redirect output to NUL:. However, there is another way. You can also redirect output to the secret null file \DEV\NUL. This works even if you don't have a \DEV subdirectory.

For example, the following two commands are equivalent:

```
DIR >NUL:
DIR >\DEV\NUL
```

Why the name \DEV\NUL? The concepts of standard input and output originated, not with DOS, but with Unix, another operating system. Within Unix, there is always a null device within a directory named "dev". The name \DEV\NUL is similar to the name that you use for the Unix null device. (The actual Unix name is "/dev/null".)

As an experiment, make yourself a \DEV subdirectory. Try to put a file named NUL into it. You can't.

Strange but true.

Copying from the Console Using CON:

In the next section, I will show you a useful example of redirection. But first, let's take a moment to discuss a quick, easy way to create short files which we will use in the next session.

In Chapter 13, I explained that the device name for the keyboard and screen (the console) is CON:. Just as we can send data directly to the printer by referring to it by PRN:, we can read and write directly to the console by using CON:.

For example, we can copy from the keyboard into a file by using a command like:

```
COPY CON: filename
```

DOS will copy everything you type directly to the file that you name. If no such file exists, DOS will create it. Be careful though: If the file already exists, DOS will replace it (as it will with any COPY command).

Of course, if you are typing directly from the console to a file, you need a way to tell DOS that you are finished. You can't depend on pressing the <Enter> key—this would simply generate a legitimate character that would be sent straight to the file. What you need to do is press a special *end of file key* when you are finished. This key is <F6>—function key number 6—followed by the <Enter> Key.

Here is an example that creates a short, two-line file. As you can see, you press <F6>, then <Enter>, to end the copying.

```
COPY CON: TEST
THIS IS A TEST
THIS IS LINE 2
<F6> <ENTER>
```

To display this file, enter:

```
TYPE TEST
```

and you will see:

```
THIS IS A TEST
THIS IS LINE 2
```

Now that we understand this quick way of creating short files, let's proceed with redirection.

A Redirection Example

For a nifty example of how redirection can be used to your advantage, let's consider something both handy and annoying about DOS's DATE and TIME commands. DATE and TIME were basically designed for us to interactively set the computer's record of today's date and the current time. These commands also do something useful in simply showing us today's date and the current time. But if we want to use these commands only to show the current date and time, we have to respond to DOS's prompt for us to enter a new setting (which we do by just pressing <Enter>, which tells DOS to leave the old date or time setting unchanged). That makes it not a very convenient way to show the current settings.

Redirection to the rescue! We can use redirection of input to hand that <Enter> key to the TIME or DATE program, so that it won't have to wait for our response. Here's how we do it. First, we create an input file that contains nothing but an empty line, the equivalent of the <Enter> key pressed alone. Let's call this file ENTER.

There are several ways that we can create ENTER. We can use one of the DOS built-in editors, EDIT (see Chapter 26) or EDLIN (see Chapter 27), or we can use another editor or a word processor. However, there is an even easier way: to copy this very short file directly from the keyboard. Type:

```
COPY CON: ENTER
<Enter>
<F6> <Enter>
```

As you can see, you have created a one-line file—and that one line is empty except for the <Enter> character.

Under the right circumstances—and you'll have to experiment thoughtfully to find them—you can use this technique to prepare canned responses to programs. This can save you both time and mistakes (since the canned responses will be correct each time).

One technique that I find handy is to keep the ENTER file in my UTILITY directory. This way, I always have an <Enter> key character to feed to any program that I want. For example, you might create a batch file to show yourself the time and date:

```
:* ----------------------------------------------------
:* NOW.BAT: batch file to show time/date
   @echo off
   time < c:\utility\enter
   date < c:\utility\enter
:* ----------------------------------------------------
```

Now you can easily display the time and date whenever you want. Later in this chapter, I'll show you how to use the FIND command to make this batch file even better.

If you decide to make use of > and < for redirection, you're likely to find, as I did, that redirecting output is a fairly safe and routine operation, while redirecting input can be much trickier (consider what happens when program needs an input response that you didn't anticipate). Still, if you are both careful and adventuresome, you can have fun with redirection and make quite productive use of it as well.

Appending to a File by Using >>

When you redirect output to a file, DOS will replace the file if it already exists. However, sometime you will want to append data to a file rather than erase what is already there. To do this, simply use two ">" characters instead of one.

For example, here is how to get copies of three directories—A, B, and C—into one file, DIRLIST:

```
DIR A >DIRLIST
DIR B >>DIRLIST
DIR C >>DIRLIST
```

The first command uses a single > to start a new file, DIRLIST. The following commands use >> to add new data to DIRLIST without erasing the old data.

From Redirection to Pipelines

If you can use redirection to send information off to somewhere other than its usual destination, can you also send it on a longer trip? Perhaps even have that information processed along the way? Yes, you can.

Programs use data, so it is natural that the output of one program might be needed as the input to another program. DOS provides a handy way of making this automatic. Before you see how DOS does this for you, let's consider how you could accomplish this with what you already have.

If you have a program named ONE, which creates data that is needed by another program named TWO, you could use > and < and a temporary file name, to pass the data like this:

```
ONE >TEMP
TWO <TEMP
```

The first program would write its data into TEMP and the second would read back from it.

This is the basic idea that DOS accomplishes with *pipelines*. A pipeline is just an automatic way of doing what we did with ONE, TWO, and the file TEMP. In a pipeline, DOS takes care of creating the temporary file to pass data through. To create a pipeline, you just write the program names on the same command line, separated by a vertical bar, (|), which is the signal for a pipeline. Here, then is how you would pipeline the programs ONE and TWO:

```
ONE | TWO
```

If you want to, you can informally think of the data as passing directly between the two programs, but actually it is stored temporarily in a file that DOS creates especially for this purpose. The first program writes out all of its data and ends operation before the second program begins working and reads the first part of the data. When the whole operation is done, DOS removes the temporary files used to pass pipeline data so they do not clutter up our disks. The whole process goes on quietly, behind the scenes, without needing any attention from you.

A pipeline can have as many programs in it as you want it to, for example:

```
ONE | TWO | THREE | FOUR | FIVE
```

There is an obvious difference between the programs at the beginning, middle, and end of a pipeline. Unless there is something unusual going on, the first program in a pipeline would be generating data. The ones in the middle would do something with the data, but still pass it on; this kind of program is called a *filter*. The last program in a pipeline could be a consumer of data, to balance the generator on the other end. Usually, though, the last program of a pipeline is a filter, just like any of the ones in the middle. If the last program is a filter, then it passes the finished result to DOS's standard output device, and it will appear on your display screen.

DOS's Filter Programs

Lets take a look at the filters that DOS provides us with. There are three main ones, called SORT, FIND, and MORE.

SORT

Each of these three programs is a classic example of a filter—it reads from standard input, does something with the data, then passes it on to standard output. SORT is quite obvious: It sorts the data that is passed to it. SORT treats each line of data as a separate entity, and so it is the order of the lines of data that SORT rearranges. Normally SORT arranges the lines in first to last order, but a switch, /R, will make the sort work in reverse order. Another switch, /+n (where n is a number), will make the sort start on the nth column of each line. A common example of the use of SORT, and of the use of the + switch, is with the DIR directory command.

Using SORT with DIR

DIR will list files in the order that they happen to be kept in this directory—not necessarily in sorted order (unless you use the /O option). But if you combine DIR with SORT, you can get the directory listing in order by file name, or by the file name extension, or by the size of the file. This pipeline will sort the files into order by name:

```
DIR | SORT
```

By using the /+n switch to shift the sorting over to the column where the file size is displayed, you can get the list in order by size:

```
DIR | SORT /+14
```

MORE

When you have information displayed on the screen, there is often more than can fit onto the screen at one time, and some of it may roll off the top of the screen before you get a chance to study it. The MORE filter is designed to display only as many lines of information as will fit onto your computer's screen, and then wait for a keystroke to indicate that you are ready to see more. Naturally MORE is only used at the end of a pipeline—it wouldn't make much sense to use it anywhere else. So, to display a long directory listing one screenful at a time, you could enter:

```
DIR | MORE
```

Or, you can combine SORT and MORE. For example:

```
DIR | SORT /+14 | MORE
```

If you list your current directory in this way, you may find some puzzling entries in the directory. Don't worry: they are the names of the temporary files that DOS has created to form the pipeline. They will disappear when the command is over.

The most common use of the MORE filter is to process the output of a TYPE command that is displaying a long file:

```
TYPE LONGFILE | MORE
```

This keeps the output from scrolling off your screen faster than you can read.

FIND

The FIND filter is used to identify the lines of data that have, or don't have, some particular data on them. To use FIND, you must specify what you are looking for, enclosed in double-quotes. FIND filters out the lines that don't contain what you are looking for, and only passes on the lines that do. Here is an example, where you use FIND in combination with the MORE filter to look for error messages:

```
TEST | FIND "ERROR" | MORE
```

As you might expect, FIND has some switches: the /V switch reverses the search so that lines with the specified information are filtered out and the others are passed through. The /N switch adds in the relative line numbers (which can help you know where the data was found). The /C switch gives a count of the lines found, without passing any other data on.

Here is an important example that puts together redirection and a filter. Remember how we automated the TIME and DATE commands by redirecting the standard input from a file, ENTER, that contained only an <Enter> key character:

```
TIME <ENTER
```

The problem is that TIME still displays the full two-line message:

```
Current time is 1:29:36.27p
Enter new time:
```

when we are really only interested in the first line. The solution is to pass the output of the TIME command through the FIND filter and extract the line that contains "Current":

```
TIME <ENTER | FIND "Current"
```

Using this technique, let us rewrite the batch file that automatically shows us the time and date. (As you remember, the ENTER file is stored in our UTILITY directory.)

```
:* ---------------------------------------------------------
:* NOW.BAT: batch file to show time/date
    @echo off
    time < c:\utility\enter | find "CURRENT"
    date < c:\utility\enter | find "CURRENT"
:* ---------------------------------------------------------
```

The output will look something like this:

```
Current time is 3:15:35.63p
Current date is Fri 12-21-1990
```

Using SORT, MORE, and FIND

While these three filter commands—SORT, MORE, and FIND—are intended to be used inside pipelines, they each can be used by themselves. For example, we can use SORT together with ordinary > and < redirection to sort the contents of one file and place it in another:

```
SORT  <FILE.OLD  >FILE.NEW
```

Similarly, MORE can be used like the TYPE command, but with automatic pauses when the screen fills.

```
MORE <LONGFILE
```

While DOS provides us with three handy filters, SORT, MORE, and FIND, these aren't the only filters we can have. Remember, any reasonable program that reads from standard input and writes to standard output can be used as a filter. If you have any ideas for useful filters, you can write programs to carry out your ideas, and then make use of them in your pipelines.

Using CHKDSK /V and FIND to Search for Files

So far, you have learned two ways to search a disk for files. First, if you are looking for a file in a specific directory, you can use DIR. For example, the following command looks for the file named MYFILE.DOC in the current directory:

```
DIR MYFILE.DOC
```

This next command looks for the same file in the \DOCUMENT directory:

```
DIR \DOCUMENT\MYFILE.DOC
```

But what if you are not sure what directory to look in? In Chapter 17,
we saw how to use ATTRIB /S to search an entire disk or part of a
tree. For example, to search the entire disk for the file MYFILE.DOC we
can use:

```
ATTRIB \MYFILE.DOC /S
```

The file specification \MYFILE.DOC says to start at the root directory,
and the /S option tells DOS to check all subdirectories. To search the
part of the tree under the \EXTRA subdirectory, we can use:

```
ATTRIB \EXTRA\MYFILE.DOC /S
```

However, what if you know only part of the file name? As we explained
in Chapter 9, you can use CHKDSK /V to list all the files on a disk. If only
there were some way to make use of this list to find the file we want.

But there is! All you have to do is send the output of CHKDSK /V to
the FIND filter, and ask FIND to go through the entire list, picking out
the names that fit your criteria.

Here is an example. You want to find a file that contains the letters FIL
somewhere in the file name. All you have to do is ask CHKDSK for a
complete list of files and then tell FIND to search for the files you want:

```
CHKDSK /V | FIND "FIL"
```

Here is some sample output:

```
D:\DOSBOOK\GENERAL\MYFILE.DOC
D:\UNIX\INFO\GENERAL\FILENAME
D:\MIRORSAV.FIL
D:\MIRROR.FIL
```

In this case, four file names contain the letters FIL. By using CHKDSK
/V /V with FIND we have avoided a long and probably error-prone
search.

20

SPECIAL COMMANDS

Introduction

So far, you've seen many of commands that let you use DOS to do work of one kind or another. There are also four special DOS commands that let you control the way your computer or your programs operate. Each of these commands has its own particular uses, and that's what we'll look at here. We'll begin with the MODE command.

Controlling Devices with MODE

MODE is a command with quite a few faces to it, but they all add up to a variation on the same concept: changing the way that some of the hardware devices work. Although it is possible to enter MODE commands from the keyboard, you usually use them in your AUTOEXEC.BAT file to automatically perform some sort of reconfiguration every time you boot DOS.

Actually MODE is best thought of as being seven commands in one. You can use MODE to:

- Set the characteristics of a parallel printer port.
- Set the characteristics of a serial port.
- Display the current status of various hardware devices.
- Redirect parallel printer output to a serial device.
- Control code page support (for non-English languages).
- Configure the display, including the number of lines.
- Set the automatic repeat rate for the keyboard.

It is likely that the usual way that the computer works is fine for you and you will not have to use MODE. However, certain occasions do arise when MODE is important and it is useful to know something about how the command works.

As you might imagine, MODE is a complex command with many options. To make things easier, we have listed the seven uses of MODE above in the order that they are explained in the DOS manual (version 5.0).

In this chapter, we will discuss the most commonly used variations of MODE. If you need more details, please refer to your DOS manual. You may also want to check to make sure that the type of MODE command you want to use is available. If you are using an old version of DOS, some of the newer MODE functions may not be supported.

Controlling Your Display

The MODE command provides a good number of ways to control the display. However, most of them are used only with the older CGA (Color/Graphics Adaptor) and MDA (Monochrome Display Adaptor) displays.

There are actually only two ways in which you might use MODE with a modern display: to set the number of columns and to set the number of lines on the screen.

However, before we start, you should know that you can't use this form of the MODE command unless you have installed the ANSI.SYS device driver. ANSI.SYS is a special program that affords you extra control over the display and keyboard. You install it by including a particular DEVICE command in your configuration file, CONFIG.SYS. This whole topic is explained in Chapter 28.

When you use MODE in this way, you can set the number of columns to either 40 or 80, and you can set the number of lines to either, 25, 43, or 50. However, you can only set 50 lines with an XGA(Extended Graphics Array) or a VGA (Video Graphics Array) display; and you can only set 43 lines with an XGA, VGA or EGA (Enhanced Graphics Adaptor) display.

The actual command looks like this:

```
MODE CON: COLS=xx LINES=yy
```

where xx can be either 40 or 80, and yy can be either 25, 43, or 50. The word CON: tells MODE that this command is to affect the operation of the console.

As an example, if you have a VGA display, you can set it to display 40 columns and 50 lines by entering:

```
MODE CON: COLS=40 LINES=50
```

If you want, you can specify only one setting; the other will remain the same. Thus:

```
MODE CON: LINES=50
```

You might think that it would be nice to get more lines on the screen whenever you want to. But there is a problem: Many programs routinely reset the display back to the regular settings. However, there are two important programs that will use all the lines they can: the DOS text editors, EDIT and EDLIN. (These programs are discussed in Chapters 26 and 27.) Using extra lines with an editor is handy as it allows you to see as much of your file as possible.

Controlling Your Printer

There are two different ways that you can control your printer with the MODE command. The first type of MODE command looks like this:

```
MODE LPT1: COLS=aa, LINES=b, RETRY=c
```

The first value, aa, is the number of characters per line. You have only two choices, 80 or 132. The second value, b, is the number of lines per inch. Again, you have only two choices, 6 or 8. The final value, c, tells DOS what to do if the printer does not respond. The choices are:

E   ->   act as if there is an error
B   ->   act as if the printer is busy
R   ->   act as if the printer is ready
NONE ->   do nothing

Of these three values, you only need to specify the ones you want. DOS will use default values for the others. The defaults are COLS=80, LINES=132 and RETRY=E.

For example, to set your printer at 132 characters per line, use:

```
MODE LPT1: COLS=132
```

The way we have written this command, it controls a printer connected to the first parallel port, LPT1:. If you have a printer connected to a second or third port, you can specify LPT2: or LPT3:.

As you can see, DOS is limited in how well it can control a printer. For one thing, MODE will work only with IBM-compatible printers. Moreover, the command offers only the most rudimentary of printer settings. It will not issue the type of signals you need to control the features of a modern complex printer, even an IBM printer.

The second way to use MODE to control your printer tells DOS where to send printed output. By default, DOS expects that your printer will be connected to a parallel port. If you have a serial printer, you will have to tell DOS to redirect output to the appropriate serial port. This form of the MODE command looks like:

```
MODE LPT1:=COM1:
```

If necessary, you can specify a different parallel port (LPT2: or LPT3:) or a different serial port (COM2:, COM3:, or COM4:).

If you have a serial printer, you will usually use another MODE command first to set up the serial port. (We will discuss this use of MODE in the next section.) Your printer documentation will tell you exactly what commands to use. It is a good idea to put commands like this in your AUTOEXEC.BAT file. This will ensure that your printer is set up exactly how you want, every time you start DOS.

Controlling Your Serial Ports

The serial ports (also known as communications or RS-232 ports) on our computers were designed as a general-purpose channel for two machines to talk to each other. Although the most common use of a serial port is to connect our computers to a telephone line, these serial ports are also used for printers, to connect a mouse, to interface with scientific and lab equipment, and zillions of other uses. In fact, the RS-232 connection is widely used as a standard interface between many different kinds of machines that have nothing to do with our PCs.

As a consequence, the serial connection was designed to be as flexible as possible, which in turn means that it can be adjusted in quite a few ways to adapt to changing needs. These adjustments—the serial port parameters—can be made under software control and often the job of setting them is taken care of for us by the programs that work with the serial port. But we also need to be able to set these communications parameters ourselves, and that is what this variation on the MODE command is able to do for us.

There are four communication parameters that we can set with MODE: speed, parity, data bits, and stop bits. In addition, we can tell DOS what to do if the serial port does not respond. This form of MODE looks like:

```
MODE COM1: BAUD=aa PARITY=b DATA=c STOP=d RETRY=e
```

All of the settings are optional except the first one, BAUD.

We have shown the command to control the first serial port, COM1:. You can use MODE to control other serial ports by using COM2:, COM3:, or COM4:.

The first setting, BAUD, specifies the speed of the line. This seems like a strange word so let's take a moment to discuss its origin. The term baud is derived from the name of a nineteenth century French engineer, J. M. E. Baudot. As an engineering term, baud is a unit of signal transmission, referring to one unit of information per second. When we discuss the speed at which data travels over a communication line, we measure it in bits per second, usually abbreviated as bps. Over the years, however, the term baud has taken on a second meaning: as a synonym for bits per second. Thus, it is common—and correct—to refer to bits per second as baud. Of course, if you are talking with a communications engineer, you should be aware that he may interpret baud as having a more esoteric and precise meaning.

To return to MODE, we specify the speed of a serial line by giving BAUD a particular value. This value is a two digit number as follows:

- 11   110 bits per second
- 15   150 bps
- 30   300 bps
- 60   600 bps
- 12   1200 bps
- 24   2400 bps
- 48   4800 bps
- 96   9600 bps
- 19   19200 bps

There is no default. If you use this form of the MODE command you must specify the speed. For example,

```
MODE COM1: BAUD=24
```

The common speeds that are used are 1200, 2400, 9600, and 19200 bits per second, the most common being 2400 and 9600. As a general rule, it takes about 10 characters to transmit a single character (including overhead). Thus, you can divide the speed by 10 to approximate the characters-per-second transmission rate.

The next three values, PARITY, DATA, and STOP are more technical. PARITY refers to a simple type of error checking, DATA refers to how many bits represent a single character, and STOP refers to how many bits are used for a particular type of timing synchronization.

PARITY has 5 different values; DATA has 4; and STOP has 3. They are:

Parity	Data	Stop
N(none)	5	1
E (even)	6	1.5
O (odd)	7	2
M (mark)	8	
S (space)		

All three of these settings are optional. The defaults are PARITY=E, DATA=7, and STOP=1.

Actually, you can ignore the details. All you have to do is make sure that the communication values used by your serial port are the same as the ones expected by the computer or device on the other end.

The last value that you can specify, RETRY, tells DOS what to do if the device attached to the serial port does not respond. The choices are:

E	->	act as if there is an error
B	->	act as if the device is busy
R	->	act as if the device is ready
NONE	->	do nothing

The RETRY value is optional with a default of E (error).

If you want to check the current settings of a serial port, enter MODE followed by the name of the port. For example:

```
MODE COM1:
```

Two Common Uses of MODE: Modems and Serial Printers

Two of the most common uses of the MODE command are to set up a serial for either a modem or a serial printer.

When you a modem to dial another computer, you must make sure that your system sends out the expected signals. A common combination, especially for bulletin board systems, is BAUD=2400, PARITY=N, DATA=8, and STOP=1. However, it is likely that your communication software will take care of the details, so you won't even have to use a MODE command.

The other common use for MODE is to prepare DOS for work with a serial printer. This takes two commands. First, you must set up the serial port. Typically, the command to use is:

```
MODE COM1: BAUD=96 PARITY=N DATA=8 STOP=1 RETRY=B
```

Next, you must redirect the printer output from the parallel to the serial port:

```
MODE LPT1:=COM1:
```

If you have a serial printer, the best place to put these commands is in your AUTOEXEC.BAT file. This way, your system will be set up the way you want it each time you start DOS.

Note: The documentation for your serial printer may use the old form of the MODE command that was used with previous versions of DOS:

```
MODE COM1:9600,N,8,1,B
```

For compatibility, DOS will accept this type of command, but it is a good idea to translate it into the more modern form which is easier to understand, especially in a batch file.

Keyboard Modes

There are two ways that MODE lets you control the operation of your keyboard—they have to do with what IBM calls the *typematic* feature. This is an old word, originally used with Selectric typewriters, that means that a key repeats itself when you hold it down. With a typewriter, this is useful for using the hyphen or underscore characters to draw lines. With a computer keyboard, it is also useful to be able to hold down the cursor-control keys (the Arrow keys). However, the typematic feature will work with any key on your computer keyboard.

In order to use this version of the MODE command, you need to install the ANSI.SYS device driver—just as when you want to change the number of lines on the screen. (ANSI.SYS is explained in Chapter 28.)

The first typematic feature that you can control is the rate at which the key will repeat. The second feature is the delay time—that is, how long you must hold down the key before it begins to repeat. The command looks like this:

```
MODE CON: RATE=aa DELAY=b
```

The RATE value can range from 1 to 32. The higher the number, the faster the repetition. RATE=1 will repeat approximately two times a second; RATE=32 will repeat approximately thirty times a second.

The DELAY value can be 1, 2, 3, or 4. This is the number of quarter seconds of delay. For instance, if you use:

```
MODE CON: RATE=32 DELAY=3
```

it tells DOS that you want a key to repeat at the fastest possible rate. The repetition is to start every time a key is help down for more than $3/4$ of a second.

Unfortunately, the DOS manual does not tell you what the normal values of RATE and DELAY are. Moreover, the MODE command offers no way for you to find out the current settings.

Showing the MODE Status

The last form of the MODE command that I will discuss is simple. It shows you the status of various devices. You can use this simple form of MODE to check, say, what the settings are for your display. The command looks like this:

```
MODE /STATUS
```

If you want, you can leave out the /STATUS option completely:

```
MODE
```

The MODE command with no options or values will also display the status report.

Controlling Interruptions with BREAK

There are times when you may need to interrupt the operation of a program—because you don't need it anymore, because you told it to do something you'd now like to stop, or because it's just running wild.

Short of turning off your computer and turning it back on, there's no foolproof way to interrupt a program. There is one standard and accepted way you can often use to break into a program's operation, and that's the <Ctrl-Break> key combination or its equivalent, the <Ctrl-C> combination.

There is no guarantee that pressing the <Ctrl-Break> key will effectively work to interrupt your computer every time, but many programs cooperate in recognizing this shut-down signal. DOS does as well, and DOS goes even further by giving partial control over when and how the break key can take effect.

This is accomplished with a feature of DOS known as the "break" switch. If the break switch is not active, DOS will recognize your pressing the <Break> key only when it is actively doing I/O work: for example, writing information to the screen. Many more sophisticated programs independently recognize the <Break> key and either act on it or, for good safety reasons, ignore it.

On the other hand, if the break switch is active, DOS does its best to recognize the <Break> key whenever you press it, and does its best to act on the key and force any program that's running to recognize it.

There are two ways you can set the break switch so that you have fairly good control over how it works. One, which we'll get to in Chapter 28, allows you to tell DOS what the default setting of the switch should be: on or off. The other, our topic here, is the BREAK command, which explicitly turns the switch on or off.

You use the BREAK command in three ways. If you type:

```
BREAK
```

DOS tells you whether the break switch is currently on or off with a message like this:

```
BREAK IS ON
```

If you type the command like this:

```
BREAK ON
```

you set the switch on, telling DOS to use every opportunity to recognize when you've pressed the <Break> key.

Alternatively, if you type:

```
BREAK OFF
```

this does the opposite, setting the switch off, so that DOS only recognizes a break action when it's doing standard I/O operations.

As I mentioned, setting this break switch with the BREAK command gives you only a limited degree of control over whether the computer can be interrupted. Whether it's on or off, other circumstances may override DOS's ability to respond to the switch. Still, at least this command gives you some control.

Remote Control with CTTY

As handy as it is to work with a personal computer in person, there are also times when it might be nice to operate a computer by remote control—say, by calling it up on the telephone, issuing commands, and getting responses back.

DOS actually makes this possible through a command called CTTY. When you're working with DOS, it is accepting input from you through the computer's keyboard and it's showing you the results on the display screen. DOS doesn't necessarily have to work with those two devices; instead, it is possible for DOS to redirect its attention to a telephone line, for example, that's hooked to another PC. When this is the case, DOS can get its keyboard-type input from the phone line, and can put its screen-type output into the phone line.

The CTTY command makes this work by letting you tell DOS what device to pay attention to. For example, with a command like:

```
CTTY COM1:
```

you can tell DOS to look to the first serial port (COM1) for its operations. If that serial port is hooked to a modem that's dialed up to another PC computer—you can control your PC remotely.

If you do use this remote control, you can switch back to the regular console (keyboard and display) by entering:

```
CTTY CON:
```

Before you get too excited about the possibilities, here comes the "however." To make all this work takes more than just the CTTY command that comes with DOS. It also means that your computer has to be set up the right way, that you have the necessary remote connection (through a modem and a telephone line, or whatever), and that the program you're running is designed to take input and send output through a standard DOS means that can be redirected by this CTTY instruction. This last part can't be done with many of the most important programs, such as spreadsheets or word processors. These programs (naturally enough) aren't designed to be used remotely. But, with the right kind of software, which might be something you've had specially prepared for your needs, you can operate your PC remotely, through the facilities of CTTY.

However, if you do need a reliable way to control a computer remotely, several companies sell software to do the job. Such software comes in handy when you want to help someone whose computer is at a remote location, or when you need to use or administer a local area network from home.

Setting the DOS Version Number with SETVER

Under certain circumstances, a program needs to know what version of DOS it is using. For instance, the program may depend upon a particular feature that is not supported by older versions of DOS. For such cases, DOS provides programmers with a way of checking what version of DOS is currently running. They can then build an automatic check into the program: if the version of DOS is not new enough, the program can warn the user and abort.

On rare occasions, you may run into a program that will work with only certain specific versions of DOS. You may be using a newer DOS and the program will not run.

Logically, such situations should not occur because new DOS versions are upwards compatible with the older ones. This means that anything that works with one version of DOS will work with all newer versions. In fact, if you could just induce the program to run, it might work just fine. However, because it runs only with specific older versions of DOS, you cannot even get it to start.

Beginning wiht DOS 5.0 there is a way around this problem. You can use the SETVER (set version number) command.

You use SETVER to tell DOS that a particular program expects a specific version of DOS. Once you do this, DOS adds the information to a special table. Whenever a program inquires as to what is the current DOS version, DOS will check this table. If the program is listed in the table, DOS will report the version number that the program expects to see. Otherwise, DOS will tell the truth and report the real version number.

In most cases, this will allow the program to run. However, there is an important point that you should understand. Presumably, such programs check the version number because they depend on certain version-specific features of DOS. SETVER does *not* make sure that it provedes such features. All it does is report a false version number to trick the program into thinking that it is working with the DOS version that it wants.

Usually, this is not a problem because, as we mentioned, new versions of DOS version are upwards compatible with older versions. However, if you run a program using SETVER, and the program uses a feature that existed only under the older version of DOS, you may get into trouble. This might happen if the programmer was using undocumented idiosyncrasies of DOS that were changed in later versions. Although the contigency is unlikely, you should be aware that the possibility does exist. Be suspicious of any program that will work only with an older version of DOS.

In order to use SETVER, you first need to initialize it as a device driver from within your CONFIG.SYS file (see Chapter 28), and then issue the SETVER command, probably from within your AUTOEXEC.BAT file (see Chapter 12). Since most people will never need SETVER, we won't go into the particulars here. If you think you need this command, check your DOS manual for the details.

When you install DOS (5.0 or later), the setup program automatically places the SETVER configuration command in your CONFIG.SYS file. The first time you use DOS, you can enter the SETVER command with no parameters:

```
SETVER
```

You will be shown a list of all the programs whose preferences come built into the SETVER table. DOS 5.0 comes with a list of 27 such programs. Actually, the list is so long that it will probably run off the top of your screen. If this happens, pipe the output to the MORE filter (see Chapter 19):

```
SETVER | MORE
```

Check the list: If you do not use any of these programs, and you do not need to use SETVER for any other programs (which will probably be the case), you can remove the SETVER configuration command from your CONFIG.SYS file. Later, if you decide you need SETVER, you can always put the command back in.

21

DOS'S MEMORY-RESIDENT PROGRAMS

Introduction

Programs, like people, can be grouped in many different ways: by their size, the work they do, the language they "speak," and so on. They can also be categorized according to how long and where they stick around in your computer's memory. Most programs do their work and then are replaced in memory by other programs. But some, which are called memory-resident programs, remain in memory until you deliberately remove them, restart DOS or turn off your computer. These programs are also called terminate-and-stay resident programs or TSRs. These memory-resident programs are one of the most mysterious elements in the world of DOS, and they are what we'll explore in this chapter.

Memory-Resident Programs and What They Do

When DOS runs a program, it finds space in the computer's memory for the program, copies it from disk to memory, and then, temporarily, turns control of the computer over to the program. Normally, when a program is finished working, it turns control of the computer back over to DOS, and DOS uses the memory where the program was loaded for the next program that you use. With memory resident programs things work slightly differently.

When a memory-resident program finishes its initial operation, it hands control of the computer back to DOS, but it also instructs DOS to not reuse the memory area where it is loaded. The program asks DOS to leave it resident. DOS, in effect, puts a barrier in place where the memory-resident program ends, and loads the next program that we use above the memory-resident program.

What do I mean by "above" the memory-resident program? Well, whenever we talk about memory, we refer to parts of it by number. These numbers start off low and get increasingly higher, much as house addresses on a street start low and get higher. DOS and memory resident programs settle in at the lower-numbered addresses, so that when I say a program is loaded above another program, I mean it is placed in a portion of memory with higher-numbered addresses.

In effect then, a memory-resident program incorporates itself into the small part of DOS that stays in the lower end of the computer's memory. All subsequent programs that you use operate at higher memory locations, leaving your memory-resident program and DOS undisturbed in lower memory locations. (However, as we will see in Chapter 29, with

DOS 5.0 or later it is possible to load memory-resident programs into a unused area in a higher part of memory.) Thus, the memory resident program stays, semi-permanently in the computer's memory, until you turn the computer off.

What is the point of having a program stay resident? Unlike most other programs, a memory-resident program stays active after it seems to have finished. The program stays in memory and, through some technical tricks, manages to continue getting work done, even though you are running other programs after it.

There are many uses for memory-resident programs. Some, like the DOS programs we will be discussing in this chapter, sit in the background, waiting to help out as they are needed. Others do nothing until you press a special key combination called a *hotkey*. Then they pop up on top of whatever you are doing. When you are finished, you press another key (often <Esc>) and the pop-up program disappears, leaving you in your original program.

Aside from the memory-resident programs that come with DOS, there are all kinds that you can buy: programs to send and receive electronic mail, check for computer viruses, provide pop-up calculators and appointment books, and on and on. We won't be covering these programs in this book, but you should be aware of them and how useful they can be.

DOS's Memory-Resident Programs

DOS has more memory-resident programs than most people realize. Table 21.1 shows the DOS commands—14 of them—that can initialize memory resident programs. It is important to recognize these programs as they can use up part of your overall memory allotment—although, for the most part, the memory requirements are small.

None of these commands is crucial. In fact, unless you have a good reason to use one of these commands you can probably ignore them. For reference, we have shown which chapters of this book discuss each command. The commands which you will be most likely to use are DOSKEY, FASTOPEN, MIRROR, and possible DOSSHELL.

In this chapter, we will be discussing four memory resident programs: PRINT, GRAPHICS, SHARE, and FASTOPEN.

**Table 21.1   *DOS Commands that Can Initialize
Memory Resident Programs***

Command Name	Chapter Reference
APPEND	Chapter 12
ASSIGN	Chapter 17
COMMAND	---
DOSKEY	Chapters 23 and 25
DOSSHELL	Chapter 30
EMM386	Chapter 29
FASTOPEN	Chapter 21
GRAFTABL	---
GRAPHICS	Chapter 21
MIRROR	Chapter 18
MODE	Chapter 20
NLSFUNC	Chapter 22
PRINT	Chapter 21
SHARE	Chapter 21

Aside from the commands in Table 21.1, there are other DOS programs called *device drivers* that are also memory resident. You install device drivers by placing certain instructions in your CONFIG.SYS configuration file. We will discuss this topic in detail in Chapter 28.

Background Printing

The first of the DOS memory-resident programs we'll consider is a command called PRINT, which acts as a variety of *print spooler*—a manager, so to speak, that handles information you want to send to your printer. The job of a print spooler is to print information without tying up the computer while the printing is going on. (The term s*pool*, by the way, comes from an old acronym meaning "simultaneous peripheral operations off-line.")

If you've used your computer's printer, you've probably noticed that it's relatively slow compared to the computer's ability to get work done. While your printer is laboriously working away, almost all of your computer's working power is going to waste because printing really doesn't require all that much attention from your computer.

The memory-resident program PRINT solves this problem by taking over the job of feeding data to the printer, while leaving the majority of the computer's power available for other programs to use. It's a bit like reading a book while you're stirring soup that's cooking. You don't have to give all your attention to stirring soup. Nor does your computer have to give its full power to printing information. What the PRINT memory-resident program does is put just enough of the computer's power to work keeping a printer busy, while turning the rest of the computer's thinking power over to any other programs you want to run.

Because of the unobtrusive way it works, PRINT is what is known as a *background program.* Once you start up the PRINT command, it sits in the computer, and uses just enough of the computer's power to print out what you've asked it to do (just as you give a fraction of your attention to stirring soup while reading a book). If PRINT finishes its work, it remains in memory, ready for more work, but not taking up any computing power. When you ask PRINT to print something else, it occupies a fraction of the computing power to keep the printer busy, and leaves the rest of the computing power for our other programs; that's how a background program works.

Despite the intricacies of its work habits, PRINT itself is easy to use.

Using PRINT

The first time that you invoke the PRINT command, it loads itself into memory, and stays there until the computer is turned off or reset. From then on, any time you invoke the PRINT command, you just tell it what you want it to do. To start PRINT, you enter the command with the /D: (device) option, specifying which printer you want to use. Most of the time you will be using the first printer, LPT1:

```
PRINT /D:LPT1
```

If you want to use another printer, you can specify LPT2 or LPT3.

If you forget to tell PRINT about your printer, it will ask for the information like this:

```
NAME OF LIST DEVICE [PRN]:
```

and wait. Here, if you want, you can just press <Enter> and PRINT will use its default, LPT1. (PRN is a synonym for LPT1.)

Once you've got PRINT settled in, tell it to print information by giving it the name of a file that you want printed. PRINT only works with disk files, so if you want to use PRINT to print the output of one of your programs, you first have to get that program to store its print-style information into the disk file. Many programs, particularly word-processing programs, are prepared to do exactly that, for your convenience.

However, if your program has its own printing facility, you are better off using that. Some programs store data in their own format and your results may not look right unless the program itself prints the data.

Assuming that your file is on disk, however, you tell PRINT to print a file like this:

```
PRINT MYFILE.DOC
```

If you want, you can specify the names of more than one file. DOS will print them in the order you specify. For example:

```
PRINT MYFILE.DOC YOURFILE.DOC
PRINT *.DOC
```

Using PRINT and the DOS Shell

In Chapter 30, we will be discussing the DOS Shell, a program that acts as an easy-to-use interface to DOS. One of the functions that the DOS Shell provides is the ability to print a file. If you want to make use of this capability, you will have to make sure that the PRINT memory resident program is initialized before the DOS Shell starts. The usual way to do this is to place the command

```
PRINT /D:LPT1
```

in your AUTOEXEC.BAT file (see Chapter 12) before the command which starts the DOS Shell. Normally, this command, DOSSHELL, will be the last command in the AUTOEXEC.BAT file.

Print Queues

PRINT has the ability to hold a list of work to be done in what is called a *print queue*. You can put up to 10 files in a print queue, and as long as there is work to be done in the print queue, PRINT will work away, passing information to your printer. When all work is done, PRINT goes to sleep, until you wake it up with a request to print some more information. If you've got some heavy-duty printing to do, you can increase the holding capacity of the print queue with PRINT's /Q switch:

```
PRINT /Q:size
```

where size can be any number from 4 to 32 (that's probably many more files than you need).

If you change your mind about printing a file in the queue, you can type:

```
PRINT filename /C
```

to cancel the job and eliminate it from the queue.

If you change your mind about printing all the files in the queue, you can type:

```
PRINT /T
```

to terminate all jobs (and the queue).

Finally, if you only want to see what's in the queue, type:

```
PRINT
```

and PRINT will tell you.

Help with Screen Printing

The next memory-resident command we'll look at is GRAPHICS. When you learned about the things your computer will do, you no doubt learned about its built-in print-screen function, which lets you use the <Print Screen> key to copy the contents of the display screen to your printer. The standard print screen operation, though, is only intended to print out normal character data, not any graphics pictures that might be on the screen.

GRAPHICS is a slightly different kind of memory-resident program from PRINT. While PRINT will work away simultaneously with your other programs (operating in the background), GRAPHICS is a program that replaces, and improves on, a standard operation you already have in the computer. Personal computers already have the ability to do the print-screen operation with text characters. The GRAPHICS program just augments that function by adding the ability to copy not just character text, but any graphics image as well.

To invoke GRAPHICS, enter the command name followed by the type of printer you have. For example, if you enter:

```
GRAPHICS LASERJETII
```

it loads itself into memory (and tells DOS to leave it resident), and then it does nothing. Nothing, that is, until you press the <Print-Screen> key, then the memory-resident GRAPHICS program goes to work, working just like the regular print-screen program, but doing it for graphics images as well. If you think you will need it, this is the type of command to put in your AUTOEXEC.BAT file.

GRAPHICS will support only a limited number of printers; check your DOS manual for a list. If your printer is not listed, you can try entering the command by itself:

```
GRAPHICS
```

This initiates support for standard IBM-compatible printers.

One last word about starting GRAPHICS: Most of the time, your screen contains white or colored characters on a black background. Normally, DOS will reverse this and print a screen as black on white. However, if for some reason you want the screen to print exactly as you see it, with a black background, you can start GRAPHICS with the /R (reverse) option.

Controlling the Sharing of Data

The next of the memory resident programs that DOS provides for is the SHARE program. SHARE is used to control the use and sharing of data and disk files between programs. SHARE takes care of problems that arise when more than one program, or more than one computer, is making use of your disks. This is a special problem that can arise if you use a network to allow several computers to share a disk and pass data around. If one program, or one computer, is reading a data file, and another is changing it, things can get into quite a muddle. SHARE's job is to coordinate the sharing of data, so that nothing goes wrong.

SHARE actually has three uses:

- To support file sharing on networks.
- With certain diskette drives, SHARE will make sure that the diskette has not been changed during critical operations.
- With DOS 4.0, you must use SHARE if you have a hard disk partition that is greater than 32 megabytes. This is not necessary with DOS 5.0 or later.

If your computer setup is such that you need SHARE, you would put it in your AUTOEXEC.BAT file. (If you do, be sure to place it after your PATH command so DOS can find the SHARE.EXE file.) The command is simple, just the name:

```
SHARE
```

Alternately, you can use the INSTALL command in your CONFIG.SYS file. (AUTOEXEC.BAT is explained in Chapter 24; CONFIG.SYS is explained in Chapter 23.)

Speeding Up Your Disk with FASTOPEN

The FASTOPEN program can enhance the performance of your hard disk. It does this by reserving some memory in which DOS can remember information about the directories that you are currently using and how the files are stored. This means that much of the time, DOS can avoid going to the hard disk for information that it has at its fingertips.

There are several technical parameters that you can use with this command. However, most of the time you won't need them; if you think you do, refer to your DOS manual for the details.

The simplest form of FASTOPEN is to list the names of the hard disk partitions that you want to speed up. Here are two examples:

```
FASTOPEN C:
FASTOPEN C: D:
```

Normally, you would put a FASTOPEN command in your AUTOEXEC.BAT file. (If you do, be sure to place it after your PATH command so DOS can find the FASTOPEN.EXE file.)

As with SHARE, you can also use the INSTALL command in your CONFIG.SYS file (see Chapter 23).

22

DOS AROUND
THE WORLD

Introduction

Personal computers are used worldwide and DOS is called on to support all kinds of different keyboards, character sets, and local conventions. IBM calls this facility National Language Support.

If you are using your computer with American English, you do not need to use the National Language Support—DOS will automatically set things up the way you need them. If you want, you can skip this chapter.

National Language Support

National Language Support allows DOS to provide the following services:

1. You can use a keyboard that is suitable for the language you are using.

2. You can have your display show characters that are suitable for the language that you are using

3. You can have DOS respect certain conventions used by the country you are in. These conventions affect:

   - The way the time is displayed

   - The way the date is displayed

   - Collating sequence (the order in which charatcers are sorted)

   - Capitalization

   - Case conversions

   - Which currency symbol is used

   - Which character is used as a decimal separator (period or comma)

   - Possible file-name characters

One thing that National Language Support does *not* do is translate what DOS displays—for example, error messages. Your country may have a translated version of DOS. However, if one is not available, the next best thing is to use the standard DOS with National Language Support that specifies your country.

If you would like to see what countries are supported, check your DOS manual. The discussion of the KEYB command shows the different keyboards that are supported. The discussion of the COUNTRY command shows the countries for which all the other facilities are supported. DOS supports 28 countries and a variety of keyboards.

How to Install National Language Support

By far the easiest way to install National Language Support is to let DOS do it for you.

Overall, you will need to use eight different commands. Three of them will have to be in your CONFIG.SYS file; five of them will have to be in your AUTOEXEC.BAT file. (These two files are used to tell DOS how you want to configure your system, and to execute certain commands automatically every time you boot DOS. CONFIG.SYS is discussed in detail in Chapter 28; AUTOEXEC.BAT is discussed in Chapter 12.)

When you install DOS (see Chapter 5), the installation program will come to a point where it asks you if you would like the default keyboard and country information. Say "No," and you will then be given a chance to pick the country you want. The installation program will then automatically put the right commands in your CONFIG.SYS and AUTOEXEC.BAT files.

If you are using an old version of DOS (before 4.0), then there is no automatic installation program. However, there is a command named SELECT that you can use. See your DOS manual for details.

Code Pages

When you use a non-American keyboard, DOS takes note of which keys you press and translates them into the appropriate characters.

But how about your data that is stored on a disk? Every time it is displayed or printed DOS will have to make sure that the data codes are translated into the right characters. This is done via *code pages*.

As I explained in Chapter 13, the standard code for storing information is called ASCII, the American Standard Code for Information Interchange. There are 256 different possible characters; ASCII defines each one of these and which symbol it stands for.

Most of the 256 characters are oriented towards American English. There are some non-American symbols included but not enough to support every country.

A code page is a table that contains 256 entries, some of which are oriented towards a particular country. We can think of the standard ASCII code as a particular code page.

DOS comes with a number of different code pages. Through a facility called *code-page switching*, DOS allows you to use the code page you want. As the name implies, you can switch from one code page to another as the need arises.

There are two types of code pages: hardware code pages and prepared code pages. A hardware code page is one that is built into a particular device. For example, a printer that is meant to be used in Portugal may come with a Portuguese hardware code page. Many of these types of devices can use only their built-in code page.

A prepared code page is one that comes with DOS. The different versions of IBM DOS and MS DOS have different numbers of prepared code pages. You will have to check your manual for details. A few of the code pages require special software supplements. The oriental code pages require an Asian version of DOS and special hardware.

By using certain commands, you can tell DOS to use a particular code page with your display and printer. To use this facility, you must have an IBM-compatible printer and a display that is one of the following:

- A PS/2 display
- Enhanced Graphics Adaptor (EGA) compatible
- Video Graphics Array (VGA) compatible
- Extended Graphics Array (XGA) compatible

If it suits you, you can prepare more than one code page. Although each device can have only one code page active at a time, you can switch whenever you want.

Commands to Start National Language Support

As I mentioned earlier, the best way to install National Language Support is to have the installation program do it for you when you install DOS. However, for your interest, here are the commands that you will be using. For the details, see your DOS manual.

In your CONFIG.SYS file, you will need:

```
COUNTRY
```

to tell DOS what country you want

```
DEVICE=DISPLAY.SYS
DEVICE=PRINTER.SYS
```

to prepare the display and printer to use the correct code pages
In your AUTOEXEC.BAT file, you will need:

```
NLSFUNC
```

to load the memory-resident program for National Language Support

```
MODE CON: CODEPAGE PREPARE
MODE LPT1: CODEPAGE PREPARE
```

to prepare the code pages you want for your display (CON:) and your printer (LPT1:)

```
KEYB
```

to tell DOS what keyboard you will be using

```
CHCP
```

to start off with the appropriate code page

Commands to Modify National Language Support

If you are using more than one code page, you can use the CHCP (Change Code Page) command to change the active code page whenever you wish.

If your display or printer loses its active code page due to a hardware error, you can prepare them again by using the

```
MODE CON: CODEPAGE PREPARE
MODE LPT1: CODEPAGE PREPARE
```

commands, and then reinstate them by using the

```
MODE CON: CODEPAGE REFRESH
MODE LPT1: CODEPAGE REFRESH
```

commands.

If you have used the KEYB command to use a non-American keyboard, you can change to the default American keyboard at any time by pressing <Ctrl-Alt-F1>. (That is, by holding down the <Ctrl> and <Alt> keys and pressing the <F1> key.) If you want to switch back to the non-American keyboard, press <Ctrl-Alt-F2>.

At any time, you can ask DOS to show you how code pages are being used by entering either of the following commands:

```
MODE /STATUS
MODE
```

You can also display the keyboard status by entering:

```
KEYB
```

with no parameters.

23

RECYCLING YOUR DOS COMMANDS

Introduction

This chapter is really the beginning of a three-chapter tutorial on commands and your keyboard. Not the basics—we have already covered those—but the more powerful techniques that can turn you into a sophisticated and confident veteran.

The tools that we will discuss are all offered by DOSKEY, a new member of our DOS toolbox, available only with DOS 5.0 or later. DOSKEY provides three major services, allowing you to:

- Recall, edit, and reenter previous commands
- Use the DOS editing keys to cut and paste a single command
- Make up your own customized commands, called macros

In this chapter, we will discuss how to start DOSKEY and how to use it to recycle your DOS commands. In Chapter 24, we will take a guided tour of the DOS editing keys. Along the way, we'll look into the other special keys, the ones that help you control the operation of your computer. And in Chapter 25, we'll look at how you can use DOSKEY to create customized macros.

The material that we'll cover in Chapter 24 pertains to all versions of DOS, so you should definitely read that chapter. However, the topics in this chapter and Chapter 25 do not apply to the older versions of DOS (before 5.0). However, even if you are using an older DOS, you may still want to skim these chapters.

Starting DOSKEY

DOSKEY is a memory resident program, like the ones we discussed in Chapter 21. To start DOSKEY, just enter the command name:

```
DOSKEY
```

Like other memory resident programs, it is best to start DOSKEY from your AUTOEXEC.BAT file. That way, it will be ready for you each time you start DOS.

The DOSKEY command comes only with DOS 5.0 or later. If you have an old version of DOS, you can use the command editing keys that we will discuss in Chapter 24, but that is all.

Recalling Commands from the History List

When you start DOSKEY, you won't notice anything in particular. But DOSKEY is working behind the scenes, remembering every command that you type. These commands are saved in what is called a *history list*. At any time, you can recall one of these commands from the list, edit it, and send it back to DOS to be executed.

To take a look at the history list, press the <F7> key. DOSKEY will display all your previous commands. A typical history list might look like this:

```
1: C:
2: CHKDSK
3: CD \DOCUMENT
4: DIR
5: TIME
6: D:
```

(Remember, we are showing our examples in uppercase but you will probably be typing in lowercase.)

As you type, the command line you are entering is called the *current line*. DOSKEY provides several ways for you to copy one of your previous commands from the history list onto the current line. This allows you to make use of old commands without having to retype them.

Consider the following example. You have entered the commands in our sample history list. As you can see, you have already run the CHKDSK program on the C: disk (commands #1 and #2). You have now switched to the D: disk (command #6) and you wish to run CHKDSK again. To do this, you need to recall command #2 and reenter it.

To recall a previous command, press <F9>. DOS will ask you what command you want to recall:

```
LINE NUMBER:
```

Type whatever number you want and press <Enter>. DOS will copy that command to the current line. In this case, type 2 and press <Enter>. DOS will copy the CHKDSK command to the current line. You will see:

```
CHKDSK
```

You can now press <Enter> to run the command again.

When you are prompted for a line number, you have several choices. If you enter a valid number, DOS recalls that command. If you press

<Enter> without typing a number, or if you type a number that is too high, DOS will recall your previous command. If you type the number 0, DOS will copy the first command. If you change your mind, just press <Esc>—the Escape key—and DOS will forget the whole thing.

Once a command is recalled, you can modify it before you press <Enter>. For example, say that you want to see a directory listing for the \DOCUMENT subdirectory. Press <F9> and then specify that you want to recall command #4. The command line will look like this:

```
DIR
```

You can now type \DOCUMENT and the line will look like this:

```
DIR \DOCUMENT
```

Press <Enter> to enter the command.

When you press <F7> to display the history list, it may be that there are more commands than can fit onto a single screen. If so, DOS will show you one screenful at a time, displaying

```
--- MORE---
```

at the bottom of each screen. When you see this message, you can press any key to move on to the next screenful.

If you decide that the history list is too large, you can press <Alt-F7>. DOS will remove all the previous commands and start afresh with an empty list.

Saving Commands to a Batch File

It may be that you have just entered a particularly clever set of commands and that you wish that you could save them to a batch file. Well, you can.

You already know that you can display the history list by pressing <F7>. Alternatively, you can enter the DOSKEY command with the /H option. (Actually, the full name of this option is /HISTORY, but /H will do just fine.)

```
DOSKEY /H
```

The difference is that with DOSKEY /H there will not be any line numbers.

Thus, the output of DOSKEY /H is suitable for being re-entered as a collection of commands. To take advantage of this, redirect the output to a file. For a batch file, make sure to use an extension of BAT. For instance:

```
DOSKEY /H >CLEVER.BAT
```

You can now enter the name of the batch file whenever you want to execute the commands. However, before you do, edit the file and remove the DOSKEY /H command at the end: Otherwise you will get yourself into a strange sort of never-ending loop. Actually, you will probably want to do other editing before you use the batch file.

More Ways to Recall Commands

As you have already seen, you can recall DOS commands by pressing <F9> and specifying the command number. However, there are other ways to recall commands.

You can recall a command that starts with a particular pattern by typing that pattern followed by <F8>. DOS will copy the most recent command that starts with that pattern to the current line. You can then edit and reenter it.

Here is an example. By pressing <F7> you see that your history list is:

```
1: C:
2: CHKDSK
3: CD \DOCUMENT
4: DIR
5: TIME
6: D:
```

If you type C and then press <F8>, DOS will search for the most recent command that started with C, and then copy it to the current line. In this case, it is command #3. However, let's say that you really wanted the CHKDSK command. Type CH and press <F8>. This time, DOS will recall command #2.

Two more ways to recall commands allow you to zip to the beginning or end of the history list. Pressing <Page Up> recalls the very first command. Pressing <Page Down> recalls the most recent command.

If you want to work your way up and down the list, one command at a time, use the <Up> and <Down> cursor control keys. (These are the keys with the up and down arrows.) The first time you press <Up>, DOS will recall the most recent command to the current line. If you press <Up> again, DOS recalls the next most recent command. You can press

<Up> repeatedly and work your way up the list. Similarly, you can press <Down> and go down the list.

By itself, <Up> is the single most useful recall key. You will find yourself using it frequently to bring back (and then edit) your last command.

Editing a Recalled Command

Once you have recalled a command, editing is simple. All you do is type whatever changes you want. You can move to the left and right by pressing the <Left> and <Right> cursor control keys.

For example, say that you enter the incorrect command:

```
FORXAT A: /Q /V:EMPTY
```

Since you have misspelled FORMAT, DOS will respond with:

```
Bad command and file name
```

To recall the command, press <Up>. DOS copies the command to the current line. The cursor is at the end of the line, just past the Y. Press <Left> and hold it down until the cursor is below the X. Type M, to replace the X. You can now press <Enter> to reenter the command.

As you edit the current line there are several keys you can use to move the cursor:

<Left>	Move one position to the left
<Right>	Move one position to the right
<Home>	Move to the beginning of the line
<End>	Move to the end of the line
<Ctrl-Left>	Move one word to the left
<Ctrl-Right>	Move one word to the right

By becoming comfortable with these keys, you can zip around the current line with dispatch. For instance, in our example:

```
FORXAT A: /Q /V:EMPTY
```

the fastest way to get to the X in FORXAT is to press <Home> <Right> <Right> <Right>.

Deleting Characters

While you are editing, there are four ways to erase characters. The first way is to move to a character you want to erase and press the <Delete> key.

Here is an example. You accidentally enter the following incorrect command:

```
FORMXAT A: /Q /V:EMPTY
```

Like our last example, you meant to type FORMAT, but in this case you typed an extra letter, X, after the M.

Press <Up> to recall this command to the current line. Next, move the cursor to the X. Now, remove the X by pressing <Delete>. You can now press <Enter> to reenter the command.

The second way to erase characters works only when you are at the end of the current line. You can press <Backspace> to remove the rightmost character. By pressing <Backspace> repeatedly, you can remove characters from the right-hand side of the line, one at a time.

Here is an example. You accidentally enter the incorrect command:

```
FORMAT A: /Q /VEMPTY
```

Since you have left out the colon after the /V, DOS thinks that /VEMPTY is one long option and you get the following error message:

```
INVALID SWITCH - /VEMPTY
```

(Remember, "switch" is another name for an option.)

To correct this mistake, recall the command by pressing <Up>. DOS will display the command

```
FORMAT A: /Q /VEMPTY
```

leaving the cursor one position past the end of the line, just after the Y. Now, press <Backspace> five times, to erase the five rightmost characters. You will now see:

```
FORMAT A: /Q /V
```

Type the correct characters, :EMPTY. The line will look like this:

```
FORMAT A: /Q /V:EMPTY
```

You can now press <Enter> to reenter the command. In other words, you can only use <Backspace> to remove characters from the end of the current line.

The final two ways to erase characters from the current line are by pressing <Ctrl-Home> or <Ctrl-End>. <Ctrl-End> erases from the cursor to the end of the line. <Ctrl-Home> erases from the beginning of the line, up to, but not including, the cursor.

For example, say that you are editing the command:

```
FORMAT A: /Q /V:EMPTY
```

and that the cursor is under the Q. If you press <Ctrl-End>, DOS will erase from the Q to the end of the line. The command line will look like this:

```
FORMAT A: /
```

If, on the other hand, the cursor is under the Q and you press <Ctrl-Home>, DOS will erase from the beginning of the line up to, but not including the Q. The command line will look like this:

```
Q /V:EMPTY
```

Overstrike and Insert Mode

Normally, what you type on the command line replaces whatever happens to be there. For example, in the last section we changed FORBAT to FORMAT by moving to the B and typing the letter M. This is called *overstrike mode.*

If you want to insert characters, press the <Insert> key. From now on, whatever you type will be inserted at the position of the cursor. As you type, everything to the right will be moved over to make room. This is called *Insert mode.* To change back to overstrike mode, press <Insert> a second time.

Here is an example. You type the command:

```
DIR \DOCUMENT
```

to list the contents of the \DOCUMENT directory on the default disk. You now want to check a directory with the same name on the A: disk.

To start, press <Up> to recall the command. You will see:

```
DIR \DOCUMENT
```

The cursor will be at the end of the line, after the T. Move one word to the left by pressing <Ctrl-Left>. The cursor is now under the \.

Now, press the <Insert> key. To show you that you are in Insert mode, DOS will change the cursor. Instead of being a blinking underscore, the cursor becomes a blinking square. You can now type A:. The current line looks like:

```
DIR A:\DOCUMENT
```

Press <Enter> to enter the command.

Normally, each time you start to edit a command DOS puts you in overstrike mode. By pressing <Insert>, you can toggle back and forth between Insert and Overstrike.

If you prefer to start in Insert mode automatically, you can activate DOSKEY with the /INSERT option:

```
DOSKEY /INSERT
```

Of course, within a particular command, you can always press <Insert> to change to Overstrike mode.

For completeness, there is a /OVERSTRIKE option but you don't need to use it, as Overstrike mode is the default.

Recalling and Editing Commands: A Summary

For reference, Table 23.1 contains a summary of the commands and keys that we described in this chapter.

Table 23.1 *Summary of Recall and Edit Facilities for DOS Commands*

Overstrike and Insert Mode

To start the command history mechanism in overstrike mode:

```
DOSKEY
DOSKEY /OVERSTRIKE
```

To start the command history mechanism in insert mode:

```
DOSKEY /INSERT
```

While editing, press <Insert> to toggle back and forth between overstrike and insert mode.

(continued)

Table 23.1   *(continued)*

Manipulating the Command History

To display the command history: <F7>
To erase the command history: <Alt-F7>
To display the command history without numbers:

```
DOSKEY /H
```

To write the command history to a file:

```
DOSKEY /H >filename
```

Recalling a Previously Entered Command

To recall a command by number: <F9>
To recall a command by pattern: pattern <F8>
To recall the:
• last command in the history list: <Up> or <Page Down>
• first command in the history list: <Page Up>
To move up and down in the history list: <Up> and <Down>

Moving the Cursor

To move one position left: <Left>
To move one position right: <Right>
To move to the start of the line: <Home>
To move to the end of the line: <End>
To move one word left: <Ctrl-Left>
To move one word right: <Ctrl-Right>

Deleting Characters

To delete a single character at the cursor position: <Delete>
To delete a single character to the left of the cursor: <Backspace>
To delete from the cursor to the end of the line: <Ctrl-End>
To delete from start of line, up to but not including cursor: <Ctrl-Home>

Note: *<Left>, <Right>, <Up>, and <Down> refer to the cursor control [arrow] keys.*

24

THE DOS
EDITING KEYS

Introduction

In Chapter 23, we discussed DOSKEY, a memory resident program that allows you to recall and edit DOS commands. However, there is another set of keys, the DOS editing keys, that also allow you to edit a previous command. These keys are:

<F1>, <F2>, <F3>, <F4>, <F5>

<Esc>, <Insert>, <Delete>, <Backspace>, <Left>, <Right>

(By the way, <Left> and <Right> refer to the cursor control (arrow) keys).

In addition, the <F6> key also has a special role to play. Strictly speaking, it is not an editing key, but it is usually discussed with the other keys and we will cover it in this chapter.

The DOS Editing Keys and DOSKEY

The DOS editing keys have two advantages over DOSKEY. First, they will work with all versions of DOS. DOSKEY comes only with DOS 5.0 or later. Second, the editing keys will work, not only with DOS commands, but with the EDLIN line editor that we will be discussing in Chapter 27. The one disadvantage is that the editing keys are not as powerful as the DOSKEY facilities.

If you have DOS 5.0 or later, you can look on the DOS editing keys as complementing the DOSKEY facilities we covered in Chapter 23. You will notice some overlap. That is because the DOSKEY facilities were conceived as an extension to the DOS editing keys.

If you are using an old version of DOS, you will definitely want to pay attention to this chapter. It describes the only editing keys that you will be able to use.

Recalling the Previous Command

The role of the editing keys is to let you recall a DOS command, edit it, and then reenter it. However, unlike the DOSKEY facilities, the editing keys can only recall the very last command. An explanation of how it works follows.

As we explained in Chapter 23, the line that you are currently typing is called the *command line*. DOS maintains the command line, interpreting each key as you press it. With DOSKEY, DOS also keeps a list of all your previous commands, called the history list.

Well, there is one more storage area that DOS maintains—a small bit of memory just large enough to hold one command. The area is called the *template* and, at all times, DOS makes sure that it contains the last command that you entered. Thus, whenever you enter a command DOS copies it to two places: the template, and (if you are using DOSKEY) to the bottom of the history list.

The conceptual difference between DOSKEY and the editing keys is that DOSKEY recalls data from the history list, while the editing keys recall data from the template.

This means that the editing keys can recall only one command—your last one. However, they do afford a fair bit of control over how the characters are to be recalled.

Recalling the Entire Command

To recall the last command you entered, press <F3>. You can now edit the command and reenter it. Here is an example.

You enter the command:

```
DIR
```

You see a directory listing of the current directory on your default drive. However, you really wanted a listing of the files on drive A:, but you forgot to specify the disk name. Simply press <F3>. DOS will redisplay the command:

```
DIR
```

and leave the cursor at the end of the line. You can now add the drive name:

```
DIR A:
```

and press <Enter>.

If you use DOSKEY, you will notice that <F3> is a lot like the <Up> and <Page Down> keys. All three of them will recall the last command that you entered. The main difference is that <F3> recalls the contents of the template, where <Up> and <Page Down> recall the last line of the history list. Most of the time, the distinction is not an important one.

Recalling One Character at a Time

By using <F1>, you can recall one character at a time from the template. For example, say that you want to check your hard disk C:. However, you accidentally enter:

```
CHKDSK X:
```

You can press <F1> seven times, to recall the first seven characters of the template:

```
CHKDSK
```

You can now type C:

```
CHKDSK C:
```

and then press <Enter>.

As a convenience, the <Right> key—that is, the cursor control key with the right arrow—performs the same function as <F1>.

Editing the Command Line

Once you have recalled all or part of your previous command, there are several ways that you can edit it. First, you can use <Backspace> to back up one character at a time, deleting as you go.

Here is an example. Again, you want CHKDSK C: but you accidentally enter:

```
CHKDSK X:
```

However, this time you do not recall the command one character at a time. Instead you recall the entire command by pressing <F3>. The cursor is now at the end of the command, just after the colon.

Press <Backspace> twice to erase the last two characters. You will see:

```
CHKDSK
```

Now, type C:, the drive name that you want:

```
CHKDSK C:
```

and press <Enter>.

When you are using DOSKEY, the <Left>, <Home>, and <Ctrl-Left> keys allow you to move the cursor within the current line. You can then insert, delete, or retype characters. With the editing keys, you cannot move within the current line. All you can do is start from the end and, moving left, using <Backspace> or <Left>, erase one character at a time.

Recalling Part of the Template

There are two keys that you can use to recall part of your last command. The first key, <F2>, copies part of the template to the current line.

You type <F2> followed by a single character. DOS copies from the template, starting with the current position, up to but not including the first instance of the character you typed. This sounds more complex than it really is, so let's look at an example.

You enter the command:

```
CHKDSK A:
```

Now that you have checked the A: disk, you want to reuse the command to check the C: disk. Press <F2> followed by the letter A. DOS copies from the template to the current line, up to, but not including the A. You will see:

```
CHKDSK
```

You can now enter C:

```
CHKDSK C:
```

and press <Enter>.

Skipping Over Part of the Template

The second key that you can use to recall part of your last command is <F4>. You press <F4> followed by any character. Within the template, DOS will skip to the next occurrence of that character, without copying anything to the current line.

At first, this is difficult to understand because you are working with something you can't see—the template—so an example to show how it works follows.

You want to display the DOS version number. By mistake, you enter DOSVER instead of VER:

```
DOSVER
```

You want to ignore the first three letters of the template (DOS) and recall the rest of the command (VER). Press <F4> followed by the letter V.
Nothing happens on the command line but, within the template, DOS
has moved up to the letter V. That is, DOS has skipped over the first three
letters. Now, press <F3> to recall the rest of the command. You will see:

```
VER
```

You can now press <Enter>.

To understand this fully, realize that DOS keeps two cursors to mark
your position within a line. The first cursor is in the command line which
you can see. The other cursor is in the template, which you can't see.

Whenever you press <F3>, DOS copies from the template to the current line. The copying takes place from the current position in the template to the end of the template. Both cursors are updated.

When you press <F1> or <Right>, DOS copies a single character from
the template to the current line. Again, the copying takes place from the
current position in the template. Both cursors are updated one position
to the right.

When you use <F4>, it tells DOS to move the template cursor to the
right without changing the current line. The result is that you have
skipped over part of the template.

It can take a while to become comfortable with all of this, so another
example follows: You have entered the command:

```
DIR C:\DOCUMENT\YOURFILE.DOC
```

However, you really wanted to enter DIR C:YOURFILE.DOC. First, recall
all of the command up to, but not including, the first \ character. Press
<F2>\. You will see:

```
DIR C:
```

Now, skip over all the characters up to, but not including, the letter Y.

Press <F4>Y. The current line will not change but, within the template,
the invisible cursor is now pointing to the letter Y. Now, recall the rest of
the command by pressing <F3>. You will see:

```
DIR C:YOURFILE.DOC
```

You can now press <Enter>.

Inserting and Deleting Characters

Whenever you type on the current line, DOS moves the cursor to the right. However, at the same time, DOS is moving the template cursor, even though you can't see it.

For instance, say that you have just entered the command:

```
DIR OLDFILE.DOC
```

You now decide to enter the command DIR NEWFILE. Press <F2> followed by the letter O. DOS copies from the template to the current line, up to but not including the letter O. You will see:

```
DIR
```

Now, type NEW. As you type, DOS moves the cursor three positions to the right, both in the current line and in the template. You will see:

```
DIR NEW
```

The template cursor is now pointing to the letter F. To copy the rest of the template, press <F3>. You will see:

```
DIR NEWFILE.DOC
```

You can now press <Enter>.

Sometimes you may wish to copy part of the template, insert a few characters, and then copy the rest of the template. By pressing the <Insert> key you can tell DOS to leave the template cursor where it is while you introduce new characters into the current line.

For example, you have just entered the command:

```
DIR OLDFILE.DOC
```

However, you forgot that the file resides on the A: disk. You should have entered DIR A:OLDFILE.DOC. Here is what you can do. First, press <F2> followed by the letter O. This copies from the template to the current line, up to but not including the letter O. You will see:

```
DIR
```

Now, press <Insert> and type A:. You will see:

```
DIR A:
```

However, the template cursor is still pointing at the O.

Now, copy the rest of the command by pressing <F3>. You will see:

```
DIR A:OLDFILE.DOC
```

You can now press <Enter>.

By using the <Delete> key, you can tell DOS to perform the opposite operation: skip over a character in the template without changing the current line. Here is an example. You have just entered the command:

```
DIR C:E:OLDFILE.DOC
```

You should have entered DIR C:OLDFILE.DOC. Press <F2> followed by the letter E to copy from the template to the current line. DOS will copy up to but not including the E. You will see:

```
DIR C:
```

The template cursor is pointing to the E.

Now, press <Delete> twice. DOS moves the template cursor two positions to the right. It is now pointing to the letter O. The current line has not changed. To copy the rest of the template, press <F3>. You will see:

```
DIR C:OLDFILE.DOC
```

You can now press <Enter>.

What to Do When You Make a Mistake

When you make a mistake, you can press either one of two keys. If you press <Esc>, DOS discards the current line but leaves the template untouched. If you press <F5>, DOS discards the current line but first copies it to the template.

Here is how it works. Say that you enter the command:

```
FORMAT C: /Q /V:EMPTY
```

Just before you hit <Enter>, you realize that this command will wipe out your hard disk. Press <Esc>. DOS will forget all about the command as if you had never typed it.

Later, you type:

```
DIR C:\DOCUQENT\BACKUP\MYFILE.DOC
```

Before you press <Enter> you realize that you have misspelled DOCU-
MENT. Of course, you can always press <Esc> and retype everything, but
it's a long, difficult command and you might as well use what you already
have. Press <F5>. DOS will copy the command to the template but will
not execute it. You can now use the editing keys to recall and correct
what is in the template. Press <F2> followed by the letter Q. DOS will
copy from the template to the command line, up to but not including the
letter Q. You will see:

```
DIR C:\DOCU
```

Now, type M to replace the Q. You will see:

```
DIR C:\DOCUM
```

The template cursor is now pointing to the letter E. Press <F3> to copy
the rest of the line:

```
DIR C:\DOCUMENT\BACKUP\MYFILE.DOC
```

You can now press <Enter>.

Typing the End of File Character

Many DOS files end with a special character that marks the end of the
file. This character is a <Ctrl-Z>. You can type this character by holding
down the <Ctrl> key and pressing the letter Z. As a convenience, DOS lets
you press <F6> instead.

The only time you will be likely to need <Ctrl-Z> is to mark the end of
text that you are copying from the keyboard directly to a file. (We discussed this idea in Chapter 19.) For example, you want to create a quick
batch file consisting of two commands. You enter the following command to copy from the console to a file:

```
COPY CON: DISKTEST.BAT
```

DOS is now waiting for your input. You type the two commands:

```
CHKDSK C:
CHKDSK D:
```

You now need to indicate that this is the end of the file. Once way is to
press <Ctrl-Z>. Another way is to press <F6>—DOS will send the end of
file character for you. Either way you will see:

```
^Z
```

(The ^ character is an abbreviation for <Ctrl>.)

Press <Enter> to end the command. You new file is complete. (In this example, you can now run the two commands by typing DISKTEST.)

A Summary of the DOS Editing Keys

For reference, Table 24.1 contains a summary of the editing keys that we described in this chapter. The editing keys not only enhance the power of DOSKEY, they make life a lot easier if you use the EDLIN text editor. At first, these commands may seem a bit awkward, but they will repay any effort you are willing to make.

Table 24.1   *Summary of the DOS Editing Keys*

At all times DOS maintains two cursors: one on the command line, and one in the template (which you cannot see). The DOS editing keys copy characters from the current position in the template to the current position of the command line.

<F3>

Copy the rest of the characters in the template to the current line.

<F1> or <Right>

Copy a single character in the template to the current line.

<Backspace> or <Left>

Delete a single character from the end of the current line.

<F2> followed by a single character

Copy from the template to the command line, up until the first occurrence of the specified character.

<F4> followed by a single character

Skip over characters in the template, up until the first occurrence of the specified character. The current line does not change.

(continued)

Table 24.1 *(continued)*

<Insert>

Start inserting characters into the command line without moving the template cursor.

<Delete>

Skip over a single character in the template. The current line does not change.

<Esc>

Cancel the current line. Do not change the template.

<F5>

Cancel the current line, but first copy it to the template.

<F6>

Insert the end of file character, Ctrl-Z, into the command line.

Note: <Left> and <Right> refer to the cursor control [arrow] keys.

25

USING MACROS TO CREATE YOUR OWN COMMANDS

Introduction

There will be times when you will want to change the DOS command set. You may wish that a command operated just a little differently. Or, you might want to combine several commands into a single new command. The DOSKEY program allows you to do all of this and more by creating what are called *macros.*

A macro is nothing less than your own customized command. Macros allow you to set up a truly personalized working environment. You can create all sorts of new commands, each of which carries out a specific task just the way you want it to.

What Is a Macro?

A macro is a name that stands for one or more specific commands. When you enter the name, DOS will automatically substitute the commands.

For example, let's say that you often need to format diskettes using the command:

```
FORMAT A: /Q /V:EMPTY
```

You can define a macro named QF (quick format) to stand for this command. Now, whenever you want to format a diskette, you can enter:

```
QF
```

DOS will recognize it as being a macro and will substitute the real command automatically.

Initializing DOSKEY

In Chapter 23, we showed you how DOSKEY maintains a history list from which you can recall and edit DOS commands. It is the very same DOSKEY program that enables you to create macros. Since DOSKEY is a memory-resident program (see Chapter 21), you must install it before it can be used. Normally, you would do this by including a DOSKEY command in your AUTOEXEC.BAT file.

In Chapter 23, we explained that you can start DOSKEY to be in either overstrike or insert mode. (This only has to do with command line editing, not macros.) To express your preference, there are two ways to start DOSKEY:

```
DOSKEY /OVERSTRIKE
DOSKEY /INSERT
```

By default, DOSKEY starts in overstrike mode, so most people leave out the /OVERSTRIKE option and just put

```
DOSKEY
```

in their AUTOEXEC.BAT file.

Since DOSKEY is a memory resident program, it remains in your computer's memory until you turn off the computer or until you restart DOS. If you decide to do without DOSKEY, you will have to edit your AUTOEXEC.BAT file, remove the DOSKEY command, and restart your system.

When you anticipate using macros, there is another option, /BUFSIZE=, that you may want to use. This controls the size of the buffer—memory area—in which DOS keeps the macro definitions and the history list. (The history list is explained in Chapter 23).

By default, DOS sets aside 512 bytes of memory. If you would like a different size, you can specify it when you initialize DOSKEY. For instance, to request 1 kilobyte (1024 bytes) of memory, use:

```
DOSKEY /SIZE=1024
```

The minimum size you can specify is 256.

Normally, there is no need to use /SIZE= unless you know that you will run out of room. If so, this option should be part of the DOSKEY command in your AUTOEXEC.BAT file.

Clearing the DOSKEY Buffer

Every time you start DOSKEY, it clears the buffer. If you want to restart DOSKEY in the middle of a work session, you can use the /REINSTALL option:

```
DOSKEY /REINSTALL
```

This will install a new copy of DOSKEY with an empty buffer. The history list will be empty and there will be no macros.

However, this is not something that you would normally do. As we explained in Chapter 23, you can clear the history list by pressing <Alt-F7>. And, as you will see in this chapter, you can clear the macro list by pressing <Alt-F10>.

Using the /REINSTALL option is a more drastic step that will actually install a second copy of DOSKEY and use up more memory. Moreover, it is almost guaranteed to cause problems if you have other memory-resident programs.

Defining a Macro

To define a macro, type the DOSKEY command, followed by the name of the macro, an equal sign (=), and the commands you want to abbreviate:

```
DOSKEY NAME = COMMANDS
```

For example, to define the macro QF to perform a quick format, you might use:

```
DOSKEY QF = FORMAT A: /Q /V:EMPTY
```

If you want, you can leave out the spaces around the equal sign.

```
DOSKEY QF=FORMAT A: /Q /V:EMPTY
```

Whenever you want to use a macro, all you have to do is enter its name. DOS will replace it by the appropriate command list. (In a moment, we'll show you how to specify more than one command in a macro.) When you enter the macro name, DOS will display the commands for you and execute them.

For example, if you use the QF macro we just defined, DOS will display the FORMAT command and then execute it, just as if you had typed it yourself. Once you type in:

```
QF
```

you will see:

```
FORMAT A: /Q /V:EMPTY
INSERT NEW DISKETTE FOR DRIVE A:
AND PRESS ENTER WHEN READY...
```

Every time you use a macro, DOS will display the real commands. There is no way to suppress this, even with the ECHO OFF command.

Displaying and Deleting Macros

At any time, you can display all your macros by using DOSKEY with the /M command. (Actually, the full name of this option is /MACROS, but /M works just fine.)

```
DOSKEY /M
```

If you will be doing much work with macros, you will find it useful to define a simple macro just to execute the DOSKEY /M command. For example:

```
DOSKEY M = DOSKEY /M
```

Now, you can see your macros whenever you want, just by entering:

```
M
```

If you want to delete all your macros, press <Alt-F10>. If you want to delete a particular macro, type DOSKEY, followed by the macro name, followed by an equal sign. For example:

```
DOSKEY QF =
```

DOS will delete the macro you specify while preserving all the others.

Using Macros to Replace DOS Commands

One of the most important uses for macros is to replace DOS commands. For example, you might want to replace DIR with DIR /P. Define a DIR macro as follows:

```
DOSKEY DIR = DIR /P
```

Now, whenever you type a DIR command, DOS will replace it with DIR /P.

You might wonder, what actually happens when you type DIR? How does DOS know if you are referring to the macro or the command? The answer is that DOSKEY looks at everything you type before it is passed to the command processor to be executed. Thus, DOSKEY has a chance to process macros before anything else happens. This allows you to redefine DOS commands, even internal commands like DIR. (Internal and external commands are explained in Chapter 6.)

One of the most important uses for macros is to prevent accidental damage. For example, the FDISK command can delete a hard disk partition. Once a hard disk has been set up, there is rarely a need to use FDISK. But this may not stop a curious individual from experimenting on your computer. To protect your hard disk, define the following macro:

```
DOSKEY FDISK = ECHO Sorry, this command is restricted.
```

Controlling Whether a Macro Should Be Processed

There may be times when you do not want a command to be interpreted as a macro. DOSKEY provides for such contingencies by observing the following rules:

If a command line starts with a space or tab character, DOSKEY will not look for a macro.

If a command line begins with any other character, DOSKEY will look for a macro.

This provides us with an important control. If you do not want a macro to be replaced, simply press the <Space> bar or the <Tab> key at the beginning of the line.

For example, say that you have replaced the FDISK command by an ECHO command that displays a warning message. Normally, whenever anyone enters:

```
FDISK
```

all they will get is the ECHO command. However, there may be a rare occasion on which you really do want to run FDISK. All you have to do is press <Space> and then type FDISK.

Remember, DOSKEY will look for macros in any command line that does not start with a space or tab character. This allows you to define a macro with any name you want—it does not need to start with a letter. For example, you might define:

```
DOSKEY @ = COPY C:\DOCUMENT\NEWFILE.DOC A:BACKUP.DOC
```

You can now execute this complex COPY command just by entering the @ (at-sign) character.

You can use just about any characters within a macro command except for three that have special meaning for DOS. They are < (the less-than sign) which redirects the standard input; > (the greater-than sign) which redirects the standard output; and | (the vertical bar) which creates a pipeline. (These three tools are discussed in Chapter 19.)

If you want to use these characters within a macro definition, you need to refer to them by the following codes:

```
<    $L
>    $G
|    $B
```

Here is an example. To copy a directory listing to the file MASTER.LST, you can redirect the output of the DIR command:

```
DIR > MASTER.LST
```

You can create a macro to do this for you by using:

```
DOSKEY DIRSAVE = DIR $G MASTER.LST
```

As we explained in Chapter 19, using a single > character tells DOS to replace the output file if it already exists. If you want to append data to the end of a file, you need to use >>. For example,

```
DIR >> MASTER.LST
```

To define this as a macro, use GG:

```
DOSKEY DIRSAVE = DIR $G$G MASTER.LST
```

Using Multiple Commands Within a Macro

Normally, you can enter only one DOS command at a time. However, you can define a macro to execute multiple commands. All you need to do is separate each command with the special code $T. (The name $T reminds you that it is a command terminator.)

Here is an example:

```
DOSKEY TESTDISK = CHKDSK C: $T CHKDSK D: $T ECHO finished!
```

If you want, you can leave out the spaces around the equal sign and the $T:

```
DOSKEY TESTDISK=CHKDSK C:$TCHKDSK D:$TECHO finished!
```

When you invoke the macro, DOS will execute the three commands

```
CHKDSK C:
CHKDSK D:
ECHO Finished!
```

one right after the other.

Using Parameters

When you enter a command, any words or values that you type after the command name are called *parameters*. For example, in the command:

```
COPY NEWFILE OLDFILE /V
```

there are three parameters: NEWFILE, OLDFILE and /V. The third parameter also happens to be an option.

In Chapter 10, we saw that we can reference the value of parameters from within a batch file by using the special names:

```
%1  %2  %3  %4  %5  %6  %7  %8  %9
```

The first parameter is represented by %1, the second by %2, and so on. The importance of parameters is that they allow us to use values that will not be set until the batch file is actually executed.

When you define a macro, DOS affords you a similar capability. Within a macro, parameters are referred to as:

```
$1  $2  $3  $4  $5  $6  $7  $8  $9
```

When DOS invokes a macro, all instances of these parameters are replaced by the corresponding values that you type on the command line.

Consider the following example:

```
DOSKEY TESTDISK = CHKDSK $1 $T DIR $1
```

Once this macro is defined, you can invoke it with a command line parameter. For example:

```
TESTDISK C:
```

DOS will substitute the parameter value for $1 and then execute the commands. In this case, DOS will execute:

```
CHKDSK C:
DIR C:
```

Here is a slightly more complex example. You extend the previous macro by placing another parameter after the DIR command:

```
DOSKEY TESTDISK = CHKDSK $1 $T DIR $1 $2
```

Now, you can specify a second parameter value that can be used as an option for DIR. For example, if you enter:

```
TESTDISK C: /W
```

DOS will execute:

```
CHKDSK C:
DIR C: /W
```

If you use parameters within a macro that are not specified when you invoke the macro, DOS will simply remove the parameters. For example, if you invoke the TESTDISK macro with no parameters:

```
TESTDISK
```

$1 and $2 will have no value and DOS will execute the following two commands:

```
CHKDSK
DIR
```

Referring to All of the Parameters

There will be times when you want to refer to all of the parameters as a single unit. To do this, use the $* code. This is handy when you want to be able to pass an indefinite number of parameters to a command.

For example, say that you are tired of typing DOSKEY every time you want to define a macro. You would rather type DEF. Use the following macro:

```
DOSKEY DEF = DOSKEY $*
```

$* represents all the parameters that you might type. You can use DEF to define macros:

```
DEF HELLO = ECHO Hi There.
```

Here is a slightly more complex example. Say that you want a customized version of the DIR command, named DW, that will always use the /W flag. Use:

```
DOSKEY DW = DIR $* /W
```

When you invoke DW with no parameters:

```
DW
```

DOS will execute the command:

```
DIR /W
```

However, if you want to specify parameters, say:

```
DIR C:\MYFILE /P
```

DOS will include them in the command:

```
DIR C:\MYFILE /P /W
```

Using a $ Character Literally

Since the $ (dollar sign) character has a special meaning, DOSKEY can misinterpret your command if you use $ by itself within a macro definition. If you want to use an actual $ character, you must represent it by the code $$:

```
DOSKEY MONEY = ECHO Please insert $$5.00 and press Enter.
```

The output will be a single $ character:

```
ECHO Please insert $5.00 and press Enter.
```

When to Use a Macro Instead of a Batch File.

Both macros and batch files allow you to create your own customized commands. In order to choose which facility to use, follow this guideline:

When you want to create commands that are simple or temporary, use a macro.

Otherwise, use a batch file.

Probably one of the most important uses of a macro is to make a customized version of a particular DOS command. For example, say that you are a Unix user and you want to create a command called LS to act like the Unix "ls" command. Like DIR, this command lists the contents of a directory. However, by default, the Unix "ls" command lists only file names, one name per line in lower case, sorted by file name. The equivalent DIR command would be:

```
DIR /B /L /O:N
```

(These DIR options are described in Chapter 9.)

The following macro will create an LS command for you:

```
DOSKEY LS = DIR $* /B /L /O:N
```

In this case, it is easier to use a macro than a batch file. Moreover, the macro will execute slightly faster because DOS will not have to read a batch file from the disk.

However, when you are doing anything the least bit complex, you are usually better off with a batch file. Here is a example of how easy it is to get in trouble with a macro if you are not careful.

Say that you often need to format disks, sometimes in drive A: and sometimes in drive B:. To make it easy, you decide to define the following macro for quick unconditional formatting:

```
DOSKEY QF = FORMAT $1 /Q /U
```

You have chosen to use the /Q /U combination because it makes for the fastest format (see Chapter 18). True, the /U option prevents you from being able to UNFORMAT the disk but, in this case, it doesn't matter because you only format old diskettes that contain unimportant data.

Then, whenever you want to format, you use QF with A: or B:

```
QF A:
QF B:
```

and DOS generates the appropriate command, one of the following:

```
FORMAT A: /Q /U
FORMAT B: /Q /U
```

But, one day when you are away, an untutored neophyte sits down at your computer and types:

```
QF C:
```

In response, DOS executes the following command:

```
FORMAT C: /Q /U
```

The next morning you come in to discover an unconditionally formatted hard disk and a new resolve to use batch files for potentially dangerous commands. (In this case, a batch file could have refused to execute the command unless a parameter was specified that was equal to A: or B:.)

If you use both macros and batch files, you should remember that macros are processed before the results are passed to the command processor. This means that where a macro can invoke a batch file, a batch file cannot invoke a macro. If you use the name of a macro within a batch file, DOS will treat it like an ordinary command. Furthermore, because macros are processed only once, you cannot use a macro within a macro. If you do, the second level macro will not be recognized.

Saving Your Macro List

Once you develop useful macros, you will want to have them accessible at all times. But the list of macro definitions is kept in memory and is erased whenever you turn off your computer or restart DOS.

The best strategy is to maintain a batch file of macro definitions in your BATCH subdirectory. (In Chapter 16, we explained how it is a good idea to keep batch files in their own directory.) That way, you can put the command:

```
CALL C:\BATCH\MACROS
```

in your AUTOEXEC.BAT file. Each time you start DOS, your macros will be defined for you automatically.

From time to time you will develop new macros that you will want to add to MACROS.BAT. However, it is a lot of trouble to have to retype each macro. Instead, all you have to do is list your macros by using the DOSKEY /M command and redirect the output to the macros batch file. For example:

```
DOSKEY /M >>C:\BATCH\MACROS.BAT
```

Notice the use of >> instead of a single > character. If you use >, the output will replace whatever happens to be in the batch file. By using >>, you make sure that DOS will append the output to the end of the file.

Once the list of macros is saved, you can edit the batch file to make each macro listing into a proper definition. In particular, you will have to put the command name DOSKEY in front of each new macro.

A Summary of Macro Definition Tools

For reference, Table 25.1 contains a summary of all the tools you can use to define macros.

Table 25.1   *Summary of Macro Definition Tools*

To define a macro:

```
DOSKEY name = commands
```

To delete a single macro:

```
DOSKEY name =
```

To delete all your macros press <Alt-F10>.

To display all your macros:

```
DOSKEY /M
```

To save your macros to the end of a file:

```
DOSKEY /M >>filename
```

To prevent DOS from processing a macro:
put a space or tab at the beginning of the command line

Within a macro, you can use the following special codes:

$L	<	(a less-than sign)
$G	>	(a greater-than sign)
GG	>>	(two greater-than signs)
$B	|	(a vertical bar)
$$	$	(a dollar sign)
$T		separate multiple commands

(continued)

Table 25.1 *(continued)*

To reference a specific command line parameter, use:

$1 $2 $3 $4 $5 $6 $7 $8 $9

To reference all the command line parameters, use:

$*

26

THE DOS EDITOR

Introduction

DOS comes with two text editors, EDIT and EDLIN. EDIT is a full screen editor, which means that you can edit a whole screenful of data at a time. You simply move the cursor to wherever you want, and insert data or make changes. EDLIN is a line editor, which means that you edit your data line by line. To work with your text, you enter commands that are applied to specific lines.

In this chapter we will discuss EDIT. In Chapter 27 we will discuss EDLIN. Almost all of the time, EDIT is the better editor to use. However, it comes only with DOS 5.0 or later. If you are using an old version of DOS, you will have to use EDLIN. And, as we will see in Chapter 27, EDLIN does have a few advantages over EDIT.

What Can You Do with EDIT?

EDIT allows you to create, modify and print text files—that is, files that contain plain ASCII characters. The most important use for EDIT is to create and modify batch files. As we discussed in Chapters 10 and 11, batch files are an important tool that you can use to customize your DOS system.

Another important use for EDIT is maintaining your initialization files: that is, the AUTOEXEC.BAT and CONFIG.SYS files. (AUTOEXEC.BAT is discussed in Chapter 12; CONFIG.SYS is discussed in Chapter 28.) These are the files that tell DOS how you want your system to be configured and initialized. From time to time, you will have to make changes and EDIT is the program to use.

A third use for EDIT is to write programs. Actually, as we will see in a minute, EDIT was really designed for programmers.

Finally, EDIT is perfect for creating short documents, such as letters or memos. In such cases, you can use EDIT instead of a word processor. Not only does EDIT come free with DOS, but it's a lot easier to learn then a word processor.

Starting the Editor: The EDIT Command

To start the editor type EDIT, followed by the name of the file you want to work with. For example:

```
EDIT AUTOEXEC.BAT
```

If the file does not already exist, DOS will create it for you.

If you are creating a new file and you aren't sure what name you want to use, you can start the editor without a file name:

```
EDIT
```

EDIT will set up an empty file with no name. Later, when it is time to save the file, you can decide on a name.

When you start the editor, there are several options that you can help EDIT use your display to advantage. They are:

/B	You have a monochrome display with a graphics card
/G	You have an old CGA (color graphics adaptor) display
/H	Use max number of lines that your display will support
/NOHI	You have a display that has no high intensity

Normally, there is no need to use an option.

EDIT and QBASIC

All of Microsoft's programming languages come with an editor program. Programmers use this editor to write their programs. Starting with DOS version 5.0, Microsoft included a new BASIC interpreter, named QBASIC, as part of DOS. And along with QBASIC, came the programmer's editor. The DOS editor is actually the QBASIC programmer's editor.

When you enter the QBASIC commands, it starts a complete BASIC programming environment. However, if you start QBASIC with the /EDITOR option, it allows you to use the MS-DOS Editor by itself, without entering the programming environment:

```
QBASIC /EDITOR
```

The EDIT command is just an easy way to use the QBASIC /EDITOR command. In fact, the options that we described above— /B, /G, /H, /NOHI—are options for the QBASIC command.

Normally, you can ignore the fact that EDIT and QBASIC are related. However, in order for you to use the Editor, DOS must be able to access

QBASIC. This means that if you want to start EDIT, you must have the QBASIC program in your DOS directory.

You might be tempted to delete QBASIC to save space if you know that you will never want to program in BASIC. However, if you do delete this program, you will not be able to use the EDIT command because there will be no QBASIC Editor. You will see the message:

```
CAN NOT FIND FILE QBASIC.EXE
```

If you have a serious need to save space and you will not be using QBASIC, you can delete the file QBASIC.HLP. This file contains help information for QBASIC. The EDIT program has its own help file, EDIT.HLP.

Learning to Use EDIT

Although the DOS manual has a chapter explaining EDIT, it is really not necessary to spend much time reading it. The program is so easy to use that, with a few hints, you can start using it right away. Moreover, EDIT comes with a built-in Help system that you can access whenever you want.

The user interface for EDIT was modeled after Microsoft Windows. You can use both a keyboard and a mouse to access pull-down menus. If you are familiar with this type of interface—which you will also find with OS/2 or with a Macintosh computer—you will feel right at home.

When you start EDIT without specifying a file name:

```
EDIT
```

you will see the screen shown in Figure 26.1.

As you can see, EDIT begins by offering you a chance to read a quick summary, called the DOS Editor Survival Guide. If you want this help, press <Enter>; otherwise, press <Esc>. If you press <Enter>, you will see the screen shown in Figure 26.2.

Within the Survival Guide is a short list of general information. In addition, as you can see, you can ask for further help in two areas: Getting Started and Keyboard. You can select one of these areas for further help, or you can press any key to continue.

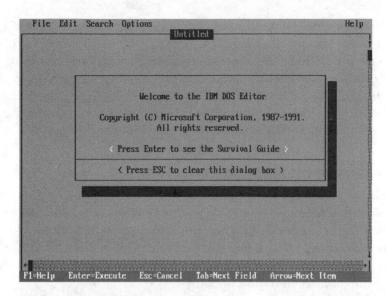

Figure 26.1.   *Starting with EDIT*

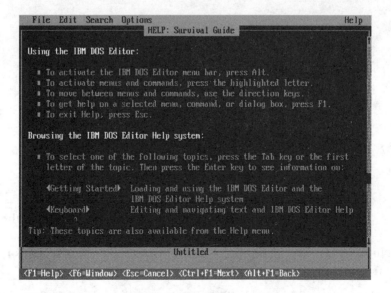

Figure 26.2   *The DOS Editor Survival Guide*

At any time, no matter what you are doing, you can press <F1> to ask for help. Most of the time, EDIT will be able to offer an explanation or some advice that deals with whatever situation you happen to be in. This is called *context-sensitive help.* By experimenting and pressing <F1> frequently, you can teach yourself just about everything you need to know. If you press <F1> in a situation for which no context-sensitive help is available, EDIT will display the Survival Guide.

Selecting Items and Moving Around

A lot of your work within the Editor involves selecting one choice or another. There are two ways that you can make a selection. Using the keyboard, you can move to your choice and press the <Enter> key. If you have a mouse, you can move to your choice and click the mouse button. As a general rule, you can do anything you want with the keyboard, a mouse, or a combination of both.

For reference, here is a list of keys that you can use to navigate within the Editor. This list shows the most important keys. For a full list, select the Keyboard help item.

<Left>	Move one position to the left
<Right>	Move one position to the right
<Up>	Move up one line
<Down>	Move down one line
<Home>	Move to the beginning of the current line
<End>	Move to the end of the current line
<Ctrl-Left>	Move one word to the left
<Ctrl-Right>	Move one word to the right
<Tab>	Move from one selection to another
<Shift-Tab>	Move backward from one selection to another

Note: <Left>, <Right>, <Up> and <Down> refer to the cursor control [arrow] keys.

Except for <Tab> and <Shift-Tab>, you will notice that these keys work pretty much the same as when you edit the DOS command line (see Chapter 23).

If you have a mouse, you can also use the scroll bars. These are the bars at the right and bottom borders of the screen. Each bar has an arrow at each end. There are two ways to use a scroll bar.

First, if you click on or near an arrow, EDIT will scroll the text in that direction. Second, between the arrows is a shaded area that contains a dark spot. You can click on the spot, hold down the button, and move the mouse in the direction of one of the arrows. EDIT will scroll the text in the same direction.

If you look at the Keyboard Help item, you will find that there are actually a great number of key combinations that you can use. The Editor recognizes the key combinations that are used with other Microsoft programs, such as Word, as well as many of the double-letter <Ctrl> key sequences from Wordstar.

When moving within a list of items, you have another alternative. You can press the first letter of the item name to move the cursor to that item. For, example, in Figure 26.2, we see a screen that gives us a choice between Getting Started and Keyboard. You can move to Getting Started by pressing the letter <G>; and you can move the Keyboard by pressing <K>. If a list has more than one item that starts with the same letter, you can press the letter more than once. Each time you do, the cursor will move to the next item that starts with that letter.

Pull-Down Menus

Once you start work, EDIT will show you a screen that looks something like Figure 26.3. As you can see, EDIT has displayed the file we are editing, NOW.BAT. In this case, we started the Editor using the command:

```
EDIT NOW.BAT
```

If we had started the Editor without specifying a file name:

```
EDIT
```

the text window would be empty and the file name would read UNTITLED.

As you can see from Figure 26.3, the top line has five items: FILE, EDIT, SEARCH, OPTIONS, and, at the far right, HELP. Each of these items can be selected to pull down a menu. There are several ways you can do this. With the keyboard, press the <Alt> key. The first item, <File>, will be highlighted. You can now select the item you want by pressing the first letter of the item name. Alternatively, you can press <Right> or <Left> to move to the item and then press <Enter>. As a shortcut, you can choose the item directly by holding down <Alt> and pressing the first letter of the name you want: <Alt-F>, <Alt-E>, <Alt-S>, <Alt-O> or <Alt-H>. With a mouse, all you need to do is point to the item and click.

Once you make a selection, a menu will appear. To select from the menu, move the cursor to a selection and press <Enter>. If you have a mouse, you can point and click. To move the cursor, you can use one of the cursor control keys. As a shortcut, one of the letters in the selection name will be highlighted—usually the first letter. You can press this letter and move right to that selection.

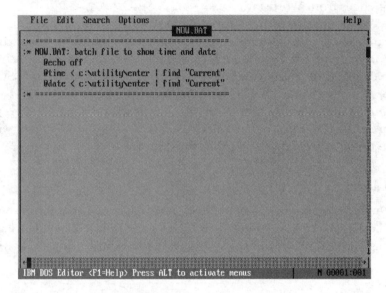

Figure 26.3. *Editing a File*

If you see a selection whose name is followed by three dots (...), it means that selecting this item will lead to another menu or information window.

As you move up and down a menu, the bottom line of the screen will display a brief description of what each selection does. For instance, if you are pointing to the Save item in the File menu, the bottom line displays the explanation "Saves current file".

Once a menu is pulled down, you can move back and forth to other menus by pressing <Left> and <Right>, or by using a mouse to click on a new selection within the top line.

In the next few sections, we'll take a tour of each of the menus. Along the way, we'll describe most of the functions of EDIT. If at any time you want to back out of a menu, simply press the <Esc> (escape) key. With a mouse, just click anywhere outside of the menu.

Within every menu, you can move to any item and press <F1> for help. EDIT will respond with a short explanation of that selection and how to use it. By selecting each item in turn and pressing <F1> you can learn everything there is to know. If you are an experienced user, this is a quick, easy way to learn to use the Editor.

The Help Menu

To pull down the Help menu, press <Alt-H> or select it with a mouse. You will see a menu like the one in Figure 26.4.

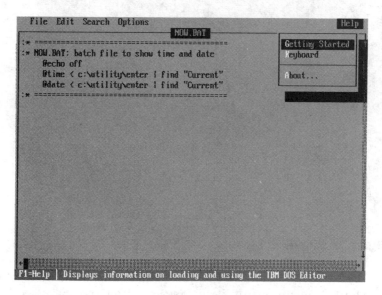

Figure 26.4. *Editing a File*

The Help menu has three items: Getting Started, Keyboard, and About. The first two items, Getting Started and Keyboard, display the same two Help screens that we met earlier within the Survival Guide. Getting Started contains a number of selections that will explain basic information. If you are a new user, it is a good idea to display each selection in turn and give yourself a basic grounding in how the Editor works.

The Keyboard selection gives you a few hints and then offers several more selections, each of which describes one aspect of using the keyboard.

The last item on the Help menu, About, displays the current version number of the Editor program.

The File Menu

To pull down the File menu, press <Alt-F> or select it with a mouse. You will see a menu like the one in Figure 26-5.

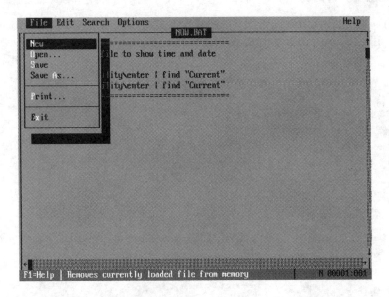

Figure 26.5. The File Menu

The File menu has six items: New, Open, Save, Save As, Print, and Exit. The first item, New, deletes the file that you are currently editing. You start fresh with a brand new empty file. If you have not yet saved your current file, EDIT will ask you if you want to save before deleting it.

The second item, Open, allows you to bring in a new file to work on. When you select Open, EDIT will display a window in which you can specify the file you want. Such a window is called a *dialog box* because EDIT expects you to enter or confirm information (see Figure 26.6).

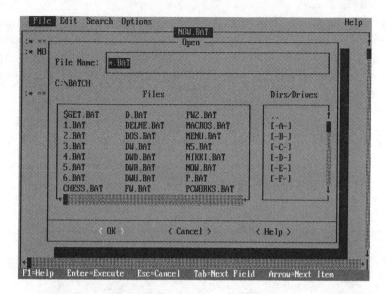

Figure 26.6.   *A Dialog Box*

Within the dialog box you can type the name of the file you want and press <Enter>. Like many dialog boxes, this one has several parts. You can move from one part of another by pressing <Tab> and <Shift-Tab> or by pointing and clicking with a mouse. If you want to learn how to use any dialog box, you can press <F1>. The context-sensitive Help will teach you everything you need to know.

The next item on the File menu is Save. When you select this item, EDIT will save your data to the file it came from. If you are working with a file that does not yet have a name, EDIT will ask you what name you want. As you edit, it is a good idea to save your file every now and then to safeguard your work.

The next item, Save As, allows you to save to a different file. When you select this item, EDIT will display a dialog box into which you can enter the name of the file you want. Choose the Save As item if you want to make an extra copy of your file.

The fifth item, Print, allows you to print your file. When you select this item, Edit will display a dialog box asking you if you want to print the whole document or just a selected portion. (We will discuss selecting text in a moment.) If you want, you can call up the File menu and choose Print while you are looking at a Help screen. This is a good way to print yourself some reference material.

The last item in the File menu is Exit. This is the selection to make to end your session with the Editor. If you have not already saved your work, EDIT will remind you and ask you what to do. If you do not want to save your work, select No from the dialog box. Your original file will be not be updated.

The Edit Menu

To pull down the Edit menu, press <Alt-E> or select it with a mouse. You will see a menu like the one in Figure 26.7.

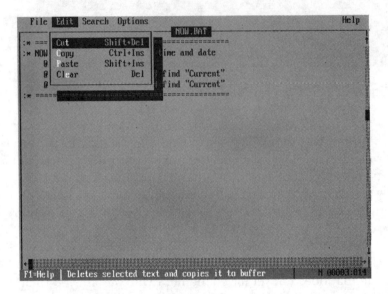

Figure 26.7. *The Edit Menu*

The Edit menu has four items: Cut, Copy, Paste, and Clear. These items work with a special storage area called the clipboard. As you edit, you can put data into the clipboard. Later, you can copy the data back into your file at whatever location you want.

To start, you must select part of your file. Selecting is easy: Just hold down one of the <Shift> keys and move the cursor. Whatever data you pass over will be selected and displayed in reverse colors.

For example, to select a five-line paragraph, move to the first line, hold down <Shift>, and press <Down> four times. As a second example, to select eight characters, move the cursor to the first character, hold down <Shift> and press <Right> seven times.

Once you have selected text, you can copy it to the clipboard. Pull down the Edit menu. (You can either press <Alt-E> or use a mouse.) To copy the text to the clipboard, select Copy. If you want to copy and then delete the text from your file, select Cut. If you want to delete the text without saving it to clipboard, select Clear.

Note: Whenever you copy anything to the clipboard—even a single character—it erases what was already there.

To copy text from the clipboard back to your file, move the cursor to where you want to insert the text. Then, pull down the Edit menu and select Paste. You can copy the same text from the clipboard as many times as you want.

Because the Edit operations are so useful, there are special key combinations you can use to speed things up. If you use these keys, you do not need to pull down the Edit menu.

Once you have selected text, you can use the following keys:

<Ctrl-Insert>	COPY: copy to clipboard
<Shift-Delete>	CUT: copy to clipboard, then delete text
<Del>	CLEAR: delete text; do not copy to clipboard
<Shift-Insert>	PASTE: copy text from clipboard

Hint: You can use the clipboard to transfer data between two files. After you select and copy data to the clipboard, open a new file. (Remember to save the old one, if it is necessary.) The contents of the clipboard will be preserved. You can now copy the data from the clipboard to the new file.

If you want to copy between files, you need to do it within the same editing session. Once you exit the Editor, the contents of the clipboard are lost.

The Search Menu

To pull down the Search menu, press <Alt-S> or select it with a mouse. You will see a menu like the one in Figure 26.8.

The Search menu has three items: Find, Repeat Last Find, and Change. The Find item displays a dialog box into which you can type a pattern. When you press <Enter>, the Editor will search your file looking for the pattern. The search starts at your current position in the file and proceeds toward the end of the file. When the end of the file is reached, the search will wrap around to the top and continue until the entire file has been searched. Within the Find dialog box, you can specify if you want the search to be sensitive to upper- and lowercase, and if you want to search only for whole words.

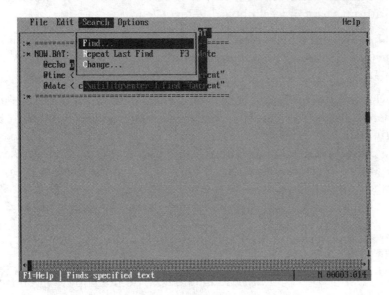

Figure 26.8.   *The Search Menu*

The next item, Repeat Last Find searches for the same pattern as your last search. As a convenience, you can press <F3> for a shortcut instead of having to use the menu. This is handy when you need to search for the same pattern over and over. Simply use Find to define the pattern, and then press <F3> to repeat the search.

The final menu item, Change, allows you to search for a pattern and replace it with another pattern. When you select Change, the Editor will present a dialog box. You can fill in what pattern you want to find, and what you want to change it to. If you want to delete the pattern, do not specify a replacement. EDIT will change your pattern to "nothing." (Remember, within the dialog box, to move from item to item without a mouse use <Tab> or <Shift-Tab>.)

Within this dialog box you can choose either "Find and Verify" or "Change All". The first choice tells EDIT to ask you for permission before making a change. EDIT will go through the entire file looking for your search pattern. Each time it finds it, you will see a dialog box asking you if you want to make the change. You can choose to make the change, skip this pattern and continue, or cancel the whole thing. The second choice, "Change All", tells EDIT to go ahead and process the whole file, making the changes automatically.

The Options Menu

To pull down the Options menu, press <Alt-O> or select it with a mouse. You will see a menu like the one in Figure 26.9.

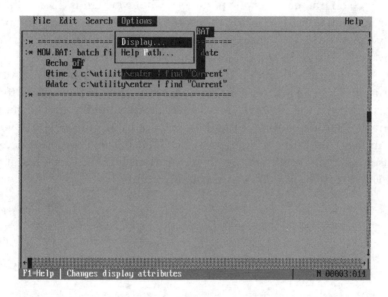

Figure 26.9. *The Options Menu*

The Options menu has two items: Display and Help Path. Display allows you to make some choices about how you want to use the display screen. First, you can specify what colors you want to use to display your text. You can choose both a foreground and a background color. As you change your choices, EDIT will show you what the new colors will look like. You can experiment and pick the ones you want. By the way, there are more colors than you can see at one time. Be sure to look through the entire list so you don't miss any of the possibilities.

The next choice you can make is whether or not you want scroll bars. As we explained earlier, if you have a mouse you can use the scroll bars to move throughout your file. However, if you do not have a mouse, you will probably want to remove the bars. This looks nicer and will leave a little more room on the screen for your data.

Whenever you have to make a yes/no type choice like this, you can move to the item and press the <Space> bar. Each time you press <Space> it toggles your selection.

The final choice in the Display dialog box allows you to change the tab settings. By default, the tabs are set to every 8 characters. You can change this to any setting you want. Whatever you choose will set the tabs evenly: every 6 characters, every 9 characters, whatever. Unlike a word processor or a typewriter, there is no provision for setting tabs to specific positions. By the way, the tabs setting you choose will be remembered permanently by the EDIT program; it is not just for a specific file.

The second choice on the Options menu is Help Path. If you select this choice, you will get a dialog box asking for the path (directory specification) for the file EDIT.HLP. EDIT.HLP is the file that contains all of the Help information for the Editor. Usually, this file will be in your DOS subdirectory. If for some reason EDIT.HLP is somewhere else, you can use this menu option to specify its location. If the Editor cannot find the EDIT.HLP file, it cannot give you any help.

27

THE EDLIN EDITOR

Introduction

An *editor* is a program that you can use to create and modify files. DOS comes with two editors: EDIT and EDLIN. Sometimes these programs are called text editors because they manipulate plain ASCII text.

Word processors may seem like text editors but they are not. When a word processor stores a document in a data file, the file contains invisible codes for formatting, underlining, boldface and so on. Within a text file, there is only ASCII text: letters, numbers and punctuation. What you see is pretty much what you've got.

This makes text editors perfect for editing files that contain programs, batch files, configuration files, and even short documents, such as letters or memos. When you need to edit your AUTOEXEC.BAT file (Chapter 12) or your CONFIG.SYS file (Chapter 28), a text editor is the program to use.

The EDLIN editor is an old program. It was available with the first version of DOS and has been a part of DOS ever since. EDLIN is a type of program called a line editor. When you work with EDLIN, you manipulate text in terms of line numbers.

Line editors were developed years ago, to use with slow terminals that printed data one line at a time. Today, line editors seem slow and clunky. This is why, starting with version 5.0, DOS now includes a screen editor, named EDIT. This is the editor that we discussed in Chapter 26. However, you may have rare occasion to find that EDLIN still has its uses and so it is still included with DOS.

Why EDLIN Is Important

Under almost any circumstances, EDIT is a better choice as a text editor. After all, it is a lot easier to work with a full screen of data than to deal with lines of text. With EDIT, you can move the cursor wherever you want and insert text or make changes. With EDLIN, as you will see, you need to enter terse commands and reference each location by a line number. But there are circumstances in which you will need to use EDLIN.

First, if you are using an old version of DOS (before 5.0), EDIT is not included. Unless you buy a separate editor program, you will have to use EDLIN.

Second, there are times when you may have only a small amount of memory available. EDLIN is a compact program that will work under almost all circumstances. EDIT requires more room and will not work properly if there is not enough memory.

You might think that this won't be a problem if your computer has plenty of memory, but there are surprises. For example, say you are working with a word processor and you want to perform a few DOS commands. Instead of ending the word processor, you may elect to put it on hold and change to DOS temporarily. (Many programs offer this facility.) The word processor will start a new copy of DOS for you to work with. When you are finished, you can type EXIT and return to what you were doing.

Now, think about what is in the computer's memory. First, the original copy of DOS you started with. Second, any memory resident programs that you may have loaded. Third, a copy of the word processor program. And now, a fresh copy of DOS. Under such circumstances, you may find that there is not enough memory left to run EDIT. But, almost always, you will still be able to use EDLIN.

Remember earlier when we mentioned that EDLIN has been part of every version of DOS since the beginning? This is the final reason why it is important to learn EDLIN. EDIT will be available only with DOS 5.0 or later. EDLIN will always be available, no matter what DOS system you use. It is nice to know that whatever PC you happen to find yourself in front of, you will always be able to do simple editing.

EDLIN and How It Works

While a full-screen editor shows as much of the file as possible, a line editor like EDLIN works in smaller units. It thinks of a file as a collection of lines. Each line can be up to 253 characters long. If you want to see or change something in the fifth line of your file, you must first tell EDLIN to show you the line, then you must tell it what change to make, then you must tell it to display the line again so you can check that the change worked. Whatever you do, when you're working with a line editor like EDLIN, you do it all in terms of commands that operate on the lines of a file.

EDLIN always refers to a file in terms of the numeric order of the lines in the file. If you had a file with three lines in it like this:

```
THIS IS THE FIRST LINE
THIS IS THE SECOND LINE
THIS IS THE THIRD LINE
```

EDLIN would refer to these as line numbers 1, 2, and 3. To help you keep track of the line numbers, EDLIN always gives the line number when it displays lines from the file. If EDLIN were to display the lines shown above, they would appear like this:

```
1: THIS IS THE FIRST LINE
2: THIS IS THE SECOND LINE
3: THIS IS THE THIRD LINE
```

The line numbers EDLIN shows are not part of the data in your ASCII text file—they are only shown for reference.

Another thing that you need to know about EDLIN and line numbers is that the lines are renumbered after any change. In our three-line example, let's say you delete line 2. The old line 3 immediately becomes the new line 2, so that the file now would look like this:

```
1: THIS IS THE FIRST LINE
2: THIS IS THE THIRD LINE
```

Likewise, if you insert a new line below line 1, line 2 becomes line 3 again:

```
1: THIS IS THE FIRST LINE
2. THIS IS THE NEW SECOND LINE
3: THIS IS THE THIRD LINE
```

To make work easier, EDLIN keeps track of its current place in a file and indicates the current line by marking it with an asterisk (*). For example, if the current location in our original three-line file were the second line, then it would be displayed like this:

```
1: THIS IS THE FIRST LINE
2:*THIS IS THE SECOND LINE
3: THIS IS THE THIRD LINE
```

When you tell EDLIN to do something, you can either tell it to work with a particular line number or to work relative to the current line. For anything you are typing into EDLIN, whether it is a command to EDLIN or data you are entering, you can use the DOS editing keys you learned about in Chapter 24 to help you.

File Protection

Before we move on to the actual use of EDLIN, you ought to know that, for your protection, a safety feature is built into EDLIN and many other editors (but not EDIT). When you use EDLIN to change a file, it does not destroy the old file. Instead, it saves the old file data under a slightly different name —the file keeps the original filename, but EDLIN adds a filename extension of BAK, short for backup copy.

If you happen to make some disastrous error in editing a file, the BAK copy will help you recover from the mistake. Because of this backup convention, you can't edit a file while it has an extension of BAK, but you can rename the file to something else with the DOS REN command. Now let's move on to see EDLIN in action.

Starting EDLIN

You start EDLIN by typing the command name, followed by the name of the file that you want to edit. For example:

```
EDLIN AUTOEXEC.BAT
```

Although many editors don't have to be given the name of a file when they're started up, EDLIN does. The file name can either belong to an existing file that you want to look at or change, or it can be the name of a new file you want to create.

When it starts, EDLIN looks for the file you've named. If the file already exists, EDLIN reads it into memory. After EDLIN begins, it will give you one of three messages. If EDLIN hasn't found the file you named, it reports:

```
NEW FILE
```

If you're creating a new file, this message is fine. But if you want to work with an existing file, this message means EDLIN wasn't able to find the file you named. Perhaps you misspelled the filename, or maybe the file does exist, but it's not in the current directory. If that's the case, you need to quit EDLIN by typing:

```
Q
```

and (as you'll soon find out in more detail) then press:

```
Y
```

to confirm your intentions. You can then either change directories to the one that contains your file (with the CD, or CHDIR, command) or restart EDLIN, giving it the full path name that will lead it to the file.

That's the first message you might see. Now, what if you requested an existing file, and EDLIN finds it? If EDLIN finds the file, and there is room enough, it reads the complete file into memory. It's unlikely you'll use EDLIN with a file too large to fit into memory, but it could happen. However, if EDLIN has enough memory space for the file, it reports:

```
End of input file
```

This message tells you that EDLIN did find the file, and had enough room for all of it.

If there isn't room for the entire file, then EDLIN gives a "message" of a different kind: no message at all. This is a little cryptic, and is the sort of thing that makes EDLIN a poor editor, but if you know how to read EDLIN's signs, no message means "the file was found, and it's too big to fit into memory." When a file is too big to fit into memory, EDLIN reads part of it into memory, leaving a cushion of about 25% of available memory to give you some working room.

Once EDLIN is up and running and has given one of its three messages, it tells you it is ready for a command by giving its command prompt. EDLIN's prompt is a simple but distinctive asterisk (*) that helps distinguish it from DOS or any other program.

Ending an EDLIN Session

At this point, since you've learned how to start using EDLIN, your next order of business might as well be knowing how to end it. There are two different commands used to end EDLIN's operation. One, E (for end), writes the file you're working on from memory to disk, replacing the old file with a new version, and saving the old version as a BAK file. E both writes the file and ends operation. To have EDLIN carry out the E command, you type in the single letter at EDLIN's asterisk prompt:

```
*E
```

and press the enter key.

The other way to end EDLIN's operation is Q (for quit), which you saw briefly already. The Q command is used when you want to stop using EDLIN, but don't want to write a file back to disk—perhaps because you haven't made any changes and don't need to save anything new, or because you've made some mistakes and want to discard them. Whatever the reason, if you want to throw away whatever record of the file that

EDLIN has in memory, you use the Q command. As a protection against accidentally losing some work you have done, EDLIN will ask:

```
Abort edit (Y/N)?
```

and unless you answer Y for yes, EDLIN will continue operation.

Be careful to keep these two commands straight, otherwise you may write a bad file to disk when you don't want to, or throw away changes you wanted to keep. E is end, including writing the changes; Q is quit, without writing any changes to the disk copy of the file. If you've been tinkering with a file and have made a mess of it (deleting lines you need to keep, or whatever), then be sure to use Q, not E, so that you discard the changes you don't want to make a permanent part of the file.

Both of the commands you have seen so far are given as single letters —E and Q. In fact, all of the EDLIN commands are single letters. This makes them very quick and easy to type. You always press the <Enter> key to tell EDLIN to carry out our commands, just as you do in entering DOS commands.

Using EDLIN Commands

While the two commands you've seen so far are used by themselves, the other EDLIN commands take some parameters that tell them where to act and what to act upon. For example, the D (Delete Lines) command needs to know which lines to delete. Before you get into the details of each command, let's see how you specify which lines you want the command to act on.

When an EDLIN command needs to know what line to act on, you have five different ways to indicate the line you're interested in:

1. Type the specific line number, such as 27 or 32500. If you type in a line number that is too big (a higher number than the last line in memory), EDLIN acts just as if you had put in the number immediately after the last line number.

2. You can explicitly refer to the line after the last line in memory by typing in a pound sign (#). This has the same effect as entering a line number that is too big.

3. Indicate you want to work on whichever line is the current line by putting in a period (.). A period means, "use the current line number." You'll recall that EDLIN indicates the current line by mark-

ing it with an asterisk. Although keeping mental track of the current line may be a little confusing at first, it will become easy after a while.

4. Leave the line number blank, and EDLIN will use some default line number. This number will be whatever makes the most sense for the specified commands.

5. You can indicate a line above or below the current line by entering a plus or minus sign and a number, such as +25 or -200. This will refer to the line which is that number of lines before (-), or after (+) the current line.

With that background, let's look at some more commands.

Adding Lines

To add some lines to a file, you use the I (Insert) command. The command is given like this:

```
Line-number I
```

This command sets you up to begin inserting lines into the file. The insertion begins before the specified line number. If you do not specify a line number, the insertion goes before the current line. Here, for example, is how a new line is inserted above line 3 in an existing file:

```
  *3I
3:*THIS IS GOING ABOVE OLD LINE 3
```

and here's what the result looks like:

```
1: THIS IS THE FIRST LINE
2: THIS IS THE SECOND LINE
3: THIS IS GOING ABOVE OLD LINE 3
4:*THIS IS THE THIRD LINE
```

If you are creating a new file, there is nothing in the file, and you would expect you could just start typing lines into it. EDLIN doesn't work that way. Even with a brand-new file, you have to use the I command to start entering lines. With a new file, the first command you give EDLIN is the I command. Here, however, you don't have to specify a line number, just type I all by itself:

```
  *I
```

When you give EDLIN the Insert command, it lets you enter not only one line, but line after line—very convenient. Along the way, press the <Enter> to signal the end of one line, and EDLIN lets you begin the next and the next and the next.

How do you stop entering new lines? You press <Ctrl-Break> or <Ctrl-C> to tell EDLIN that you have finished inserting. One special warning about breaking out of insert mode, though: Press <Ctrl-Break> only after you have pressed <Enter> for the last line you inserted. If you press <Ctrl-Break> with a line partly entered, the line will be thrown away. Keep that in mind—losing the last line you've entered is very easy to do until you're familiar with EDLIN's rules.

Once you press <Ctrl-Break>, EDLIN switches back into command mode, where it waits for your next command. To signal this, EDLIN shows its command prompt, the asterisk.

Removing Lines

The opposite of the I command is the D (Delete) command. D removes one or more lines from the file you are editing.

To delete one line, you enter the command like this, with one line number:

```
line-number D
```

For example, you would delete line 3 of our earlier example like this:

```
*3D
```

When you press <Enter>, that one line will be deleted; naturally, all the following lines will be renumbered. For example:

```
1: THIS IS THE FIRST LINE
2: THIS IS THE SECOND LINE
3: THIS IS GOING ABOVE OLD LINE 3
4:*THIS IS THE THIRD LINE
```

When you enter the 3D command, you will get this result:

```
1: THIS IS THE FIRST LINE
2: THIS IS THE SECOND LINE
3:*THIS IS THE THIRD LINE
```

If you want to delete a group of lines, you give two line numbers, separated by a comma, like this:

```
starting-line-number,ending-line-number D
```

For example:

```
5,15D
```

Both of the lines specified, and any lines in between, will be deleted.

You'll recall that we can always leave a line-number specification blank, and a default will be used. If you enter just a D, without a line number, like this:

```
D
```

then the current line is deleted. With the range form, if you leave out the first number, like this:

```
,ending-line-number  D
```

then lines are deleted from the current line through the line specified.

The reverse doesn't work. If you specify

```
starting-line-number,  D
```

it will only delete one line, and not (as you might think) a range of lines from the starting point to the current line.

Listing a File

Naturally, you can't edit a file blindly; you need to be able to see what you are doing. The L (List) command lets you display lines from the file. Remember that EDLIN doesn't voluntarily reveal anything about the file you're editing. It will only show you exactly what you ask to see, and nothing more. Screen-editors such as EDIT (see Chapter 26) display much more information.

The L command has a format similar to the D command. You can enter it with no line number, or one line number, or a range of lines:

```
L
line-number  L
starting-line-number,ending-line-number  L
```

As I mentioned, each command has its own defaults, which are tailored to what makes the most sense for it. The defaults are quite different for L than they are for D. Generally, the L command lists one screenful of lines at a time. As I explained in Chapter 18, when I covered the MODE CON: command, you can display either 25, 43, or 50 lines per screen (if you have the appropriate display). EDLIN will take advantage of all the available lines to show you as much as possible at one time. EDLIN will show one less than the number of lines that will fit on the screen. The last line is reserved for you to enter a command. If you give no numbers, then EDLIN lists one screenful of lines, centered around the current line. This is an easy and convenient way to get a quick snapshot of the lines you're currently working on in the file.

If you enter only the first line number, with or without a comma, EDLIN also shows one screenful of lines, but starting with the specified line, no matter where the current line is. If you put in just the second line number (with a comma before it, to indicate that it is the second number), then lines are displayed from one-half screenful before the current line, up to the specified line.

Do you find this a little confusing? One of the problems with EDLIN is that, at first, its rules are truly a nightmare (even more so than what you've seen). This is a common problem of line-based editors, but with some practice you'll find that the commands like L may even begin to seem reasonably easy to use. When you think about it, you will see that the commands are rational and do follow a rational design.

Changing Lines

The next thing you need to learn about EDLIN is how to make changes to a line that is already in the file. Say you've used the L command to find the part of the file you're interested in, and now you are ready to make changes. You've seen how to delete and insert whole lines, but how do you change part of an existing line?

You make such changes with the Edit - Line Command. For this command, you don't use a letter of the alphabet; instead, you just enter the number of the line you want to edit. In response, EDLIN displays a copy of the line, as it exists, and then gives you a (seemingly) blank line with the same line number. You can then use the DOS editing keys to make changes to the line, including copying any part of it that you don't need to change. When you have the line the way you want it, press <Enter> and the line is changed. If we decide we don't want to make any changes to the line, we can just press <Enter>, without typing in any changes and the line will be left as it is.

So that you can see what this process looks like, let's assume you want to change the word "second" in line 2 of our earlier example from lower-case to capital letters. First, let's list the file:

```
*L
  1:*THIS IS THE FIRST LINE
  2: THIS IS THE SECOND LINE
  3: THIS IS THE THIRD LINE
```

Now, tell EDLIN you want to change line 2:

```
*2
```

This is what you see:

```
2:*THIS IS THE SECOND LINE
2:*
```

To make the change, let's just copy the whole line (with the <F3> editing key we discussed in Chapter 24), then backspace to erase characters and retype the end of the line. First, press F3 to copy all:

```
2:*THIS IS THE SECOND LINE
2:*THIS IS THE SECOND LINE
```

Then, backspace to get this:

```
2:*THIS IS THE SECOND LINE
2:*THIS IS THE
```

Finally, correct the line:

```
2:*THIS IS THE SECOND LINE
2:*THIS IS THE SECOND LINE
```

and list the result:

```
  1: THIS IS THE FIRST LINE
  2:*THIS IS THE SECOND LINE
  3: THIS IS THE THIRD LINE
```

The Edit Line command has a default line number, just like any other command. So, when the asterisk prompt is displayed, if you just press <Enter> without typing a line number, EDLIN will assume that you want to edit the current line. It will display the current line and you can then change it, as we just did, using the DOS editing keys if you want.

Also, if you repeatedly press <Enter>, EDLIN will switch back and forth between command mode (with the asterisk prompt) and editing the current line. Each time it switches, the current line location is moved down one. This makes it possible to move through the file, line by line, by repeatedly pressing <Enter>. As each line is set up to be edited, you can either change it or move on to the next line. This is a convenient and quick way to go through a small file, making changes as you need to.

Finding Text

One of the things an editor needs to be able to do is search through a file to find the location of some text you are interested in. EDLIN has two commands to do this: the S (Search) command and the R (Replace) command (which is really a search-and-replace command). We'll start with the S command. There are several variations on the S command. The simplest one is like this:

```
start-line-number,end-line-number S search-pattern
```

The search command searches through the range of lines, looking for the search pattern. If it is found, then the line with the information is displayed (and made the current line).

For instance, you could search for the word "third" in our example like this:

```
*1,4Sthird
```

and EDLIN would display this:

```
3: THIS IS THE THIRD LINE
```

If EDLIN doesn't find what it is searching for, then it will display the message: "Not found." Each of the three parameters is optional. If the starting line is left off, the search begins with the line following the current line; if the ending line is left off, the search goes on to the end of the file in memory. If the search pattern is left off, then EDLIN uses whatever you last told it to search for.

These three default values make it very easy to continue a search after one instance has been found. After you have had the Search command search once, just entering the command S with no more parameters, will continue the search from where EDLIN left off.

EDLIN will only report exact matches of the information that you ask it to search for. If you had typed the Search command like this:

```
*1,4Sthird
```

EDLIN wouldn't have found it. It can find a word in the middle of a sentence, but it can't make the connection between "THIRD" and "third". Thus, for example, EDLIN can find a match if the word you're looking for is capitalized at the beginning of a sentence. Some editors can make matches in either upper- or lowercase, but EDLIN does not—it requires exact matches.

There is another variation on the S command, when we put a question mark just before the S; for example

```
1,35?SWHERE
```

S is prepared to repeat the search over and over when the question mark is used, until it finds the instance that you are looking for. Each time EDLIN finds an occurrence of the search text, it displays what it found, and asks:

```
O.K.?
```

If you answer N for no, then EDLIN will go on looking. If you answer Y for yes, then EDLIN will stop looking, so you can work with the line it found. Here's another opportunity for confusion. To me anyway, this yes/no convention seems backward. Whether you find it logical or not, remember the rule: Y-yes means stop and work here; N-no means continue searching.

Related to the S command is the R (Search and Replace) command. This command is entered like the S command, including the optional question mark. But Replace is designed to replace what it finds with something else, thus you have to enter two sets of characters after the R command. The two items are separated by a special character, Ctrl-Z. You can enter it either by holding down the <Ctrl> key and pressing Z, or by pressing the <F6> DOS editing key. In either case, Ctrl-Z will appear in your command like this: ^Z. (Even though it's represented as two characters, ^ and Z, DOS considers the two together as one Ctrl-Z character.)

To see what the R command looks like, let's go back to our example and tell EDLIN to replace "THIRD" with third. Here's the command:

```
*1,4RTHIRD^Zthird
```

and here is the result:

```
3:*THIS IS THE third LINE
```

Now, here's something to remember. The S command stops at the first instance that it finds, so that you can do whatever you want with what it found. But the R command has something active to do, so it will automatically repeat its search-and-replace operation all through the range of lines that you give it. For example, if you had a 300-line file, and you used the command:

```
*1,300Rjellybeans^Zlicorice
```

Every time EDLIN finds "jellybeans" anywhere in lines 1 through 300, it will replace it with "licorice". Each replacement will also be displayed, so you can see what is going on.

While the ordinary form of the R command will replace each instance that it finds, the question mark version will stop each time and ask you "O.K.?" If you answer Y, the replacement is made; if you answer N, the line is left as it was, unchanged. But the search and replace continues, even if you answer N to any particular query.

You will notice that this is an important difference between the S and R commands. With S, answering yes stops the search, while no continues it. With R, answering yes lets the replacement take place, while no prevents that one replacement, but the search still continues, whether the answer is yes or no. So while these two commands are very similar, they respond very differently to the yes-or-no answer.

As you might imagine, it is very easy to make an accidental mess using the S and R commands. Proceed cautiously until you are comfortable with them.

Working with Large Files

There are two commands that are used in that special case I mentioned at the beginning of this chapter: When a file is too large to fit into memory. One command is used to write some of the file back to disk, to make more room in memory, and the other is used to read in more of the file.

The W (Write) command is used to write some lines out of memory. The command is given like this:

```
number-of-lines W
```

As many lines as were specified are written from the beginning of the lines in memory. If you don't specify a number of lines, then EDLIN will write just enough lines to get the 25% working cushion that it likes to have. After the lines are written, the part of the file that remains in memory is still numbered from line one. As a result, your line numbers don't tell you where the lines are relative to the beginning of the entire file—only relative to the beginning of the part that is in memory.

When some space has been made free by writing out part of a file (or by deleting some lines), you can then read in more of the file into memory. This is done with the A (Append) command. The A command is given just like the W command:

```
number-of-lines A
```

If there is enough room, EDLIN reads in as many lines as you asked it to. If you don't specify the number of lines, then EDLIN will automatically read until memory is 75% full, leaving its 25% cushion of working space.

If EDLIN finds the end of a file while reading it with the A command, it will report it with the message "End of input file," just as it does when it first begins editing a file.

Advanced EDLIN Commands

From the commands that you've seen so far, it would appear that EDLIN doesn't give you any way to move data around or to duplicate it. If you need to rearrange your file data, it looks as though you would be stuck. Not so. You have three special commands, C (Copy), M (Move), and T (Transfer), that let you move lines of a file from one place to another.

The (Copy) command lets you duplicate lines, copying them to another part of the file. There are four parameters in this command:

```
start-line,end-line,where-to,how-many-times C
```

Each of the four parameters is optional, expect for the "where to" specification, which must be given. If either the starting or ending lines are left off, then the current line is assumed. If the number of times is left off, then only one copy is made. The copied material is placed before the specified "where to" line, just as it is with the I command.

You would usually use the Copy command only to duplicate material once, but there are times when you might want to use the "how many

times" parameter to make several copies. As an example, if you were creating a table or list in a file, you might create a skeleton line (with all the
repeated information), copy it as many times as needed, and then fill in
the details in each line.

To show how you would use this command, here's an example using
the lines you've been seeing throughout this chapter. Let's say you
wanted to make three copies of lines 2 and 3 at the end of your short file.
Here's the command:

```
*2,3,4,3C
```

which, translated, means "take lines 2 and 3 (2,3,), go to line 4 (4,), and
make three copies (3C)." This is what you'd get:

```
1: THIS IS THE FIRST LINE
2: THIS IS THE SECOND LINE
3: THIS IS THE THIRD LINE
4: THIS IS THE SECOND LINE
5: THIS IS THE THIRD LINE
6: THIS IS THE SECOND LINE
7: THIS IS THE THIRD LINE
8: THIS IS THE SECOND LINE
9: THIS IS THE THIRD LINE
```

Obviously, you'll have better uses for the command.

The M (Move) command performs a similar function to the C command, but takes lines out of their current place, and puts them somewhere else. With a C, the original copy stays in place; with M, it is gone.
Duplication makes sense for a C command, but not for M, so M doesn't
make multiple copies. There are three parameters for the M command:

```
starting-line,ending-line,where-to M
```

As with C, the third parameter, "where-to," is required and not optional.
The starting and ending line numbers will default to the current line if
they are not specified.

Here's our three-line example once again, this time with lines 2 and 3
moved above line 1. First, the Move command:

```
*2,3,1M
```

meaning, "take lines 2 and 3 (2,3) and move them before line 1 (1M)."
This is the result:

```
1:*THIS IS THE SECOND LINE
2: THIS IS THE THIRD LINE
3: THIS IS THE FIRST LINE
```

The third special command that can be used to rearrange data is the T (Transfer) command. T is used to read the contents of another file, and to place it into the file being edited. The command is given like this:

```
line-number T file-name
```

The contents of the file are placed in memory, ahead of the specified line number, just as it is with I, C, and M. The file must be specified, naturally enough, but the line number is optional. If it is not specified, then the current line indicates where the new data is to go. For example, if you had a two-line file named NEWDATA that looked like this:

```
1:*THIS IS THE NAME LINE
2: THIS IS THE ADDRESS LINE
```

and you wanted to place it at the top of our much-edited three-line sample file, the command would be:

```
*1TNEWDATA
```

and the result would be:

```
1:*THIS IS THE NAME LINE
2: THIS IS THE ADDRESS LINE
3: THIS IS THE SECOND LINE
4: THIS IS THE THIRD LINE
5: THIS IS THE FIRST LINE
```

There is one further advanced command which EDLIN provides, the P (Page) command. The P command is intended for browsing (paging) through a file, and it works just like the L command, with one handy exception. The L command leaves the current line unchanged, which might be far from what is being displayed on the screen. The P command makes the last line displayed the current line, so that the working location in the file follows what is displayed. This means that you can page through a file by entering the P command repeatedly. If you enter the L command repeatedly, you just see the same lines over and over.

28

THE CONFIGURATION FILE

Introduction

In Chapter 2, we discussed what happens when DOS starts. A tiny program called the bootstrap loader begins to execute. The bootstrap loader starts up a small portion of DOS, which starts up the rest of DOS. (This is why we talk of "booting" a computer. The process is somewhat like pulling yourself up by the bootstraps.)

Once DOS gets going, it does two things before it settles down, ready for you to start work. First, it modifies its configuration according to your specifications. Second, it executes your initialization commands. It is only when all of this is completed that DOS displays the prompt, ready for you to type in your first command.

In order to control how DOS starts, there are two files you need to understand: the CONFIG.SYS file that contains your configuration specifications, and the AUTOEXEC.BAT file that contains your initialization commands. We discussed the AUTOEXEC.BAT file in Chapter 12. The CONFIG.SYS file—how to use it and what it contains—is the subject of the chapter.

The Configuration File

The CONFIG.SYS file itself is a plain ASCII text file containing a series of commands to DOS that tell it how you want it to be customized. These commands fall into two groups, those that perform particular functions, and one, named DEVICE, that allows you to load external software (device drivers) into DOS. In the next section we'll look at the various distinct commands, and then we'll finish up this chapter with a discussion of the device drivers.

When you install DOS, the installation program builds you a CONFIG.SYS file. The commands in this file will be based on the choices you selected during the installation. If you would like to look at your CONFIG.SYS file, enter the following command:

```
TYPE C:\CONFIG.SYS
```

If you already have DOS and you are updating to a newer version, you will have both a CONFIG.SYS and AUTOEXEC.BAT file. The installation program will either modify your existing files, or save them and create new ones. Check with the documentation for your particular version of DOS.

Configuration Commands

There are fifteen special-purpose commands that you can put into your CONFIG.SYS file. Some of them are very technical and you will probably never encounter them in your work (although they may be inserted automatically when you install DOS). In this chapter, I will explain the commands that are the most important for you to understand. Let's begin with the REM command.

REM

Just as you can use REM to insert comments (remarks) in batch files (see Chapter 11), you can do the same in your CONFIG.SYS file. This is handy for two reasons: First, you can put in explanatory notes so you can understand what you did the next time you read the file; second, if you are experimenting, you can disable specific commands by putting "REM" in front of them.

BREAK

As you already know, you can press <Ctrl-Break> to cancel or interrupt something. When you press this key combination, it generates a signal for DOS. If a DOS command is executing, DOS will abort it. If a program is executing, the signal is passed to the program to interpret as it sees fit. (Many programs choose to ignore this signal.) Under most circumstances, the same signal is also generated by <Ctrl-C>.

When you press <Ctrl-Break>, it cannot take effect until DOS notices. Sometimes it seems as if you get an instant response; at other times, you have to wait. The reason has to do with how often DOS looks for the signal. You can control this by using the BREAK command within your CONFIG.SYS file. You can use either BREAK=OFF or BREAK=ON.

By default, BREAK is set off. With BREAK=OFF, DOS will check for <Ctrl-Break> every time it reads from the keyboard, or writes to the display or printer. If you want a better response, you can set BREAK=ON. DOS will check for <Ctrl-Break> at extra times: in particular, whenever it reads or writes to a disk.

Although BREAK=OFF is the default, there is no reason why you should not make a habit of setting BREAK=ON. Thus, it is a good idea to always include this command in your CONFIG.SYS file.

Aside from setting BREAK within the CONFIG.SYS file, there is a regular DOS command, BREAK, that you can enter at the DOS prompt. (We discussed this command in Chapter 20.) If you'd like, you can forgo setting BREAK with CONFIG.SYS. Instead, you can use a BREAK-ON command in your AUTOEXEC.BAT file. (Notice that you do not need an equal sign.) Whether you set BREAK in CONFIG.SYS or in AUTOEXEC.BAT, the results are the same. The choice is up to you.

If you want to check how BREAK is set on your system, you can type:

```
BREAK
```

at the DOS prompt. DOS will display the current status.

BUFFERS

To improve the performance of your programs—especially its own performance—DOS sets aside some memory space for disk buffers, which can, under the right circumstances, reduce the amount of reading and writing of disk information that has to be done. To conserve memory, DOS by default doesn't set aside many disk buffers, usually just two or three. But for many PC users, particularly those with hard disks, DOS's default buffers are far from enough for efficient operation. Fortunately, you can control the number of disk buffers that DOS uses, by including the BUFFERS command in CONFIG.SYS.

This command lets you set the number of buffers you want, from a minimum of 1 to a maximum of 99. In my experience, a PC with a hard disk needs at least 16, maybe even 20, 30, 40, or more. There is a price to be paid in setting aside buffers, though: Each buffer takes about one-half K of memory away from your main programs. Still, if you have enough memory and the right number of buffers, they can greatly speed up much of your computer's disk work.

You can easily test to see if you need more or fewer buffers in your machine. Set up a CONFIG.SYS file with this BUFFERS command in it like this:

```
BUFFERS=8
```

Then, reboot your machine and try some of the program you use the most. If you don't know what program to try, use the DOS program CHKDSK as a test. Observe how much time DOS takes to start up, how long it takes to load programs, and how long it takes the programs to do their disk-intensive work. Next, try using the values:

```
BUFFERS=16
BUFFERS=32
BUFFERS=64
```

and see what happens with each. Don't worry about minute differences, but if you see a dramatic change, you know you've hit pay-dirt.

The BUFFERS command can be fine-tuned in various ways and, as you might imagine, it is often difficult to pick the optimal values you need. Your DOS manual contains a section that explains how the buffers work and gives you hints on what numbers to choose. However, if you are not sure what to do, the best thing would be to just accept the BUFFERS command that is put into your CONFIG.SYS file by the installation program. This is fine for most people.

COUNTRY

The next CONFIG.SYS command to consider is the COUNTRY command, which we looked at in Chapter 20. As the use of personal computers and DOS has spread from America to the rest of the world, there's been a growing need to have DOS (and the programs that run under it) adapt to different customs and conventions used in each country. Originally DOS did everything in the way that was most congenial for Americans, but now DOS can adapt to the country it is working in. This is done with the COUNTRY command, like this:

```
COUNTRY=061
```

which happens to set up DOS for Australia. The default code for the United States is 001 and there are codes for all the countries that DOS has been developed for.

Setting the country code allows DOS to adjust its own operations—for example, the way it shows the date and time on the screen when you use a command, such as DIR, that displays date and time information. In America, dates are shown in the form: month, day of the month, and the year, as in 10-11-91. But some other countries use the convention of the year first; others, put the day of the month first.

The COUNTRY command not only adjusts some of the way DOS works, it allows other programs to adjust the way they work, too. To do this, a program (behind the scenes and invisible to us) asks DOS for a table of country-specific information, which DOS passes along to the program. This table of information includes not only things like the preferred format for date and time, but also the currency symbol that's used (such as the dollar sign, $, or the pound sign, <£>) and many other things as well. Few programs make use of this feature of DOS, but it's there, available to any program that wishes to adjust to local national conventions.

The Other CONFIG.SYS Commands

There are also CONFIG.SYS commands that allow you to expand or contract some of DOS's internal limits. The FILES command lets you control how many disk files DOS will allow a program to use at one time. DOS's default is 8 files. You can specify up to 255.

Another similar command, FCBS, controls a more old-fashioned limit on how many files a program can be using at once. Unless you get error messages indicating trouble in this area (which is possible, but unlikely), you can ignore this facility.

A similar command, called LASTDRIVE, lets you tell DOS how many logical disk drives to allow for. DOS will always accommodate as many disk drives as your machine has, and will also always accommodate as many apparent drives as the device drivers need. (We'll get to them in the next section.)

Beyond that fixed requirement, you can make disk drives seemingly come and go by using the SUBST command (see Chapter 17). DOS, though, can't accommodate new drives indefinitely. It needs to know in advance how many drives will be called for, and that's what the LASTDRIVE command is for. It's used like this:

```
LASTDRIVE=letter
```

where you would make LASTDRIVE equal to a single letter from A to Z which allows for a total of 26 drives. If you do not use a LASTDRIVE command, DOS will default to LASTDRIVE=E. This gives you up to 5 drives: A, B, C, D, and E.

For many people, this is enough, and the LASTDRIVE command can be ignored entirely. However, if you are using a network or if you have extra devices, you may need to use the LASTDRIVE command to ask for extra drive names. The minimum that you can specify is the number of physical drives on your system. If you specify less than this, DOS will overrule you and ignore the command.

DOS makes certain assumptions about the physical drives on your system. If you want to change the specifications for a drive, you can do so by using the DRIVPARM (drive parameter) command.

The last two miscellaneous CONFIG.SYS commands are SWITCHES and STACKS. Normally, you would not need to use these commands so we'll mention them only in passing. SWITCHES tells DOS to pretend that your keyboard is an old-style one. You would use SWITCHES in the unlikely event that you have a modern keyboard and one of your programs will work only with the old keyboard. If you use Microsoft Windows, you can use the SWITCHES command to specify that the special file WINA20.386 is not in the route directory.

STACKS controls how much memory is set aside for processing certain hardware signals. Like SWITCHES, this is a command you can ignore. If the DOS installation program puts a SWITCHES command in your CONFIG.SYS file, you can leave it there. If you have problems check with the DOS manual for help.

SHELL

The next CONFIG.SYS command is an interesting one. It allows you to control some of the workings of DOS's command interpreter, COMMAND.COM which, if anything is, can be called the heart of DOS. The SHELL command is used like this:

```
SHELL=C:\DOS\COMMAND.COM C:\DOS /E:512 /P
```

There is actually a variety of things that the SHELL command allows you to do. First, if you want to activate a command processor other than DOS's standard COMMAND.COM, you can use the SHELL command to give the name and disk location of that program. Even if you are using COMMAND.COM, in the SHELL program, you can specify a special disk path or drive where you want DOS to find the command processor.

Within the SHELL command, you specify the full path and filename of the command processor (In our example, C:\DOS\COMMAND.COM). Following this, you specify the name of the directory that contains the command processor (in our example C:\). DOS will use this pathname to set the COMSPEC variable (see Chapter 12).

Note: With versions of DOS before 5.0 you do not specify the pathname separately.

The two options allow you to control two features of COMMAND.COM. The first one, /E tells DOS how much memory to set aside for the DOS environment. As we explained in Chapter 12, the environment is where DOS stores the information that is set by the PATH, PROMPT, and SET commands. By default, DOS sets aside 256 bytes of memory for the environment. (Although if you have an old version of DOS, the default is smaller.)

Should you need a larger environment, you can specify the size using the /E:size option. The size must be a multiple of 16 and can range from 160 to 32768. If you do not specify a multiple of 16, DOS will round up your number to the nearest such multiple. In our example, we specified an environment of 512 bytes. If you do not want to change the default size of the environment, you do not need to use the /E option.

The second option, /P, tells DOS that the command processor is to be stored permanently in memory. With /P, DOS will follow the normal procedure: execute the commands in your AUTOEXEC.BAT file, then display the DOS prompt and wait for new commands. You must always use /P with the SHELL command.

Device Drivers

DOS automatically knows certain things about your computer and the devices (such as printers, and disk drives) that are attached to it. These are the default devices, and DOS knows about them because IBM designed them into DOS. But, of course, you can attach all sorts of other devices to your computer. How does DOS learn about them and any special commands that they might require? The answer is the DEVICE command, which you can put in the CONFIG.SYS file.

Unusual devices call for special support programs that are called device drivers. DOS is able to incorporate device drivers into itself, through the use of this DEVICE command. For any device driver that you might want to incorporate into DOS, you have to have the program code of the driver stored in a file on your DOS disk. Typically, the driver is stored in a file with the extension of SYS. For example, to use the device driver named ANSI.SYS, which is stored in the \DOS directory, you would put the following command in your CONFIG.SYS file:

```
DEVICE = C:\DOS\ANSI.SYS
```

When DOS encounters the command in the CONFIG.SYS file, it will read the device driver and absorb it as a native part of DOS.

As you might imagine, writing a device driver is a highly technical subject, for expert programmers only. Any device driver has to follow strict DOS rules, so that it cooperates with the rest of DOS. Normally, people like you and me don't write device drivers; instead, we get them as part and parcel of any equipment we want to attach to our computers that happens to require a special device driver.

This equipment might be an unusual type of disk drive, a mouse, or whatever. For example, if you equip your computer with a tape backup system, you'll find that it comes with a diskette that includes the device driver program that DOS needs to support the hardware. Similarly, some other exotic hardware add-ons for your PC may come with their own custom device drivers.

Device Drivers as Software

The concept and use of device drivers is even more broad than what I've suggested. Device drivers can be used strictly for hardware, such as the tape system I mentioned, but they can also be used to perform services that are more closely related to software. In the next few sections, I will describe several such device drivers that are included with DOS.

RAMDRIVE.SYS

The first DOS device driver is RAMDRIVE.SYS. You use this device driver to create a virtual disk. (With older versions of IBM PC-DOS, this driver is called VDISK.SYS.) A virtual disk is an area of regular memory in which DOS simulates a very fast disk. We discussed virtual disks in Chapter 4.

Using RAMDRIVE, specify how much memory should be used for the disk, as well as some of its internal characteristics. You can also choose if you want to put the disk in extended or expanded memory (which we will discuss in Chapter 29). You can use more than one RAMDRIVE specification to set up as many virtual disks as you need.

Most of the time, you will create a virtual disk by using a command like:

```
DEVICE = C:\DOS\RAMDRIVE SIZE
```

The size you specify is measured in kilobytes. You can use any size from 16 kilobytes to 4096 kilobytes (4 megabytes). For example:

```
DEVICE = C:\DOS\RAMDRIVE 4096
```

If you do not specify a size, the default is 64 kilobytes.

By default, DOS will create a virtual disk in regular (conventional) memory. If you want DOS to use extended memory, use the /E option; for expanded memory, use /A.

When you install a virtual disk, DOS gives it the next available letter for a drive name. For example, say that you have one hard disk partition and you install a single virtual disk. The hard disk will be Drive C and the virtual disk will be Drive D.

As a more complex example, say that you have two hard disks, each with two partitions, and you install two virtual disks. The hard disk partitions will be Drives C, D, E, and F; the virtual disks will be Drives G and H. In this case, you would have to use a LASTDRIVE=H command.

ANSI.SYS

Our next device driver is called ANSI.SYS. It's a very special kind of device driver, and can do wonders for you. What ANSI does is provide two special facilities to modify the routine keyboard input and screen output that goes on in your computer. The full details are complicated and surprisingly hard to explain, but the essence is this: If you have ANSI.SYS installed as a device inside your DOS, you can give it commands that make it perform two special kinds of magic.

One kind of magic is keyboard translation, which can turn one keystroke into something quite different, including a long series of keystrokes generated by ANSI.SYS. For example, you could tell ANSI.SYS that every time you press the ! key, that single keystroke should be changed into this entire phrase: "Now isn't that magic!" (However, if you have DOS 5.0 or later, you can do the same sort of thing using the DOSKEY command to create a macro. This should probably be your first choice. See Chapter 25 for the details.)

The other magic ANSI.SYS can do is accept special commands that fully control the information that appears on the display screen—including such things as where the cursor is located, or what color is being written on the screen. Some programming languages, such as BASIC, include features like this, but ANSI.SYS can give this kind of screen-control to any program that wishes to use it.

The ability of ANSI.SYS to perform screen-control magic was created to provide a standard way for programs to gain full control over the capabilities of the computer's display screen, without having to know just how the screen works. This could assist people in writing programs to be used on a wider variety of computers. I always recommend that people install ANSI.SYS. First, some programs require it and it's nice to know that it's always there for you. For example, as I explained in Chapter 18, you must have ANSI.SYS to use the MODE CON: commands. Second, ANSI.SYS can be a lot of fun to play with. Your DOS manual will have a description of all the facilities and how you use them.

DRIVER.SYS

Another device driver that comes with DOS is called DRIVER.SYS. DRIVER.SYS allows you to create another disk drive letter (for example, drive F) and make it refer to one of the disk drives you already have. This may sound silly, but it has its uses.

You already know that for PCs with only a single disk drive, DOS makes that one disk drive act as both drive A and drive B. This makes it easier for you use the same disk drive to copy files from one disk to another.

Now suppose that you decide to add an extra disk drive to your computer. For example, if your computer uses 3 1/2-inch disks, you might add a 5 1/4-inch disk drive so you can read older disks. The DRIVER.SYS device driver would allow you to tell DOS to treat that drive as two drive letters (say, drives E and F), so you can use it to copy files on its particular kind of disk. That's a handy facility!

SMARTDRV.SYS

The SMARTDRV.SYS driver creates a disk cache. This is a section of memory that acts as a high-speed interface to your disks. As data is read from a disk, it is copied to the cache. If DOS needs the data again, it is a lot faster to read it from the cache, which is in memory, than from the relatively slower disk. On some occasions, DOS will even copy data from the disk to the cache ahead of time, anticipating that you will need it soon.

Using a disk cache can speed up your programs significantly—it is well worth any extra memory you can give it. However, SMARTDRV.SYS will only work with extended or expanded memory, not conventional memory. (We will discuss the different types of memory in Chapter 29.)

The simplest way to define a cache is to use the command:

```
DEVICE = C:\DOS\SMARTDRV.SYS SIZE
```

The size you specify is in kilobytes, from 128 to 8192. The default cache size is 256 kilobytes. As with VDISK.SYS, SMARTDRV requires the size to be a multiple of 16. If it is not, DOS will round it up to the nearest such multiple. By default, DOS will install the disk cache in extended memory. If you want to use expanded memory, use the /A option.

National Language Support: DISPLAY.SYS and PRINTER.SYS

In Chapter 22, we discussed the commands that you need to prepare DOS to use a language other than American English. Within the CONFIG.SYS file, there are two drivers that you may need to support code page switching: DISPLAY.SYS for your display, and PRINTER.SYS for your printer. If you need these drivers, check with your DOS manual for the details.

Also related to National Language Support are two more drivers, COUNTRY.SYS and KEYBOARD.SYS. However, these drivers are installed automatically by DOS—do not load them with a DEVICE command. If you do, it will cause problems.

EGA.SYS

This is a special purpose driver only for those people who use EGA (Extended Graphics Adaptor) displays. In Chapter 30, we will be discussing the DOS Shell, a user interface program that comes with DOS. If you are using DOS 5.0 or later, the DOS Shell supports what is called task switching, to allow you to press a hotkey and switch from one program to another. When you do this, DOS must be able to save and restore the data that is on your screen. If you have an EGA display, DOS needs you to load the EGA.SYS device driver to perform this job. Otherwise, you do not need this device driver.

HIMEM.SYS and EMM386.SYS

In Chapter 29, we will be discussing the important topic of extended and expanded memory. For now, let's just say that these two specifications allow DOS to use extra memory that would otherwise not be available. To manage extended memory, you need the HIMEM.SYS driver. For expanded memory, you use EMM386.EXE. In many cases, you will want to install both drivers.

Notice that the expanded memory driver is an EXE file, unlike the other drivers which have an extension of SYS. This is because EMM386 is not only a driver but an executable program that you can use from the DOS prompt.

SETVER.EXE

In Chapter 20, we described the SETVER command—available with DOS 5.0 or later—which tells DOS that certain programs expect to use specific versions of DOS. If you use SETVER, you must initialize the table it keeps by invoking the SETVER.EXE device driver from within your CONFIG.SYS file.

The DOS and DEVICEHIGH Commands

In Chapter 29, we will be discussing the upper memory area. This is the portion that lies between regular (conventional) memory and extended or expanded memory. We will also be talking about the high memory area, just above upper memory.

Under certain circumstances, you can tell DOS to load device drivers, as well as part of DOS itself, into these alternate memory areas. This frees extra room for your programs.

Once you load the HIMEM.SYS and EMM386.EXE drivers, you can use the DOS command to set up extra support for the upper memory and high memory areas. And once you use the DOS command, you can use DEVICEHIGH to load device drivers into upper memory.

By using DEVICEHIGH, instead of the usual DEVICE command, you free regular memory for your programs. For example, to load the ANSI.SYS driver into high memory, use:

```
DEVICEHIGH = C:\DOS\ANSI.SYS
```

All of this sounds complex—and it is. That's why we'll defer the details for now.

Installing Memory-Resident Programs

In Chapter 21, we discussed memory resident programs. At that time, we mentioned that it is a good idea to initialize such programs from within your AUTOEXEC.BAT file.

Alternatively, you can perform these initializations from within the CONFIG.SYS file. You may prefer to start memory resident programs from CONFIG.SYS in order to keep you AUTOEXEC.BAT file shorter and easier to manage.

Most of the time, how you initialize memory resident programs is a matter of personal preference. However, you should be aware of one limitation. In Chapter 29, we will be discussing high memory. At the time, you will see how to use the LOADHIGH command from within your AUTOEXEC.BAT file to load memory resident programs into high memory. This frees extra memory for your programs. If you install programs from your CONFIG.SYS file, you do not have this option.

To install memory-resident programs with CONFIG.SYS, you use the INSTALL command:

```
INSTALL = filename parameters
```

That is, you specify the program you want to install and any parameters it needs.

You can use the INSTALL command with FASTOPEN.EXE and SHARE.EXE, and with the National Language Support commands KEYB.COM and NLSFUNC.EXE. Here is an example:

```
INSTALL = C:\DOS\FASTOPEN.EXE C:
```

You can use INSTALL with any memory resident programs, not just the ones that come with DOS. However, be sure you test that the programs load properly. If they do not, initialize them in the regular manner, from your AUTOEXEC.BAT file.

Summary of CONFIG.SYS Commands And Device Drivers

For your reference, the following two tables summarize what you need to know about the CONFIG.SYS file. Table 28.1 shows the commands you can use. Table 28.2 shows the device drivers that come with DOS.

Table 28.1   *Summary of CONFIG.SYS Commands*

Command	*Purpose*
BREAK	Control the checking for <Ctrl-Break> signal
BUFFERS	Set the number of disk buffers
COUNTRY	Set country specific conventions
DEVICE	Install a device driver
DEVICEHIGH	Install a device driver to upper memory
DOS	Set up high memory and upper memory usage
DRIVPARM	Specify the characteristics of a disk drive
FCBS	Set maximum number of file control blocks
FILES	Set maximum number of open files
INSTALL	Install a memory-resident program
LASTDRIVE	Set the maximum number of disk drives

(continued)

REM	Insert a descriptive comment (remark)
SHELL	Specify the command processor
STACKS	Set memory used to handle hardware signals
SWITCHES	Use a new keyboard as if it were an old one

The following commands are new to DOS 5.0:

DEVICEHIGH, DOS

The DRIVPARM command was included with IBM PC-DOS 4.0 but not with MS-DOS.

The SWITCHES command was included with MS-DOS 4.0 but not with IBM PC-DOS.

Table 28.2 *Summary of DOS Device Drivers*

Command	*Purpose*
ANSI.SYS	Extended control of the keyboard and display
DISPLAY.SYS	Code page switching for the display
DRIVER.SYS	Create an extra name for a diskette drive
EGA.SYS	Support DOS Shell task switching with EGA
EMM386.EXE	Manage expanded memory
HIMEM.SYS	Manage extended memory
PRINTER.SYS	Code page switching for a printer
RAMDRIVE.SYS	Create a virtual disk
SETVER.EXE	Initialize the SETVER table
SMARTDRV.SYS	Create a disk cache

The following device drivers are new to DOS 5.0:

EGA.SYS, EMM386.EXE, HIMEM.SYS

Before version 5.0, IBM PC-DOS uses VDISK.SYS instead of RAMDRIVE.DOS.

With IBM PC-DOS 4.0, XMA2EMS.SYS and XMAEM.SYS were used to manage expanded memory.

IBM PS/2 computers come with a disk cache program called IBMCACHE.SYS that you can use instead of SMARTDRV.SYS.

29

MANAGING MEMORY

Introduction

In Chapter 1, we described how the processor is the "brain" of your computer. It is the processor that executes your programs and manipulates your data. However, processors need somewhere to store their data. This is the job of your computer's memory.

Within the memory, you will find the various parts of DOS, as well as device drivers, memory-resident programs, regular programs, data, and so on. Each time you start your computer, DOS makes sure that everything you need is read into the memory from the disk.

Every operating system has a memory management scheme to control how data is stored in the memory, and to make the data available to programs as they execute. The DOS memory management design was created in 1980, and was based on the characteristics of the processor that was used in the original IBM PC. As we will see in a moment, this design restricted DOS to being able to work with only 640 kilobytes of memory. To this day, the same restriction is still in effect on every one of the 50 million or so DOS computers around the world. In fact, DOS's limited ability to use memory has become the biggest single factor inhibiting the growth of personal computers.

In this chapter, we will examine the DOS memory problem and take a look at what has been done to solve it. Then we'll discuss what you need to know in order for you to make the best use of the memory on your own PC.

Understanding Memory

Before we start, let's take a quick refresher course on PC memory and how we talk about it.

Computer memory is stored within electronic chips. These chips are inside your computer, either on the main board or on an add-in board that is inserted into an expansion slot.

There are two types of memory chips in your PC. The first type contains important data that never changes: the data is "burned in," so to speak. These chips always retain their data, even when you turn off the power. You can read the data, but you can never change it. For this reason, we call this read-only memory, usually abbreviated as ROM.

The largest program in the ROM is called the Basic Input/Output Services, or the BIOS. The BIOS helps DOS take care of the low-level interfacing to all the standard devices. Because these services are so important, every PC is built with the BIOS built into read-only memory.

The second type of memory consists of chips that lose their data each time the power is turned off. However, you can read and write to these chips, which makes them more versatile than ROM. This type of memory is called random-access memory, or RAM.

Unfortunately, RAM is a poor name: all computer memory, even ROM, is random access memory. (This means that you can read anywhere in the memory.) What we call RAM should really be called "read-write memory"; but RWM is too hard to pronounce, so we are stuck with RAM.

Most of your computer's memory is RAM. When someone asks how much memory your computer has, they mean how much RAM does it have. All PCs come with some ROM needed for your computer to run properly, but most of the time we don't really pay attention to it.

As we discussed in Chapter 1, memory is organized into bytes, each of which can hold a single character. We measure memory in kilobytes and megabytes. A kilobyte is 1024 bytes. A megabyte is 1024 kilobytes, or 1,048,576.00 bytes. We abbreviate kilobytes as KB or, more simply K. We abbreviate megabytes as MB.

Much of the time, it is convenient to think of "kilo" as meaning thousand and "mega" as meaning million. Although it is not exactly true, we can say, for example, that 640 K is about 640,000 bytes, and that 2 MB is about 2 million bytes.

The Original DOS Memory Management Scheme

All the bytes in your computer's memory have an address—a number by which they are known. Your processor accesses memory by specifying what number byte it wants to read or write. For example, the processor might say, I want to read byte number 245212, or I want to write this data to byte number 144256. It is the operating system that decides how bytes should be numbered and how memory should be addressed.

This leads us to the most important single idea in memory management: The processor can only use memory that has an address. The problem with DOS is that there are not enough addresses to go around.

All of the processors for IBM-compatible PCs are manufactured by the Intel company. These processors are—from oldest to newest—the 8088, the 8086, the 286, the 386, and the 486.

The original IBM PC was designed around the 8088, which had the limitation of being able to address only 1024K (1 megabyte) of memory. Thus, the original designers of DOS knew that they had 1024K worth of addresses to use.

They decided to use the first 640K addresses for the general working space that would hold the programs and data, including DOS itself. The remaining 384K (1024–640) addresses would be set aside for special uses. For example, some of these addresses would be used to access the ROM, including the BIOS. Other addresses would be used to access the memory that holds what is being shown on the display screen.

Thus, DOS was set up to allow programs direct access to the first 640K memory addresses. The higher addresses, starting with 641 K, were already spoken for and were considered to be forbidden territory. In effect, this set an upper limit on how much RAM—regular memory—DOS would be able to manage.

At first, this wasn't much of a problem. When DOS was designed, 1024K was considered to be an enormous amount of memory. It seemed inconceivable that a personal computer would ever use more than a few hundred kilobytes. In fact, the original PC contained only 64K.

Of course, what happened was that memory became cheap and processors were developed that could address many megabytes of memory. But DOS, which has to manage it all, is still limited by the original design. DOS can access up 1024K of memory, but only the first 640K can be RAM.

You might ask, why don't they just change DOS so that it can use more than 640K of RAM? The reason is that this could not be done without relocating the data items that are stored in the upper 384K, above the 640K boundary. But these items cannot be moved because thousands and thousands of programs have been written to work with the system the way it is.

What made the situation intolerable is that, as the personal computer industry matured, programs and data files became larger and larger. DOS itself grew bigger. Memory resident programs became available. New device drivers were brought out. All of these things required memory, and all of the memory had to come out of the 640K address space for RAM.

The situation today is ironic. Modern PCs have plenty of memory. Modern processors can use many megabytes of RAM. However, DOS still has only 640K of addresses to use. The result is memory shortages in the midst of plenty—a situation that is whimsically referred to as "RAM cram."

Two Solutions to the Memory Shortage Problem

As a general rule, if something doesn't work well, there are two things you can do: make a new one or fix the old one. With DOS, both solutions were used.

First, IBM and Microsoft created a new operating system, OS/2, as a replacement for DOS. OS/2 has many advantages over DOS, one of them being the capability to use a lot of memory. However, OS/2 is being accepted rather slowly and DOS will be here for years to come.

Second, certain PC companies developed ways to extend DOS's memory management so that programs could access memory above the 640K boundary. These are the solutions that we will be discussing in this chapter.

Before we do, let's take a minute to clear up a point that can be confusing: how DOS allots addresses for memory over 640K.

How Is Extra Memory Addressed?

The RAM chips in your computer supply the main part of your system's memory. The first 640K bytes are assigned the addresses 0 through 640K. But what happens if you have extra memory?

The rest of your RAM cannot be assigned addresses starting from 640K because, as we explained, all the addresses from 640K to 1024K are already reserved. Thus, any RAM over 640K bytes must be assigned to addresses starting at 1024K.

For example, say that your PC comes with 2048K (2 megabytes) of memory. The first 640K bytes is assigned the addresses 0K through 640K. The remainder, 1408K bytes, is assigned the addresses 1024K through 2432K.

Imagine that you are walking down a street and you notice that, all of a sudden, the house numbers skip from 640 to 1024. When you ask why, you are told that when the street was first designed, the numbers between 640 and 1024 were reserved for other uses. Houses were expensive and nobody ever dreamt that the numbers would get anywhere near 640.

Eventually, more than 640 houses were built but the extras had to be numbered starting from 1024. There were so many important arrangements based on the original numbering scheme that it was impossible to change.

Thus, any RAM that your machine has over 640K bytes, is addressed starting at 1024 K. The unfortunate confusion that results from such an arrangement comes from the fact that the same units of measurement—

kilobytes and megabytes—are used to describe both physical memory and memory addresses.

The Different Types of Memory

With DOS, we use different names to describe the various ranges of memory addresses.

- 0K to 640K is called conventional memory.
- 640K and 1024K is called upper memory.
- Everything above 1024K is called extended memory.

An old term for upper memory is reserved memory. This name reminds us that these addresses have been set aside for special purposes.

It is important to realize that these names are used only with DOS. With other operating systems, memory is memory: there is only one type of addressing, so there are no special names.

DOS allows your programs to access as much conventional memory as is in your PC. If you have more than 640K of RAM, the extra memory will be extended memory. There are two ways that this memory can be used. First, the memory can be used by programs that follow a certain protocol called Extended Memory Specification, or XMS. Since DOS cannot manage extended memory, a special XMS memory manager is required. Starting with DOS 5.0, such a program is furnished as a device driver. This driver has two main jobs:

- To make extra memory available to programs that adhere to the XMS standard
- To arbitrate when programs make conflicting memory requests

As we explained in Chapter 28, a device driver is an extension to DOS that allows it to oversee the operation of a particular device. In this case, the "device" is extra memory.

The XMS driver is named HIMEM.SYS. Like all device drivers, you install it by using a DEVICE command in your CONFIG.SYS file. We will go over the details in a moment.

The second way to use extended memory is to treat it as expanded memory. Expanded memory is extra memory that operates according to the Expanded Memory Specification, or EMS. Like XMS, EMS memory requires its own device driver to act as a memory manager.

Expanded memory was originally conceived as a way to use extra memory for DOS programs and data. A small 64K portion of the upper memory area is used as a "window" into the extra memory. Programs request access to extra memory in chunks called pages, which are copied back and forth into the 64K window.

Since the window is within the upper memory area (which DOS can access), programs that are written to take advantage of EMS have a way to use extra memory. However, as you might imagine, it is slower to work with memory in 64K chunks that are constantly being swapped in and out, than it is to work with memory that can be accessed directly. But at the time expanded memory was developed, there was no other way for programs to use extra memory. (The XMS standard has not yet been invented.) The EMS standard was an important breakthrough.

Expanded memory was first sold on special add-in boards that plugged into a slot in your computer. These boards contained RAM chips along with all the extra hardware necessary to perform the swapping operations.

Today, it is possible to use a device driver to simulate expanded memory using regular, extended memory. Such a program, called EMM386.EXE comes with DOS. However, as the name implies, you can use EMM386 only with a 386- or 486-based PC.

So, where does that leave us? Let's summarize:

- DOS and your programs can use up to 640K of RAM.
- Extra RAM can be used as extended memory by programs that follow the XMS standard, and as expanded memory by programs that follow the EMS standard.
- Expanded memory comes on special add-in boards. If you have a 386- or 486-based computer, you can use a device driver to simulate expanded memory from extended memory.

How do you know which scheme you want to use to take advantage of your extra memory? It depends on your programs. Extended memory is fast and is efficient for programs that can use it. Expanded memory involves lots of swapping and is slower. However, many programs are designed to use expanded memory as the EMS standard was introduced earlier than the XMS standard.

Unfortunately, most programs can use neither expanded nor extended memory. They are confined to the conventional 640 K. Does this mean that, except for special programs, all our extra memory goes to waste? The answer is no—because DOS comes with a few facilities to lets everyone take advantage of extra memory. How that is done—what extras are available—is the topic of the rest of the chapter.

HIMEM.SYS: The Extended Memory Manager

Starting with DOS 5.0, you can place certain device drivers, memory resident programs, and even part of DOS itself into extended, expanded and upper memory. This allows you to use as much of the 640K conventional memory as possible for your programs and data. In fact, these features are so important that they provide a compelling reason to upgrade from an older DOS to 5.0.

However, before you can take advantage of these savings, you must install the requisite device drivers. The first one is HIMEM.SYS, the extended memory driver.

To install HIMEM.SYS use the following command in your CONFIG.SYS file:

```
DEVICE = C:\DOS\HIMEM.SYS
```

HIMEM.SYS has a number of highly technical options that you probably won't need, so we won't cover them here. If necessary, you can look them up in your DOS manual.

EMM386.EXE: The Expanded Memory Simulator

The EMM386.EXE driver will simulate expanded memory from extended memory. However, you can only use the program if you have a 386- or 486-based computer. The less powerful 8088-, 8086-, and 286-based computers do not have the sophisticated capabilities needed to run this program.

Because EMM386.EXE depends on being able to use extended memory, you must install HIMEM.SYS before you can use it. Like HIMEM.SYS, EXE386.EXE has a number of highly technical options that you will probably never need. The usual way that you will install this driver is by using the following command in your CONFIG.SYS file:

```
DEVICE = C:\DOS\EMM386.EXE SIZE
```

The size you specify is the number of kilobytes that you want to convert to expanded memory. You can specify an amount between 16K and 32768K (which is 32 megabytes). Of course, you can't specify more than the amount of extended memory you have. The size you specify must be a multiple of 16K. If it is not, DOS will round the amount down (not up) to the nearest such multiple. If you do not specify a size, DOS will use a default of 256K.

Here are two examples. The first installs the EMM386.EXE driver and specifies that 1024K (1 MB) of expanded memory should be simulated. The second accepts the default of 256K:

```
DEVICE = C:\DOS\EMM386.EXE 1024
DEVICE = C:\DOS\EMM386.EXE
```

Note: EMM386.EXE will manage the expanded memory that it creates. However, if you have an expanded memory board, do not use EMM386. Use the expanded memory manager that comes with the board. Each type of memory board requires its own manager.

Using EXE386.EXE to Manage Upper Memory

As we explained earlier, the 384K of memory addresses in upper memory are reserved for accessing special types of memory like the ROM, the display memory, and so on. However, in most cases, not all of this space is used. This means, in principle, the unused addresses can be mapped onto extra memory and used for something else.

Aside from managing expanded memory, EMM386.EXE is able to manage upper memory in a way that lets you take advantage of any unused address space. You can use this space to hold device drivers and memory resident programs. This frees up extra conventional memory for your programs and data.

To tell EMM386 that you want it to manage upper memory, specify either RAM or NOEMS when you install the driver. For example:

```
DEVICE = C:\DOS\EMM386.EXE 1024 RAM
DEVICE = C:\DOS\EMM386.EXE NOEMS
```

Either of these commands initialize the upper memory feature. The difference is that you use RAM when you want expanded memory, and NOEMS when you do not want expanded memory.

Within upper memory, each range of available addresses is called an upper memory block, or UMB. A program, like EMM386, that manages upper memory, makes it possible to use the UMBs. Such programs are called UMB providers.

Thus, we can say, EMM386.EXE that is an expanded memory simulator, an expanded memory manager, an upper memory manager, and a UMB provider.

Using the DOS Command to Make the Most of Extra Memory

To take full advantage of extended memory and such upper memory blocks (UMB's) that are available, you need to use the DOS command. This command is only for the CONFIG.SYS file. You cannot enter it at the regular DOS prompt.

The DOS command has four forms:

```
DOS HIGH, UMB
DOS HIGH, NOUMB
DOS LOW, UMB
DOS LOW, NOUMB
```

When you use UMB, it sets things up so you are able to load device drivers and memory resident programs into free UMBs. Using NOUMB says you do not want this service.

HIGH indicates that the operating system should load part of itself into a special area of extended memory. LOW indicates that all of DOS should be in regular, conventional memory.

The defaults are to provide neither service. So, if you do not use a DOS command, it is as if you specified LOW, NOUMB.

Most of the time you will want to take advantage of both services and use:

```
DOS HIGH, UMB
```

By the way, the area of extended memory that can hold part of DOS is the lowest 64K. Since extended memory starts at 1024K, we are talking about the addresses from 1024K to 1088K. For certain technical reasons that we won't go into here, this 64K, and only this 64K, of extended memory can be accessed by DOS. Since this part of extended memory is special, it has its own name, the high memory area, or HMA. If this seems confusing, forget it. Just use the correct commands in your CONFIG.SYS and let DOS worry about the details.

How to Arrange Your CONFIG.SYS File

If you do not have a 386- or 486-based computer, you cannot use EMM386.EXE. Most of the memory management facilities are not available, so don't worry about them.

If you do have a 386- or 486-based computer, all you have to do is set up your CONFIG.SYS file according to the following checklist. Put the commands in the order that they appear in the list and everything will work as efficiently as possible.

1. If you need to use the SETVER facility (see Chapters 20 and 28), initialize the SETVER table by using the command:

   ```
   DEVICE = C:\DOS\SETVER.EXE
   ```

2. Install HIMEM.SYS. Use the command:

   ```
   DEVICE = C:\DOS\HIMEM.SYS
   ```

3. Install any device drivers that use extended memory. If you use RAMDRIVE.SYS, you need to specify the /E option. With SMARTDRV.SYS, no option is necessary—extended memory is the default. (See Chapter 28 and your DOS manual for the details.) The following are two sample commands:

   ```
   DEVICE = C:\DOS\RAMDRIVE size /E
   DEVICE = C:\DOS\SMARTDRV size
   ```

4. Install EMM386.EXE. If you do not want expanded memory, use:

   ```
   DEVICE = C:\DOS\EMM386.EXE NOEMS
   ```

   If you want expanded memory, use:

   ```
   DEVICE = C:\DOS\EMM386.EXE size RAM
   ```

   If you do not need expanded memory, do not ask for it. If you want it for certain programs, ask for only as much as you need.

5. Use the DOS command to make use of upper memory blocks and to load part of DOS in extended memory:

   ```
   DOS = HIGH, UMB
   ```

6. Install any device drivers that use expanded memory. If you have a choice, as you do with RAMDRIVE and SMARTDRV, choose extended memory instead.

7. Install whatever drivers will fit into upper memory by using DEVICEHIGH commands (see Chapter 28). For example:

```
DEVICEHIGH = C:\DOS\ANSI.SYS
```

8. Install whatever other device drivers you need, using the usual DEVICE commands.

For reference, Table 29.1 shows a summary of these recommendations. Remember, these are only for 386- and 486-based computers.

Table 29.1   Summary of How to Configure Your CONFIG.SYS File

1.	SETVER.EXE (if necessary)
2.	HIMEM.SYS
3.	Extended memory device drivers
4.	EMM386.EXE
5.	DOS = HIGH, UMB
6.	Expanded memory device drivers
7.	Device drivers loaded with DEVICEHIGH
8.	Other drivers loaded with DEVICE

Loading Memory-Resident Programs into Upper Memory

If your CONFIG.SYS file uses HIMEM.SYS, EMM386.EXE, and the DOS command to access upper memory, you can use the extra upper memory blocks (UMBs) to load device drivers and memory resident programs.

To load device drivers into upper memory, use the DEVICEHIGH command (see Chapter 29) in your CONFIG.SYS file, as we did in the previous section. To load memory resident programs into upper memory, use the LOADHIGH command in your AUTOEXEC.BAT file. All you need to do is put the word LOADHIGH in front of the command that initializes the program. If you want, you can use LH instead of LOADHIGH.

For example, in Chapters 23 and 25 we used the DOSKEY memory resident program. Usually, you would initialize this program by using the command:

```
DOSKEY
```

in your AUTOEXEC.BAT file. However, when DOSKEY is loaded in this manner, DOS will place it in conventional memory. If you want DOS to place the program into upper memory, use:

```
LOADHIGH DOSKEY
```

That's all there is to it. If the program requires parameters or options, just put them on the same line. For example:

```
LOADHIGH DOSKEY /INSERT
```

As we mentioned in Chapter 28, you can load memory resident programs from your CONFIG.SYS file by using the INSTALL command. Loading from CONFIG.SYS can be more convenient but there is no way to load into upper memory. To do that, you must use LOADHIGH. Since LOADHIGH is a DOS command, it cannot be used in your CONFIG.SYS file.

Using MEM to Find Out About Memory Usage

In Chapter 7, we explained how you can use the MEM command to display how much memory your machine has and how much is available. If you are using extended, expanded, or upper memory, there are three options for MEM that can help you by displaying extra information.

The /PROGRAM option displays the memory status of all the programs that are currently loaded into memory. If you want, you can use /P instead of /PROGRAM:

```
MEM /PROGRAM
MEM /P
```

The /CLASSIFY option classifies programs by memory usage. This option lists the size of each program, displays a summary of what memory is being used, and shows you the largest available blocks of memory. This option is particularly useful if you have trouble setting up upper memory block (UMB) support. If you want, you can use /C instead of /CLASSIFY:

```
MEM /CLASSIFY
MEM /C
```

The /DEBUG option shows even more information. Along with the status of programs, /DEBUG displays the memory status of device drivers. If you want, you can use /D instead of /DEBUG:

```
MEM /DEBUG
MEM /D
```

Although the extra memory statistics can be useful, there are two problems. First, the output is difficult to understand (although /CLASSIFY is probably the most useful). Second, the output is so long that it will scroll off the top of your screen before you can read it. The best idea is to pipe the output to the MORE command (see Chapter 19):

```
MEM /P | MORE
MEM /D | MORE
MEM /C | MORE
```

A useful alternative is to use DOSKEY to create macros to do the job for you (see Chapter 25). For example:

```
DOSKEY MEMP = MEM /PROGRAM $B MORE
DOSKEY MEMD = MEM /DEBUG $B MORE
DOSKEY MEMC = MEM /CLASSIFY $B MORE
```

Once you have these macros it is easy to display whatever type of memory statistics you want.

command:	MEM	basic statistics
macro:	MEMP	basic + loaded programs
macro:	MEMD	basic + loaded programs + drivers
macro:	MEMC	classified summary of memory usage.

30

THE DOS SHELL

Introduction

A *shell* is a program that surrounds or shields you from another program, much like the shell of an oyster surrounds and protects its insides. The reason people use shells is that they are designed to be easier to use, and sometimes more powerful, than the underlying program. In other words, a shell acts as a user interface.

Strictly speaking, the DOS command processor, COMMAND.COM, is a shell. It acts as your user interface with DOS. It reads your commands, makes sure they are carried out, and shields you from the insides of DOS. In fact, as you remember, in Chapter 28 we learned how to use the SHELL command within a CONFIG.SYS file to set up COMMAND.COM.

However, shells can be used to surround other shells. In particular, DOS comes with a program called the DOS Shell that you can use as an alternate user interface.

In this chapter, we will take a look at the DOS Shell and describe what it has to offer. You can decide if you like the shell enough to use it, or if you prefer standard DOS-prompt interface.

The Different Versions of the DOS Shell

The first DOS Shell was designed for DOS 4.0 by IBM. For DOS 5.0, Microsoft designed a completely new shell. Both shells use the keyboard and, optionally, a mouse. Both use pull-down menus and follow the standard graphical user interface design.

One big difference is that Microsoft planned the DOS 5.0 shell to look and to work like Microsoft Windows. Although the shell is not as powerful as Windows, it uses the keyboard and mouse in the same way.

In this chapter, we will discuss the new DOS Shell. If you have the version 4.0 shell, much of what we say will pertain to your work. However, the screen will look somewhat different and there will be some differences, most of which will be self-evident.

Why Use the DOS Shell?

The DOS Shell was designed for people who want a simple windowing interface. Since the shell comes free with DOS, you can use it or not as you see fit. The DOS Shell provides a menu-based interface for working with DOS. You can use either the keyboard, or a mouse, or both. When you use the shell, most of your interaction with DOS will take the form of selecting items from menus and lists, rather than typing commands.

Generally speaking, there are three reasons why you would choose to use the DOS Shell:

- To provide a simple menu-based interface to DOS
- To customize the work environment, either for yourself or for someone else
- To access a function that is not available with regular DOS commands

The DOS Shell is excellent for offices and organizations that provide computing services for many people. Each person can have his own customized shell, set up to access only those programs he is interested in. Moreover, you can install passwords to ensure that only authorized users access certain facilities. Alternatively, you can set up one standard environment that can be used by many people.

Starting and Stopping the DOS Shell

To start the DOS Shell, you use the DOSSHELL command. Just enter:

```
DOSSHELL
```

When you install DOS, you will be asked if you want to use the shell. If you do, the installation program will add the DOSSHELL command to the end of your AUTOEXEC.BAT file. If you get tired of using the shell, simply remove the DOSSHELL command.

On the other hand, if you are currently not using the shell, you can start by placing a DOSSHELL command in your AUTOEXEC.BAT file. Be sure that DOSSHELL is the last command in the file.

From within the shell, you stop by pressing either <F3> or <Alt-F4>. This will return you to COMMAND.COM and the DOS prompt. If you are using a mouse, select the Exit item from the Files menu. If you want to restart the shell, enter the DOSSHELL command again.

If you want to put the shell on hold and temporarily enter commands at the DOS prompt, press <Shift-F9>. You can now enter as many DOS commands as you want. When you have finished, enter:

```
EXIT
```

to return to the shell. You don't need to enter another DOSSHELL command. The shell is already waiting in the background for you to return.

The DOS Shell Initialization File

When the DOS Shell starts, it reads from a special initialization file called DOSSHELL.INI. This file holds your preferences for how the Shell should be set up. Normally, this file is stored in your DOS directory and maintained automatically, so you don't need to worry about it.

However, if the need should arise, there is a way for you to keep this file in a different directory. This can come in handy if more than one person is using the same computer and each person has his own initialization file.

Simply use the SETcommand to set the value of a variable named DOSSHELL in the DOS environment. For example, if your initialization file is in the directory C:\TOM, you would put the following commands in whatever batch file starts the DOS Shell:

```
SET DOSSHELL=C:\TOM
DOSSHELL
```

Learning How to Use the DOS Shell

Along with your DOS documentation will be a tutorial teaching you how to use the DOS Shell. Using this tutorial is a quick way to get up to speed. On the other hand, the DOS Shell is so easy to use that if you have any experience with a window-oriented system, you might find it easier just to start work and experiment.

The DOS Shell has an extensive context sensitive help system. Wherever you are, you can ask for help by pressing <F1> or by selecting Help with a mouse. Whenever possible, the shell displays a message pertaining to your exact situation. Within some messages, there are other Help topics than you can select.

In this chapter, we will introduce you to the facilities that the shell has to offer. However, the best way to actually learn to use the shell is to read the tutorial and then experiment for yourself.

Using the DOS Shell

When you start the DOS Shell for the first time, your screen will look something like the one in Figure 30.1. You will notice that the second line from the top contains five choices: File, Options, View, Tree and Help. This is the menu bar. Each of these choices can be selected to pull down a menu. Within the menu, you can select from several items.

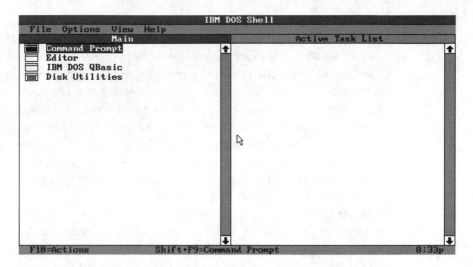

Figure 30.1. *Starting with the DOS Shell*

With a mouse, you point to what you want and click. With a keyboard you use the same keys that we described in Chapter 26 for the DOS editor. The general idea is to move to what you want and then press <Enter>.

In general, the keys you use to move around are:

<Up> and <Down>   (the cursor control keys)
<Tab> and <Shift-Tab>

Most of the time, you use the cursor keys to move within a list, and the tab keys to move from one window to another. But this rule does not always hold. If you are ever in a position where the cursor keys don't seem to work, try <Tab>.

To select a menu, you can hold down the <Alt> key and press the first letter of the menu you want: <Alt-F>, <Alt-O>, <Alt-V>, <Alt-T>, or <Alt-H>.

Each of these menus has a list of items which we will discuss in turn. For now, let's take a look at the DOS Shell screen display. Look first at the third line of the screen. Notice that it shows the default drive and the current directory. At all times, you can look here and find out just where you are within the DOS file system.

The next line contains a list of disks. In our example, you can see that there are two disk drives (A: and B:), two hard disks (C: and D:), and a virtual disk (E:). You can switch the default drive from one disk to another by selecting the one you want. (Move to it and press <Enter>, or point and click with the mouse.) As a shortcut, you can hold down the <Ctrl> key and press the letter of the disk you want. In our example, you can choose among <Ctrl-A>, <Ctrl-B>, <Ctrl-C>, <Ctrl-D>, and <Ctrl-E>.

After this line is the main part of the screen. This part consists of either two or more large windows. These windows hold either a list of programs you can start, or information about your directories and files. We will take a closer look in a moment.

Finally, take a look at the bottom line of the screen, the status bar. On the right is the time of day. On the left is a reminder about two important keys and what they do. <Shift-F9>, as we have already mentioned, will put the shell on hold and start a fresh copy of DOS so you can type in commands.

The other key <F10> performs Actions. This means that you can press <F10> and then select one of the menus along the top. For example, if you want to access the Help menu you can press <F10>, move to Help, and press <Enter>. Alternatively, you can just press <Alt-H>. As a convenience, pressing the <Alt> key by itself works the same as <F10>.

Now that we've oriented ourselves to the DOS Shell screen, let's take a tour of each of the menus to see what they have to offer. By the time you understand each menu and each item, you will know most of what the shell can do for you.

The Help Menu

The first menu you need to become familiar with is the Help menu. As you know, you can press <F1> at any time to get context-sensitive help. The Help menu complements this system. By selecting from this menu, you can ask access an extensive library of on-line documentation.

To pull down the Help menu, press <Alt-H>. Each item on the menu displays a list of Help topics from which you can make a selection. Here is a list of each choice and what it offers:

Index	A master index (includes all topics)
Keyboard	Learning how to use the keyboard with the shell
Shell Basics	The basic operation of the shell
Commands	The various DOS Shell functions, grouped by menu

Procedures   The various DOS Shell functions, grouped by task

Using Help   Instructions on how to use the help system

About Shell   Shows the version of the shell you are using

To start teaching yourself, first read about Using Help, then read about Shell Basics.

The View Menu

Most of the time, your work within the DOS Shell centers around one of two activities: selecting a program to run, or performing a file system task. The main part of your screen will consist of a list of programs, file and directory information, or both.

You can control what is displayed on your screen by making choices from the View menu. When you are displaying a file list, the shell will show you the directory tree on the left, and a list of files on the right. A typical file list is shown in Figure 30.2. In this example, we are looking at the files in the \DOS subdirectory on the C: disk.

```
                          IBM DOS Shell
 File  Options  View  Tree  Help
 C:\DOS
  A    B    C    D    E

        Directory Tree                      C:\DOS\*.*
    C:\                         ↑        4201    .CPI       6,404   01-30-90  ↑
        BATCH                            4208    .CPI         720   08-08-90
        DBASE                            5202    .CPI         359   02-12-91
        DOS                              ANSI    .SYS       8,965   02-12-91
        DW5                              APPEND  .EXE      10,710   02-12-91
        EXCEL                            ASSIGN  .COM       6,351   02-12-91
        FASTBACK                         ATTRIB  .EXE      15,732   02-12-91
        FW3                              AUTOEXEC.BAT          86   03-01-91
        GAMES                            BACKUP  .COM      35,948   02-12-91
        HIJAAK                           BASIC   .COM       1,065   10-11-89
        IBMLINK                          BASICA  .COM      64,160   08-28-90
        LOG                              CHKDSK  .COM      16,120   02-12-91
        NC                               COMMAND .COM      48,568   02-12-91
        NG                               COMP    .COM      13,722   02-12-91
        NORTON                           CONFIG  .SYS          93   03-01-91
        QBASIC                           COUNTRY .SYS      16,981   02-12-91
        TELIX                            DEBUG   .COM      20,586   02-12-91
        UTILITY                  ↓       DISKCOMP.COM      10,572   02-12-91  ↓
 F10=Actions  Shift+F9=Command Prompt                              11:24a
```

Figure 30.2. *The DOS Shell Showing a File List*

You can traverse the directory tree, moving from one directory to another. As you do, the shell updates the right side of the screen to show the files in whatever directory you are pointing to.

The choices on the View menu that pertain to displaying file lists are:

Single File List	Display one large list of files from selected directory
Dual File Lists	Display two lists of files, in whatever directories you want
All Files	Display a single list of all the files on the disk

If you choose Dual File Lists, the shell divides the screen into two parts. The top half shows one file list, the bottom half shows another list. You can move from one directory tree to another and display the files in two different directories. If you want, you can even have the two file lists point to different disks. You can see this in Figure 30.3. Choose the All Files selection when you want to look at one large alphabetical list of all the files on a disk.

Aside from file lists, you can display a program list. This shows the names of all the programs you can start from the shell. You can add and remove programs from the list as you see fit.

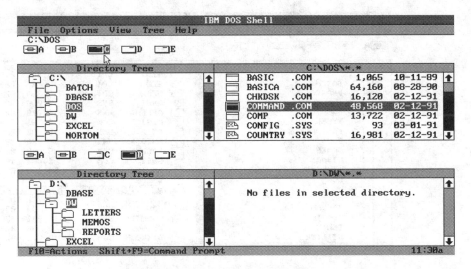

Figure 30.3. *The DOS Shell Showing Dual File Lists*

Just as every directory can have subdirectories, a program list can have a sublist, called a group. For example, you might have a main list consisting of different groups, one for each department in an office. Each group would be a separate list that contains the programs used by that department.

The choices in the View menu that have to do with program lists are:

Program/File Lists   Display one program list and one file list

Program List   Display one large program list (no file lists)

Generally, you will find that the most useful view is the one that shows both a file list and a program list. This allows you work with files and start programs at the same time. You can see such a screen in Figure 30.4.

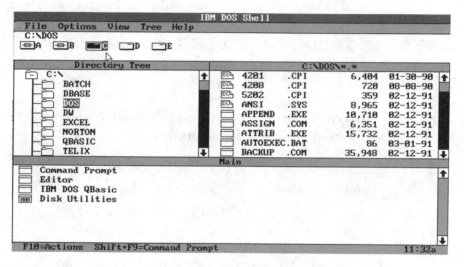

Figure 30.4.   *The DOS Shell Showing a Program List and a File List*

The final two View choices tell the shell to re-display whatever is on the screen.

Repaint Screen   Rewrite the screen without changing any information

Refresh   Re-scan the default disk and then rewrite the screen

Select Repaint Screen if, for some reason, your screen becomes garbled. Select Refresh if the file information needs to be updated; for example, if you are working with drive A: and you have just changed the diskette. As a convenience, you can press <Shift-F5> for Repaint Screen, and <F5> for Refresh.

The Tree Menu

This menu is used only when you are moving within a directory tree. The choices allow you to display or not display part of the directory tree, so you can look at as much or as little detail as you want.

Expand One Level	Display the subdirectory under the selected directory
Expand Branch	Display all the subdirectories under the selected directory
Expand Tree	Display the entire directory tree
Collapse Branch	Hide all the subdirectories under the selected directory

As a convenience, you can move to a directory and press the following keys instead of choosing from the menu:

Expand One Level	<+>	(plus sign)
Expand Branch	<*>	(asterisk)
Expand Tree	<Ctrl-*>	(Ctrl-asterisk)
Collapse Branch	<->	(minus sign)

If you use the numeric keypad (on the right side of the keyboard), you will find these keys easy to access.

The File Menu: Executing and Associating Files

The last menu to discuss is the File menu. This is the menu that you will be using most of the time. From this menu, you can initiate all file and directory operations, as well as define and launch programs.

This menu actually has two versions: one for dealing with files and directories, and one for working with programs. The shell displays whatever menu is appropriate when you select File. We'll discuss each variation, starting with files and directories.

This version of the File menu allows you to perform the regular operations, as well as a few that cannot be done from the DOS prompt. One of these allows you to associate a data file with a program. How it works follows.

An easy way to execute a program or batch file is to move to the EXE, COM, or BAT file and press <Enter> (or point and double click with the mouse). DOS checks to make sure that file is executable and then runs it.

For example, suppose you point to an executable COM file and double click. The shell puts itself on hold and runs the program. When the program ends, you will automatically be returned to the shell.

By associating files, you tell the shell to execute a specific program whenever you select a file that has a particular extension. The name of the file you select is passed to the program as a parameter.

For example, say that you tell the shell that whenever you select a file with an extension of TXT, you want to start the DOS editor. Now, you point at a file named MEMO.TXT and double click. (Or, you move to the file name and press <Enter>.)

The shell executes the following command:

```
EDIT MEMO.TXT
```

The result? You can edit a file just by selecting it.

On the file list version of the File menu, there are three choices that let you run programs.

Associate	Associate a file extension with a program
Open	Execute a file, or the program associated with a file
Run	Enter and execute a single DOS command

The File Menu: Operating on Files and Directories

Most of the file commands you use require you to select a file, a directory, or a group of files to act upon. To select a file, move to it and press the <Space> bar. With a mouse, point to the file and click. For example, you can delete a file or directory by pointing to it, clicking, and then choosing Delete from the File menu.

If you want to select a group of files, point to the first one in the group, hold down the <Shift> key and move up or down. The files you pass over will be marked as being selected. With the mouse, point to a file, hold the button down, and move up or down.

Normally, whenever you select files, all other files are automatically unselected. If you want to select a noncontiguous set of files you must collect them into a group, one at a time.

Start by pressing <Shift-F8>. You will see the word ADD appear on the right side of the bottom line (the status bar). This means that you can now accumulate selections. Now, move to a file and press the <Space> bar. The file will be selected. Repeat this as often as you want. Each time you do, the file will be added to the group.

When you want to stop selecting files, press <Shift-F8> once again. The status bar will stop displaying the ADD notice.

Once you have selected the file, directory, or group of files you want to act upon, choose an item from the File menu. The choices are:

Print	Print a file
Search	Search for a particular file
View File Contents	Display the contents of a file
Move	Move a file from one directory to another
Copy	Copy a file
Delete	Delete a file or directory
Rename	Rename a file or directory
Change Attributes	Change the attributes of a file or directory (see Chapter 17)
Create Directory	Create a new directory
Select All	Select all of the files in the current directory
Deselect All	Un-select all of the files in the current directory

Notice that you can rename a directory—something that you cannot do through a regular DOS command.

As a convenience, you can select a file, directory, or group of files, and press the following keys instead of choosing from the menu:

Move	<F7>
Copy	<F8>
Delete	<Delete>
View File Contents	<F9>

Select All	<Ctrl-/>	(Ctrl-Slash)
Deselect All	<Ctrl-\>	(Ctrl-Backslash)

The File Menu: Working with Program Lists

As we explained earlier, the main part of the screen contains either a program list, a file list, or both. You move from one area to another by pressing <Tab> or <Shift-Tab>. You can define whatever items you want to be on a program list. In order to do so, you specify the information that the shell needs to run that particular item.

The most important items are:

- The title that you want to appear in the program list
- The commands you want to execute when this selection is chosen (you can specify more than one command)
- The directory from which you want to start the program
- If you want a password for this item
- Help text for this item
- A shortcut key for task switching (explained later)

Later, when you select an item from the list, the shell executes it according to your specifications.

Aside from adding new items to the main program list, you can define groups. A group is an item on the list that, when selected, displays a sublist. For example, say that your computer is used by two people named Harley and Kimberlyn. Within the main program list, you create two groups named Kimberlyn and Harley. Within each group you set up the programs used by that person.

When you select the File menu while you are working with a program list, you will have the following choices:

New	Create a new item, or create a new group
Open	Start a program, or move into a different group
Copy	Copy an item from one group to another
Delete	Delete an item from a group
Properties	Modify the information associated with a particular item

Reorder	Change the order of an item within the program list
Run	Enter and execute a single DOS command
Exit	Stop the shell and return to the DOS prompt

As a convenience, you can move to an item in the program list and press the following keys instead of choosing from the menu:

Open	<Enter>
Delete	<Delete>
Exit	<F3> or <Alt-4>

The Options Menu

The Options Menu allows you to express various preferences to the shell. You will probably not use this menu very often. Most people make their choices once and leave them alone unless conditions change. Whatever choices you make are automatically stored in a special initialization file. Every time you start work, the shell reads this file and sets itself up just the way you specified. By far the most useful option you have is to turn on task switching. We will deal with this facility separately in the next section.

Here are the choices that you have with the Options menu:

Confirmation	Ask for permission before certain file operations
File Display Options	Specify how files should be displayed within a file list
Select Across Directories	Allow the selecting of files in more than one directory
Show Information	Show detailed file, directory, and disk information
Enable Task Swapper	Turn task switching on or off
Display	Specify which display mode you want to use
Colors	Specify which set of colors you want to use

Task Switching

When you use the standard DOS interface—entering one command after another at the prompt—you can work with only one program at a time. One of the most important facilities offered by the DOS shell is task switching. This allows you to switch back and forth between programs.

Be sure that you do not confuse task switching with multitasking. With task switching, all the programs but one are paused. When you switch away from a program, it stops until you return.

With multitasking, more than one program can execute simultaneously, sharing the resources of the processor. Of course, you can interact with only one program at a time, but the others can still be running in the background.

DOS does support limited multitasking via memory-resident programs (see Chapter 21). For example, you can use the PRINT command to oversee background printing while you are working with another program.

If you have a true multitasking system, you can—for example—recalculate a large spreadsheet in the background while you are typing a letter. On its own, DOS cannot do this, but if you add an operating environment like Microsoft Windows, it becomes possible with a 386- or 486-based PC. Using the task switching provided by the DOS shell, you can change from a spreadsheet to your word processor, but as soon as you do, the spreadsheet stops executing.

Still, task switching is a useful capability. You can load up a set of programs and, by pressing a hotkey, switch back and forth as you wish. Once you get used to being able to switch in midstream, you will not be satisfied with one program at a time.

Working with the Task Switcher

To start the DOS Shell task switcher, call up the Options menu and choose Enable Task Swapper. This menu item acts like an on/off toggle. If you decide that you want to stop the task switcher, stop all of your programs and return to the shell. Select the same item from the Options menu—in this case, Enable Task Swapper—and the option will be turned off.

The reason that you have a choice is that the task switcher takes up a small bit of memory. Those people who do not want the facility do not have to give up the extra memory.

As soon as you start task switching, the shell divides the program list area into right and left sections. The left section contains the program list. The right section, the Active Task List, shows you whatever programs are currently running.

Take a look at the sample screen in Figure 30.5. On the left side of the screen, we see that the program list has ten items. Two of these items, Harley and Kimberlyn, are groups that contain other program lists. On the right side of the screen, we see that three programs have been started.

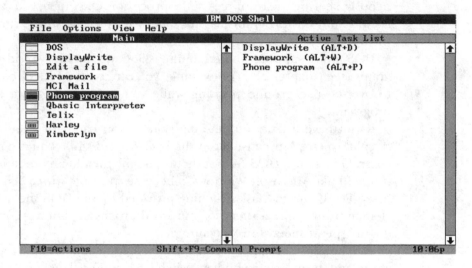

Figure 30.5. *The DOS Shell Showing Task Switching*

As always, you move from one area of the screen to another by pressing <Tab> and <Shift-Tab>, or by pointing with the mouse. To start a program, all you have to do is move to it and press <Enter> (or double-click the mouse).

The shell will disappear into the background and start the program. When you stop the program, you will automatically be returned to the shell.

Whenever you want to switch to another program, simply press <Ctrl-Esc>. Your current program will pause and you will be returned to the shell. You can now select and start another program.

You can press <Ctrl-Esc> whenever you want to return to the shell. Once you are back in the shell, you can use the menus, start a new program, or switch to a program that is currently on hold. To switch to a program, simply select it from the Active Task List.

A word to the wise: Although the shell allows you to skip back and forth between programs, very few DOS programs are written with task switching in mind. It is altogether possible that a program will get mixed up when you switch back to it after doing something else. For instance, it may lose track of its file allocation on the disk. Such events are not supposed to happen, but they do. As a precaution, it is a good idea to save your work before you switch to a new program.

Task Switching with Hot Keys

When you set up an entry in your program list, you have the option of defining what the shell calls an Application Shortcut Key. You can use any combination of <Shift>, <Ctrl> or <Alt> followed by a single letter, for example, <Ctrl-H> or <Alt-K>.

These combinations act as *hot keys* to allow you to switch from one program to another. For instance, say that you are working with one program and you want to switch to another. All you have to do is press the appropriate hot key and you will instantly switch to the other program. You will not be returned to the shell.

When you set up your own hot keys, be sure that you do not pick a combination that is used by your programs. For example, if you have a program that uses <Ctrl-K> for something, you will not be able to use it as a hot key.

Aside from customized hot keys, there are five that are built into the shell itself. The first one, <Ctrl-Esc>, we have already met. You use it to switch back to the shell.

The other four are <Alt-Esc>, <Shift-Alt-Esc>, <Alt-Tab>, and <Shift-Alt-Tab>. These keys switch you to another program without returning to the shell. <Alt-Esc> switches you to the next active program. By pressing <Alt-Esc> repeatedly, you can cycle through all your active programs, one after the other. When you get to the bottom of the list, you wrap around to the top. <Shift-Alt-Esc>, cycles through your active programs, but in the opposite order.

<Alt-Tab>, on the other hand, switches to the last active program. By pressing <Alt-Tab> repeatedly, you can switch back and forth between the same two programs. <Shift-Alt-Tab> switches to the next active program.

Summary of the DOS Shell Shortcut Keys

As a reference, the following table contains a summary of the shortcut keys that we have discussed in this chapter. These are keys that you can use to avoid having to select items from menus.

Table 30.6   *Summary of DOS Shell Shortcut Keys*

Keys of general usefulness

<F1>	Ask for help
<F3>	Stop the shell and return to DOS prompt
<Alt-F4>	Stop the shell and return to DOS prompt
<Shift-F9>	Pause the shell to enter DOS commands
<Shift-F5>	Redraw the screen

To change the default drive

<Ctrl-drive>	for example, <Ctrl-A> for drive A:

When working with a directory tree

<+>	Expand directory one level
<*>	Expand full branch of the tree
<Ctrl-*>	Expand entire directory tree
<->	Hide a branch of the tree
<F5>	Re-scan the disk and then redraw the screen

To select files or a directory

<Space>	Select a single file
<Shift-Up>	Select a group of files
<Shift-Down>	Select a group of files
<Ctrl-/>	Select all files in list
<Ctrl-\>	Un-select all files in list
<Shift-F8>	Start/stop selecting non-contiguous files

(continued)

Table 30.6 *(continued)*

After having selected files

<F7>	Move
<F8>	Copy
<F9>	Display
<Delete>	Delete
<Enter>	Execute program or associated program

After having selected a directory

<Delete>	Delete

When task switching

<Enter>	Start a program, or switch to a program
<Ctrl-Esc>	Switch to the shell
<Alt-Esc>	Switch to next program in active list
<Shift-Alt-Esc>	Switch to the previous program in active list
<Alt-Tab>	Switch to last active program
<Shift-Alt-Tab>	Switch to the next active program

31

AVOIDING PITFALLS

Introduction

Everything you do on your computer involves information of some sort. Programs, facts, and figures—they're all types of information. But there are danger areas in using a computer, areas where just the wrong moves could wipe out a lot of valuable information. We'll use this chapter to do something a lot of computer books don't do. Let's look at some of the ways you could make a dangerous mess of things and lose much of your data. We'll see the sources of these pitfalls and dangers and, as we go, you'll see what you can do to avoid them.

Disastrous Interruptions

An easy way to destroy your data is by interrupting the writing of disk information before it is complete. There are several ways this can happen. One way is if the power goes off on your computer while something is being written. In this case, anything that hasn't been saved on disk is gone, irretrievably. Other than buying a backup power supply, there's little you can do about this except save your work frequently.

It's also possible to lose data if you remove a disk while it is being written to, or if you use <Ctrl-Break> to tell DOS to interrupt the write operation. Here, however, even though your disks are spinning, the computer may not necessarily be writing to them at the time of the interruption—it might have been reading from the disk, and that can't do you any harm. If it was writing, damage might be done, but even then you might get off scot-free.

In general terms, any of the interruptions I have mentioned run the risk of damaging a file, but there is less risk that any of these interruptions will ruin everything on the disk. Sometimes no harm is done at all, and you are lucky. Occasionally one file, the file that was being written, will be messed up. Very rarely will there be more harm, but in either case you can check both the disk and the file you were writing.

Checking a Disk

The first and best way to check a disk is with the CHKDSK command. CHKDSK will tell you if there is any logical scrambling of the disk for one file or any others. If CHKDSK gives no error messages, then you know that the disk as a whole is okay, and that the one file that was being written might be all right. But you don't know for sure yet, so the next check to do is to use the DIR command to look at the file's directory entry. If you know which file was being written, ask for it; if you don't, then ask for the full directory listing (DIR *.*).

When you see the directory listing, the main thing to check for is a reasonable size for the file (or for all files). If a file size is given as zero, then the creation of the file was cut off in midstream, and the data that was being written (or any old data that the file had before) has been lost.

Suppose you do find that your file has a size of zero bytes. Does that mean you have to start all over from scratch? Not necessarily. Some application programs create automatic backup copies of files you are using, and you may find a backup version of your lost file. If so, all you've really lost are the changes you made to update the file. Then, too, files are sometimes created under a temporary working name and only given their official name when the creation process is finished. If you suspect that a file was cut off as it was being created, you should check for unusual file names; common possibilities are names with extensions of BAK, $$$ or TMP. If you do find such a file, at least some of your work may be salvageable. (Backup files may have to be given a different extension with the DOS RENAME command before you can load them into your usual application program.)

Switching Diskettes

There is one kind of interruption of the computer's writing to diskette that can do much more harm: if you switch disks in the middle of an operation. The problem relates to the disk's record of its used and unused space, which we covered in Chapter 13. After a file is written, a record of the space the file occupies is written to the disk—this record applies to every file, and not just one. If this space table, called the File Allocation Table or FAT, is lost or damaged, then every file will be damaged or permanently lost.

This problem can occur in quite an innocent way, and I know of many people who have had it happen to them. You think that you are just beginning to write out a file, and DOS reports that something is wrong with the diskette, so you substitute another disk. DOS finishes writing out the file and the File Allocation Table. However, DOS doesn't know you switched diskettes, and so it writes the FAT that was read from the first disk onto the second disk. Every file that was stored on the second diskette is now lost.

Newer versions of DOS provide protection against this problem, but the danger still exists. The way to protect against this danger is simple: Whenever DOS tells you that there is trouble with a disk, never switch to a disk with good data on it. Either fix the original disk, switch to a blank disk, or abort the operation. Don't put in a good disk with existing files, because they may all be lost.

This potential problem with disks is a good reason for always keeping a supply of formatted blank diskettes handy. Unless you are using a program that gives you access to DOS, encountering diskette troubles while trying to save hours of work may put you in a no-win situation: In order to format a good diskette on which to save your work, you have to quit the program. But if you quit the program, you lose your work anyway, so you don't need the diskette.

Ordinary Ways to Lose Your Data

So far, I've mentioned the more interesting and exotic ways that you can lose your data. Now we'll get down to the dull, prosaic, and common dangers. There are exactly three ordinary ways to lose your disk data: by copying over it, by erasing it, and reformatting a disk.

Of these three dangers, the least frequent is to copy old or bad data onto new, good data. Although there are a million ways you could do this without meaning to, the most common is when you intend to make a backup copy of your data, but copy in the wrong direction: Instead of copying from your newly updated original to the backup disk, you copy from an old backup, overwriting your latest data.

The best way to protect against this problem is to use batch files to make sure that the copy is made correctly. For example, here is the batch file that was used to back up files used during the revision of this book.

The files all have an extension of DOC and I want to copy them from the hard disk to a diskette. I am using XCOPY with the /M option so DOS will copy only those files that have been modified since the last backup.

```
:*=======================================================
:* SAVE.BAT: batch file to backup new files to diskette
    @echo off

:* display all the DOC files
    dir d:\dosbook\*.doc

:* copy files that have been modified to a diskette
    xcopy d:\dosbook\*.doc a: /m

:* display the files on the diskette
    dir a:
:*=======================================================
```

The next problem, and probably the most common destroyer of data, is the DEL/ERASE command. It is incredibly easy to accidentally erase files you didn't mean to erase. This happens most often through the unintended, or misguided, use of the asterisk wildcard, which will match any filename or any extension. DOS does contain one small precaution against this: If you use the DEL/ERASE command and enter the complete wildcard name *.*, then DOS will pause to ask for confirmation. That's not a lot of safety. It's pretty easy to think to yourself, "Of course that's what I want to do," press Y for Yes, and a second later—a second too late—wish with all your heart you hadn't done that.

There are three things that you can do to protect against losing files through erasure. First, you can use a delete tracking system, like the one we discussed in Chapter 18, or the more sophisticated one built-in to the Norton Utilities. Second, avoid using the DEL or ERASE command manually. If you have any routine need to erase files, don't do it by entering the command by hand; instead, build a batch file that will then have the names of the files being erased specified correctly. If you use a batch file, instead of manually entering the erasure command directly, you guard against an accidental mistyping of the names to be erased (provided you get it right in the batch file).

The third way to keep from losing files is a neat trick that another computer writer showed me. You find the files you want using DIR, and then you use DEL and the <F3> key to automatically delete just those files that you found. How it works follows:

Say that you want to delete all the files that start with the letter S and have the extension BAK. First, you enter the DIR command with the pattern that describes these files:

```
DIR S*.BAK
```

Now you have a chance to see what files the pattern matches. It may be that they are exactly the files you wanted. However, there may be a file or two that you forgot about that you want to keep, but that would have been erased if you had simply entered:

```
DEL S*.BAK
```

If the DIR command does not show you what you want, you can change it and enter it again and again until it exactly matches the files you want to delete.

Now, here's the trick: Once you get the files you want, you type "DEL" and then press the <F3> key (function key 3). As I explained in Chapter 22, <F3> is a DOS editing key that repeats all or part of the previous command.

In this case, because you have typed the three characters "DEL", <F3> will repeat all but the first three characters of your previous DIR command. But these are exactly the characters that match the files you want. Thus, you are assured that the pattern following the DEL command is exactly the pattern you want to delete.

The last of the dangers I'm going to cover is the danger of reformatting a disk that has valuable data on it. This is one of the worst of all the dangers to your data. If you erase your data, you may be able to unerase it. If you copy over your data, some of it may still be left on the disk. But when you format a disk, everything that was on that disk is gone. If you have the Norton Utilities or DOS 5.0, you might be able to unformat if you do it right away (see Chapter 18). But this is certainly not something to count on for day-to-day work.

The best way to protect against formatting over your data is to use the FORMAT command only through a batch file, and have that batch file first check the disk for any files that are there. Here is an example of what such a batch file might be like:

```
:*=======================================================
:* FORMAT.BAT: batch file to format a diskette
   @echo off

:* ask the user to insert the diskette to be formatted
   echo Insert diskette to be formatted into drive A
   pause

:* display any files that might already be on the disk
   dir a:

:* tell user to cancel if this is the wrong diskette
   echo If you do not want to format this diskette
   echo stop the procedure by pressing Ctrl-Break
   pause

:* format the diskette
   c:\dos\format.com a: /v
:*=======================================================
```

There are a few points that I would like to make about this batch file.

The filename—FORMAT—is the same as the name of the DOS command, FORMAT. However, if you set up your DOS search path the way we suggested in Chapter 16, DOS will find your batch file directory before it finds the DOS directory that contains the FORMAT command. That is, DOS will find C:\BATCH\FORMAT.BAT before it finds C:\DOS\FORMAT.COM.

This means that whenever you enter:

```
FORMAT
```

DOS will execute the batch file instead of the command. The only time this isn't true is if you happen to be in the DOS directory. In this case, DOS will search the current directory and find FORMAT.COM without even looking at the search path. (By the way, you cannot simply put FORMAT.BAT into your DOS directory along with FORMAT.COM. DOS will give priority to a COM file over a BAT file within the same directory.)

In the last line, we had to specify the full path name of the FORMAT command. If we had simply used FORMAT and not C:\DOS\FORMAT.COM, we would have restarted the FORMAT.BAT batch file and entered an endless loop.

If you use this batch file with a brand new disk, DOS will not be able to display a directory listing. The DIR command will generate the following message:

```
General failure reading drive A
Abort, Retry, Fail?
```

If this happens, press A to abort the DIR command. (Do not press Enter after the A.) FORMAT.BAT will proceed with the next command in the batch file.

After the formatting is complete, DOS will ask for a volume label (because we included the /V switch). If you are formatting a disk simply to keep until needed, I suggest you use the label "EMPTY". This way, if you display the directory, DOS will show the message:

```
Volume in drive A is EMPTY
```

Once the disk is formatted, DOS will ask if you want to format another. Answer "n" for No. If you do want to format another disk, use the batch file again.

This batch file only formats disk. What if you want to format a hard disk?

The answer is, you would rarely, if ever, want to format a hard disk. But, if the situation should arise, you have two choices: Either enter the full path name of the FORMAT program, or change to the DOS directory and run the FORMAT command from there.

Beyond all these things, the best protection for your data is simply meticulous care. Be careful to always label your disks, indicating what is on them. Be careful not to do physical damage to your disks. Be particularly careful about the particularly dangerous operations of copying, erasing, and formatting. Finally, do not let your disks come into contact with a magnet. (By the way, a ringing telephone generates a magnetic field.)

32

AVOIDING OTHER MISTAKES

Introduction

If you are new to computing or even if you aren't, you may be worried about making expensive mistakes with your computer. First, expect to make plenty of mistakes, and don't worry too much about it. Personal computing is still a young field, and many people don't have a lot of experience with it. Making mistakes comes with the territory; expect it, and be prepared for it. What I'll try to do in this chapter is to help you avoid some mistakes that are especially shortsighted or especially costly.

Hardware Mistakes

Since computer equipment is so modular and computers are so expandable, it is hard to make a mistake by getting too little equipment. If you end up needing an expansion feature that you didn't need at first, you can always add it. This seems to argue in favor of under-buying at first and adding on to your computer later. The simple fact is, it usually works the other way: You are generally better off buying more equipment than you think you might need. Why is this so? Here is the simple reason. Only rarely do people buy a piece of computer equipment and then later realize they never needed it at all. Conversely, it is a common experience for computer users to waste time because they don't have a piece of equipment that they need but are reluctant to add to their system, or to waste money by replacing some part of their system with a bigger, better, or faster component. The market for used parts of personal computers is weak, so that if you need to replace your printer or disk drive with a better one, you may not be able to recover much, if any, of the cost of your first one.

Unless your budget is severely constrained, it is wiser to over-buy in computing than to under-buy. The history of computing shows that people almost always need more, more, more as time goes by. If you get plenty to start with, you are usually better off. Obviously, you shouldn't buy everything in sight and spend your money wildly. Yet it is a simple fact of computer life that you are better off, when equipping your computer, to get more rather than less—more speed or more capacity than you might think you will need.

What mistakes are you most likely to make in under-buying? Too little memory, for one, although these days PCs tend to come fully loaded with more than their maximum complement of standard memory, 640K. If the computer you choose doesn't necessarily come with that much memory, I'd recommend you make sure the system you buy has it added.

Memory is relatively cheap, so you can get plenty. Of course, memory is something you can add on but rarely have to replace, so there's no great problem in adding it later. Usually, though, there is a large savings in buying memory in big chunks. For example, if you add 1 Mb of memory to your system, and then later add another 1 Mb, it will probably cost more than if you had bought 2 Mb to begin with.

Another common under-buy is too little disk capacity. Your data storage needs are likely to grow beyond anything you imagined possible. Adding disk storage is likely to mean discarding your old disk devices, and this can be a real money waster. If you can add capacity by adding equipment, don't worry about under-buying. But if adding capacity will mean replacing equipment, you would be better off over-buying than under-buying.

The third most likely under-buy is printer quality. Printers that produce a high-quality appearance, especially what's called letter-quality printing, are sometimes expensive. This is a natural area for computer buyers to economize, but is also one of the most common areas in which people become dissatisfied with their equipment. Since printers can be expensive, it is harder to recommend that you buy a better printer than you may need. I do recommend that you think carefully. Upgrading to a better printer can be a real waste of money. In my own experience, this is where I have wasted the most money—buying printers that were in the price range I might have preferred, but were less useful than what I needed.

The biggest thing to consider, of course, is the computer itself. If you are choosing between one model of computer and another, consider deeply the expansion options and the raw computing horsepower. The last thing you want to have to replace, and the most expensive thing to replace, is the computer itself. So if you are choosing between one computer and another, err on the side of more power and more expandability, rather than less.

If at all possible, buy a computer based on a 386 or 486 processor. The extra functionality provided by these processors is important. There are significant capabilities that you miss out on without a 386, such as the memory management tools we discussed in Chapter 29. If you use an enhanced operating environment like Microsoft Windows, you will have a lot more power with a 386. Moreover, the design of the 386 ensures that it will be a practical choice for at least the next few years. Unless you have no choice, avoid buying a PC based on the older 8088, 8086, or 286 processors.

To recap, the most common and expensive mistakes that are made in buying personal computer hardware are buying too little disk storage capacity and too low a quality of printer. An even more common mistake, though a less costly one, is to buy too little memory; this won't waste much money, but it can waste your time. Finally, the most expensive mistake of all is to buy too little computer—too little expansion capability or an older, less powerful processor.

Software Mistakes

Making mistakes in buying software can be very expensive, and even more wasteful of your time and effort than of your money. It's easy to waste your money in basket loads, if you make the wrong moves in buying software for your computer. You are more likely to make mistakes in buying software than in buying hardware.

By far the most common and most important mistake is accepting an old version of DOS along with a new computer. Unfortunately, many computers come equipped with old software. If you have read this far in the book, you will have noticed numerous examples of new features that just are not available with old versions of DOS. (These are summarized in Appendix A.) When you buy a computer, make sure that you have the latest version of the operating system. For now, that means at least DOS 5.0.

Another important mistake is in underestimating how much you will want to tie your software uses together. By that, I mean how much you'll be using one piece of software in conjunction with another. Integration is the key here; the more integrated the software, the better.

This is a strong argument in favor of multifunction packages. You may, quite wisely, want to buy the best available word processor and the best spreadsheet program. But you may be even wiser to get an integrated package that does both, even if neither the word processor nor the spreadsheet is the most sophisticated program available. The same rule obviously applies to accounting packages. If you are going to need payroll processing in the future, it would be very short-sighted to buy a general ledger that doesn't have an accompanying payroll module, no matter how superior the general ledger might be.

Another common software mistake is to underestimate how important speed and ease of use will become to you. When you start out in computing, speed may not seem extremely important. You may think that it is no big deal if it takes a few keystrokes to tell one program to do some operation, while another program can do the same thing automatically through a batch file. As time goes by, it is likely that your use of the computer, and your dependence on it, will grow. Then, the speed and ease of use of your computer programs will become major factors in how efficiently you can get your work done.

Still another shortsighted mistake in buying programs is to underestimate how important it is to be able to transfer programs to fast-access storage, such as hard disks and virtual disks. As the number of programs you use grows and the amount of time you spend working with your computer grows, the worth of hard and virtual disks grows.

Operational Mistakes

There are three main mistakes that you can make in organizing the operation of your computer. The first one I don't really have to hammer into you, since you will hear it from so many sources: Make backup copies of your data. You'll hear it again and again and again.

Computers are so thoroughly reliable it is easy to feel that your data is quite secure, but that isn't the case. Your data is in danger, two ways. The lesser danger is from failure of the computer—or its programs—resulting in destruction of your data. The greater danger is from inadvertent erasure of your data. As I've mentioned, it is extremely easy to lose your data by a mistaken DEL/ERASE or FORMAT command.

The all-around solution to this operational danger is to make frequent backup copies of your data. Because this can be a time-consuming process, it is tempting to skip or put off doing it—*don't*. As you saw earlier, the best and safest way to safeguard your data is to incorporate backup procedures into your working methods, through batch files.

The second shortsighted mistake in the operation of your computer is not taking the time to get organized. It is easy to think that you don't need to devote much effort into organizing your use of the system. But the simple fact is that one of the best investments you can make of your time is to carefully organize how you use your computer, including placing the right programs together on your disks and, especially, working out the most effective batch-processing files. Once you've done that, do it again when your work patterns change, or when you develop a better way to get organized. The payoff in smooth, easy work is tremendous. I find that it pays off for me to take the time to refine my working procedures roughly once a month. Even after a full year of heavily using the same computer, I still reorganize every month or so. It takes me about a half-hour's effort, and then what I'm working on goes more smoothly.

The third operational mistake is about neglecting to use batch files altogether. There is nothing else in the DOS operating system that can more enhance the smooth and effective operation of your computer system than automating working procedures with batch processing files. When you think you've got the hang of putting them together, try some out. Start with the easy, but useful commands like DIR, PROMPT, PATH, and COPY. Leave the tougher ones—the IFs, SHIFTs, and GOTOs—for a more experienced you.

33

OPTIMIZING YOUR SYSTEM

Introduction

No matter how fast computers get, it always seems as if they are never fast enough. In this chapter, we'll go over a few hints that you can follow to help make your computer run as quickly and as efficiently as possible.

The material in this chapter is not necessarily anything you need to worry about if you are a beginner. But after you have a few months of computer experience under your belt, it's worth your while to take a few hours and see what you can do to optimize your system.

At the end of the chapter, there is a list of each topic we will mention and where you can reference it in this book.

Use Windows Wisely

If you use Microsoft Windows, the first thing you should do is make sure that you are using at least version 3. The older versions will not be able to get as much performance out of your computer. This is especially true if you have a 386- or 486-based PC.

Second, make sure that your DOS is at least version 5.0. Windows will not work as well with an older DOS. As you read the DOS manual, look for specific advice for Windows users. Remember, both DOS and Windows were developed by Microsoft to work together.

Within the Windows documentation, there will be lot of guidelines for configuring your system. If any of these hints conflict with the DOS manual, do what the Windows manual says.

Speed Up Your Disks

The BUFFERS command goes in your CONFIG.SYS file to tell DOS how much space to set aside for the disk work area. Generally speaking, you will get better performance with more buffers, up to a point.

When you install DOS, the installation program will set the BUFFERS value to some reasonable amount. If you want to set it for yourself, use the following rules of thumb:

```
SET BUFFERS = 15.
```

If you have a lot of subdirectories,

```
SET BUFFERS = 25
```

Use FASTOPEN to speed up DOS's access to each of your disks. If possible, use the LOADHIGH command to load FASTOPEN in upper memory.

Use SMARTDRV.SYS to set up a disk cache. Give the cache any extra memory you aren't using for anything else. Put the cache in extended memory.

If you have a program that reads the same files repeatedly, use RAMDRIVE.SYS to create a virtual disk and copy the files to the disk. A good example would be keeping the dictionary used by your spelling checker on a virtual disk. Do not use a virtual disk to hold volatile data—if the power goes off, you will lose all your work.

Put the virtual disk in extended memory.

Use TEMP to Point to a Temporary Storage Area

If you have DOS 5.0 or later, there are two variables that you can set that DOS can use to enhance its operation: TEMP and DIRCMD. You set these variables by using the SET command within your AUTOEXEC.BAT file.

Set TEMP to point to a directory on a fast disk. DOS will use this directory as a temporary storage area whenever possible. For example, when you combine programs using a pipe, DOS will store the temporary files in this storage area. Even better, if there is room, the DOS Shell will use this area to hold its swap files when you are task switching.

The best idea is to define a virtual disk and set TEMP to point to this disk. For example, if E: is a virtual disk, put the following command in your AUTOEXEC.BAT file:

```
SET TEMP=E:\
```

Use DIRCMD to Customize the DIR Command

The second variable, DIRCMD, is used to tell DOS that you want to certain default parameters with every DIR command. You can specify any parameters you want—not only options, but even a filename specification.

For example, say that you always want DIR to use the /W and /P options. Put the following command in your AUTOEXEC.BAT file:

```
SET DIRCMD=/W /P
```

Here is a trickier example. By default DIR will list the files in the current directory if you do not specify a file name. If you want DIR to list different file names by default, you can specify them. For instance:

```
SET DIRCMD=C:\BATCH\*.BAT /W
```

This says that, by default, DIR should list all the batch files in the \BATCH subdirectory on the C: disk, using the /W option. If you enter:

```
DIR
```

it is the same as:

```
DIR C:\BATCH\*.BAT /W
```

If you define a default file specification, you can override it whenever you want. Just specify the files or directory you want. For example:

```
DIR MYFILE.DOC
```

In this case, the C:\BATCH*.BAT default will be ignored, but the /W option will still be respected.

If you want to override a default file specification to list the files in your current directory, use a single period to stand for the current directory:

```
DIR .
```

Another example: By default, you want DIR to list only files with the extension of DOC, in reverse alphabetical order. Use:

```
SET DIRCMD=*.DOC /O:-N
```

When you want to override this to list all files, use:

```
DIR *.*
```

One last example. If you want to drive someone crazy, put the following command in their AUTOEXEC.BAT file:

```
SET DIRCMD=/A:H
```

From now on, DIR will list only hidden files. If you want to make some money, bet that you know a secret command to bring the DIR command back to life. Then, override the default by entering:

```
DIR /A:-H
```

To examine all your variables, enter:

```
SET
```

To delete a variable, use the SET command with nothing after the equal sign:

```
SET DIRCMD=
```

Use Upper Memory and Extended Memory

With DOS 5.0 or later, free up conventional memory by loading device drivers and memory-resident programs into upper memory. To load device drivers, use the DEVICEHIGH command in your CONFIG.SYS file. (But do not try to use DEVICEHIGH to load HIMEM.SYS or EMM386.SYS.)

To load memory-resident programs, use the LOADHIGH command in your AUTOEXEC.BAT file. Be aware that if you use the INSTALL command to load programs from your CONFIG.SYS file, you cannot load into upper memory.

Whenever you have a choice over where to load a program, choose extended over expanded memory.

Use Macros

With DOS 5.0 or later, you can use DOSKEY to define macros. It is worth your while to spend some time creating macros. Once you get the hang of it, you can create all sorts of useful commands, to make up for DOS's deficiencies.

For example, there is no command to display how much space is available on a disk. However, the last line of the DIR command output gives just such a statistic. Define a DF (disk free) macro as follows:

```
DOSKEY DF=DIR $* $B FIND "FREE"
```

You can now use commands like:

```
DF
DF C:
DF D:
```

The output of DF looks like this:

```
20228300 BYTES FREE
```

To make it easy to define macros, use:

```
DOSKEY DEF=DOSKEY $*
```

Now, you can define a macro by using DEF. For example:

```
DEF DF=DIR $* $B FIND "FREE"
```

To make it easy to see your macros, use:

```
DOSKEY MAC=DOSKEY /M
```

Now, you can display your macros by entering:

```
MAC
```

As you can see, macros can be a lot more powerful than most people realize. Whenever you create a macro you like, be sure to save it to a batch file, so you don't have to retype it.

References

The following chapters explain the commands and the optimization ideas mentioned in this chapter:

Chapter 9:
- The DIR command and its options

Chapter 12:
- The AUTOEXEC.BAT file
- The DOS environment and the SET command

Chapter 21:
- Memory-resident programs
- Using FASTOPEN to speed up disk access

Chapter 25:
- Using DOSKEY to define macros

Chapter 28:
- The CONFIG.SYS file
- BUFFERS
- Using DEVICEHIGH to load into upper memory
- Using RAMDRIVE.SYS to create a virtual disk
- Using SMARTDRV.SYS to create a disk cache

Chapter 29:
- Memory management
- Using LOADHIGH to load into upper memory

34

ALTERNATIVES
TO DOS

Introduction

Throughout this book we have concentrated on DOS, particularly version 5.0 and later. However, there are other operating environments that you can use with IBM-compatible computers. These fall into two classes, operating system and shells.

In this chapter we'll take a look at these alternatives to DOS. Then, we'll discuss two of them—Microsoft Windows and OS/2—in detail and compare them to DOS.

PC Operating Systems

There are more PC operating systems than you might think. First, of course, there is DOS. Close to DOS is DR-DOS, from Digital Research Corporation. This is a DOS-compatible operating system, which offers extra functionality over standard DOS.

Next is OS/2, developed by IBM and Microsoft. OS/2 was originally conceived as a replacement for DOS, but has since changed its focus. We will discuss OS/2 in more detail in a moment.

The next branch of the operating system tree holds the Unix systems. The original Unix was developed at AT&T's Bell Labs and later at the University of California at Berkeley, Computer Science Department. Today, there are a variety of Unix and Unix-like operating system available. For PCs the most important systems are:

- SCO Unix, from the Santa Cruz Operations
- Interactive Unix, from the Interactive Systems Corporation
- AIX PS/2, from IBM
- Coherent, from the Mark Williams Company

The first three operating systems can be configured to run DOS programs. The software that provides this functionality is either VP/ix (from Interactive) or DOS Merge (from the Locus Computing Corporation).

The fourth system, Coherent, is an important one if you have your own small system. The other Unixes are based on the AT&T standard and are complex, large, and relatively expensive. Coherent, however, was written from scratch to work just like Unix, but it does not incorporate AT&T software. Coherent is small, less complex and a lot cheaper than the other Unixes. However, it cannot run DOS programs.

The next group of PC operating systems are the ones that run local area network servers. On a network, the PC workstations usually use a standard operating system, like DOS or OS/2. However, the computer that stores the bulk of the data, the file server, does not run DOS. It has its own special operating system that knows how to cooperate with workstations.

The most well-known of the PC network operating systems are:

- Netware, from Novell
- LAN Manager, from Microsoft
- LAN Server, from IBM
- PC LAN, from IBM
- Vines, from Banyan
- 3+Open, from 3Com
- LANtastic, from Artisoft

The MS-DOS 5.0 installation manual comes with instructions for using DOS with a number such operating systems.

Finally, there are less well-known, niche operating systems that have small bands of fervent supporters. Once such system is the Pick operating system, designed around database management.

Shells and Graphical User Interfaces

As we discussed in Chapter 30, a shell is a program that surrounds or shields you from another program. In the DOS world, there are a number of shells that can provide a user interface that is easier and more powerful than the standard DOS prompt.

First, there is the DOS Shell, which comes free with DOS 4.0 or later (See Chapter 30). Next, there are programs like the Norton Commander, that not only provide a more powerful front end to the standard DOS functions, but include a host of extra features.

Finally, there are large, complex operating environments that stand completely between you and DOS. With these programs, you interact with your PC using a keyboard and a mouse, pull-down menus, windows, and icons (small pictures). Such an environment is often referred to as a graphical user interface, or GUI (pronounced "goo-ey").

The most important GUIs are:

- Microsoft Windows, from Microsoft
- Desqview, from Quarterdeck
- New Wave, from Hewlett-Packard
- Presentation Manager, from IBM and Microsoft

The first three are DOS operating environments. New Wave runs with Windows, so it is actually a shell (New Wave), on top of a shell (Windows), on top of another shell (COMMAND.COM).

Presentation Manager (PM) is the standard OS/2 interface and comes free with that system. PM and Windows look similar when you use them. However, internally, there are big differences, as you would see if you were writing programs to run with one or the other.

If you want to use a GUI with DOS, you will find that it will work best if you have:

- a mouse (this is practically indispensable)
- a 386- or 486-based computer
- as much memory as possible
- software that is specially designed for your GUI
- the newest version of your GUI
- DOS 5.0 or later

Microsoft Windows

Windows is a graphical user interface designed to provide a pull-down menu, windowed-type operating environment for IBM-compatible computers.

With DOS 5.0, you get the DOS Shell for free. Windows is a different product that must buy separately. To help you compare, here is a list of the additional capabilities provided by Windows+DOS, compared to DOS alone.

- **Access to more memory** By itself, DOS can access 640 K of RAM, along with extra memory utilized via the EMS (expanded memory) and XMS (extended memory) standards. (See Chapter 29.)

  If you have enough RAM, Windows can use up to 16 megabytes (16,384K) of memory.

- **Work with multiple programs** With DOS, you can work with only one program at a time. The DOS Shell allows you switch between tasks but only one program is visible at a time.

  Windows allows you to use multiple, overlapping windows on a single screen. Each window contains a program. You can move the windows about, size them, and switch from one to the another whenever you want.

- **Multitasking** With the DOS Shell, you can switch from one program to another. However, except for memory-resident programs, only one program at a time can be active.

  With a 386- or 486-based PC, Windows provides true multitasking. A program can remain active at all times, even when you are working with another programs.

- **Cut and Paste between applications** Windows makes it easy to copy data from one program into another. For example, you can copy part of a spreadsheet into a word processor document.

- **Graphics** Windows offers a software library that allows programmers to take advantage of the full graphics capabilities of whatever computer is being used. Windows programs tend to be more picture-oriented than regular DOS programs.

- **Dynamic Data Exchange** Dynamic Data Exchange allows Windows programmers to design software that shares data between different programs. For example, a graph in a spreadsheet might be automatically updated whenever the certain database information changes.

OS/2

OS/2 was originally conceived by IBM and Microsoft as a replacement for DOS. Aside from being able to access megabytes of memory, OS/2 comes with a built-in graphical user interface called Presentation Manager (PM) that has all the facilities of Microsoft Windows, (including full multitasking for all programs) plus a lot more. In addition, the OS/2 family contains a sophisticated Communications Manager and Database Manager.

OS/2 contains all the facilities listed above for Windows, as well as the following programming tools:

- **Multi-threading** This allows programmers to have several parts of a single program executing at the same time.

- **A high-performance file system** A new, optional file system that eliminates virtually all of the limitations of the DOS file system.

- **Interprocess communication** A variety of methods for programs to share data as they execute. The programs can be on the same computer or on different computers connected by a network.

As we mentioned, OS/2 was developed to replace DOS. However, OS/2 never really caught on as a mass market operating system. In spite of the fact that OS/2 can run DOS programs, too many people preferred what they already had.

As a result, OS/2 has shifted its focus to areas in which a powerful single-user, multitasking operating system is a necessity. Today, you will find OS/2 used in large enterprises that require network workstations and connections to midrange or mainframe computers.

Nevertheless, OS/2 is an excellent operating system for a single PC and you might want to use it if you get a chance. One caveat: Try to use OS/2-specific software. OS/2 can run DOS programs, but OS/2 programs are preferable. New versions of OS/2 will be able to run all OS/2, DOS, and Windows programs.

A

THE HISTORY OF DOS

What Is an Operating System?

Collectively, the parts of a computer system that make up a machine are called the hardware. The hardware consists of all the devices we mentioned in Chapter 1: the processor, the memory, the disks, input/output devices, and adaptors. Indeed there are many more hardware parts which we haven't yet mentioned, and many of those just sit there inside your machine, silently performing their jobs.

By itself, a computer without programs is a lifeless hunk of metal and plastic. If you were to turn on a bare computer, nothing would happen. What makes a computer come alive are the programs—the lists of instructions that the computer is to follow in order to get its work done.

The role of an operating system—in this case, DOS—is to coordinate the hardware and the programs by:

1. Making it possible for programs to use the hardware

2. Providing an interface so that you can use the computer

3. Managing the entire system as efficiently as possible

In other words, DOS is the master control program, running the system, fielding requests from programs, and following your orders.

Who Makes DOS?

When IBM was developing the first PC—in 1980/81—they hired the Microsoft company to create an operating system for the new computer. At the time, Microsoft was quite small, consisting of only two people. When the PC debuted, IBM actually offered three different operating systems. The idea was that customers should be able to choose the working environment they preferred. The three systems were DOS, the p-System, and CP/M.

The p-System was developed at the University of California at San Diego and was based on the Pascal programming language. CP/M was used on other small computers and supported a large number of business-oriented programs. Thus, IBM offered two existing operating systems along with DOS, a brand new system written especially for the PC.

Within a short time it became clear that users and vendors preferred DOS which, along with the PC, became a roaring success. In fact, both DOS and the PC were far more successful than anyone had anticipated.

Today, DOS is the principal operating system used with IBM-compatible PCs. In fact, DOS is the most successful operating system in the history of computers, managing tens of millions of computers around the world. And since 1980, Microsoft has grown from a two-man shop to the largest independent software company in the world.

From the beginning, DOS was a collaboration between Microsoft and IBM. The deal was, and still is, that IBM will market one version of DOS—called IBM DOS or PC-DOS—strictly for IBM computers. Microsoft will market another version of DOS—called MS-DOS—for all the other compatible computers.

Microsoft does not sell MS-DOS directly. (However, starting with version 5.0 Microsoft sells upgrades to DOS.) Mostly, Microsoft licenses DOS to other companies who then sell the operating system along with their computers. Most of the time, these companies sell MS-DOS pretty much as they receive it from Microsoft. In some cases, a company may make small changes so that the DOS they sell will work better with their computers. However, for the most part, MS-DOS works the same way from one computer to the next.

There are differences between the IBM DOS and the generic Microsoft DOS. In this book, we make sure to point out where one DOS is different from the other. As we mentioned in the introduction, just about everything in this book will work no matter what type of DOS you have.

The first DOS, version 1.0, was developed by Microsoft based on IBM's specifications. This was the case through DOS version 3.3. Microsoft developed each new version of DOS which they sold as the generic MS-DOS. Each new MS-DOS was sent to IBM where it would be modified to become PC-DOS.

With version 4.0, IBM reversed the process. They became the primary developers of PC-DOS 4.0 which they sent to Microsoft to turn into MS-DOS 4.0. Currently, the ball has passed back to Microsoft. The newest DOS, version 5.0, was developed primarily at Microsoft and then modified by IBM.

Why switch back and forth? Well, it all depends on how the two companies decide to allocate their resources. When it came time to develop DOS 5.0, IBM decided to concentrate their programming resources in other areas; in particular, they wanted to develop a lot of new software for the OS/2 operating system.

Why Are There Different Versions of DOS?

As we explained above, one of the main roles of an operating system is to coordinate the operation of the hardware. This means that as hardware evolves we would expect that the operating system would need to be updated.

As we discussed in Chapter 29, DOS has a facility that allows the operating system to be configured to support new hardware. In a sense, you can use this facility—called a configuration file—to enhance DOS in a way that allows it to support the particular hardware of your system. However, for major hardware upgrades, such as a brand new type of computer system, nothing less than a brand new version of DOS will do.

For this reason, the first eight versions of DOS (1.0 through 3.3) were developed to support new hardware. Since then, Microsoft and IBM have changed their philosophy. The last several DOS versions (4.0 through 5.0) have been oriented towards enhancing the overall level of services. Although new hardware is still supported, the primary motivation now for a new version of DOS is the requirements of PC users.

Along with new hardware support, each new version of DOS improves upon its predecessor in three important ways:

- New commands are added
- A number of existing commands are enhanced
- Bugs (errors in DOS itself) are corrected

Probably the most important reason why DOS has become so successful is that it has been improved and enhanced so many times. As hardware and user requirements have changed, IBM and Microsoft have made sure that DOS has kept pace. To be sure, some people wish that the changes could come faster and be more extensive. Still, like the family of computers that it controls, DOS is an evolving product that will be useful for years to come.

The Different Versions of DOS

The first version of PC-DOS, version 1.0, was released with the original IBM PC (August 1981). The PC was very successful and IBM soon brought out an enhanced model that used larger capacity disks. (Some people refer to these first two PCs as the "PC-1" and the "PC-2," even though these were never official IBM names.)

With the second PC, the so-called PC-2, IBM released a new PC-DOS, version 1.1, to support the new disks. Just as important, Microsoft, at this time, released the first MS-DOS, which they called version 1.25. MS-DOS 1.25 was used on the first wave of IBM-compatible computers, which were called *clones*.

As we track the subsequent versions of DOS, we see that most of them were released at the same time as new computers. Version 2.0 supported the PC XT (the first PC with a hard disk); version 2.1 supported the PC

Jr; version 3.0 supported the PC AT; version 3.1 supported local area networks; version 3.2 supported the PC Convertible (a laptop computer); and version 3.3 supported the new line of PS/2 computers.

Version 3.3 marked the last time that a version of DOS was brought out specifically to support a new computer. The next two versions, 4.0 and 5.0, offered other enhancements, mostly having to do with being able to access large amount of memory and large-capacity disks.

Table A.1 summarizes all of this information. However, we've included the table only for your interest, and you don't need to know anything about the various DOS versions in order to learn how to use your computer. All you need to do is to make sure that you are using a modern version of DOS.

The whole point is that operating systems evolve. There are always new commands and new features being added (and problems being fixed). We strongly recommend that you use the newest version of DOS. Right now, that means DOS 5.0. If you are using an older version, you can upgrade directly to 5.0; if you are buying a new PC, you should insist on 5.0 right from the start.

Most of what is covered in this book will work with any modern version of DOS; however, DOS 5.0 is an important improvement and it's a good idea for just about everybody to upgrade.

Table A.1   A Summary of the Different Versions of PC-DOS and MS-DOS

	PC-DOS	*MS-DOS*	*New Hardware*
August, 1981	1.0		PC-1
May, 1982	1.1	1.25	PC-2
March, 1983	2.0	2.0	PC XT
May, 1983		2.01	
November, 1983	2.1		PC Jr
November, 1983		2.11	
August, 1984	3.0	3.05	PC AT
March, 1985	3.1	3.1	local area networks
December, 1985	3.2	3.2	PC Convertible
April, 1987	3.3	3.3	PS/2 family
September, 1988	4.0		
November, 1988		4.01	
June, 1991	5.0	5.0	

Note that, until DOS 4.0, all new versions of PC-DOS were released to support new hardware, usually new computers.

For those who care about technical esoterica, here are a few supplementary notes:

- Starting with version 5.0, IBM changed the name PC-DOS to IBM DOS.

- MS-DOS 1.25 was similar to PC-DOS 1.1 except that the Microsoft DOS did not offer the DISKCOPY and DISKCOMP commands.

- MS-DOS 2.01 offered extra support for non-American languages, including Japanese Kanji.

- MS-DOS 2.11 (which was very popular) combined versions 2.01 and 2.1.

- At one time, Compaq issued its own version of MS-DOS, version 3.31. This DOS, which was for Compaq computers only, allowed disk partitions that were greater than 32 megabytes. Eventually DOS 4.0 offered this same capability.

- Before the American version of PC-DOS 4.0 was released, Microsoft offered a special MS-DOS 4.0 but only in Europe. This version of DOS added rudimentary network support.

- IBM released PC-DOS 4.0 before Microsoft. Soon after, it was discovered that there were some bugs in how expanded memory was being handled. These bugs were fixed. When Microsoft released its version of DOS 4.0, they called it MS-DOS 4.01 to show that the bugs had been fixed. IBM, too, fixed the bugs but did not change the version number, which remained at 4.0.

The Important Advantages of DOS 5.0

Since DOS 5.0 is the most recent DOS, let's take a brief moment to discuss the new facilities that this new version brings to the table. Don't worry if you don't understand the more technical details. This section is provided primarily for the experienced user who wants to know what's new with DOS.

The most important advantages of DOS 5.0 are:

- **Replacement for older versions** DOS 5.0 has been designed as a replacement for all preceding versions of DOS. As we mentioned earlier, there have always been some differences between IBM DOS and MS-DOS. With DOS 5.0, both IBM and Microsoft are now selling the same DOS—even the documentation is similar. For the first time, IBM DOS and MS-DOS are virtually identical. IBM and Microsoft want everybody to upgrade to version 5.0, and we believe this is a good idea.

- **Memory** DOS 5.0 requires significantly less memory than earlier versions of DOS. Moreover, DOS 5.0 offers much better support for expanded and extended memory. We discuss these topics in Chapter 30.

- **Editor** DOS 5.0 offers a new, full-screen editor named EDIT. The old editor EDLIN is still included. We discussed EDIT in Chapter 27 and EDLIN in Chapter 28.

- **DOS Shell** DOS 5.0 has a completely new DOS Shell. We discussed DOS Shells (versions 4.0 and 5.0) in Chapter 31.

- **Basic** DOS 5.0 replaces the old BASICA and GWBASIC interpreters with QBASIC. QBASIC is similar to, but not exactly like, the Microsoft QuickBASIC interpreter. QBASIC will run most but not all BASICA and GWBASIC programs.

- **Data recovery** For the first time, DOS now offers a way to recover data that has been accidentally lost—at least some of the time. We covered this topic in Chapter 19.

- **Online Help** DOS 5.0 has new commands and command options that provide online help. It is easy to list all the DOS commands, along with a short description of each; you can also display specific help for any particular command. We covered the new Help facilities in Chapter 8.

B

NARRATIVE GLOSSARY

Introduction

This narrative glossary is intended to provide a brief rundown of the most common and fundamental terminology used in discussing computers. You can use this narrative glossary in two ways—either by reading it all, or by scanning the **boldface** words for the terms you are interested in, and then reading the surrounding discussion.

Numbers and Notation

Computers work only with **binary numbers**—numbers made up of zeros and ones (0's and 1's). These binary digits are called **bits** for short. No matter what a computer is doing, it is working with bits. Even if the subject matter is alphabet characters, or decimal arithmetic, the method is still binary numbers.

Writing many bits, for example 01010101101001001000010111010, is inconvenient, so several shorthand notations have been developed. The most common is **hexadecimal**, or base-16, notation. Hexadecimal digits have 16 possible values, from 0 through 15; they are written as 0 through 9, followed by A (representing the value of 10), B (meaning 11), and C through F (values of 12 through 15, inclusive). Hexadecimal digits, also called **hex**, represent four binary digits, or bits, at a time.

The bits that a computer uses are grouped into larger units. A group of eight bits is called a **byte**. Since hex notation represents four bits at a time, it takes two hex digits to represent the value stored in a byte (hex digits are sometimes whimsically called nibbles). A byte can be used to store 2^8 values—256 different values. The values can be interpreted as numbers or as characters (such as letters of the alphabet). One byte can hold one character, and therefore the terms bytes and characters are sometimes used interchangeably. The letters of the alphabet and the ten digits, together, are called the **alphanumerics**, although the term is sometimes used loosely to mean any text data.

When bytes are used to hold characters, some code must be used to determine which numeric value will represent which character. The most common code is the American Standard Code for Information Interchange (**ASCII**). In ASCII, the capital letter A has the value 65 (in hex notation, 41); B is 66, and so forth. ASCII includes codes for letters, numbers, punctuation, and special control codes.

ASCII proper has only 128 different codes, and needs only 7 bits to represent then, but since ASCII characters are almost always stored inside 8-bit bytes, there is actually room for the 128 ASCII codes, plus another 128 codes. The other codes are sometimes called **extended ASCII**. ASCII codes are standardized, but extended ASCII varies from computer to computer.

Large IBM computers have not used ASCII coding to represent characters. Instead, they used **EBCDIC** (the Extended Binary Coded Decimal Information Code). Although EBCDIC has been very little used in personal computers, it is important when data is transferred between the two types of machines.

ASCII data, or an ASCII file, is data that consists of text—letters of the alphabet, punctuation, and so forth—rather than numbers or other data. Sometimes the term ASCII is used loosely to mean text data. Properly speaking, an ASCII file contains not only the ASCII codes for letters, spaces, punctuation, and so on, but also contains the standard ASCII codes for formatting, such as carriage return and end-of-file.

When a byte is used to represent a number, the 256 different byte values can be interpreted as either all positive numbers ranging from 0 through 255, or as positive and negative numbers, ranging from −128 through 127. There are referred to as **unsigned** (0 to 255) or **signed** (−128 to 127) numbers.

To handle larger numbers, several bytes are used together as a unit, often called a word. For different computers, different meanings are given to the term *word*, but most often it means either two bytes (16 bits) or four bytes (32 bits). For the IBM-PC family of computers (and compatibles) a word means a two-byte, 16-bit number.

A two-byte word has 2^{16} different possible values. These can be used as unsigned numbers, with a range of 0 through 65,535, or signed numbers, with a range of -32,768 through 32,767.

Integers, or whole numbers, are not satisfactory for some tasks. When fractional numbers are needed or a very wide range of numbers is needed, a different form of computer arithmetic is used. This is called **floating-point**. Floating-point numbers involve a fractional portion, and an exponent portion, similar to the scientific notation used in science and engineering. To work with floating-point numbers, computers interpret the bits of a word in a special way. Floating-point numbers generally represent approximate, inexact values. Often more than one format of floating-point numbers is available, offering different degrees of accuracy. Common terms for these formats are **single-precision** and **double-precision**. Floating-point numbers are also sometimes called **real numbers**.

Due to the nature of computer arithmetic and notation, items are often numbered starting from 0 for the first element; this is called **zero-**

origin. Counting from zero is done especially when figuring a memory location relative to some starting point. The starting point can be called many things, including **base** and **origin**. The relative location is most often called an **offset**. Starting from any base location in memory, the first byte is at offset 0, and the next byte is at offset 1.

Computer Fundamentals

All of the mechanical and electronic parts of a computer system are called **hardware**. The programs that a computer uses are called **software**.

The idea of a computer starts with the concept of **memory**, or storage. A computer's memory consists of many locations, each of which has an **address** and can store a value. For most computers, including the PC family, each location is a byte; for others, each location is a word.

The addresses of the locations are numbers. The values stored in each location can either be examined (read) or changed (written). When a value is read or written, the address of the location must be given.

Some computers organize their memory storage into large modular units, often called **pages**. IBM PC computers running DOS do not use pages, but for addressing purposes they divide their memory into units of 16 bytes, called **paragraphs** (a term that was chosen to suggest a smaller division than a page). The memory-addressing mechanism for these computers uses two parts: a **segment value**, which points to a paragraph boundary, and a relative value, which points to a byte located at some displacement, or **offset**, from the segment paragraph. The two values, segment and displacement, are needed to specify any complete address; together, they are sometimes called an **address vector**, or just a **vector**.

Amounts of computer memory are frequently referred to in units of 1,024 because 1,024 is a round number in binary notation, and almost a round number in decimal notation. The value 1,024 is known as one **K**, from the metric *kilo*. 64K is 64 units of 1,024, or exactly 65,536.

When referring to general capacity, K almost always means 1,024 bytes. However, when referring to semiconductor chips, K means 1,024 bits. When magazine articles refer to 16K and 64K chips, they mean 16K bits (equivalent to 2K bytes) or 64K bits (equivalent to 8K bytes).

A computer has the ability to perform operations on the values stored in its memory. Examples of these operations are arithmetic (addition, subtraction) and movement from location to location. A request for the computer to perform an operation is called an **instruction**, or **command**.

A series of computer instructions that together perform some work, is called a **program**. Programs are also called **code**.

The part of the computer that interprets programs and performs the instructions is called the **processor**. A very small processor, particularly one that fits onto a single computer chip, is called a **microprocessor**. The development of microprocessors made personal computers possible. Properly speaking, a computer is a complete working machine that includes a processor and other parts, but the processor part of a computer is sometimes also called a computer.

The memory of a computer is used to store both programs and data. To the memory, there is no difference between programs and data; however, to the processor, only those stored values that represent valid instructions can be a program. The processor reads and writes from its memory both to carry out a program and to access the data that the program uses.

Many modern computers, including the PC family, use a **push-down stack** to hold status information. Data is pushed onto and popped off of the top of the stack, on a last-in-first-out (or **LIFO**) basis.

When a computer uses a common data path to pass data from one part to another, this path is called a **bus**. The first PC models had an 8-bit bus; the AT-class of PCs (which use the 286 microprocessor) have a 16-bit bus, while the 386-class of PCs use a 32-bit bus. This bus width is a partial reflection of the speed and power of a PC.

The newest, most powerful buses are MCA (Micro Channel Architecture) and EISA (Extended Industry Standard Architecture). MCA was developed by IBM and is used in most PS/2 personal computers and some midrange and mainframe computers. EISA was developed by a consortium of companies led by Compaq. The EISA bus is used in certain high-performance PCs.

The memory and processor are the internal parts of a computer. There are many external parts, generally called **peripheral equipment**, or **peripherals**. Most peripherals must be connected to a computer through some supporting electronic circuitry, called an **adapter**. For a complex peripheral, such as a diskette drive, the adapter will include some special logical circuitry called a **controller**. A controller is often a specialized computer in its own right.

Peripherals may be of many kinds, but they fall into a few simple categories. **Storage peripherals** are used to hold programs and data that can be moved into the computer's internal memory. Examples of peripheral storage devices are **diskette drives**, **cassette tape backup drives**, **hard disks**, and **optical drives**. (For more on this, see the Disk Vocabulary section of this Glossary).

Other peripheral equipment is used to communicate with people. The pieces of equipment used to communicate between people and computers are usually called **terminals**. A terminal most often consists of a typewriter-style **keyboard**, and a television-like **display**. A **printer** of some kind may be used instead of or in addition to a display. A display screen is sometimes called a **monitor**, or **CRT** (cathode-ray-tube). A color display may accept its color signal information in a combined form, called **composite**, or separated into its red, green, and blue components, called **RGB**.

Large computers may have many terminals, but small personal computers usually work with only one terminal, which may be built right into the computer system. Having only one terminal, called the **console**, is a large part of what makes a personal computer personal.

Other kinds of peripherals, besides storage and terminals, are **printers** and **telephone connections**. Connections between computers and telephones are referred to by the names of some of their parts, such as **modems** and **asynchronous adapters**; all of these terms, in general use, refer to the entire computer–telephone connection, which is generally called **telecommunications**. The most common format for communications connections follows a design standard known as **RS-232C**. The speed, or data rate, of a communications line is measured in **baud**, which is bits-per-second, or **bps**. 9600 and 2400 BPS are common speeds for personal computer telecommunications; 9600 is about 960 characters per second. On personal computers, an **RS-232C** connection is also called **serial**, since it transmits data one bit at a time. A **parallel** connection can transmit several bits at one time.

Computer printers come in many varieties. Many personal computers use an inexpensive **dot-matrix** printer, which creates its printed results by writing a series of dots. **Letter-quality** printers produce results comparable to good typewriters.

There are two newer kinds of printers that are used a good deal more than traditional dot-matrix and daisy-wheel printers. One type is the **inkjet** printer, which squirts very tiny drops of ink, and paints information with these small dots. Some ink-jets print as crudely as dot-matrix printers, while others print as finely as a typewriter that uses a fabric ribbon. The other new printer technology is called **laser printing**. A laser printer is essentially a computer-driven photocopier, but while a photocopier gets its image from taking a camera-like picture of an original, a laser printer creates an original image of what you want to print. A computer-controlled laser beam paints the image inside the photocopier, which then prints the image onto paper.

An **interface** is a connection between any two elements in a computer system. The term interface is used both for connections between hardware parts, and software parts, as well as the human interface.

Much of the equipment that can be connected to a computer is generally referred to as **input/output** or **I/O**.

The smallest physical parts that make up a computer may be called **chips**. Chips and other parts are connected together electrically and held mechanically on **boards**. If there is one principal board, it is called the system board, or **motherboard**. Openings for the addition of more boards are called **expansion slots**, into which are placed memory boards, disk boards, asynchronous communications boards (telephone connections), and other expansion or peripheral boards.

A microprocessor interacts with its world through three means: **memory accesses**, **interrupts**, and **ports**. Ports have a port number or port address, and are used for passing data to and from peripheral devices. Interrupts are used to get the computer's attention. There are three kinds of interrupts (although all three are handled in the same way). An **external interrupt** is from the outside world (for example, from a diskette drive). An **internal interrupt** reports some exceptional logical situation within the computer (for example, trying to divide by zero—something that isn't allowed). A **software interrupt** is a request from a program for some service to be performed. A software interrupt is an alternative to using a program call to activate a subroutine. Memory accesses are used to read or write from the computer's memory.

The computer's memory can be of several types. Ordinary memory, which can be read or written to, is called **RAM** (random access memory). Memory that contains permanent data is **ROM** (read-only memory). Memory can be dedicated to some particular use, say, to hold the data that appears on the computer's display screen. If a display screen itself uses the computer's memory to hold its information, then it is a **memory-mapped display**.

Because of design limitations, DOS can directly access only 1024K worth of addresses. Out of this 1024K, the first 640K are used for programs and data. This is called **conventional memory**. The remaining 384K is reserved for special purposes. It is called **upper memory** or **reserved memory**.

The memory addresses over 1024K refer to **extended memory**. Programs that follow the **Extended Memory Standard (XMS)** can use extended memory. Some types of extended memory can be used as **expanded memory**, an old way to make use of extra memory. Programs that follow the **Expanded Memory Standard (EMS)** can use expanded memory. To use extended or expanded memory, DOS requires a special program called a **memory manager**.

Sometimes, the first 64K of extended memory is called the **high memory area** (HMA). If there are unused portions of the upper memory, they are called **upper memory blocks** (UMBs).

Programs and Programming Languages

Series of computer instructions are called **programs**. Parts of programs that are partially self-contained are called **subroutines**. Subroutines are **procedures** if they only do some work. They are **functions** if the work they do results in a value. ("Open the door" is an example of a procedure, while "tell me your name" is analogous to a function). Subroutines are also called subprograms, and routines.

Many subroutines use **parameters** to specify exactly what work is to be done; for example, a subroutine that computes a square root needs a parameter to specify what number to use. Many subroutines will indicate how successful their operation was through a return code.

Computers can only execute programs that appear in the detailed form known as **machine language**. However, for convenience, programs can be represented in other forms. If the details of a machine-language program are replaced with meaningful symbols (such as the term ADD or MOVE) then the programming language is known as **assembly language** (also called **assembler**).

Assembler is considered to be a **low-level language**, because assembly programs are written in a form which is very close to machine language. Other forms of programming languages are more abstract and produce many machine instructions for each command written by the programmer. These are called **high-level languages**, and examples of these are **BASIC**, **Pascal**, **C**, **C++**, and **PL/I**.

Programs that translate high-level programs into a form usable by the computer are called **compilers**; for low-level languages, the translators are called **assemblers**. There is no conceptual difference between a compiler and an assembler—they both translate from a human programming language to a form of machine language.

When a person writes a computer program, the form it takes is called **source code**. When the source code is translated by an assembler or a compiler, the result is often called **object code**. Object code is nearly ready to be used by the computer, but it often has to undergo a minor transformation, performed by a **linker** to produce a **load module**, which is a finished, ready-to-use program.

An error in a program is called a **bug**, and the process of trying to location and correct errors is called **debugging**.

A program works with symbolic entities called **variables**. In effect, a variable is the name of a place that can hold data of some type. Specific data can be moved into and out of a variable, and the purpose of a variable is to provide a mechanism for manipulating data. Variables usually have a fixed **type**, which indicated what sort of data it can accommodate: for example, **integer** type, **single-** and **double-precision floating-point** type, and **string** type. In a program, a **file** is just a special kind of variable which can be connected to a diskette file or some device, such as the monitor.

Human Roles

On a personal computer, one person can do everything that is to be done. However, in traditional large computer systems, there is a division of labor, separating human involvement with a computer into various roles. Users of personal computers may wonder about the meaning of various job titles used.

The **user** is the person for whom computer work is done.

The **systems analyst** determines the details of the work that the user needs to have done, and decides on the general strategy of how a computer will perform the work.

The **programmer** converts the analyst's general strategy into the detailed tactics and methods to be used. This usually includes writing (and testing) the actual program. However, actually writing and testing the program is sometimes left to a coder.

A **coder** turns the programmer's detailed methods into the program instructions.

The **operator** runs the computer and makes sure that special requests, such as mounting a tape, are fulfilled.

With a **network** (in which computers are connected together) or a **time-sharing system** (in which multiple users share a computer), the **system manager** or **system administrator** controls and maintains the central resources.

With a **bulletin-board system (BBS)** (to which you can connect via a modem and share files), the person in charge is called the **sysop**.

Data Organization

Data is organized and viewed differently, depending upon who or what is looking at it. To the computer itself, data consists of just bits and bytes. To programmers who manipulate data, there are some traditional logical boundaries for data. A complete collection of related data is a **file**. One complete unit of information in a file is called a **record**; in a mailing-list file, for example, all of the information connected with one address would be a record. Finally, within a record are **fields**, which store information of one type. For example, the ZIP code would be one field in an address record in a mailing-list file.

The records that a program reads or writes are **logical records**. Logical records are placed in the storage medium's **physical records**—the data actually read from or written to a disk. A program sees logical records, while the operating system performs any necessary translating between logical and physical records. On a disk, a physical record is called a **sector**.

The terms **database** and **database manager** are used, and abused, so widely that they have no precise meaning. When data is large, complex, and spread across several files, it might be called a database. A database manager is a program—usually large and complex in itself—that can control and organize a database.

Disk Vocabulary

Data on a disk is stored on sectors, which can be individually read from or written to. Typically for DOS, a sector is 512 bytes. Sectors are the disk's physical records—the units that are actually read or written. A **track** is the collection of sectors that will fit into one circle on a disk; a typical disk format has nine sectors in a track. If there is more than one surface on a disk drive, then a **cylinder** is all of the tracks that are the same distance from the center on each surface. Sectors that are in the same cylinder can be read without moving the disk drive's **read/write head**, or read/write mechanism. Moving the read/write heads from one track or cylinder to another is called **seeking**, and is a relatively slow process. Typically there are 40 or 80 tracks on each surface of a diskette and several hundred on a hard disk.

A disk needs a table of contents for its files. This is called a **root directory** in DOS. Some means must be used to keep track of occupied and unoccupied space on a disk, and with DOS it is done with the **FAT** (**File Allocation Table**). The first sector of each disk is dedicated to holding the first part of the operating system's startup program, called the **bootstrap loader**, or **boot record**. On each disk, there are four kinds of sectors—boot record, FAT, directory, and data storage space.

The inside recording surface of a diskette is flexible, and so an older name for a **diskette** was a **floppy disk**. A **hard disk** has one or more rigid platters in place of the flexible plastic of a diskette; the rigidity allows more precise data recording, and thus, higher density and more capacity. IBM calls the hard disks in their personal computers **fixed disks**; everyone else calls them hard disks.

There are two sizes of diskettes. The first is $3^1/_2$-inches across. It is small enough to fit into a pocket and is enclosed in a hard plastic shell. The second type is the older, $5^1/_4$-inch disk, which is enclosed in a truly "floppy" plastic covering.

Very old 5.25 inch disks hold 360K bytes of data. The **high density** $5^1/_4$-inch diskettes hold 1.2 megabytes. The most common type of $3^1/_2$-inch disks hold 1.44 MB (megabytes) of data, but there are some that hold only 720K. The very newest $3^1/_2$-inch diskettes hold 2.88 MB.

Aside from the standard hard disks and floppy disks, there are several important variations. A **removable hard disk** has a cartridge that can be changed like a diskette.

An **optical disk** uses compact disk technology and is read from and written to using a laser. An optical disk whose data cannot be changed by the user once it is manufactured is called a **CD-ROM** (compact disk–read only memory). Some optical disks can be written on once by the user, but then never changed. These are called **WORM** disks (write once, read mostly). An optical disk that can be read and written multiple times is said to be **erasable**.

A **floptical diskette** provides much more storage than a regular diskette. Such disks combine standard magnetic disk technology with optically-written position markings on the disk surface.

A **virtual disk** isn't a disk at all: It is an area of memory, created by a device-driver, which the computer uses to emulate an actual disk. Such disks are extremely fast, but transient—they disappear when you turn off the power. Virtual disks are also called **RAM disks**.

Operating Systems

An **operating system** is a program that supervises and control the operation of a computer. Operating systems are complex and consist of many parts.

One element of the DOS operating system is the **BIOS**, or Basic Input-Output System. The BIOS is responsible for handling the details of logical records to a peripheral device's records. At the most detailed level, the BIOS contains routines tailored to the specific requirements of each peripheral device; these routines are called **device drivers**.

Usually an operating system is organized into a hierarchy of levels of services. At the lowest level, the device handlers insulate the rest of the operating system from the details of each device. At the next level, relating logical data to physical data is performed. At a higher level, basic services are provided, such as accepting output data from a program to be placed in a file.

Besides device and data handling, an operating system must supervise programs, including loading them, relocating them (adjusting their locations in memory), and recovering from any program errors, though an **error handler**.

Another element of an operating system is the **command processor**, which accepts and acts upon commands given by the user. Commands usually amount to a request for the execution of some program. The command processor is the part of an operation that most people think of as the operating system. In DOS, the command processor is a program named COMMAND.COM.

A program that provides an easy-to-use or special interface to the operating system is called a **shell**. A shell comes between the user and the command processor and acts as the user's window into the computer. A Shell that provides a graphical interface usually featuring windows, pull-down menus, and icons (pictures) is called a **graphical user interface** or **GUI**.

C

COMPAQ MS-DOS 5.0

Starting with DOS 5.0, MS-DOS and IBM PC-DOS is essentially the same. However, a few companies add features to their version of MS-DOS. In this appendix, we will describe the most important new features that you will find if you are using Compaq's version of DOS 5.0. As you can see, Compaq MS-DOS is virtually the same as MS-DOS and PC-DOS, with just a few minor differences.

1. **Support of COMPAQ hardware** Most of the modifications to DOS have to do with supporting specific Compaq computers and peripheral devices such as extra hard disks. The Compaq MS-DOS manual describes these features. The MODE command has extra facilities to control Compaq hardware.

2. **Improved online help system** The MS-DOS HELP command has been replaced by a sophisticated full-screen help system, based on a loadable video graphics library. With this technology, the help information is stored in a file and is accessed by a special database engine.

3. **Installation Program** Compaq MS-DOS has its own installation program called FASTART. The MS-DOS installation program is called SETUP.

4. **Extended use of displays** The MODE command allows you to take advantage of the higher resolution of VGA displays. You can specify either 25, 28, 43, 50, or 60 rows; and 40, 80, or 132 columns. The ANSI.SYS and DISPLAY.SYS drivers, and the CLS, DOSSHELL, QBASIC, and EDIT commands have been enhanced to support the higher resolution.

5. **Expanded memory management** Compaq worked with Microsoft to develop EMM 386. They took this memory manager, modified it for Compaq computers, and renamed it CEMM.

6. **As with IBM DOS,** the two hidden system files are named IBMBIO.SYS and IBMCOM.SYS (not IO.SYS and MSDOS.SYS). Compaq worked with Microsoft to develop EMM 386. They took this memory manager, modified it for Compaq computers, and renamed it CEMM.

7. **Disk Caching** Compaq provides an enhanced disk caching driver, called CACHE.EXE, that offers higher performance on Compaq hardware.

D

USING DEBUG

Introduction

In this appendix, we delve into the technical part of DOS. Our topic is the DOS programmer's tool command, DEBUG. DEBUG is really a quite advanced tool, and is not intended for the ordinary DOS user. But DEBUG may provide capabilities you need, or you may just want to know what can be done by DEBUG. This chapter will give you a low-level introduction to DEBUG.

If you don't need to know about technical matters like this, or you're not interested in them, don't feel you have to read through what's in this appendix. If you don't need it, you won't be cheating yourself—this is technical material for those who want to know everything about DOS.

DEBUG works very much like the DOS text editor EDLIN, thus some of the methods we'll be going over here, and particularly the very linear style of using the commands, should already be familiar.

In fact, EDLIN and DEBUG have similar uses for different types of files. We use EDLIN to examine and change ASCII source files; we use DEBUG to examine and *change* binary program files (that is, executable files of machine instructions). DEBUG comes as a program, DEBUG.EXE, that is installed in your DOS directory. With older versions of DOS, the program is DEBUG.COM.

Some DEBUG Background

Almost everything in DOS is designed for civilian use by the likes of you and me. But there are some special things that need to be done by qualified, technically expert people, and DOS's DEBUG is designed to provide the means to accomplish many important tasks that can't be done without such a sophisticated and complicated tool.

In order for a truck to do its job, it can't be made as pretty, or as easy to drive, as an ordinary car, and so it is with DEBUG. Much of what DEBUG works with is technical by nature, thus the use of DEBUG is equally technical. This isn't to say that DEBUG is necessarily over your head; you can judge that for yourself. I can assure you that it is substantially more complicated and technical than any other element in DOS.

The details of using DEBUG are closely tied to the details of the particular microprocessor that is in your computer. Our discussion here will be based on the Intel series of processors, which are used in IBM-compatible computers. Most of the features of DEBUG require a rough understanding of the processor; some of them call for a very thorough understanding.

Hexadecimal Arithmetic and DEBUG

The first thing you need to know about DEBUG is that it does all of its work in hexadecimal arithmetic. Unfortunately, DEBUG doesn't even give you the option of using decimal numbers; everything in DEBUG is done in hexadecimal, or hex, as it is called.

Hexadecimal arithmetic uses 16 as its base, or radix, instead of 10, which we use. All computers work with binary numbers, and so they need to be given, in one way or another, binary numbers. Hexadecimal is simply a shorthand for binary, with each hexadecimal digit standing for 4 separate binary digits (bits). While our decimal arithmetic uses the ten digits 0 through 9, hexadecimal arithmetic uses 16 digits, which are represented by 0 through 9, followed by A (with a value of 10) through F (with a value of 15).

Table D-1 gives a quick outline of the hexadecimal digits.

Table D.1   *Hexadecimal Digits and Equivalents*

Hex Digit	Decimal Equivalent	Binary Equivalent
0	0	0000
1	1	0001
2	2	0010
3	3	0011
4	4	0100
5	5	0101
6	6	0110
7	7	0111
8	8	1000
9	9	1001
A	10	1010
B	11	1011
C	12	1100
D	13	1101
E	14	1110
F	15	1111

Hex numbers are interpreted like decimal numbers, but with a base of 16, rather than 10. Thus, whereas you could interpret decimal 12 as a number meaning "one times ten plus two equals twelve," the hexadecimal 12 would be interpreted as "one times sixteen plus two equals eighteen."

DEBUG will work with numbers up to four hexadecimal digits long, so they can range from 0 to FFFF, which is equivalent to the decimal number 65,535.

DEBUG and Memory

The use of DEBUG involves referring to locations in memory called addresses. For computers like the IBM PC family that are based on the Intel 86 family of microprocessors, complete memory addresses are five hex digits long, but they have to be represented by numbers no longer than four digits. This is accomplished by using two numbers to represent an address. The first number, called the segment part, is treated as if it were shifted onc place over, the equivalent of multiplying it by 10 base 16. The second number, called the relative part, is added to the segment part (shifted over), to get a complete address. It is done like this:

```
 1234
  5678
179B8
```

When addresses are written out, they are shown with the two parts separated by a colon, like this:

```
1234:5678
```

When DEBUG shows you addresses, it always shows them in that form. When you give DEBUG addresses, you can type them in that way, or you can leave off the segment part and the colon and give only the relative part. In that case, DEBUG will use a default segment value, which will be the first free segment.

There is one other way you can specify the segment part of addresses. The microprocessor has registers, which are used to hold numbers for addressing memory. Each of the registers has a symbolic name; for example, CS is the name of the code-segment register, which customarily provides the segment portion of addresses within a program itself (as opposed to the program's data). Any of the standard symbolic register names can be used, if you know and understand them.

There is much more of a technical summary we could go into, but rather than lay it all out here, we'll let it emerge as we cover the commands that DEBUG can perform.

The DEBUG Commands

You begin operating DEBUG in one of two ways. You can give the command name, DEBUG, and DEBUG will begin operation by showing you its command prompt, which is a hyphen (-). DEBUG, like EDLIN, has its own command prompt, different from the main DOS command prompt. When you see a hyphen prompt, you know that DEBUG is asking for a command.

The other way to start DEBUG is similar to the way you start EDLIN. You give the name of a file after the command, like this:

```
DEBUG filename
```

When you start DEBUG this way, it begins by reading the file into memory, so you can work with the data in the file.

After you've started DEBUG, you need to know how to stop it. The Q (Quit) command tells DEBUG to end its operation. In response to DEBUG's hyphen command prompt, you type Q, press the enter key, and DEBUG ends. As a matter of fact, all of DEBUG's commands are single-letter abbreviations (as with the EDLIN editor), except for four expanded memory commands which are two letters.

Now, the first thing you might want to do with DEBUG is display the information stored in some of your computer's memory. Displaying is done with the D (Display) command. You have to tell DEBUG what you want displayed. It's always part of your computer's memory, but DEBUG needs to know two things about what to display: where in memory to start, and how much of it to show.

You must specify where to start as an address (as you saw in the last section), but there are three ways to tell DEBUG how much to display. You can leave this part of the command blank and DEBUG will show a standard amount, 128 bytes. You can give the relative part of a second address, and DEBUG will display through that address. You can indicate the number of characters you want displayed by keying in L (mcaning you're specifying the length you want displayed) followed by the number of bytes, which must be given in hexadecimal.

Here are examples of all three ways of invoking the D (Display) command:

```
D F000:6000           Display from an address, default length
D F000:6000 6800      Display from one address, through another
D F000:6000 L 100     Explicit length, for 100 (hex) bytes
```

These three ways of specifying a section of memory are collectively called a range, and several more of the DEBUG commands use ranges; whenever we indicate that DEBUG needs a range, you can give it to DE-BUG in any of these three formats.

As a convenience, D keeps track of where it has displayed last, so that just entering the D command, with no parameters, will display successive parts of memory—convenient for browsing. (The U command, which we are coming to, gives us another way of seeing memory, but let's concentrate on D here.)

The information shown by D shows the contents of memory in both hexadecimal and character formats, so you can read what is there either way. Here is what a typical D command shows:

```
D
0:0
0000:00004331E3003F017000-C3E200F03F017000C1c.?.p.Cb.p?.p.
0000:00103F01700054FF00F0-47FF00F047FF00F0?.p.T..pG..pG..p
0000:0020A5FE00F087E900F0-DDE600F0DDE600F0%~.p.i.pf.pf.p
0000:0030DDE600F0600700C8-57EF00F03F017000f.p'..HWo.p?.p.
0000:004065F000F04DF800F0-41F800F0560200C8ep.pMx.pAx.pV..H
0000:005039E700F059F800F0-2EE800F0D2EF00F09g.pYx.p.h.pRo.p
0000:0060000000F6860100C8-6EFE00F0F2007105...v...H~~.pr.q.
0000:007053FF00F0A4F000F0-2205000000000F0S..p$p.p"......p
```

Here's a D command that will show the date of your computer's built-in BIOS programs, if you have one of the models with a standard date-stamp:

```
D FFFF:6 L 8
```

The information from D, and all other DEBUG commands, appears only on your computer's display screen, but you can save a record of it in several ways. One is to turn on your computer's echo-to-printer switch, which we covered in Chapter 22. Another is to redirect the output of DEBUG—say, to a file. The display shown here is actual DEBUG output, which was captured in a file using redirected output and then incorporated into the text of this chapter. The only problem with redirecting the output is that you must be completely familiar with DEBUG. Remember, you won't see any output on the display and it is easy to get lost.

Besides displaying memory, DEBUG also lets you compare two parts of memory with the C (Compare) command. To work, C needs a range to indicate the location and length of one part of memory, and a second address to indicate the location of the other part of memory. DEBUG will then compare them, byte for byte, and report any differences. Here what the C command looks like:

```
C F000:1000 L 200 F000:2000
```

Similar to the C command, is the M (Move) command, which will copy the data in one part of memory to another. Like C, the M command needs a range to indicate the move-from locations, and an address to indicate the move-to locations. For example, this would move 1K of read-only BIOS data into the regular memory:

```
M F000:0 L 1000 100
```

Since you have to use hexadecimal numbers with DEBUG, it would be nice to have some aids. Unfortunately DEBUG offers no help in converting between decimal and hexadecimal, so you are on your own in this department and must turn to a programmer's pocket calculator, or to BASIC (which has easy ways to convert decimal and hex). Alternatively, many people buy memory-resident utilities that allow them to "pop up" a hex calculator whenever they want it.

Even if it doesn't convert back and forth between decimal and hexadecimal, DEBUG does give you a tool to do addition and subtraction in hexadecimal—the H (Hexarithmetic) command. To use the H command, you key in H followed by two hex numbers. H will then display their sum and their difference, which gives you easy access to hex addition and subtraction—something very useful in working with addresses. For example, the command,

```
H 1234 ABCD
```

will get you the result

```
BE01 6667
```

One of the things you might want to do with DEBUG is make changes to the information that is stored in memory. DEBUG gives you two ways to do this, the Enter and Fill commands, E and F. Let's start with E.

The E (Enter) command lets you make direct changes to memory. There are two ways to use this command, one that lets you just enter data, and one that lets you first see what you are changing.

The first way of using the E command is done like this:

```
E  address  list-of-data
```

With this command, the list of data is entered in memory, starting at the address, and continuing until everything in the list has been placed in memory. For your convenience, the list-of-data can be any mixture of character and hexadecimal data. If you use characters, just enclose them in quotation marks to make them distinct from hex numbers. Here is an example:

```
E 0F32:0100 25 "If you figure this out, you're" 20 63 6C 65 76 65 72 21
```

The other way to use E is interactive, with DEBUG showing you the old contents of each byte of memory before you change it. This is very important and useful, because it provides a safeguard against changes to the wrong part of memory. One way in which you might use this form of the command is if you receive a program patch—changes that need to be made to a program. Patches are often given in the form of DEBUG's interactive E commands, so that you can confirm that you are changing what you are supposed to, and not something else.

The interactive form of the E command is invoked by giving E an address, but no list of data to store. E will then display, in hex only, the data at that address and wait for you to key in a new value, also in hex. You either key in a new value, or press the spacebar to leave the value unchanged. DEBUG will continue, presenting you with byte after byte, until you call the process to a halt by pressing <Enter>.

You can confirm the changes you make in two ways. You can do it later by using D to show where you made the changes, or you can confirm the changes on the spot by using another feature of E, the hyphen. While you are using the interactive form of the E command, keying in a hyphen will move you back one byte (just as pressing the spacebar will move you forward one). This makes it easy to back up and confirm what you have done.

The F (Fill) command can also be used to change the contents of memory. F is used like the automatic form of E, except that you specify a range of memory and not just a single starting memory address:

```
F range list-of-data
```

The reason for the range is that F will duplicate the list-of-data as many times as necessary to fill up the range of memory. The list of data can be as long and complicated as you wish, but the most common use for the F command is to set a block of memory to one byte value, such as zero.

If, instead of putting something into memory, you want to search through memory for some particular data, you can do so with the S

(Search) command. S needs the same kind of parameters as F: a range (indicating what part of memory to search) and a list of data, in hex or character formats. S will report the address location of each set of data in the range that matches the data list. If you are using DEBUG for snooping—two of the most popular uses of DEBUG—then the Search command is definitely for you.

DEBUG and Registers

Besides the main memory, your computer also has registers, which it uses to hold working addresses and temporary results of arithmetic operations. DEBUG provides the R (Register) command to let you display and change the register values. If you enter the R command by itself, DEBUG will display the contents of all the computer's registers, along with some related information. If you enter R followed by the name of one particular register, then DEBUG will display its contents, and give you an opportunity to enter a new value similar to the way you do with the interactive E command. To use this command successfully, you must understand quite well how registers are used by your computer, and you must understand how DEBUG uses the registers when it is working.

Here's an example of how DEBUG shows the register values to you:

```
AX=0000BX=0000CX=0000DX=0000SP=FFEEBP=0000
SI=0000DI=0000DS=4531ES=4531SS=4531CS=4531IP=0100NV UP EI PL NZ NA PO NC
4531:0100 0A496E OR CL,9BX+DI+6E:DS:006E=20
```

DEBUG and Ports

One of the ways your computer talks to its various parts—and also to the world around it is through an element known as a port. Ports are data paths into and out of your computer's microprocessor, so that each port can pass data in or out. Each port has an address that identifies it, an address that is similar to, but completely distinct from, memory addresses. There are very many possible ports, and your particular computer will use some of them for special purposes. Generally, you must have a detailed knowledge of your particular computer's inner workings to be able to understand and use ports.

If you know enough about the ports in your computer, DEBUG gives you two commands to move data through them: I (In) reads data from the port, and displays it; O (Out) sends data out the port. The commands are used like this:

```
I port-address
O port-address data
```

DEBUG and Disks

While DEBUG gives you the means to display and change data in memory, often your real goal is to display or change data that is on disk. DEBUG provides you with a way to read and write disk data to and from memory. The L (Load) and W (Write) commands are used for this. L and W work in two distinct ways. They can read and write either entire files or specific parts of the disk storage. Let's cover the file part first.

Reading and Writing Disk Data

As you'll recall from the beginning of this chapter, when you start DEBUG, you can either start it by itself, or with the name of a file you want DEBUG to read into memory automatically. If you make changes to the file's data in memory, how do you write it back to the disk? The W (Write) command, without any parameters, writes the memory copy back to the disk, replacing the original disk copy of the file.

Important—when DEBUG executes the W command, it expects the BX and the CX registers to contain the number of bytes to be written. Each of these registers can hold four hex digits. The combination BX+CX is treated as one long 8-digit hex number. BX contains the leftmost part of the number; CX contains the rightmost part of the number.

When you start DEBUG, these registers are properly set up for you. However, they may be changed if you use the G (go) and T (trace) commands. If this happens, you will have to reset both BX and CX before you enter a W (write) command. The smart thing to do is to write down the initial BX and CX values immediately after you load the file. You can display the registers with the R (register) command.

Suppose you want to read another file into memory? How can you do this? Oddly enough, it takes a combination of two commands. The first command, N (Name), tells DEBUG the name of the file to be read; the second command is L, without any parameters (just like writing a file is done with W, with no parameters). To read a file, you do something like this:

```
N filename L
```

and then the file is read into memory, just as it would be if you had used that file name when you started DEBUG.

Reading Disk Data

The "naked" form of L and W is used to read and write complete files, but another form of these commands is used to read specific parts of the disk data. In this case, you specify the memory address you want the data read into, and what part of the disk you want to read from. The command is like this:

```
L address drive-number sector-number sector-count
```

The address is the location in memory the data is to go to. The drive-number is the equivalent of the letter that DOS uses to identify disk drives, with 0 representing the A drive, 1 the B drive, and so forth. This indicates which disk drive the data is to be read from. The sector-number indicates what part of the disk is to be read; the exact number used depends upon your particular computer, the particular disk format, and the version of DOS. The sector-count indicates how many disk storage units, or sectors, are to be read into memory.

Writing to specific locations is done with the W command, using the same kind of specifications used for a L command.

DEBUG and Programs

Everything discussed so far has been about, and has been working with, abstract data. DEBUG also has the ability to work with programs in several interesting ways.

With the D command, you saw how to display data in a combined hex and character format. That is just fine if what you are displaying is data, but it doesn't tell you much if the information is part of a program. To translate raw programs into a more intelligible format, DEBUG gives you the U (Unassemble) command.

The U command translates the hexadecimal of machine language programs into the form of assembly language. Ordinary users still won't be able to comprehend the result, but anyone who can at least stumble through assembly language programs will be able to decipher some or all of what is being done. Here is an actual example of an Unassemble.

```
F600:0000 E98F7E JMP   7E92
F600:0003 E8A76B CALL  6BAD
F600:0006        CB RETF
```

The display, as you can see, includes the address locations, the data in hex format, and the equivalent assembly language instructions, such as JMP and CALL. The assembly language format does not strictly follow what is needed to create an assembly program, but it is a close equivalent.

DEBUG also provides the flip side of U, the A (Assemble) command. The A command allows you to key in assembly-like instructions, like the JMP 7E92 that appears in our example, and have them translated into machine language and stored in memory. While anyone can use the U command, and some will also be able to understand it as well, only those who are fluent in assembly language can use the A command successfully. It is more difficult to use DEBUG's A command than it is to write ordinary assembly programs, since an assembler provides more aid and assistance than DEBUG can. The Assemble command is only for proficient experts.

There are two more program-oriented commands that DEBUG offers. Both of them are quite advanced, and are really only for use by very proficient assembly-language programmers. Even then, these two commands are used only in fairly extreme circumstances, when programming problems can't be solved by more routine methods. These two commands are T (Trace) and G (Go).

The T command is used to execute a program step by step. With a program ready in memory, T will execute the program's instructions, one at a time, and display the status of the computer, as reflected in its registers. T can be told to stop after each instruction or to continue for a number of instructions, displaying the results of each one. The T command is mostly used when a programmer is uncertain about the exact results of some instructions in a very small part of a program. T is too laborious to be effective for extensive program testing.

The G command also executes a program, but without tracing its results. G will execute, or carry out, a program as quickly as DEBUG is able to. With the G command, you can specify locations in the program, called *breakpoints*, where DEBUG will stop executing it. This is the difference between executing a program by itself, and executing it under the control of DEBUG's G command. With breakpoints set, you can run a program and then stop to check the results when it reaches an interesting or important part.

This has been a quick, and only slightly technical overview of what the facilities of DEBUG are. In the next section we'll look at how to use DE-BUG to patch, or change programs.

Using DEBUG to Patch

Whatever else you might do with DEBUG, there is one common use that anyone might need it for: modifying or patching programs.

There are two different kinds of patching that you might be doing with DEBUG. One is making actual detailed changes in hexadecimal to correct a program, or to alter its operating characteristics. For example, some editing and word-processing programs are patched with DEBUG in order to customize the way they operate. When you do this kind of patching, you should be following very careful and detailed instructions that tell you exactly how to make the patches.

The other kind of patching you might do on your own. In this type of patching, you don't have to know the exact details of the program that you are changing. Instead, you want to change something more obvious and more easy than the program code. One example of this kind of patching is changing a message that a program displays.

A Patch Example

In order to illustrate how this is done, let's imagine a typical example of how such patching might be done. Suppose you have a program, called SUPER, and you find that this program really is super in every respect but one: SUPER insists on reading its data from your disk drive B, when you would like it to use whatever default disk drive DOS is currently using. If you can change SUPER so that it doesn't specify a disk drive, then you can move SUPER's data to a hard disk or a virtual disk or, in fact, any disk other than the B drive that SUPER insists on.

Here is what you would do to try to change SUPER. You don't know in advance if this is going to work—the method is experimental, but there is a very good chance that you will succeed and do no harm in the process.

First find the SUPER program. It ought to be in a file named SUPER.COM or SUPER.EXE. If SUPER happens to be a BASIC program, it might be stored in a file named SUPER.BAS. Whatever the name, find it and make a copy (so that you can safely change it without endangering your main copy). In the process, you should note the size of the program file.

Next, you have to consider one detail. If the program file has an extension of EXE, then DEBUG will treat it in a special way that makes it possible for DEBUG to use the T and G commands. You don't want this, for reasons that are rather technical. The main thing is, if you have an EXE file, you don't want DEBUG to know about it. If the file has an extension of EXE, you get around it by using the DOS RENAME command, to change its extension to anything other than EXE. Let's assume that SUPER is an EXE file, so you rename it like this:

```
REN SUPER.EXE SUPER.XXX
```

Next, start DEBUG and tell it to load the program file. The command is like this:

```
DEBUG SUPER.XXX
```

At this point, DEBUG has a copy of the SUPER program file in memory. You suspect that inside this program file are specific references to the B drive, in this form: "B:". Now you are going to ask DEBUG to search for them. To use the search command, you have to tell DEBUG how much to search, and that is the length of the SUPER.XXX file. If you can translate decimal into hexadecimal, figure it out. If you can't, tell DEBUG just to search as much as possible. Here is the **S** command that you use:

```
S 0 L FFFF "B:"
```

Step by step, this is what you are asking DEBUG to do: The "S" tells DEBUG you want to search for something. The "0" tells it to look from the beginning of its working memory. The "L" tells it to search for some length. The "FFFF" tells it to search for as many bytes as possible. (If you knew the exact length of the file, in hexadecimal, you would substitute the length here.) The last part, in quotes, tells DEBUG to look for the drive specification "B:".

In response to this command, DEBUG will report where it found "B:". If it doesn't report it anywhere, you are out of luck, and you have to give up. But instead, DEBUG is likely to report one or even several addresses. Now, if you want to, you can display the data following each address. If DEBUG reported an address like this: 04EF:0220, then you would use the D command to show information from there:

```
D 04EF:0220
```

using exactly the same address that S gave you.

When you do this display, you may see only the "B:", but more likely you will see a complete filename, with the "B:" at the front. You're likely to see something like this:

```
04EF:0220 42 3B 46 49 4C 45 4E 41-4D 45 32 32 32 32 32 32 B:FILENAME
```

The combination of the "B:" and the file name is a tip-off that you have found what you want. Your goal now is to remove the "B:" part. You can use the E command to replace it with blank spaces, which you do like this:

```
E 04EF:0220 ""   ""
```

Repeat this process for each memory location at which the search command reported that it found "B:". When you are done, you write the file back to disk with the W command.

Now you have your modified program file, ready to test. If you re-named it from an EXE file, you need to change its name back—with the RENAME command:

```
RENAME SUPER.XXX SUPER.EXE
```

Finally, you are ready to test your version to see if it works. To play it safe, make copies of any current data that SUPER uses, just in case the new, modified version gets up to any mischief. You'll test the new SUPER with one copy of your data, knowing that if anything goes wrong, you have another, undisturbed copy. Then you try running the SUPER program, and see if it now looks for its files—not on the B drive—but wherever you have pointed the DOS default drive. If the test works, you can start using the modified program with your ordinary data.

The same methods I've described here can be used to locate and change messages that are built into programs. I can think of two plausible reasons why you might want to do this sort of thing. One would be to replace DOS's starting message with your company's own logo; if you want to do that, you'll find the DOS starting message located in the COMMAND.COM file. Another reason would be to translate program messages from English into another language. Whatever your reason, you can use the techniques here to make any kind of reasonable changes that you want. Even if you have no real reason to do this sort of patching work, you might want to give it a try, simply to learn the skill of how to do it. It's a skill that might come in handy some day.

Making patches or changes to programs, however, is a potentially dangerous process, for you take the risk of ending up making a program unusable—either due to some error on your part or some trick in the program. You need to proceed with caution when you do this kind of work. Under normal circumstances, though, what I have described works fine and is surprisingly easy to do.

You should also be aware that with certain software, it is illegal to unassemble or patch the actual programs. You will have to check the specific licensing agreement to be sure.

Realistically, you will probably stay out of trouble if you keep your modifications to yourself. But if you change commercial software and then start distributing it to others, you are probably breaking the law. And common sense should tell you that it is illegal and impolite to remove copyright notices.

Using Expanded Memory

Starting with version 4.00, DOS provides support for expanded memory (see Chapter 25). DEBUG has four commands, all starting with the letter "X", which allow you to work with expanded memory.

The details are complex and I won't go over them here. But, for your reference, here are the commands and their functions:

XA	Allocate a specified number of expanded memory pages to a handle
XD	Deallocate a handle
XM	Map an expanded memory logical page from a specified handle to an expanded memory physical page
XS	Display the status of the expanded memory

DEBUG Error Codes

DEBUG has a number of different error messages, most of which are easy to understand. However, four of the messages are simple two-letter codes that you are supposed to know. Here they are with their meanings:

Table D.2   *DEBUG Error Codes*

CODE	MEANING
BF	Bad flag You have tried to change a flag but have typed an unacceptable value
BP	Too many breakpoints You have specified more than the maximum number of breakpoints (10) with the G (go) command
BR	Bad register You have used the R (register) command with a bad registration
DF	Double flag With the RF (registerflag) command, you have typed two values instead of one.

INDEX